HOME AND BEYOND

Northwestern University
Studies in Phenomenology
and
Existential Philosophy

HOME AND BEYOND

Generative Phenomenology after Husserl

Anthony J. Steinbock

Northwestern University Press
Evanston, Illinois

Northwestern University Press
Evanston, Illinois 60208-4210

Printed in the United States of America

ISBN cloth 0-8101-1319-8
paper 0-8101-1320-1

Library of Congress Cataloging-in Publication Data

Steinbock, Anthony J.
Home and beyond : generative phenomenology after Husserl / Anthony J. Steinbock
p. cm. — (Northwestern University studies in phenomenology & existential philosophy)
Includes bibliographical references and index.
ISBN 0-8101-1319-8 — ISBN 0-8101-1320-1 (pbk.)
1. Phenomenology. 2. Life. 3. Husserl, Edmund, 1859–1938. I. Title. II. Series.
B829.5.S665 1995
142′.7—dc20 95-20681
CIP

The paper used in this publication meets the minimum requirements of the American National Standard for Information Sciences-Permanence of Paper for Printed Library materials, ANSI Z39.48-1984.

To
Arthur R. Luther
with profound respect and in loving friendship

Mais quant à moi, j'avoue que je préfère m'accrocher aux passages où Husserl indique là encore une "difficulté". . . . Là encore, ce qu'il y a d'indiqué, c'est plutôt une difficulté qu'une solution euphorique. L'inconvénient de l'euphorie, c'est que, dans la circonstance, l'euphorie nous ramène à des positions qui sont, je dirais, pré-husserliennes, à une philosophie qui serait l'idéalisme transcendantal, non pas seulement dans le sens de Husserl, mais dans le sens presque kantien du mot. Mais le mérite de Husserl, il me semble, est d'avoir indiqué où commençait quelque chose d'autre.

Maurice Merleau-Ponty

Es möchte mir scheinen, daß ich, der vermeintliche Reaktionär, weit radikaler bin und weit mehr revolutionär als die sich heutzutage in Worten so radikal Gebärdenden.

Edmund Husserl (1935)

Contents

Acknowledgments

The research leading to this work was sponsored in part by a generous fellowship from the *Deutscher Akademischer Austauschdienst* (DAAD) during a two-year period at the Ruhr-Universität Bochum, BRD (1987–89). I would like to express my sincere gratitude to Bernhard Waldenfels for providing a hospitable and exciting environment in which to carry out my research. His presence in particular was invaluable. I would also like to thank Klaus Held at the Bergische Universität Wuppertal for his invitation to discussion and his amicable encouragement at the beginning stages of this work.

This project was also supported by a generous grant from the French Government under the auspices of the Bourse Chateaubriand (1989–90). I profited from seminars and conversations particularly with Claude Lefort at L'Ecole des Hautes Etudes en Sciences Sociales, Françoise Dastur at the Université de Paris I (Sorbonne), and Marc Richir at the College International de Philosophie.

A deep expression of thanks is due to Donn Welton for his meticulous and generous comments on earlier versions of this manuscript. I have also benefited from Edward Casey's philosophical acumen and genuine openness. Let me also thank Seyla Benhabib for her attentive reading of a previous draft of this work. My thanks also extend to Franz Mayr who is exemplary of unselfish, engaging philosopical inquiry.

I owe debts of thanks to the Husserl-Archief at the Katholieke Universiteit Leuven, to the assistance of its friendly staff, to Rudolf Bernet for his kind support, and to Professor Samuel Ijsseling for permission to consult Husserl's manuscripts. I am particulary grateful to Anne Montavant and Michael Weiler for their arduous work in checking the manuscript transcriptions against Husserl's original Gablesberger stenography, and for paginating the former according to the latter. I would also like to thank the Archives-Husserl at the Ecole Normale Supérieure, the director, François Courtine, and his assistant Alain Pernet for their permission and help in using their facilities. Let me also acknowledge the Husserl-Archives at the New School for Social Research, with special thanks to Gail Soffer for putting Husserl's *Nachlaß* at my disposal.

I have been privileged with extremely capable study partners and close philosophical friends with whom I have participated in prolonged reading groups and who have either discussed with me various phases of this work, or endured lengthy drafts of the manuscript. From a host of homeworlds and alienworlds they are Junichi Murata, Ichiro Yamaguchi, Rudi Visker, Shin Nagai, Irene Klaver, Philippe Huneman, Jean-Luc Lannoy, Tom Brockelman, and Jerry Raustiala. My distinction goes even further in having been able to share in the engaging discussions, companionship, affection, and support of Leslie Brown whose subtle and incisive style of thinking I constantly strive to emulate.

To my parents Marie and Sam Steinbock, as well as to my sister Teresa Steinbock Harrison, I give my heartfelt thanks for the manifold ways they have shown their love and encouragement.

My highest acknowledgment of gratitude I offer in the form of a dedication to Arthur J. Luther. My hope is that this work will stand up to his patient reading of earlier drafts, his attention to my studies, and his trust and continued friendship so formative of my endeavors.

Abbreviations

This work relies to a great extent on untranslated and unpublished material from Husserl's manuscripts. In order to maintain consistency and accuracy in translations, all translations of Husserl's texts, as well as translations of commentaries on Husserl's works, are mine unless otherwise noted.

Husserl's works that are published in *Husserliana* are cited as "H" and are followed by volume and page number:

H I *Cartesianische Meditationen und Pariser Vorträge*

H II *Die Idee der Phänomenologie. Fünf Vorlesungen*

H III *Ideen zu einer reinen Phänomenologie und phänomenologischen Philosophie. Erstes Buch*

H IV *Ideen zu einer reinen Phänomenologie und phänomenologischen Philosophie. Zweites Buch*

H V *Ideen zu einer reinen Phänomenologie und phänomenologischen Philosophie. Drittes Buch*

H VI *Die Krisis der europäischen Wissenschaften und die transzendentale Phänomenologie*

H VII *Erste Philosophie (1923/24). Erster Teil: Kritische Ideengeschichte*

H VIII *Erste Philosophie (1923/24). Zweiter Teil: Theorie der phänomenologische Reduktion*

H IX *Phänomenologische Psychologie. Vorlesungen Sommersemester 1925*

H X *Zur Phänomenologie des inneren Zeitbewußtseins (1893–1917)*

H XI *Analysen zur passiven Synthesis. Aus Vorlesungs- und Forschungsmanuskripten 1918–1926*

H XIII *Zur Phänomenologie der Intersubjektivität. Texte aus dem Nachlaß. Erster Teil: 1905–1920*

H XIV *Zur Phänomenologie der Intersubjektivität. Texte aus dem Nachlaß. Zweiter Teil: 1921–1928*

H XV *Zur Phänomenologie der Intersubjektivität. Texte aus dem Nachlaß. Dritter Teil: 1929–1935*

H XVI *Ding und Raum. Vorlesungen 1907*

H XVII *Formale und transzendentale Logik. Versuch einer Kritik der logischen Vernunft*

H XXII *Aufsätze und Rezensionen (1890–1910)*

H XXV *Aufsätze und Vorträge (1911–1921)*

H XXVII *Aufsätze und Vorträge (1922–1937)*

H XXIX *Die Krisis der europäischen Wissenschaften und die transzendentale Phänomenologie: Ergänzungsband. Texte aus dem Nachlaß 1934–1937*

LU I *Logische Untersuchungen. Band I: Prolegomena zur reinen Logik*

LU II/1 *Logische Untersuchungen. Band II: Untersuchungen zur Phänomenologie und Theorie der Erkenntnis. I. Teil*

LU II/2 *Logische Untersuchungen. Band II: Untersuchungen zur Phänomenologie und Theorie der Erkenntnis. II. Teil*

EU *Erfahrung und Urteil. Untersuchungen zur Genealogie der Logik*

Manuscripts used in this work are indicated by "Ms." and are cited according to archival organization and documentation found at the Husserl-Archief Leuven. I follow the original pagination where available and, when not available, I cite the pagination given on the manuscript transcriptions. In either case, when referring to Husserl's manuscripts, I provide the relevant German text in footnotes. See the Bibliography for detailed bibliographical and publication information.

Introduction

Toward a Non-Foundational, Transcendental Philosophy of the Social World

Questions concerning the philosophical problematic of identity and difference are never so poignantly formulated as when they bear directly on the dimensions of social life. It is here that such questions gain a privileged experiential weight because they are framed in terms of our very coexistence. The problematic of identity and difference is formulated when we ask, for example, what it means to belong to a family, to a group of friends, or to an organization. How is it possible to say "we" or to speak of "our" community? Is unity asserted to the exclusion of difference? Who counts as a stranger? If we tend to be the same for ourselves, how is it that we can experience ourselves as different?

When we pose such questions we are also inquiring into sharply contended political and historical issues: What is the sense of ethnic wars and attempts at so-called ethnic purification? How are human beings to act responsibly in relation to other species and toward the Earth? When individuals or groups are identified as "different," say, women, who is claiming the voice of "the same"? Does asserting one's national identity of necessity result in crimes of hate, neo-Nazism, or totalitarianism? Is the ability to make cross-cultural and cross-historical critiques precluded by the recognition of difference?

Social theory in its myriad forms has attempted to grapple with these and similar questions which have at their root the relation between social forms of identity and difference. Inspired primarily by Hegel and Marx, perhaps some of the most incisive analyses of the twentieth century regarding the problem of social existence have issued from those early theorists associated with the "Frankfurt School," most notably, Theodor Adorno, Max Horkheimer, Herbert Marcuse, Walter Benjamin, Leo Lowenthal, and Friedrich Pollock. But if Adorno—perhaps the most intellectually subtle and diverse of all these figures—is to be any gauge, then phenomenology and especially Husserlian phenomenology can contribute very little to the problems confronting social life in its concrete historical forms.[1]

With the crisis of Marxism and vituperative critiques of Enlightenment rationality, social and critical theories have sought a clarification of the social world and of their own style of theorizing by appealing to phenomenology. There are essentially two ways in which social theorists have attempted to employ phenomenology to these ends. The first is a direct appeal to Husserlian phenomenology and/or to key notions explicated in Husserl's works. Enzo Paci's assimilation of Marxism and Husserl's *Krisis* analysis,[2] Jürgen Habermas's utilization of the "lifeworld" in his theory of communicative rationality,[3] Niklas Luhmann's reliance on the horizonal structure of meaning,[4] and Michael Theunissen's as well as Bernhard Waldenfels's use of Husserl for the development of a "social ontology"[5] are divergent cases in point.

The second tendency to use phenomenology in theories of the social world is marked by an appeal to the efforts of subsequent phenomenologists and their phenomenological theories. Drawing less directly on Husserl and his commitment to transcendental philosophy, contemporary theorists draw more extensively on figures such as Maurice Merleau-Ponty, Jean-Paul Sartre, Alfred Schutz, Aron Gurwitsch, even Martin Heidegger and their versions of phenomenology which seem more favorably inclined toward social phenomena. Efforts in this direction would include Anthony Giddens,[6] Richard Bernstein,[7] and Richard Grathoff.[8]

What both of these approaches have in common, it seems, is an attempt to mollify Husserlian phenomenology where theories of the social world are concerned. More precisely, there is a discernible reluctance to treat Husserl on his own in the context of social theory because of a conviction that the "transcendental" or "foundational" feature of Husserl's thought is ill disposed to deal adequately with the socio-historical dimensions of our lives. In short, perhaps one of the major criticisms facing phenomenology today is that it cannot treat problems of contemporary concern.

It has long been held that Husserl, following Descartes, remained committed to a philosophical perspective that recalcitrantly reduces structures of meaning and sense to a purely subjective foundation, to the so-called "transcendental ego." As "transcendental," as "foundational," one objects, phenomenology is deaf to the question of history and to its own place in a historical context; it vitiates otherness and the social world; it is unable to treat the political life, ethics, gender, ecology, and so forth.

That the realm of social existence, in particular, is a blind spot for Husserl is a commonly held conviction resulting from such an appraisal of Husserl's philosophy. For example, while acknowledging his indebtedness to Husserl, Luhmann echoes the widely shared judgment that "by claiming a transcendental character for subjective intentionality, the problem of intersubjectivity was, for Husserl, left unsolvable and the concept of constitution vague."[9] On this view, if one wished to apply phenomenological analyses to questions concerning historicity or social reality, one would either have to make broad allusions to phenomenology or appeal to figures ostensibly more amenable to the question of social existence. Habermas, to cite just one example, significantly supplements his version of the lifeworld with extended forays into the thought of George Herbert Mead, Emile Durkheim, and Talcott Parsons in order to explain the dimension of normativity and the social "reproduction" of the lifeworld.

These efforts in contemporary social theory are and undoubtedly will remain fruitful contributions to the problem of the social world. However, I would like to take a different approach, and judging from current trends, one that will surely appear unorthodox to both conventional social theorists and Husserlian purists.

I would like to develop a *transcendental phenomenological* philosophy of the social world that is, as one says today, *non-foundational*, and I wish to do this by working on the basis of Husserl's writings.

Husserl's own work can make a significant contribution to the problem of the social world and social ontology because there are analyses in Husserl's writings stemming from the last decade of his life that not only go beyond his "static" egological account of social existence reminiscent of the *Cartesianische Meditationen*, or even his "genetic" methodology, which reveals the facticity of the individual and the world of contemporary subjects, but also the first published *Krisis* text where the question of the lifeworld is concerned.[10] In Husserl's *Nachlaß*, we find a novel dimension of phenomenology being explored and anticipated, a dimension Husserl captures with the expression "generativity" [*Generativität*]. Stated in a provisional manner, by generativity or "generative" Husserl means both the process of becoming—hence the process of "generation"—and a process that occurs over the "generations"—hence specifically the process of "historical" and social becoming that is circumscribed geologically (whereby "geological" I mean the constitutive role of "Earth" and cultural "landscapes"). These analyses contribute to contemporary discussions in social theory by investigating the social, historical, and material dimensions of identity and difference through "generative" phenomena that are *normative, intersubjective, geological, and historical.*

The major generative phenomena or "matters" are most generally the co-relative concepts of "homeworld" [*Heimwelt*] and "alienworld"

[*Fremdwelt*]. By taking static, genetic, and generative phenomena as "leading clues" [*Leitfäden*], I formulate a new dimension of phenomenological methodology that I call a "generative phenomenology."

A non-foundational phenomenology of the social world is a phenomenology that describes and participates in geologically and historically developing structures of existence and coexistence, as well as their respective modes of constitution, without reducing those modes of constitution or structures to consciousness or to an egological subjectivity as a foundational account does. If this is the case, however, then phenomenology cannot remain merely a descriptive enterprise, but as Husserl contends, must itself be situated within generativity, detecting and responding to systemic cultural crises, ultimately, of ethical communities in an effort to sketch possible directions of generation as homeworlds relate to alienworlds. Thus, generative phenomenology becomes a normative undertaking.

In the accompanying charts, I sketch the different possibilities open to transcendental phenomenology. This outline will delimit roughly the various methodological strategies and their phenomena open to phenomenology.

The material I use to outline these diverse dimensions of transcendental phenomenology comes from Husserl's published and unpublished writings that range from the so-called "transcendental turn" about 1905–7 to refections occupying Husserl near the end of his life. I will work through these dimensions as well as their systematic interrelation in detail throughout the course of this study. Let me say a word concerning the development of Husserl's thought in relation to these methods and matters [*Sachen*] outlined in these charts.

The dimensions of transcendental phenomenology adumbrated above are not unambiguous or unproblematic. True, there are privileged moments when Husserl does explicitly distinguish between, say, a static and genetic method, or when he criticizes his "Cartesian way" in light of new methodological alternatives. My point is rather that they do not represent discretely demarcated developmental stages in Husserl's thought. This makes a simplistic distinction between an "early" and a "late" Husserl problematic. We find not fixed, clear-cut stages, but strains of thought or methodological motivations running throughout his work, often becoming interwoven with other strains or motivations. When developed systematically and consistently, however, these strains have quite distinct and irreducible implications. What I address, criticize, and develop in my analysis are not so much the "stages" of Husserl's thought as the systematic lines of methodological issues.

Some of these strains or systematic lines of methodological issues are indicated on the charts. For example, there is a Cartesian approach

Methodological Scope:

transcendental procedure / phenomenological method	Cartesian	Phenomenological Psychology	Critical	transcendental procedure / ontological analysis
static——> constitutive	*xxxxxxx* **progressive-intuitive**	*psychology* **progressive-intuitive/ psychological-regressive**	*lifeworld ontology* **regressive**	<——*ontological leading clue*
genetic——> constitutive	*xxxxxx* **xxxxxxx**	*psychology* **psychological-regressive-reconstructive/ progressive-intuitive**	*psychology sociology, etc.* **regressive-reconstructive**	<——*ontological leading clue*
generative——> constitutive	*xxxxxxx* **xxxxxxx**	*xxxxxxx* **xxxxxxx**	*anthropology* **regressive-intersubjective-geo-historical**	<——*ontological leading clue*

Thematic Scope:

transcendental procedure / phenomenological method	Cartesian	Phenomenological Psychology	Critical	transcendental procedure / ontological analysis
static——> constitutive	*xxxxxxx* **a-temporal structures of consciousness**	*region of psycho-physical life* **conscious intentional life**	*lifeworld structures, typicalities, etc.* **relations of lifeworldly foundations**	<——*ontological leading clue*
genetic——> constitutive	*xxxxxx* **xxxxxxx**	*region of psycho-physical life* **self-temporalization, monadic facticity; normality, abnormality**	*world as totality of facts\ earth as physical-body* **world as horizon/ lived-body as ground (aesthetic clue to earth-ground)**	<——*ontological leading clue*
generative——> constitutive	*xxxxxxx* **xxxxxxx**	*xxxxxxx* **xxxxxxx**	*anthropological world* **generativity: homeworld/ alienworld**	<——*ontological leading clue*

to transcendental phenomenology that begins with indubitable intuitive givenness and progresses on this foundation to secure epistemic acquisitions. In stark contrast, Husserl also takes a critical approach, which begins from the problem of "world," and questions back into modes of pregivenness that are presupposed. In the former approach, Husserl brackets the world from the very start, not allowing mundane disciplines to play a role in transcendental phenomenology. But when Husserl keeps "being" or the "beings of beings" in play, he can let different mundane and ontological disciplines guide constitutive analyses in transcendental phenomenology. Thus, psychology, sociology, and, most important, anthropology can function as "leading clues" [*Leitfäden*] to constitutive analyses. It is such an interplay between ontology and phenomenology that allows Husserl to formulate his own "regressive" approach to transcendental phenomenology.

Constitutive analyses, as we will see, entail static, genetic, and generative methods. Each of these in its own way examines a different dimension of experience. Moreover, as phenomenology begins, static analysis can function as a leading clue to a genetic one, and likewise a genetic to a generative. Nevertheless, it will be the task of this work to show if and in what respect these methods are distinctive methods, as well as the phenomena they describe, distinctive dimensions of experience. It will also be necessary to examine how they are interrelated, and to what extent, for example, static and genetic methods and matters require modification from the perspective of a generative phenomenology which itself is in the process of generation.

The second point I would like to make is that in practice Husserl does not first conceptualize a method and then execute it. Rather, the conceptualization of method is accomplished through its execution: the particular methods develop as he attempts to describe a vast array of phenomena. Thus, Husserl works out the meaning of the methods, say, genetic or generative, through phenomenological investigations themselves. Ultimately, however, a generative phenomenology by its very nature will have to transcend even the historical figure "Husserl."

The primary sources upon which I draw in order to develop a generative phenomenology include, first, the writings in which Husserl distinguishes between static and genetic methods. While these distinctions hold much promise, they still enable Husserl to engage in a progressive phenomenology of intersubjectivity that is egological and foundational (section 1).

The second set of writings upon which I draw concern the transcendental modalities of the lifeworld. Even though the lifeworld in the *Krisis 1* text is for the most part still a provisional concept, this is where almost all commentaries on the lifeworld problematic rest. After determining the systematic interrelation of these provisional concepts in light of a regressive procedure, I take up the transcendental character of the lifeworld that is expressed as "world-horizon" [*Welthorizont*] and "earth-ground" [*Erdboden*]. This characterization is introduced in *Krisis 1,* but also deepened in other manuscripts written around the same period. These reflections explicate the transcendental concept of the lifeworld as "territory" (section 2).

The third main contribution toward a generative phenomenology stems from a heretofore neglected systematic study of normality and abnormality in Husserl's works. The notions of normality and abnormality in Husserl's reflections, originating prior to the *Logische Untersuchungen,* crystallize around the years 1917–21 and extend to the years following 1930. Moreover, the generative concepts of homeworld and alienworld are not just any lifeworlds or territories, but *normatively significant* territories. While the problem of normality and abnormality permeate Husserl's reflections on constitution, it is virtually unrepresented in the literature on Husserl. This is all the more surprising since the concepts of normality and abnormality are essential for Husserl, not only where the sense constitution and genesis of the lived-body is concerned, but also in relation to the generation of common worlds.[11] My sources for this dimension of study include the copious collection of unpublished manuscripts gathered under the rubric of "primordial constitution" (section 3).

The fourth contribution toward a generative phenomenology (section 4) comes from an examination of generative matters. Generative phenomena include the role of birth and death as constitutive features in world constitution, the generative concept of constitution as the process of historical appropriation of sense and reconstitution of normative lifeworlds, historicity, tradition, the roles of communication and narrative, which usurp the foundational role of intropathy, transgression, renewal, and the ethical participation of phenomenology itself as critique in the development of the generative framework. Conceptually, the most distinctive generative phenomena are the notions of homeworld and alienworld. Among the assorted works that have introduced the concepts of homeworld and alienworld, I have not found any that treat them as the topic of a sustained, systematic analysis of intersubjectivity, nor do they place them in the context of a new *generative* constitutional account.[12] Finally, they do not explicate the problem of normality and abnormality as constitutive features of the problematic of homeworld/alienworld.[13]

This final section treats these generative matters mentioned above in terms of the basic problem of generativity. I do this by consulting the published and unpublished writings stemming primarily from the years 1930–37. On the basis of this analysis, phenomenology is revealed in its generative dimension as a normative venture concerned with socio-historical changes. In my concluding chapter I formulate the dimension and significance of a generative phenomenology.

Having outlined the basic enterprise of this work, let me remark that if generative phenomenology, as I have sketched it out here, is to be at all possible, it cannot begin with the overly hasty identification of "foundation" with "transcendental." In other words, it must begin by examining whether foundational and transcendental undertakings are necessarily implicated in one another. Let me first give the concept of foundation sharper definition. Doing this will help us to grasp the notion of foundation in a more critical manner. I will then specify the scope of transcendental phenomenology.

Foundational Phenomenology and the Social World

The term "foundation" [*Fundierung*] was first introduced by Husserl in the Third Logical Investigation characterizing logical relations or the essential laws obtaining between parts and parts, and parts and wholes. For example, if part P cannot exist without supplementation [*Ergänzung*] by or association with Q in an encompassing unity, then P is said to require foundation by Q. Relationships of foundation can be either reciprocal or one-sided. Reciprocal relations are those in which, for example, two parts mutually found one another such that neither could exist without the other. This is the case, for instance, where color and extension are concerned (LU II/1 §16). This mutual dependency, linked with the inability to present the moments separately, is not a subjective feature due to the limits of mental representation, but an "objective" or "ideal" one (LU II/1 238).[14] In the case of one-sided relations of foundation a part can be independent, that is, separately presentable.[15]

The search for a one-sided relation of foundation in terms of a universal or all-encompassing foundation that has no further presuppositions was not undertaken in the *Logische Untersuchungen* (1900–1901). But in the work of *Ideen I* around 1912 we find such a concern clearly articulated. In his introduction to phenomenological philosophy, Husserl links the notion of foundation to that of "evidence." Evidence is the fulfilling "self-presence" of something to consciousness as it is itself and remains a lasting acquisition that Husserl calls cognition or knowledge

[*Erkenntnis*]. One of the significant consequences of uniting the concept of foundation with evidence is that the technical and quite specific concept of "*Fundierung*" as elaborated in the *Logische Untersuchungen* becomes essentially synonymous with an epistemological "grounding" [*Begründung*]. Through evidence, foundation becomes ground [*Grund*] (cf. H III 52).

At the same time that Husserl ties the notion of foundation to evidence, he puts forward a Cartesian idea of transcendental philosophy. Briefly stated, the Cartesian idea is based on the "maxim of indubitability" culminating in the "Cartesian way" of transcendental philosophy: Consciousness emerges as an evident, absolute, and independent sphere of being, and hence foundational (i.e., grounding) for a relative, dubitable, and likewise dependent sphere of being, the world (H III §§44, 46, 49).

The terminology used to express a relation of foundation—being "foundational for" and being "founded upon"—avails itself to metaphors of layering or stratification, structural metaphors Husserl employed liberally. These metaphors can appear quite innocent when clarifying typically different acts. For example, in the context of Habermas's distinction between illocutionary and perlocutionary speech-acts, one can say that perlocutionary acts are founded upon illocutionary acts. An act is perlocutionary when it takes the illocutionary content as a means to a strategic end. If the strategic element is absent, the act nevertheless remains a complete act, precisely as communicative action oriented toward reaching understanding.[16] According to Husserl, the upper levels of the foundational whole, say, of a perlocutionary act, can "fall away" [*fortfallen*] without diminishing the completeness or independence of the underlying intentional experience, what Husserl designates as the "remainder." An illocutionary act, then, could retain its intentional integrity should the perlocutionary component be removed (H III 237).[17]

Yet the tendency to understand relations of foundation becomes pernicious when it is extended to the relation of consciousness to world and of ego to alter ego in a relation of founding *qua* grounding. This is uniquely a "Cartesian" move. This Cartesian move not only gives credence to the contention of §33 in *Ideen I* that the "phenomenological residuum" after the epoche is an absolute sphere of being, but justifies the claim espoused in the oft censured §49 that absolute consciousness is the residuum of world-annihilation. Because the being-sense of the world is founded on subjectivity in the foundational unity cogitatio-cogitatum, noesis-noema, or eventually subjectivity-world, the world can "fall away" without diminishing the integrity of the subject! Put differently, the residuum, the being of consciousness, retains its independent existence as founding *qua* grounding as absolute, "independent" being or concrete consciousness.

Finally, the contention that one can remove one-sidedly the founded layering where subject and world are concerned has dire repercussions for a theory of the social world. For the purposes of this introduction one need only look as far as *Ideen II* for an example of how the one-sided relation of foundation-as-ground plays itself out in the social sphere. In this text Husserl maintains that within the communicative environing-world [*Umwelt*], every person has an "egoistical environing-world." There is accordingly, he continues, a "*one-sided removability*" ["*einseitige Ablösbarkeit*"] of an environing-world in relation to another environing-world, which makes the egoistical world out to be "an *essential core* of the communicative environing-world" (H IV 193, my emphasis). By articulating social phenomena in terms of foundation, one is led to assert the primacy of the ego upon which the social whole is grounded.

What we usually understand by a "foundational" account, then, is a *one-sided* relation of foundation. By contrast, a "non-foundational" account would include what Husserl calls a relation of "reciprocal" founding, or what we might call a relation of "co-founding"—which to our customary way of thinking does not express *a* foundation at all.

A foundational account would roughly correspond to those three areas on the accompanying chart intersected by the Cartesian and phenomenological psychological ways, and static and genetic methods. If the problem of intersubjectivity were asserted in a Cartesian or psychological register and in a static research perspective, the account would yield the structure of ego and alter ego as presented in Husserl's Fifth Cartesian Meditation: a foundational, transcendental account of social relations for which Husserl is particularly renowned and criticized. Here sense bestowing consciousness or the subject is understood as the constitutive condition for the possibility of sense or meaning, in particular, for the sense of the other. For reasons I will specify in section 4, a generative phenomenology cannot exist in a Cartesian or phenomenological-psychological form.

Having briefly stated the difficulties with Husserl's Cartesian account of intersubjectivity tied to the notion of foundation, it should be stated that it remains another question whether or not phenomenological method is intrinsically dependent upon *this* particular idea of foundation or upon *this* idea of philosophy; and it remains a question whether and to what extent *transcendental* philosophy is essentially and inherently a philosophy of foundation. Under the next heading I will sketch the main features that make an analysis transcendental on Husserl's account.

The Scope of Transcendental Phenomenology

Let me note at the outset that the problem with speaking of Husserl's notion of the "transcendental" is that Husserl does not have a singular theory of transcendental philosophy. Or at least this is my contention. As we will see later in more detail, what transcendental phenomenology means depends to a large extent on the ways in which it is carried out in concrete contexts of phenomenological research. These different methodologies are most generally static, genetic, and generative. Nevertheless, it is possible to outline the basic characteristics of transcendental phenomenology. These traits are basically two: It must be an inquiry into the constitution of sense and it must identify a priori structures. These two aspects correspond to two kinds of "reductions" or approaches to phenomena peculiar to phenomenology: a "constitutive" and an "eidetic" reduction.

Husserl's employment of the term 'transcendental' is neither casual nor lacking in suggestive allusion to Kant and critical philosophy. This is not the place to sustain a discussion of the important differences obtaining between Kant and Husserl. I emphasize only two key components peculiar to both Kant and Husserl that provide a clue to transcendental philosophy where Husserl is concerned.

According to Kant's *Kritik der reinen Vernunft*,[18] philosophy is characterized as transcendental insofar as it is occupied with our mode of knowledge of objects and insofar as this mode of knowledge is to be possible a priori (B 25). In other words, first, Kant is not merely concerned with objects or transcendences but more importantly with the *mode or the way* in which these objects are known [*unsere Erkenntnisart von Gegenständen*]. He addresses this concern in part through the transcendental deduction of the pure concepts of the understanding and the schematism (B 116 f., B 177–87). Second, this mode of knowledge must be the condition for the possibility of experience and experiential knowledge, not derived from experience, but possible a priori.

These two moments marking transcendental philosophy for Kant can be seen in Husserl, though in different formulation and consequence. Let me delineate these two points.

1. Husserl brackets or holds in abeyance the question concerning the real determination or existence of objects. For Descartes, existence is an operative assumption sustained in doubt; but for Husserl like Kant, existence or being is not operative as a real predicate—it is not determinative of the thing. When one holds being in abeyance, one does not change anything in the thing, while if one excludes, say, the shell-like fracture and smooth surface from obsidian glass, the thing would be substantially

modified. For the geologist or volcanist, it makes quite a bit of difference whether this obsidian rock exists or not, but for the phenomenologist who holds the question of being in abeyance, being does not alter the essence of this rock, nor does it change how this igneous stone is given to me.

There is, nonetheless, a crucial difference between Kant's and Husserl's proposition that being is not a real predicate. For Kant, excluding being as a real predicate goes no farther than possibilizing reality, since "the real contains no more than the merely possible." To play on his example, one thousand real dollars add nothing more to the value of one thousand dollars than one thousand possible dollars, even though one thousand real dollars do alter my financial position (B 627 ff.).

Yet for Husserl, possibility is not totally neutral with respect to being. On the one hand, it is indeed opposed to all positing acts, acts that posit being, such as perception, judgment, doubting, etc.; compared to them, phantasy does not directly posit reality (cf. H III § 134; H VIII 130, 134). On the other hand, phantasy is a positional act or "quasi-positional" act insofar as it accepts being in the modality "as if."[19] For this reason Husserl must still consider the "possibilization" of being as the assertion of being. The difference between the real and the possible remains "naive" because it continues to presuppose the world or being. Such an acceptance, as real or merely possible, must be bracketed too (H VIII 115–19).

What Husserl terms the "*epoche*" is the suspension of belief in the world, not in the sense that now one posits the non-being of the world instead or the possible being of the world, but in the sense that one refrains from positing its being *or* non-being altogether. Rather than simply fixing on *what* objects are, real or possible, Husserl turns toward the *way* in which objects are given, and ultimately toward the *way* in which the world as a whole is given.[20]

Husserl echos Kant's transcendental inquiry on another note, namely, as an attempt to determine the power and limits of the subject. For Husserl, this determination is pursued by the method of the "reduction" under the title of "constitution." Constitution is not a metaphysical creation of transcendences, and the subject is not a creator of their being. Rather, the theory of constitution, "the greatest of all transcendental problems" (H III 212–14), is an account of how objects in the world and the world itself take on sense. Transcendental philosophy inquires after how objects get accepted *as* real, *as* identical, or how objective sense comes to pass (H VII 279). The point, as Husserl writes in *Krisis 1*, is not to secure objectivity, but to understand it (H VI 193).

Describing being in terms of how something takes on sense points immediately to ways in which sense is given. That is, it points from the modalities of constitut*ed* sense to ways of sense-constitut*ing*. It is to the end of analyzing *how* such transcendences are accepted in terms of their *modes of givenness* that the role of the "subject" is introduced into the phenomenological account of the object. The turn to the subject, in other words, is only one (initial) consequence of this basic concern with *transcendence. Transcendental phenomenology is a phenomenology of transcendence.*

True, for some time Husserl identified the dimension of sense-constituting with consciousness and egological subjectivity. Through his genetic analyses this sense-constituting dimension was investigated in terms not only of active synthesis, but also passive synthesis on the level of the lived-body, in terms of phenomenology of association and in the temporal dimension of facticity. But through his generative analyses we see a variation in constitutional descriptions, from the more familiar static form-matter schema, to a more dynamic temporalizing model of primordial constitution, to the constitutive roles of appropriation and renewal of sense that stems from normative territories and traditions. Here homeworld and alienworld become constitutive conditions for the possibility of sense emergence, conditions that are themselves formative of "subjectivity." My basic point here, then, is that transcendental phenomenology is a phenomenology of transcendence, and not necessarily of subjectivity.

2. The second aspect peculiar to transcendental philosophy for Husserl is provided by the concept of "a priori." "A priori" for Kant describes the way in which we know. The "way" entails necessity and universality (B 3 f.), features that experience cannot supply and that appearances do not exhibit. Pure concepts of the understanding claim validity a priori, without borrowing anything from experience (A 88); they relate a priori to objects, determining how objects are thought or known at all as objects. In this way, pure concepts like the forms of intuition are conditions, a priori, for the possibility of experience.

For Kant, then, "a priori" is used adverbially, modifying modes of knowledge.[21] While adverbial and adjectival uses do occur in Husserl's writing, the expression 'a priori' preeminently appears as a noun and is identified by Husserl with the notion of "structure," "essence," or "eidos" revealed through an "eidetic reduction." I do not wish to engage in a debate concerning Husserl's contentious and perhaps misleading identification of a priori with essence. I only wish to state that in order for phenomenology to be transcendental, it must also undertake eidetic inquiries that identify fundamental structures, rules, or conditions for the possibility of sense-emergence. By the time phenomenology becomes generative, phenomenology does not only describe essences, and in particular social essences, but participates in the ethical becoming of social structures or essences that the phenomenologist describes. In this sense, a generative phenomenology becomes a normative project of contributing to the way in which the a priori structures of society develop historically as they are being described.

Finally, the role of identifying eidetic or a priori structures differs according to whether they are employed as a *leading clue to* a constitutional analysis, or as a *result of* a constitutional analysis. For example, in a Cartesian account, all ontology or empirical disciplines that identify (mundane) structures of existence are bracketed in advance (see charts). In the phenomenological psychological or critical approaches, the "world" and the ontology of worldly beings are left in play in order to function as guides for a constitutive phenomenology. Thus, a life-world ontology will guide the empirical sciences which in turn provide leading clues to a constitutive-phenomenological undertaking: psychology for phenomenological psychology; biology and physics for the phenomenology of the lived-body; sociology for a constitutive study of the field of contemporaneous individuals; and anthropology for a generative phenomenology.[22]

The ways in which ontology and constitutive analyses interrelate will be treated throughout the course of this study. My general point here is that there are two reductions, the phenomenological and the eidetic that make up the fundamental form of all particular transcendental methods and thoroughly determine the sense of transcendental phenomenology (H I 106).

Certainly, foundational and transcendental enterprises taken together can yield an apodictic foundation, the universal eidos, "the transcendental ego" as ground. My contention, nevertheless, is that "foundation" and "transcendental" are essentially distinct. This can be seen by tracing the leading clues of static and genetic matters and methods in the direction of generative phenomena, which in turn lead to the formulation of a generative phenomenology. It is through generative phenomenology that it will be possible to present a non-foundational phenomenology of the social world as transcendental historicity, materiality, and sociality.

PART 1

FROM CONSCIOUSNESS TO WORLD

This work is the development of a generative phenomenology whose "matter" [*Sache*] is generativity. The principle generative matter of generative phenomenology is the intersubjective and historical becoming of the framework, homeworld and alienworld. The "co-constitutional" or "non-foundational" relation of homeworld/alienworld stands in stark contrast to the foundational relation of I and Other. One of the key differences in these two diverse formulations of intersubjectivity is the difference between the emphasis on "world," in the first instance, and "consciousness" *qua* egological subjectivity, in the other.

The first part of this work will show the transition in phenomenology from its emphasis on consciousness to that of world. In the first section, I offer a systematic account of phenomenology's theory of intersubjectivity as it is expressed in a foundational relation of ego to alter ego. This structure has been taken, from Adorno to Theunissen, as transcendental phenomenology's definitive stance on intersubjectivity. There are many factors which lead phenomenology to its foundational formulation of the social world: its immanent intuitive reflection or "progressive" procedure, its privileging of immanent being as a point of departure, and its methodological approach to phenomena through static and genetic analyses. In section 1, I explicate these moves and highlight the results for the problem of intersubjectivity.

In the second section, I show the motivations for taking up a "regressive" procedure, a procedure that arises in the context of static and genetic methods. This procedure will offer a new emphasis and a new starting point for phenomenology: the natural world of life or the "lifeworld." In the final discussions of section 2, I adumbrate the transcendental concepts of the lifeworld that are particularly significant for a generative phenomenology.

Section 1

First Philosophy: The Problem of Ego and Alter Ego

> I think, therefore, I am not—I am distinct from all that is, I am other than what is, and no *being* can be compared to me.
>
> Valéry[1]

In this section I explicate the methods involved in articulating phenomenology's foundational account of intersubjectivity. I do this for two reasons: First to contrast the matters of static and genetic analyses with those of a generative analysis, and second to define the differences between the methods themselves, that is, static, genetic, and ultimately generative.

Static method need not be, but actually was associated with, a "progressive" procedure by linking it with a Cartesian idea of intuition. In chapter 1 I show how the progressive procedure of intuitive reflection yields the absolute immanent being of consciousness. Chapter 2 takes up a dynamic concept of the "absolute" as the process of self-temporalization. Since such an introduction of self-temporalization requires phenomenology to distinguish explicitly between static and genetic approaches, I will formulate the difference between static and genetic methods. The considerations of genetic method and matters will provide the means for posing the question concerning the "other" in the so-called "second way" of phenomenological first philosophy (chapter 3). In the final chapter of this section (chapter 4) I articulate the salient points of a foundational theory of intersubjectivity propounded in Husserl's Fifth Cartesian Meditation.

1

Progressive Procedure and the Turn toward Immanence

Husserl's conception of phenomenology is perhaps best captured by the shibboleth, "back to the things themselves"![2] By going back to the things or matters themselves, Husserl evoked a style of thought that did not take its impetus from common prejudices or preconceptions about the world, and still less from academic discussions about what other philosophers had written.

Hegel seems to have been the first to have articulated this mandate. Inveighing against other philosophical positions for glossing over "the thing itself," Hegel advanced the distinctiveness of phenomenological exposition. Rather than ignoring the immanent content of "*die Sache*" through pre-fabricated tables of predication, rather than multiplying and manipulating pure determinations of thought whereby one "never experiences what the thing itself . . . is," rather than going from thinker to thinker passing judgment and avoiding "the matter," Hegel calls the budding philosopher back to the thing itself: If philosophy wants to be more than the beginning of cognition, asserts Hegel, if it should be valid as actual cognition, it cannot circumvent the thing itself, and indeed, grasped in a process of becoming. For Hegel, *die Sache selbst* is in the process of becoming only through an exposition [*Darstellung*] of the matter. Such an exposition, which tarries with the matter as it expounds it, is phenomenology as the way to full-fledged science.[3]

Going back to the things themselves for Husserl (and not, for example, to the formulae or thinkers themselves) had a philosophically liberating function: It strove to open the philosopher to the matter at hand as it is lived in evident self-givenness, or put differently, it sought initially to achieve clarity by going back to adequate fulfilling intuition.[4]

If phenomenology works within the strictures of "givenness," securing knowledge and progressing on the basis of a firmly given foundation, phenomenology is said to engage in a "progressive" style of phenomenology. In short, a progressive procedure is one that exercises an immanent intuitive reflection through which the matter or thing itself is *given* as the absolute being of consciousness.

Carried out systemically, this procedure permits Husserl to privilege the ego as a starting point for a foundational account of intersubjectivity. To show how this is the case, let me begin by explaining how immanent reflection relates to the givenness of consciousness.

Immanent Reflection and the Givenness of Consciousness

Of the many notions from the philosophical tradition reevaluated in the *Logische Untersuchungen,* the notion of intuition in particular stands out as cutting across old epistemological divisions. First, the traditional difference maintained between thought, which is inextricably tied to the realm of meaning, and perception, which customarily belongs to the province of sensuous reality, is overcome by a distinction between signifying acts and acts of fulfillment—both of which pertain to the so-called "intellectual" and "sensuous" dimensions. Second, the traditional division between sensibility and the understanding is itself recast by their designation as "simple" [*schlicht*] and "categorial" spheres that function in a relation of foundation as founding and founded, respectively.

On the one hand, truth is no longer conceived under the strict principality of judgment (as rationalists would claim), but is expanded to the sensuous or simple level. Let us recall that prior to Husserl, judgment had been revered as the locus of truth. Kant, for example, maintained that truth is not in the object insofar as it is intuited, but in the judgment about the object insofar as it is thought. Consequently, truth as well as error are only to be met in judgment.[5] For Husserl, on the other hand, judgment is not where truth or evidence begin.

On the other hand, intuition is not defined by the characteristics peculiar to sensible perception (as empiricists would claim), but includes "higher" acts of understanding such as judgment. Truth is experienced in both simple and in categorial acts, pre-predicative as well as predicative spheres to the extent that their respective objects are given in the way they (the objects) are intended.[6]

Thus, Husserl accounts for truth not by judgment, but by appealing to intuition. And he characterizes intuition not by virtue of sensibility per se, or even by virtue of understanding per se (one might think here of Descartes's rational/intuitive "light of nature"), but by its ability to fulfill a "signifying" or "intending" act.[7] As Levinas succinctly expresses, we can speak of truth or falsity of judgments to the extent that the judgment can or cannot be fulfilled in intuition; a judgment is true not *qua* judgment, but *qua* intuition.[8] Intuition, accordingly, is not reducible to sensuous insight, but is defined as the fulfillment of any intended sense or meaning.

We need not rehearse here the striking similarities between, on the one hand, iDescartes's mandate for radical self-responsibility and search for a secure epistemological foundation in the knowing subject, and on the other, Husserl's definition of originary giving intuition as the legitimating source of all cognition.[9] Let it suffice to note that because intuition is a meaning-fulfillment, that is, an act through which the object is presented corresponding to the modality in which the object is meant, intuition is distinguished from a "flash" of insight. For this reason, Husserl writes that intuition or evidence cannot be understood on the model of a Cartesian "theological" theory of evidence (H VIII 341) in which one appeals to a transcendent being or to some "mystical voice" from another world telling us "here is truth" (H III 354).

Because meaning or intending can be a meaning or intending *more* than what is actually given—thus "anticipating" the subsequent fulfilling acts in the direction of an ever more complete presentation of the object—by *Ideen I* Husserl allows for many different grades of evidence, and not only adequate givenness. Nevertheless, only some modes of evidence are considered appropriate for providing the beginning of philosophy, that is, for securing knowledge and grounding the sciences, especially logic: original, immediate, adequate, and apodictic evidence.[10] Evidence of the latter types are given in immanent reflective intuition. Let me now address more specifically the role of immanent reflection. The clarifications that follow—as we will see—are based in a "static" analysis.

Reflection is the title for conscious acts yielding the knowledge of consciousness in general, acts in which lived-experiences are grasped in evidence. By definition, adequate givenness takes place where what is meant comes to complete givenness, where the object is intimately enclosed in perception (H III 85, LU II/1 355, LU II/2 239 f.). For this explanation to gain appropriate specificity, let me note that there are essentially two ways in which something can be given to consciousness: Something can be given transcendently (externally) or immanently.

"External perception is a constant pretension to accomplish something that by its very nature it is not in a position to accomplish. Thus, it harbors an essential contradiction, as it were." This begins Husserl's introduction to a phenomenology of "passive synthesis" (H XI 3). External or transcendent perception is a constant pretension because it feigns to give the object completely in every appearance, and because there is always *more* (from the side of the object) to what I can mean (H XI 11). It does this because presenting consciousness is structurally coupled with a non-intuitive indicating that points mediately to other aspects of the object, that is, to "inner" or "outer" horizons of the object that are non-original.[11] By inner horizons Husserl understands, for example, the back side, the top, or the interior of an object, say, a boulder. By outer horizons Husserl would understand other objects that form the backdrop of or surround the object in question, for example, the clump of trees or other boulders implicit in or at the periphery of my focus on the boulder. A horizon in general, as we will see, is understood as a nexus of referential implications.[12]

Complete givenness, therefore, is impossible for transcendent objects (and here Husserl is thinking primarily of a spatial object) because the transcendent object only manifests itself one-sidedly through a perspective or what he calls a perspectival adumbration [*Abschattung*]. Inadequate givenness of transcendent objects is not a defect that cannot be overcome by a superhuman intellect, Husserl contends; due to the very structure of transcendence, even God would have to perceive transcendent objects perspectivally and inadequately (H XI 18 f.).

Immanent perception, however, is of a different caliber. It is directed toward immanent contents that include intentional acts and non-intentional sensations. Whereas the transcendent (spatial) thing can be given in an unlimited number of ways, it can be given originally in the present; since it can appear from different sides or in different aspects, the immanent object has only one possible way to be given in the original. In the case of transcendent perception we are conscious of the thing only through an appearance such that there is a rupture in what is exhibited and the exhibiting (H X § 44). For the immanent object, on the other hand, that which appears and the appearance cannot be dissociated. The lived-experience does not exhibit itself through perspectival adumbrations (H III 101).

Immanent perception is directed toward immanent contents. It has the peculiar structure that it, as a lived-experience, is directed in reflection toward other lived-experiences. Since the immanent objects that are intended by the intentional lived-experience belong to the same stream of consciousness to which the lived-experience itself belongs, Husserl claims that there is nothing like an infinite regress (H III 85). The *cogitatio* belongs so inherently, so intimately to my perception of it that "object" and "act" form essentially the same immediate unity. Only immanent perception has the structure of intimate inclusiveness: Where an immanent being is given in a closed lived-experience, all chance of error or conflict is precluded (H III 352).

Not all immanent objects have this indubitable mode of givenness; an immanent object in the mode of the past—for example, the remembered boulder—is not presented, but "presentified." The latter act is called presentification [*Vergegenwärtigung*] because it literally re-presents an object that is not given in the original as present. Re-presenting introduces a schism in givenness and hence the possibility of error so that its actuality is contingent and its non-being, conceivable (see H X § 22 and 151–54).

In contrast to consciousness as an object of presentification, consciousness as an object of immanent perception is given in such a way that its non-being is inconceivable; its actuality is absolute, not presumptive. On the one hand, Husserl maintains that the domain of consciousness is an originary self-*presence* grasped in an adequate intuition; on the other, he asserts that consciousness is the sphere of "absolute position," of "absolute *being*" (H III 108–10, 352). The "being of consciousness" and every lived-experience in general is "immanent being." "Immanent being is thus indubitable in the sense of absolute being" (H III 115).

Up to this point, the analyses of consciousness that I have invoked are those that regard the phenomena shorn from temporal considerations. This will be called a "static" analysis. Before defining the place of static method in phenomenology, I want to suggest how Husserl is able to posit consciousness as a absolute sphere of being accessible through immanently intuitive reflection.

The reduction to the transcendental dimension exercised as an intuitive reflective method that abstracts from temporal considerations discloses conscious constituting life as an immanent sphere of absolute being. This sphere is immanent because it is revealed in a self-enclosed reflection through which consciousness has privileged access to itself in evidence, immediately and directly (H III § 44 and 135). Since immanent perception is said to guarantee necessarily the being of its object, its negation is inconceivable and thus indubitable (H III §§ 43 and 46).

In contrast to the privileged mode of intuitive access consciousness enjoys, the world is disclosed as a sphere of transcendent relative being. This sphere is "transcendent" because it is not enclosed intimately in consciousness; its mode of intuitive access for reflecting consciousness is attenuated by the phenomenon's inability to give itself exhaustively in a single intuition. In spite of its immediate form of evidence, it is nonetheless "merely phenomenal," dubitable being since its non-being is conceivable (H III §§ 44, 46, 105, 109). Moreover, the world is "relative" because it is essentially dependent or founded upon consciousness. The result is that immanence becomes virtually identified with absoluteness and transcendence with relativity and presumptuousness (H III 107, 117): the former with necessary being, the latter with contingent being (H III § 49, 108 f., 116 f.).

Having highlighted the contrast between the immanent sphere of absolute being and the transcendent sphere of relative being, I would like to emphasize that the progressive procedure undertaken statically issues in the one-sided relativizing of the world with respect to (absolute) consciousness. This results from the following two considerations.

1. Husserl arrives at the phenomenologically suspect and troubling position of asserting an absolute being of consciousness because he usurps "the principle of presuppositionlessness" with the "maxim of indubitability."

Let me define the principle of presuppositionlessness from the *Logische Untersuchungen* as a mandate to abstain from asserting propositions taken over naively from psychological or natural scientific assumptions (cf. LU II/1 19 ff.). Within transcendental phenomenology, this principle need only mean that instead of taking for granted objects, or eventually the world in their being, one regards their *modes* of givenness. It functions essentially as a "critique" of presuppositions.

When transcendental phenomenology was pursued in a "Cartesian" manner, however, what began as epistemic self-responsibility could not be maintained without a hemorrhage in the tissue of this principle. For this reason, Husserl confesses later that he replaces the former principle with the "*Cartesian maxim of indubitability* that Descartes used at the beginning of his Meditations as the principle of complete legitimation" (H VIII 35, my emphasis). To establish a secure beginning, presumably a critical one, Husserl asserts a new presupposition, a "stratum of *being*," taking the "Cartesian way" beyond the scope of phenomenological inquiry. Let me explain.

To be consistent, when Husserl asks in *Ideen I* whether something can still be posited in its being after the epoche, after the totality of reality [*Weltall*] remains bracketed, he should not be able to answer in the affirmative, asserting immanent being (H III 70 ff.). It is one thing to clarify the existence of consciousness phenomenologically in terms of self-presence, and another to assert its being. Husserl's mistake is to equate transcendent being restrictively with the "external world," forgetting that consciousness too is mundane and is part of the "objective world," and accordingly must be bracketed (H III 69–72, 118 f.). If it is not, consciousness can emerge as an independent absolute sphere of being, and can be given epistemic priority over a dependent relative sphere. The so-called "immanent being" that Husserl asserts as a residuum founding the world and functioning as a philosophical foundation for a rigorous science (H III 72 and § 49) is not, properly speaking, a *phenomenological* presence at all, but a *metaphysical* assertion derived from Cartesian loyalties. One is left wondering whether the ego cogito is not given rather in a "*naive evidence*" (H VIII 30, 33, 276) peculiar to the natural attitude rather than truly phenomenological evidence. For indubitability, like doubt, probability, etc., is still a way of accepting being (H VIII 148). Like Descartes, Husserl implicitly conceives of an end to the critical epoche. Rectifying this mistake is one of the motives for pursuing phenomenology through the "second way," that is, "intentional phenomenological psychology" (chapter 3).[13]

2. Let us put this inconsistency aside for the moment and examine some methodological reasons for asserting the priority of consciousness over the world. As noted in the introduction to this work, there are two moments that characterize transcendental philosophy: the notion of constitution (disclosed by the method of reduction in the broad sense) and the notion of the a priori won by the "eidetic reduction." Stated concisely, Husserl writes: "Thus we arrive at the insight concerning method that *along with the phenomenological reduction, eidetic intuition is the fundamental form of all particular transcendental methods* . . . that both determine thoroughly the legitimate sense of a transcendental phenomenology" (H I 106). According to this text and the explanation given in *Phänomenologische Psychologie* (H IX 289 f.), the first step consists in clarifying all being as constituted and identifying consciousness as the constituting dimension, while the second step is understood as "the eidetic formulation of the problem." Here the results of the constitutive analysis are raised to an eidetic level so that they can be applied to every conceivable ego and to every conceivable world.

I contend that Husserl's Cartesian assertions regarding the priority of consciousness stem methodologically from the *order* in which these two moments are carried out.[14]

All inconsistencies aside, Husserl's procedure requires that one bracket the level of factual existence that discloses modes of givenness and then proceed immediately to the factual presence of my consciousness as a constituting dimension of the world-being; from here one works out the transcendental problems of constitution (the relation of consciousness to objects and to the world as a whole) on the level of my consciousness as constituting consciousness (H III 109). After accounting for the sense of transcendence by recourse to the transcendental constitutive dimension of my consciousness, one moves to another step in transcendental analysis, namely, to the eidetic level, to the transcendental ego as such. In this procedure, the phenomenologist passes from factual existence to self-presence and then to essential self-presence.

As we will see, Husserl later reverses the order in method, and rather than moving from a constitutive analysis to ontology where consciousness is concerned, the phenomenologist will move in a regressive procedure from ontology to phenomenology. We will see as well that insights into the regressive procedure also enable Husserl to impugn the yield of the "Cartesian epoche" precisely because it attains pure self-presence "in one leap" (H VI § 43). The transcendental dimension attained by the "Cartesian way" is apparently empty of content, and one is at a loss, Husserl laments, as to what should have been gained by it, and in particular, how one has gained a new fundamental science: "As the reception of my '*Ideen*' has shown, one succumbs all too easily at the very outset . . . to the very tempting relapse into the naive-natural attitude" (H VI 158). One relapses, in short, into the one-sided assertion of the absolute being of consciousness over against the relative existence of the world.

By leaping to the transcendental ego, transcendental subjectivity is worked out from the very start on the level of individual sense-constitution. Transcendental phenomenology in its progressive strain, even after raising its results to the eidetic level, remains an egology. The only difference is that it now becomes a generalized egology. At most, a phenomenological view of intersubjectivity can offer a multiplicity of individuals. Springing to consciousness does not allow one to take up the role of others or of the world in sense-constitution, except as constituted correlates. What counts in this method is the givenness of the world to consciousness, and the givenness of consciousness to itself as self-presence, since, according to its methodological restrictions, nothing can precede consciousness phenomenologically. Within the Cartesian way, phenomenology cannot inquiry into modes of *pre*-givenness, into facticity, to speak nothing of generativity. For example, Husserl's Cartesian cogito has no phenomenologically significant ancestors or successors and cannot account for the world-constituting significance of birth and death.

In section 4, I examine the possibility of transcendental progenitors and descendants where different modes of world are examined in their sense constituting roles. Let it suffice for the purposes of this section to have simply outlined some of the difficulties with attempting to carry out phenomenological method within the strictures of immanent intuitive reflection.

In the following chapter, I show the shift in the conception of absolute consciousness from a static version we have just seen to a self-temporalizing absolute or to monadic facticity. I then examine the differences and interrelation between static and genetic analyses that attempt to handle such a characterization. Finally I show how problems raised in a genetic analysis for a philosophy of transcendence provoke the problem of the "other" or intersubjectivity.

2

The Absolute as Facticity and the Necessity of Genetic Analysis

This chapter will examine the motivation for genetic method as well as the relation between static and genetic analyses for two principal reasons. First, in order to understand (1) the significance of generativity and generative method for phenomenology, (2) the latter's relationship to genesis and genetic methodology, and (3) the relation of generativity to static analysis, it is necessary to understand not only what belongs to static and genetic domains, but to articulate just how the methods themselves are related to each other methodologically. Second, in a more restricted scope, the issues raised by a genetic analysis are significant because they enable Husserl to grapple with the problem of the "other."

The Self Temporalization of the Absolute and the Concept of Monadic Facticity

The analyses carried out in *Ideen I* posit an immanent sphere of being as "absolute." This absolute is the presence of the pure ego given in intuitive immanent reflection. In this section, I wish to show that in a Cartesian framework absolute consciousness, which is given immediately and adequately in immanent reflection, is not the ultimate or definitive absolute. One reason that the reduction could have been conceived as complete when it yielded the indubitability of consciousness was the restriction of consciousness to the Now-phase. When temporal considerations are entertained, however, the "static" absolute is supplanted by the concrete factical life of the ego.

Husserl admits in *Ideen I* that he arrived at the "absolute" by "necessarily . . . concealing an entire dimension," a dimension of "exceptional difficulty" (H III 197). He writes: "The transcendental absolute [the absolute being of consciousness] that we have brought out through the reductions is in truth not the ultimate absolute; it is something that is constituted in a certain deep-lying and fully peculiar sense, and has its primordial source in an ultimate and true absolute" (H III 198).[1]

What is this ultimate and true absolute? What dimension of phenomenological analysis exceeds the style of investigation undertaken in *Ideen I* such that it misses a more profound sphere? Why does Husserl contend that phenomenology must "necessarily" remain silent at this stage concerning this other dimension? Husserl does not name this new absolute explicitly here, but it is not difficult to identify this absent dimension. The missing dimension is the *temporal* dimension. This supposition is confirmed by the section heading in which Husserl's caveat is issued: "Phenomenological Time and Time Consciousness" (H III § 81). The reason why Husserl contends that phenomenological time *must* be missing will be explained in the following section.

It is characteristic of the methodology employed in *Ideen I* to describe the immanent object merely negatively, as non-spatial, but not yet positively as temporal. As we know, transcendent objects are perspectival and of necessity cannot be given adequately. Husserl makes this point primarily with examples of spatial adumbrations. On the other hand, sensations, for example (such as the color-sensation of gray or *Gefühlserlebnisse* such as pain or pleasure), are not disclosed in (spatial) adumbrations. Ostensibly, they do not have an appearance that points beyond (non-intuitively) to other horizons. They can be registered simply in the Now-phase (H XI 17 f.; H III § 37). Moreover, because the originary phase of the Now is said to be given without adumbrations it is understood as *Undurchstreichbar*, not capable of being canceled (H III 102).

We learn as early as Husserl's lectures on time consciousness (ca. 1905) with his examples of tone-sensations that not only do transcendent objects have non-intuitive horizons, but that immanent "temporal objects" do too. In particular, time consciousness is said not only to exist in the Now-phase, as presented in immanent intuitive reflection; it is also characterized as having temporal horizons. Where time constituting consciousness is concerned, these horizons that occur prior to active ego participation are called "retention" and "protention."

Retention extends from Now-consciousness as a "comet's tail" so that what is retended takes on the character of being "just-past" (H X 36 ff.). Moreover, Husserl maintains that retention is not intentional in the precise sense, since it does not have the form of being-directed toward something; retention as such is never modified (H XI 74, 90, 93).[2]

Retentional consciousness retains the past, enabling active remembering "to reawaken" past experiences, re-presenting them (H VIII 148 ff.). It is what Husserl calls "primary remembering" and is to be distinguished from an active remembering or "secondary remembering" that is a modalization of presentation as a presentification.

Retention is like the presentifying act of active remembering, insofar as it, like remembering, attends to what has been. But whereas the pace of retention is fixed, remembering is more or less free since it can jump around or go slower or faster. This is distinct from phantasy, which in this respect is completely free. Moreover, whereas active remembering posits the reproduced object and gives it a place in relation to the current Now and to the temporal field to which secondary remembering itself belongs, phantasy is not a positional consciousness in this way: It does not posit a reproduced Now and does not coincidence with a past given Now. Finally, active remembering is unlike retention and like phantasy to the extent that both phantasy and secondary remembering are modes of presentification and are "spontaneous" acts (H X 48 ff.).

Not only does consciousness have a past horizon, it has a future horizon as well. Like retention, protention is "passive" consciousness and not a result of ego activity; and like retention, it is "empty" of present self-givenness, a "*Leervorstellung*." Although protention is to be distinguished from active expectation, protention unlike retention is an intentional consciousness as forward directing and is essential to passively constituting consciousness. For this reason Husserl insists that "[w]e are not and we cannot be entirely without a forward directing apprehension. *The temporal halo also has a future*" (H X 167).

In sum, by virtue of retentional and protentional modes of time consciousness, consciousness is necessarily horizonal, simultaneously just past and on the verge of. . . . As such consciousness cannot be given immediately as completely self-present in a Now, for it entails a "*non-intuitive* pointing." Accordingly, it cannot maintain its status as adequately given in intuition; it is always *more* than what can be given.

Consciousness cannot claim to be the ultimate absolute. In *Zur Phänomenologie des inneren Zeitbewußtseins*, Husserl observes: "The perceptual 'given' is necessarily temporally *extended* and not a mere temporal point" (H X 168). Again he asserts in a reprimanding tone: "That all reality lies in an indivisible Now-point, that everything in phenomenology is reduced to this point, is pure *fiction* and leads to absurdities" (H X 169). Finally, Husserl will even go so far as to write that the momentary phase is an *abstraction* that we must first construct and is, too, dubitable, subject to being "canceled out": "The *Undurchstreichbarkeit* peculiar to the moment is thus not something primary"![3]

Consciousness is not a mere temporal point contained in the Now and the intuitive presentation of consciousness in the Now is not absolute for two reasons. First, consciousness is constituted with past and future horizons; due to these horizons, it cannot be given simply in the present. Or more precisely, Husserl is required to extend the presence of consciousness to the more encompassing notion of the "living present" [*lebendige Gegenwart*].[4] A living present for Husserl is not just this minute, this day, or even this year; it can also be an entire coalition of years as long as it has an individual, typical self-contained unity, one that stands in contrast to another typical unity which is understood as a past living present.[5]

Second and more important, as a living absolute, time consciousness is not merely constituted; rather, it is *self-temporalizing*, that is, time constituting. As a result, consciousness as time constituting is not "in" a Now or "in" a past or a future. Rather it "belongs to" its temporal phases as it constitutes them; as constituting, it is not itself temporally objective (H X 74 f.).

Time constituting consciousness is pre-phenomenal and prior to the temporality of immanent objects. It is the process of temporalization and as such the "origin" of the past, present, and future. This matter, Husserl emphatically asserts, is "perhaps the most important matter in the whole of phenomenology" (H X 334). Husserl wants to maintain that there must be a peculiar self-appearance of the flux itself, graspable in the flowing: "Constituting and constituted coincide." And yet, he continues, "naturally, they cannot coincide in every respect" (H X 83).

If constituting consciousness and constituted consciousness cannot coincide in every respect, then it would seem that it cannot be completely present to itself in immanent intuitive reflection; it would necessarily escape from itself not only in the constitution of time, but also when the reduction turns toward time constituting consciousness. We are dealing with a peculiar absolute, indeed, with a coincidence in non-coincidence, with an absolute that withdraws from itself in the process of showing itself. The "true" and "ultimate" absolute consciousness has, as Merleau-Ponty would say, a "*punctum caecum*," a blind spot.[6]

To say that the absolute has a blind spot is to say that it is not timeless or a mere series of Now-phases, but constitutes itself temporally in a unity of life. If this ultimate absolute, time constituting consciousness, is pre-phenomenal it must also in some sense transcend phenomenological analysis, at least as it has been presented where the temporal dimension is shorn from consciousness. And if such temporal considerations are admitted into phenomenological investigations, if they are deemed to be among the most important matters of phenomenology, then phenomenology itself must engage in a new dimension of analysis. In other words, Husserl needs to thematize a method for the phenomena already being disclosed. As we will see shortly, he will call this method "genetic."

When Husserl begins to thematize genesis and distinguish it from stasis, he is particularly occupied with describing and defining the concept of a "monad," an expression taken, of course, from Leibniz.[7] For Husserl a monad is a being that is in temporal becoming or genesis, constitutes itself in a temporal unity of life as a structure of habitualities, and is ultimately a concrete ego, "individuated" or "factical." Let me explain this concept of the monad that becomes the genetically "true" absolute.

1. Husserl defines a monad as a "simple" individual being [*Wesen*] "that is what it is as *continually becoming in time*" (H XIV 35, my emphasis). The monad, he tells us, is not only what it is Now, but is also what it is as having been [*als gewesene*] in a living present, and immediately transcending what it has been in the process of becoming (H XIV 36). This living present is the unity of the temporal phases impression, retention, and protention. On the basis of this initial characterization, Husserl will distinguish between the "pure" ego as a timeless pole peculiar to a static analysis and an ego as temporally "extended" or "enduring" [*dauernd*], signaling a departure from a static analysis (H XIV 42). As temporally enduring, the monad is not fixed in a Now-point.

2. To say that the monad as a temporalizing process is not exhausted in a Now-point does not mean that it exists in a mere series of Now-phases. Rather, self-temporalizing consciousness constitutes itself primordially as a unity of becoming in and through its experiences, that is, through its diverse living presents. The immanent time of an ego, asserts Husserl, can never be unfilled, have gaps, or fall apart into several separated streams leaving the monad fragmented in disjoined pauses. "In the monad, everything is connected to everything else" (H XIV 36). More precisely, every experience is connected by virtue of the "background" or "horizon" feature of experience that meets the demands of unity and temporal becoming (H XIV 34). Living through temporal horizons, the monad is constituted as a "living unity" that carries in itself an ego as the pole of effecting and being affected, as a unity of capabilities or "dispositions" and of that which is "concealed" or "unconscious" (H XIV 34).

Because the monad has a concealed or unconscious life, it has to be investigated phenomenologically not only in terms of its "givenness" or its being-sense (the limit of a static analysis), but also in terms of its "*pre-givenness*" and the sense of its "*pre-being*." Moreover, a genetic approach, which inquires into the pre-givenness of temporalization or the latency of pre-being, Husserl explains, belongs to the "deeper levels of phenomenology" and transcends "first phenomenology" (i.e., static phenomenology) (H XV 611 fn. 1). What lies deeper than being "in the manner of constituting anonymity, in latency, is a μὴὄν." This "non-being" is not the thesis or conscious positing of being, he contends, but the pre-positing or "presupposition" of being out of a forgotten temporalization; it is not yet the temporalization of an ὂν or being, but a becoming that makes being possible.[8]

3. The monad is prior to being insofar as it is a process of genesis that makes the position of being possible. Where constitutive phenomenology is concerned, genetic method has to be seen as more profound than static method. Characterizing the monad as a living unity prior to static being implies still further that the monad is not simply a unity of acts, but a unity of acts and affections. This feature allows Husserl to claim that the monad is a "substratum of *habitualities*" (H XIV 43, H I 100–102). Habitualities are "*Niederschläge am Ich*"—deposits, precipitations, sedimentations that accrue to the ego.

Husserl tends to illustrate the interaction between act and affect, which yields the habitual structure of the ego, with the process of making a rational judgment that on the one hand quickly passes, but on the other leaves behind the "precipitations" of a person who has made the judgment, that is, a person who has this or that conviction (cf. H I 100 ff.). His point is to show that even though the act process streams away, the decision "solidifies" or "consolidates" as new abiding characteristics formative of the being who I am in rational, volitional, or axiological spheres—as long as I have not given up that conviction. Thus, habitualities result from conscious acts such as judgments that become integrated into an "abiding style" of life (H XIV 53, cf. 36, 46).

This might be seen more clearly with an example of bodily comportment. Just as I have to learn actively the proper techniques in order to make a climb, these actively learned movements become retained passively, structuring my future movement such that over time I acquire a distinctive *style* of comportment and am disposed more easily to certain action. This is more than a matter of simply remembering my acts, for they become integrated into my general comportment, whether I return to them in the future through active remembering or whether I ignore them and carry out other acts.

Similar to Aristotle's conception of ethical virtue as a product of habit [ἔθος] which is inextricably related to character [ἕξεις],[9] Husserl maintains that the monad acquires the style of "personal character" in the unity of a life through active decisions that become sedimented as an "abiding *habitus.*" As the unity of act and affect, of disposition and predisposition, the I is structured as an "*I can.*"

4. The temporal synthesis of present impression, retention, and protention, which structures the living present and the unity of the ego as the synthesis of living presents, are still "formal" treatments of the ego, and to this extent remain abstract (H XI 126 ff.). With the introduction of affection, the constitution of the monad through self-temporalization becomes more rich in content. For to assert that the monad has habitualities means that the monad as a temporal synthesis does not lose its identity from moment to moment, but retains it at least passively.

Becoming identical as enduring through immanent time, the temporal unity of the monad in genesis is necessarily concrete and not an empty form. In his discussions of monadic genesis, Husserl will differentiate between the "pure I," the temporally "enduring I," the "habitual I," and a fourth dimension that is peculiar to the temporalizing monad, namely, the concrete ego. "This *concrete* ego is the actual ego of inner experience . . . and the pure I is *abstractly* identical" (H XIV 43, 47, my emphasis).

Husserl writes that "[i]f the monad necessarily has the form of a unity of becoming [*Werdenseinheit*], of a unity of an incessant *genesis,* then it has a *concrete* structure only from 'elements' that are themselves unities of becoming and that have an *abstract* structure according to phases like the entire monad" (H XIV 34). In other words, just as the elemental unities (living presents) are concrete in relation to its phases (impression, retention, protention), which taken by themselves are abstract, so too is the monad in genesis a concrete unity of becoming made up of phases that are unities of becoming (i.e., living presents, phases which in relation to the monad are abstract).

The concrete ego constitutes itself as a unity of life in and through its phases which, when taken separately, are abstract. Only in their interdependent unity are they concrete. Thus, contends Husserl, everything concrete in the monad is *non-independent* such that the concept of independence cannot be identified with the concept of the concrete (H XIV 37). Husserl refers here explicitly to his *Logische Untersuchungen,* and implicitly to his Third Logical Investigation on the relation between parts and wholes, and specifically to his contention in § 17 of this investigation (as well as § 15 of *Ideen I*) that what is absolutely independent is concrete and that an non-independent being is abstract. His analyses of the monad would seem to challenge the privileged position of the pure ego that is given in present immanent reflection as an "independent" and one-sided foundation. It is only as non-independent that the ego can be said to be concrete; the pure ego once touted as a concrete foundation must be disclosed now as an abstraction.

5. In a final dimension of monadic genesis following from concreteness, Husserl understands the self-temporalizing life of the absolute monad as "individuated." Individuation of the monad means that the monad is a "unity of its living becoming, a unity of its *history*," and that it bears in its primordial present a "*heritage* of the past," that is, its whole "*sedimented history as a horizon*" (H XIV 36, my emphasis).

Husserl means by history [*Geschichte*] in this context that there is density of temporal becoming or development that is expressed in the style of a unique and irreducible monadic life. He does not mean by history a social, diachronically unfolding generational becoming as will be the case when he approaches "generative problems" in the framework of a generative phenomenology. While Husserl uses the term "history" here, I reserve this expression, for systematic reasons, for the dimension of temporality peculiar to *generative* phenomena. It is in fact more accurate to call this *genetic* dimension of temporality peculiar to the self-temporalization of an individual monadic life, "*facticity*."[10]

On the one hand, to maintain that genetic phenomenology treats facticity means that this type of phenomenology can treat individual development, including the developmental stages of the child to the adult.[11] But the boundaries of genetic phenomenology—what Husserl calls "first genesis"—are restricted to the development of the *individual* life; it does not question after the socio-historical context into which that life is born or out of which it dies: "In first genesis everything that lies prior to human childhood remains unquestioned."[12]

Just as consciousness is not an isolated act, but a temporal process inclusive of horizons, so too is absolute monadic life not isolated from others. Reasoning on the basis of what has been said concerning a monad, Husserl asserts that while each individuated monad is unique by virtue of its self-temporalization and concrete factical structure, a monad is nevertheless bound with other monads in a community of monads (H XIV 36). Just as a concrete monadic unity of becoming is made up of non-independent phases which, when taken separately, are abstract, so too is a community of monads a concrete unity of becoming made up of individual monadic unities, which when taken independently are abstract. Precisely because the individuated monad as concrete is dependent upon other individuations (H XIV 37), a theory of intersubjectivity in this framework could not admit of an independent concrete foundational sphere for others—unless of course the method for determining the theory were in some ways abstract. Still, where social being is concerned, genetic method is restricted to a synchronic temporality of individuals, to contemporaneous monads; it does not handle the development of social being historically. For this a generative method will be necessary.

I will not pursue this line of thought any further here. It is sufficient to note that Husserl's understanding of the absolute monad as self-temporalizing, as a unity of life, as a substratum of habitualities, as concrete and as factical exceeds the boundaries of a static analysis of a pure ego. In the next section I show how Husserl attempts to address this situation by proposing a methodological distinction between static and genetic analyses.

Static and Genetic Analyses

Husserl had already engaged in genetic analyses before phenomenology became aware of itself as having a quite distinct genetic dimension. In particular, an explicit return to the question of temporality and time constitution, the concern with pre-predicative dimensions of experience as forming the basis for the active genesis of thought, the explication of passive genesis through a phenomenology of association as well as a rekindled interest in the problems of normality and abnormality all coalesce around the years 1917-21 and exceed the bounds of a static method.[13]

Under this heading I describe static and genetic dimensions of phenomenology in terms of method and their matters, without, however, treating the interrelation of those dimensions. Thus, I describe these dimensions themselves *structurally* or *statically*. To treat them dynamically I will have to introduce the notion of "leading clue"; this will require treating the phenomenology of method itself methodologically in a genetic style (and ultimately generatively). But first I will address the structural differentiation between the first two levels of phenomenological method: static and genetic.[14]

To the best of my knowledge, the first systematic attempt to dissociate a genetic from a static method occurred in the manuscript B III 10 written at St. Märgen in 1921.[15] In these writings Husserl circumscribes various fields of investigation according to method. First, Husserl maintains that he can describe the structure of the stream of experience [*Erlebnisstrom*] "noetically-noematically" in its general "fixed" typicality, he can examine its possible modifications, investigating in the phenomenological-eidetic reduction the frameworks of structures—all this *without* inquiring into the genesis of their constitution, the genesis of the constituted objects or the facticity of the monad (H XIV 37). Let me cite the passage in which he begins to tease apart static and genetic approaches. We read:

> I can indeed characterize phenomenological investigations *statically*, investigations that trace the correlation between constituting consciousness and constituted object [*Gegenständlichkeit*], and exclude *genetic* problems altogether. From this, I can distinguish phenomenological investigations that consider the typicality of different self-exhibiting shapes of experience and of geneses according to their structural possibilities, compatibilities, etc., without however regarding the problems of the individual in this framework. Finally, we have the phenomenology of monadic individuality, included in this, the phenomenology of a *genesis* that is coupled to it, a genesis that grows in the unity of the monad, in which the monad *is by becoming* [*in der die Monad ist, indem sie wird*]. (H XIV 38, my emphasis)

To gain a clearer idea of the difference between static and genetic analyses, let me briefly describe the province of each method.

Under the rubric of "static phenomenology" Husserl has two methodological strategies in mind. The first is a *constitutive* analysis that inquires into the *way* or *how* something is given and not *what* something is. The second is a static phenomenology that analyzes "structures." Structures may include formal and material essences or morphological types. Common examples of phenomenological structures are the noesis or the noema, intentionality, modes of fulfillment and disappointment, the relations of foundation among acts, or the pregiven foundational layers of the lifeworld. Thus, static analysis can be both a constitutive and an ontological enterprise.[16]

A static analysis might begin with an experience like viewing a boulder. Taking this experience as having a relation to a meant object, I can move to the meant features found in perception such as the color gray or the sensation of hardness. In addition, I can observe that these aspects are tied to an extended spatial structure such that if it proves to be a mirage cast by light and shadows of blowing trees, the color, texture, and anticipated point of stability for movement immediately vanish; the boulder no longer has the same way of occupying space.[17]

In another step, I can follow out the correlation of the unity of the appearing object to the manifold types of consciousness in which the appearances are united. I observe, for example, that the boulder is presented primarily to my visual and tactile spheres. Here we thematize the noetic components of this correlation in terms of its sense bestowing and sense fulfilling functions.

In yet a further step, I can construe through eidetic analyses the structural possibilities of this particular object and grasp it as an example of an essence: "This" mossy green or gray, is expressive of the predicate or essence "color"; this round or sharp is an expression of "form"; this hard substance exemplifies solidity; etc. I can further identify certain typicalities in the diverse rocks I find around me and arrive at essential types of rock such as igneous, metamorphic, and sedimentary. Or by varying this instance of rock in imagination, I can reach the essence of rock in general, say, "solid mineral matter." Finally, I can attain the highest material essence of rock, namely, the region of being, "physical thing."

While I can also grasp such experiences in terms of their essential possibilities for a subject who emerges in and through them, Husserl insists nevertheless that "I do not inquire here into the genesis of the monad, into the way in which such phenomena originate or develop [*entspringen*]" (H XIV 40). That is, I can vary myself as monad *qua* correlate of the objects, but I do not inquire into its genesis as self-temporalizing or developing. Here the monad is treated simply as a "fixed" essential possibility, as an "already 'developed' subjectivity." In this instance it is regarded in terms of the types of relations that can hold for me and other self-temporalizing subjects approaching the boulder.[18]

Throughout these descriptions I can hold in abeyance questions concerning their existence or being, and inquire into how they are constituted as accomplishments of subjectivity in manifold modes of consciousness.[19] Thus, even though the analyses concerning the essential correlations between object and subject are static, because I question after the modes of givenness, the questions raised in a static analysis can be "overall *constitutive* questions." It is for this reason that Husserl is able to maintain that a static analysis can be a constitutive analysis without being an inquiry into genesis. In a very revealing and instructive remark, Husserl asserts: "*Following out constitution is not following out genesis, which is precisely genesis of constitution and operates as genesis in a monad.*"[20]

My intention thus far has been simply to show that within a static analysis two methodological strategies are possible. First, one can pursue structural descriptions: These can include the assessment of how acts or objects exist in relationships of foundation, or they can entail eidetic descriptions, that is, a formal or material ontology. All this can be carried out *within the natural attitude* where being is taken for granted. Second, one can undertake a static constitutive analysis. These two possibilities represent the distinctive static projects Husserl undertook in *Ideen I* and *Ideen II*. That Husserl understood there to be an "inner relation of constitutive phenomenologies to a priori ontologies" is clear (H III 379). Just how they are related is not. This is a topic I address below under the heading "Leading Clue." At this juncture, let me move on to some features of a genetic analysis.

Before characterizing the concept of genesis as Husserl came to understand it in the years following 1917, let me briefly cite the instances in which Husserl used the expression prior to this time.

In the first instance, Husserl employed the term genesis negatively. In the *Logische Untersuchungen*, for example, he criticized empirical psychology for imputing subjective genesis in consciousness to ideal objects rather than understanding mathematical and logical entities as self-given to consciousness in intuition.[21] By *Ideen III* (1913), Husserl used the term positively in an effort (1) to distinguish an ontological investigation into essences that remains mundane, from a constitutive or phenomenological analysis of the noema in terms of intention and fulfillment (H V 129), and (2) to describe the relations of foundation obtaining between the "categorial" affair-complexes that presuppose "simple" objects of perception.[22]

But it was not until after 1915 that Husserl used the concept of genesis in his "proper" sense. Now genetic analyses explicate monadic becoming for the full concretion and individuality of experience. Because genetic analyses concern the concrete, self-temporalizing *qua* factical ego, the investigations undertaken in *Zur Phänomenologie des inneren Zeitbewußtseins* from 1905 are not by themselves genetic in the strict sense; they are at best transitional. True, the time lectures do go beyond treating consciousness as a series of many Nows by explicating the transition obtaining between the Nows, as it were.[23] Nevertheless, these investigations are not genetic because they are still too abstract, only treating the ego as a temporal form, that is, as the form of time: impression, retention, protention, and their forms of temporal connection, namely, succession and coexistence. Husserl himself declares that "[m]ere form is surely an abstraction, and thus the intentional analysis of time consciousness and its accomplishments is an abstractive analysis from the very start." This analysis of time is abstract and not genetic in the proper sense "because it abstracts precisely from content" (H XI 128, cf. 126 f.). I will return to the significance of this "abstraction" below.

According to Husserl, in order for the analysis of temporalization not to risk remaining a conceptual idealization (H XI 387), it must be completed by a phenomenology of primordial phenomena. Such primordial phenomena include motivation, apperception, and affective association. In other words, it requires a constitutional analysis of temporalization, an inquiry into how sense unities come into relief and through their "affective force" provoke a combination with other senses. It requires an inquiry into how past sedimentations can be reawakened through the affective force of the present, and how the sense of a present perception relies on the past institution of sense in order for the sense of an object to develop. In short, a concrete analysis of self-temporalization requires an analysis of sense constitution through a "phenomenology of association" (H XI 129 ff.).

Having merely suggested the basic tenor of genetic analyses in association, let me now note that within a genetic phenomenology Husserl distinguishes between three levels of genesis or relations of motivation (H XI 342 ff.). First, Husserl reserves a dimension of investigation for purely active genesis. In active genesis, the ego is regarded as functioning in rational acts that constitute both ideal objects (such as numbers through counting, predicative affair-complexes through predicating, conclusions through deducing), and "real" objects (including so-called cultural objects, i.e., books, printing presses, etc.) that are constituted socially (H I 111).

Second, Husserl proposes a level of investigation that bridges passive and active genesis. On the one hand, what Husserl seems to have in mind is the process of becoming stimulated affectively, say, by a flash in the sky from a shooting star, and then the active turning toward it in attention (cf. H XI 162 ff.). But Husserl's foray into genesis is sufficiently ambiguous at this time enabling him to understand by the expression "passive" both "disinterested-inactivity" of the ego *and* "receptivity," or "affectivity."[24] Thus, this dimension of genetic analysis can also include the investigations into the *origins* of active genesis in "passivity," for example, the origins of ideal geometrical shapes and deductive geometrical theorems as developed from the experience of spatial shapes and pre-predicative assertions.[25] Husserl will understand this latter process as a method of questioning back [*Rückfrage*] into the founding layers of validity "and therefore a questioning back into genesis" (H XV 614).[26]

Finally, Husserl distinguishes a sphere of genetic development that is fully passive. This analysis of genetic constitution concerns the "primordial institution" [*Urstiftung*] of sense but blossoms into a phenomenology of "primordial constitution" [*Urkonstitution*] as a phenomenology of apperception.

Passive genesis is called "primordial constitution" because it occurs "prior to" rational constitution carried out by spontaneous, "free" participation of the ego. The analyses of passive synthesis are placed in the domain of what Kant called before Husserl a "transcendental aesthetic." Sensitive to the ancient Greek sense of αἴσθησις, Husserl envisions primordial constitution and passive synthesis as a unique kind of lived "perceptual" engagement with the world prior to and to some extent independent of judgmental understanding (cf. EU § 14). Passive synthesis and primordial constitution covered in a transcendental aesthetic—a "phenomenology of the so-called unconscious" (H XI 154)—is distinct from what Husserl will call (following Kant) a "transcendental logic," exploring the phenomenon of active genesis.

Under passive genesis, then, we would include the description of modes of givenness, say, of the boulder in its modes of orientation of space and time. It has sense for me by being near or far to my lived-body, left or right, above or below, in front or in back; it can be in motion or rest by virtue of my lived-body as a point of orientation, which is to say, a zero-point of sense-givenness (cf. H XIV 35). In a genetic analysis, moreover, it becomes clear that I do not have all the perspectives in the same way; some are eclipsed to the extent that others appear; some are affectively prominent, while others become distorted, vague, or peripheral. Rather than having a perceptually "flat" world, through genetic analyses my relation to the world is disclosed as a "depth" structure.

Not only does phenomenology investigate the object "aesthetically," that is, in relation to the perceptual lived-body, but it also describes the lived-body "kin-aesthetically," that is, the apperceptive motivations and transformations for movement. I investigate my bearing toward the boulder as an "I can," for example, "I can climb," and inquire into how one movement is motivated by another, provoking new sense givenness in the object. By examining the interplay of intention, fulfillment, and disappointment, new features determine the object ever more richly such that my perceptions that unfold concordantly amid discontinuities of perception form a general acceptance of "the boulder itself." In turn, the futural "in-itself" of the boulder, which is generated by the past acceptances, guides teleologically the unfolding of my kinaestheses.

Having distinguished these three interrelated spheres of genetic analysis, and having illustrated what a genetic analyses might entail, it remains to specify the relation between ontological and constitutive analyses within a static method, as well as the relation between static and genetic methods.

Leading Clue

Husserl characterizes the connection between ontological and constitutive analyses, as well as the connection between static and genetic methods as a relation of *Leitfaden* or "leading clue." The notion of leading clue articulates the relationship of motivation obtaining between methods and matters. Put differently, rather than offering a static view of the methods, the concept of leading clue is itself a dynamic notion and illustrates a "genetic" understanding of the relation between methods. In order to understand the dynamic relation between static and genetic matters and methods (and eventually between these dimensions and a generative phenomenology), let me begin with the interrelation between ontological and constitutive strategies within the strictures of a static method.

The relation between a structural and a constitutional undertaking is addressed, albeit in an oblique manner, in the concluding chapter of *Ideen I.* There the notion of leading clue describes three different relationships: (1) the relation between formal and material ontologies: A formal ontology can function as a leading clue to the structure and determination of objects in a regional ontology (H III 362–64, 378).[27] (2) The relation between ontology and constitutive analyses: A region of being, for example, the region "material thing," is said to offer a leading clue to the constitutional problems of individual objects or groups of objects within that region (H III 364, 379 f.). Thus, eidetic analyses in the natural attitude can function as a leading clue to phenomenological inquires in the transcendental attitude (H III 369), and the natural and human sciences can function as leading clues to a phenomenological science (H III 376). (3) The relation between constitutive analyses and ontology: A constitutional analysis of objects and their modes of givenness can function as a leading clue to the formulation of a material essence, that is, a region (H III 358 ff., 364, 372).

Since I am interested in showing the generation of phenomenology through a phenomenology of generativity—and thus how static and genetic methods function initially as leading clues to generativity and a generative phenomenology—it will not be necessary to delve into all these relations of leading clue here. Let me simply note that the reason Husserl asserts that a constitutive endeavor can guide an ontological one is due to the fact that regions are disclosed according to the way in which objects or affair-complexes are given. So, for example, because the way in which the thing is given differs from the way in which the lived-body (which is simultaneously constituting and constituted) is given to itself, the difference in the modes of constitution "indicate" regional differences of being.[28] In this case, the psycho-physical sphere of being distinguishes itself internally from the sphere of material nature.

This movement from constitutive phenomenology to ontology, however, is hardly mentioned in comparison to the inverse methodological turn that seems to carry much more import for Husserl at this time:

letting ontology function as a leading clue for constitutive analyses.[29] This is a more significant insight in terms of Husserl's method because it implies a phenomenological "regressive" procedure that enables phenomenology to move from a lifeworld ontology to transcendental analyses of the "lifeworld," and in the final analysis to approach the problem of intersubjectivity through homeworld and alienworld (cf. H XXIX 152–60, 173 fn. 2).

Let me begin by noting, then, that ontological analyses can provide leading clues to constitutive analyses in general. This means that the fundamental concepts of ontology serve as "indexes" for how we can examine the various strata of constituted objectivities, first in a static and then in a genetic method: "*Is not static phenomenology precisely the phenomenology of leading clues,* the phenomenology of the constitution of guiding [*leitender*] types of objectivities in their being and of the constitution of their non-being . . . ?" (H XIV 41; cf. 40).

For Husserl, one must first establish static matters: structures like intentionality, etc. They then guide the formulation of the matters in their becoming as well as the formulation of appropriate methods. In a manuscript composed in the 1930s, Husserl writes: "Thus, that is *static* phenomenology. I analyze *ontologically* the being-sense world and correlatively I inquire into the certainties of being, specifically, I inquire concretely into the modes of givenness. *Ontological analysis* is the *leading clue* for the analysis of correlative validities of being."[30] In this case, Husserl can understand a "static" formal ontological or regional analysis as providing a leading clue for a "static" constitutive analysis.[31]

But to say that the phenomenologist recognizes ontological concepts or principles as leading clues for constitutive frameworks does not mean that the phenomenologist judges ontologically, warns Husserl. This would be to reduce logical or structural relations of foundation to the empirical process of thought (H III 379 f.). There will be occasion to examine how historicity is related to the task of phenomenology when I take up the matter of generativity. At this time let me examine the relation of leading clue obtaining between static and genetic methods. To understand the relation of static to genetic methods, note that when Husserl reflects back on the emergence of genetic and static methods he orders them by understanding static method as providing a leading clue to constitutive phenomena and its method.

Husserl's methodological strategy has the peculiar trait of privileging the "simple" over the "complex" as a way of easing into phenomenological descriptions. For example, he will begin with the object in rest as opposed to the object in motion in descriptions of spatiality and kinaesthesis; he will begin with monothetic acts and then proceed to synthetic ones; he will describe the constitution of normality and abnormality by beginning with individual senses rather than the whole lived-body; and he will take as his point of departure a slice of single conscious intentionality rather than the factical individual monad when describing the phenomenological notion of the "Absolute." He explains: "With all that a certain manner of phenomenological observations is sketched out according to the exercise of the phenomenological reduction that forms the point of departure. I must proceed step by step; initially I do not even see that a conscious stream is immanently [*innerlich*] constituted; I have still not fixed it scientifically, to say nothing of monadic individuality, and the ego of dispositions that is constituted in it, etc." (H XIV 35).

Static phenomenology in the sense of ontology and constitutive phenomenology can provide leading clues for a genetic constitutive analysis. For example, as leading clues, the structure noesis:noema, intentionality, and modes of intention and fulfillment point to how consciousness develops actively and passively through transitions in retention, impression, and protention, or through remembering and expectation. Genetic phenomenology will use the language of genesis to express the laws of association and reproduction through which the monad constitutes itself in a concrete individuated unity. Once we become clear about *what* consciousness is as a structure and *how* this "what" is constituted, maintains Husserl, the results of our static analyses can function as leading clues to *how* consciousness arises out of consciousness through genetically functioning modes of "motivation," that is, the relations of conditioning obtaining between the motivated and the motivating (H XIV 41).[32] Thus, types of possible objects and subjects (natural, psychic, and cultural-spiritual) function as leading clues for the constitutive becoming of individual life and monadic communities, as well as for the teleology of reason, etc. (H XI 344).

When thematizing the progression or genesis of method, Husserl writes that the basic question concerns "how the investigations are to be ordered"; that is, it "concerns the leading clues of the system" (H XI 344). While Husserl assumes that a static method must precede a genetic one, what he describes as a foregone conclusion and necessity of connection is actually the description of his own philosophical progression, that is, the genesis of phenomenological method in his hands. For Husserl, a static phenomenology really did function as a guiding clue or way into a genetic phenomenology before it became conscious of itself as such.

Here is how a genetic method comes to be formulated. Husserl finds himself already in the process of "describing" phenomena *that exceed the restrictions of the method propounded at that time.*[33] Now, to describe these new matters, Husserl must already be employing a new method in order for those phenomena to give themselves in this new way, but without being conscious of exactly how it is a new method or when it became so. To be more specific, it is not uncommon for Husserl to advance a particular theme during a certain period of research and not treat it again systematically until a decade later. Or, during a given period of time, Husserl will experiment with incompatible approaches mixing themes and importing past conclusions into new methods of procedure. The result is that certain phenomena Husserl wants to take up in fact exceed the boundaries of the operative method. He may begin, for example, by describing phenomena that are static such as the structure of conscious intentionality. But by moving to the question of the form of temporal synthesis or habituality, new methodological assumptions are brought into play implicitly. Perhaps they are not quite fully "genetic," but they are certainly beyond what static analyses were able to offer. Looking back, Husserl tends to acknowledge retrospectively what methodological advances must have taken place in order to be able to describe the phenomena he did. He then clarifies the method for future investigations of those same themes and for the enrichment of phenomenological method as a whole.[34]

Understanding the general development of method in this way is helpful because it can account for how Husserl was not only able to describe genetic, but also generative phenomena that exceeded the bounds of genetic phenomenology, and how Husserl could implicitly carry out a generative method without explicitly distinguishing the latter from a genetic method or articulating this dimension of phenomenology *as* a generative phenomenology. According to his own notion of *Leitfaden*, generative phenomenology is anticipated by the emergence of genetic phenomenology and generative problems. This is actually the state of a generative phenomenology in the 1930s. What I do in section 4 is take the next step and formulate this generative dimension as a generative phenomenology on the basis of genetic leading clues and matters that themselves exceed the bounds of genetic analysis.

Let me add one further point. It may seem circuitous to take up the problem of world and the transcendental modalities of the lifeworld (section 2), and then develop normality and abnormality from a genetic phenomenological perspective (section 3) before ever touching on "generative problems"; having already defined static and genetic methodologies, it would seem that I should jump straight to the matter of generativity and formulate a generative phenomenology.

The reason it is not possible to do this concerns the very nature of generativity and the process of leading clue. Because Husserl never explicitly formulated a generative phenomenology, it is necessary to undertake the phenomenological work of following out the leading clues that lead to generativity and the formulation of generative phenomenology. Once this is done, the task of phenomenology and the directionality of method can and must be modified as generativity generates. While the relation between matters and methods, even between static and genetic methods, can only be determined from a generative phenomenology and the problem of generativity, let me advance some provisional conclusions.

When Husserl begins to describe genetic phenomena, he implicitly abandons his strategy of ordering the movement of leading clue from the simple to the complex. Instead, the movement seems to occur from the "concrete" to the "abstract." Such a shift, in other words, implies that the movement of leading clue goes *from genetic to static* dimensions. For example, when evaluating the process of self-temporalization from his time lectures, Husserl judges them to be merely "formal" and "abstract" (H XI 126 ff.). Or again, from the perspective of the "*concrete* ego" as unity of becoming, the "pure ego" is only "*abstractly* identical" (H XIV 34, 43, 47).[35] In view of a genetic method, Husserl will even go so far as to question whether it is even possible to undertake phenomenology systematically in a static framework, that is, where genesis is fully ignored.[36] Eventually, as we will see, even the process of self-temporalization and facticity will be viewed as "abstract" by Husserl in relation to the concrete dimension of generativity.

The point I wish to make here is that once there is some explicit awareness that phenomenology is genetic such that one can compare static and genetic matters and methods, phenomenology itself undergoes a methodological transformation. Along with the fact that the operative notions of leading clue become "concrete" and "abstract" rather than "simple" and the "complex," phenomenology takes on a new directionality, as it were. Phenomenology cannot and must not only proceed in one direction, from static to genetic; it can and must also double back on itself.

But when it "goes back," it must do so in a critical manner. It has to reevaluate the results it won from a static analysis through the disclosures of a genetic analysis. For example, the hyle/morphe distinction peculiar to a static model of constitution can be called into question in the direction of the phenomenology of association, the process of habitualization, sedimentation, reactivation, and the fundamental role of horizons in the constitution of sense. Or, as we have seen above, the static model of the "Absolute" as the "being of consciousness" can be usurped by another "Absolute" more profound, the process of self-temporalization and monadic facticity. Now, rather than the "complex" (say, the process of passive synthesis of temporal horizons) presupposing the "simple" (e.g., the impressional present), the latter as "abstract" presupposes the "concrete," factical monadic becoming. Confirming this view, Husserl charges that a static clarification, which at first functioned as a leading clue to a genetic analysis, now presupposes a genetic analysis: "Preceding this is the static elucidation of world-apperception and of the sense-giving that is executed in it. But, it seems, an absolute consideration of the world, a 'metaphysics', can only first be carried out, and the possibility of a world can only first be understood *through the genetic consideration of individuation*" (H XI 343, my emphasis). Such a view on the relation between static and genetic analyses means that even when one is undertaking static analysis, one is *already* at the level of genetic method, only abstractly; or put differently, it is possible to say that we have indeed always already been dealing with genesis, only structurally. Thus Husserl writes: "To a certain extent, every such [static] analysis is already in itself genetic analysis" (H XIV 480). This situation would seem to imply that a genetic phenomenology certainly does entail a "surpassing" of static method, and that it does not necessarily leave "intact" that which was previously discovered.[37]

How genetic method and matters function as leading clues to generativity and the formulation of a generative phenomenology will be taken up below. In order to address generative phenomena which are social and historical, it will be necessary first to see how a systematic concern with the "other" is implied by a genetic method. It will then be possible to view how a generative phenomenology's reconfiguration of intersubjective phenomena in terms of homeworld and alienworld entails reevaluating the matters disclosed by a genetic phenomenology.

In the next chapter, I introduce the notion of the "other" as a genuine mode of transcendence. I then explain how Husserl's "second way" of carrying out the reduction entertains the problem of intersubjectivity. In order to clarify the consequence of Husserl's theories of intersubjectivity, I want to introduce a systematic distinction between the "other" and the "alien." This distinction will facilitate explaining in what sense first philosophy (as the "second way") remains moored to the "Cartesian way."

3

The "Other" as the Theme of First Philosophy

Transcendence in the "Genuine" Sense

Transcendental phenomenology is a philosophy of transcendence. Genetic method has allowed the reduction to extend beyond my punctual present life and therefore beyond a mere present mode of transcendence. The gesture to expand the reduction to modes of transcendence, particularly the gesture to include temporal as well as spatial horizons implied by and extending beyond the perceptual present, requires a shift from a static analysis to a genetic analysis. Despite this fact, Husserl will persist for some time in attempting to frame a phenomenology of intersubjectivity in a static mode. What need concern us here is that when incorporating modes of transcendence that exceed the present into the reduction, it is necessary to recast the schema of transcendence in immanence in order to account for these other modes. An initial reevaluation is suggested by the attention Husserl gives to the modes of givenness in remembering.

Husserl sought to secure justified knowledge in the originary givenness of perceptual evidence. Though conflicts and discrepancies may arise that question the integrity of what was had as evident, evidence can only be canceled out and replaced by another evident perception. Original evident perception is the ultimate court of appeal for the legitimation of objective knowledge (H III § 141). Conversely, remembering and all reproductive acts, including intropathy [*Einfühlung*] which gives the other, are not original but derived and mediate. They eventually make their contribution to evidence only by their sanguine ties to originary evidence in an original present.

Yet in lectures postdating the *Ideen,* Husserl challenges this, his own assumption: To be sure, one may have indubitability and non-annullable validity in the present, "[b]ut what good is it, since it is only a momentary one? That which is immanent flows off and is gone. But where we speak of a true self and of a presentation that is verified definitively, there we reach beyond the momentary consciousness through rememberings in which we repeatedly come back to the same presentation and to its same meant object" (H XI 110). Husserl already recognized this predicament in 1905 when the temporal considerations were explicitly in play: With the acquisition of a point of time, one does not yet have a unitary objective time (H X 69). "For the realization [*Zustandekommen*] of this consciousness [of objective transcendence] reproductive remembering . . . plays an important role" (H X 69).

Reproductive remembering, which was portrayed as parasitic on originary perception and thus inadequate for establishing the security of a beginning in immediate evidence, is enlisted to succor originary perception in securing objectivity. The identical "One" that is constituted merely in perception as it is prior to all remembering is not yet an "object" ["*Gegenstand*"]. An object, instead, is the correlate of a knowing lying originally in synthetic identification, "which presupposes remembering" (H XI 327; cf. 321).

Mere perception is thus inadequate for establishing the unity of a manifold of appearances; by coming back to the same meant object, remembering can achieve a persistent unity through difference. Transcending mere momentary consciousness, remembering constitutes an objectivity that can be obtained "always and again." Accordingly, objectivity is not a-temporal, but temporal since it is achieved through repetition in temporalizing remembering. "We learn from this consideration," writes Husserl, "that the question concerning how something having the character of an object [*Gegenständlichkeit*]—an object being in itself—is constituted, how it can reveal itself as such originally, leads overall, entirely, and in principle first of all to the problem of the constitution of the in-itself of remembering" (H XI 110–11).

With attention to the intricate detail of the variegated syntheses of association, Husserl describes the objective sense or "in-itself" of the object constituted through remembering as a constant possible telos, motivating relations of intention and fulfillment and grounding the possibility of a futural in-itself, surpassing the in-itself valid for the past (H XI 203–8). The lived-experience of remembering occurs in the immanence of the living present, but what this lived-experience presentifies, namely, the past, is transcendent in relation to this experience. "This yields a curious paradox" (H XI 204).

While the paradox to which Husserl refers arises in his lectures on passive synthesis, it is nothing other than the peculiar situation of temporalizing consciousness already cited in *Zur Phänomenologie des inneren Zeitbewußtseins:* Consciousness as a temporalizing process is a coincidence in non-coincidence; it exists as an intertwining of temporalizing and temporalized, of immanence and transcendence. Husserl explains: "The stream of consciousness lives with *streaming*, and is *simultaneously objective* [*gegenständlich, objektiv*]; it [the stream of consciousness] becomes it [objective] as the *transcendent* self that comes to *incomplete* and *approximate* self-givenness in rememberings and in syntheses of remembering of a particular present" (H XI 204, my emphasis).

Consciousness as temporalizing is not temporally objective or constituted in time; nevertheless, in a temporally lived-experience such as remembering, consciousness gleans something of itself as being transcendent to itself. As a consequence, consciousness is incompletely given. It is the essence of temporalizing consciousness to coincide with itself, yet "not in every respect" (H X 83).

This peculiar chiasmatic relation of temporalization lands Husserl in the "paradoxical" situation of having to assert that the stream of consciousness as immanent time is "the first transcendence in the manner of a primordial source" [*das erste, urquellenmäßige Transzendente*] (H XI 204).[1]

While such a transcendent 'Self' is de facto approximate in terms of its objectivity, its actual incompleteness does not preclude the "idea" of a true Self (of a past consciousness) as the idea of complete, final self-givenness.[2] Yet even this idea, Husserl qualifies, is itself "essentially streaming" in a peculiar way, and thus not final. The idea must be dynamic, evolving, because consciousness is an ongoing process. Accordingly, the phenomenologist carrying out genetic method has the paradoxical task of describing the development of individual becoming while it is taking place such that its description becomes a participation in the disclosure of this matter's structure.

If immanent time consciousness is first in the manner of a primordial source, the status of what Husserl calls "transcendence in the usual sense," that is, transcendence peculiar to static phenomenology is usurped from its privileged position in the schema of immanence and transcendence. The back side, say, of the sandstone always extends beyond my presenting acts; it is appresented along with the perceived front side. Certainly, these horizons transcend immediate givenness. But regarded in terms of a more encompassing genetic phenomenological method that considers temporal implications, the transcendence peculiar to what Husserl understands as spatial phenomena becomes a "second level" transcendence founded in "the primordial transcendence of remembering" (H XI 205).[3]

Now, granted that the transcendence of remembering is primordial in relation to what we more typically regard as the static transcendence of the world, we need to ask whether the transcendence of remembering is *transcendence* in the *genuine* sense. This question must be linked to another: Is the objectivity acquired by remembering *objectivity* in the *genuine* sense? The question concerning genuine transcendence is connected with the question concerning a genuine mode of objectivity, for the strength of objectivity is proportionate to the integrity of transcendence, the ability of something to transcend *my* perceptual consciousness.

A reply to the second question regarding objectivity can be fashioned in the following manner. The mode of objectivity gained through remembering is insufficient to establish a truly objective world by Husserl's standards because it is attained by a mode of transcendence limited to an individual consciousness. A mode of objectivity can be posited that goes beyond the present and that holds for the past and a presumptive future, but it does not transcend my ego; it is not valid beyond the "original sphere" of the ego.

Transcendence "in the customary sense" always points to a possible fulfillment or to a fulfillment in original perception that was previously possible. It is always the object of a possible perception whether or not it is, had been, or has not yet been perceived: A missed event, this present peach, the back side of a cliff, the inside of quartz crystal, or a future bar mitzvah. It is still delineated, even presumptively, within the sphere of original experience.

According to Husserl, my own subjectivity is not transcended where the presumptively posited world of original experience is concerned; nor is it transcended through remembering. "Pure subjectivity is absolutely for itself, and everything originally experiencable belongs to it, even what is presumptive insofar as it has the character of being fulfilled in original experience." "But," Husserl hastens to add, "*intropathy* [*Einfühlung*] leads beyond this original sphere, leads to another ego, to other original experiences; thus, it transcends the own ego and its immanence and what is intentional on an original level." This other ego Husserl calls "a *second transcendence,* the genuine transcendence" [*Eine zweite Transzendenz: die eigentliche Transzendenz*] (H XIV 442, Husserl's emphasis).

Husserl often writes of the congruous nature of remembering and intropathy, and often evokes intropathy by analogy to remembering and appresentation. But whereas the former can become or could have been able to be present, the other subjectivity is, in principle, unable to be given in a possible original perception. The back side of the monolith, for example, is always co-given by apperception. The past or future are given in modes of presentification; still, the latter were once or can be part of my present. The other as transcendence, by contrast, essentially exceeds the bounds of my original sphere, being itself its own original sphere, its own chiasmatic relation of immanence and transcendence. For these reasons Husserl contends that the "other" is transcendence in the "genuine" sense.

Now Husserl asks: "How is this true and genuine transcendence possible, and how can my world take on a new sense whereby it [the world] itself comes to be the truly transcendent world, the inter-subjective [*zwischensubjektive*] world?" (H XIV 442).

In order to respond to this question it will be necessary to inquire into Husserl's theory of intersubjectivity and the experience of the other. Let me begin by showing how Husserl's second way is intended to open up the phenomenological reduction to the problem of the other.

The "Second Way" as an Intersubjective Reduction

According to Françoise Dastur's trenchant article entitled "Réduction et intersubjectivité," the notions of the reduction and of intersubjectivity do not form two separate concerns, but rather one and the same problematic.[4] It is more than happenstance that the first text introducing the three-volume collection devoted to the problem of intersubjectivity (Husserliana XIII, XIV, XV) stems from the 1905 "Seefelder Manuscripts"—the same period that Husserl, according to his own account, discovered for the first time the phenomenological reduction.[5] This opening text (H XIII 1–3) concerns the problem of individuation and the problem of objectivity, and inquires not only into how objects are given to others, but how *others*, how "alien psychic phenomena," are given to me. The method of the reduction makes problematic the development of an objective space and time and essentially draws into the analysis the problem of the other for the possibility of the objective world.

If it is true, as Dastur cites, that well before the 1920s (i.e., 1910–11) Husserl proposed extending the reduction to intersubjectivity,[6] it is just as true that he was at a loss as to how he should carry out such a reduction systematically. The phenomenological reduction, he concedes, had been limited to an egology: "For years I saw no possibility of shaping it into an intersubjective reduction" (H VIII 174 fn. 2). It was not until the early 1920s with the advent of a genetic method and in his lectures on "first philosophy" [*Erste Philosophie*] that Husserl took up a "second" way. The second way was intended to encompass another subjectivity allowing transcendental phenomenology to become a phenomenology of transcendental intersubjectivity.

The "second way" falls under the rubric of "phenomenological" or "intentional psychology."[7] The way of intentional psychology is portrayed by Husserl as essentially "richer" and "deeper" than the Cartesian reduction. The latter, Husserl admonishes, is based on the possible non-being of the experienced world, thereby directing attention one-sidedly to an experiencing subjectivity (H VIII 164 f.). By putting out of play in one stroke all types of validity or worldly acceptances, those directly given and those indirectly given or implied, the Cartesian reduction focused only on single accomplishments excerpted from a full intentional life (cf. H VIII 153). Phenomenological psychology, by contrast, proposed to focus more explicitly on the psychic phenomena whose nature is precisely intentional: The intended object is not merely present, but points beyond itself in intentional acts to implied senses, surpassing the immediately given one.

If the Cartesian way had the pretension of shutting off all circuits of validity (a pretension because it allowed consciousness to emerge as an independent sphere of being), the new "second way" does not. On the contrary, even if the world did somehow sneak obstinately into a Cartesian analysis, vexing it negatively, so to speak, the world now plays a positive role, affirmed in a purportedly new procedure. Intentional psychology lets the world remain in play, or put differently, it actively affirms consciousness as worldly in order to uncover conscious life beyond its present and beyond its singularity. Intentional psychology does this—in contrast to the first way—by asserting the proposition "the world is" as a point of departure for phenomenological method (H VIII 40 f.; 283).

The way of intentional psychology departs from the being or the positivity of the world within the natural attitude. To say that psychology, the science of the *soul*, begins with the proposition that the *world* is, is not a contradiction. For the human sciences [*Geisteswissenschaften*] (of which psychology is a branch), like the natural sciences, are sciences of the world or "positive sciences" (H VIII 287). To be sure, intentional psychology is a positivity of a higher reflective level than the "primary positivity" of "mere nature"; and it is presumably this "higher reflection" that distinguishes it from an empirical psychology of neuro-physiology and behaviorism, a "higher reflection" that introduces the concept of intentionality to the notion of psyche. Nevertheless, it remains "positive" because it deals with persons or human beings and with their actions as presupposed or taken for granted; it treats simply the straightforward directedness of the ego to the object.

In order to arrive at the pure psychological ego, Husserl proposes that one does not (yet) reduce the natural ego by the phenomenological epoche, that is, I do not inhibit my positing of the world (H VIII 143); rather, I abstract from everything objective or non-egological. What I obtain through this abstraction is psychic intentional life. When it is modified in eidetic form through eidetic variation, I attain psychic being as the ground for a pure phenomenological psychology (cf. H VIII 445). But since I only abstract and do not employ the phenomenological epoche, I still remain in a naive-natural psychological attitude (H VIII 449).

The task now, according to Husserl, is to raise what I reached through psychological abstraction to a transcendental level by a genuine reduction. This entails bracketing pure psyches and transforming them into transcendental phenomena: Phenomenological psychology must be transformed from an incomplete particular science to a universal, complete science; it must no longer reflect on single acts and single regions but undertake a *universal* reflection on the entire life (H VIII 158, 160, 293).

Admittedly, it is unclear what is to be gained by a detour through phenomenological psychology as a propaedeutic to transcendental phenomenology *if* the transcendental ego is to be understood merely as a universalized duplicate of a regional psychological ego. For transcendental and psychological phenomenology seemed to cover the same general scope, offer the same mode of accessible presence to consciousness, and contribute no difference to the quality of evidence. It is even more perplexing to follow Husserl parrying these objections by insisting on the fundamental difference between and "complementariness" of these two egos, implying a dualism of natural and transcendental egos (cf. H IX 342 ff., §§13–14).

One can, however, ascertain the import of a methodological step from psychological to transcendental phenomenology, even if it is not clearly expressed by Husserl. First, because one abstracted from everything objective to gain the ego, Husserl insists that the object needs to be reintegrated into the account because it has to be recognized in terms of its modes of givenness as an essential intentional correlate of subjectivity (H VIII 290). Second, prior to the transcendental reduction the subject is regarded as "worldly," asserted in its being (H VIII 183). Without this transcendental reduction, Crowell observes, the subjectivity of phenomenological psychology is unable to address the epistemological question concerning the foundation of *all* worldly knowledge, including its own.[8]

The difference between psychological and transcendental phenomenology then is a difference between particularity and universality or between incompleteness and completeness, as Husserl sometimes asserts. By completeness and universality Husserl means that *both* the object and the subject *that* are, are clarified as phenomena in their *modes* of givenness. Since this change in attitude implies a process of "going back" from the constituted to the dimensions of constituting, Husserl claims that what needs to be reached is "genuine constituting consciousness," "*transcendental* subjectivity," and not a subject taken for granted (H VIII 286–88).[9]

It is not my intention to get unduly embroiled in an extenuated exegesis of phenomenological psychology, since it would only detract from the present discussion without promise of a fruitful yield. I must hold a host of questions in abeyance concerning phenomenological psychology in order to focus on its general significance for motivating the problem of intersubjectivity and the account given in the Fifth Cartesian Meditation.

Let me reassert the advantage of the so-called "second way": It refrains from bracketing the world from the very start, allowing the phenomenologist to pursue the *implications of intentional life,* taking this life beyond the singularity of this act or the punctuality of this Now. By beginning within the validity of the world even the immediacy in which I am given to myself as ego is disclosed as having levels of intentional implications (H VIII 175). The extreme difficulties that accompany exposing "latent implications" or "implicit potentialities"—to be specific, the difficulties of time and the other—Husserl asserts, have to be weighed against the failure to uncover the "deeply hidden mediations of intentional implications"; for without the latent implications, constituting subjectivity would remain "fully incomprehensible" (H VIII 123 f., 168, 182, 294). In particular, if the other were not included in the reduction, phenomenology could not clarify the constitution of the world.

The psychological reduction, then, has the advantage of opening up the structure of subjectivity itself, disclosing the horizons of intentional life. This purportedly gives a fuller picture of constituting life when one finally submits natural life and its acceptances to a universal, phenomenological epoche.

So, rather than abstracting from temporal dimensions, transcendental subjectivity can now be clarified through the reduction in terms of its earlier and futural life, covering intentional modes such as remembering and expectation. Opened in the first instance by phenomenological psychology are the temporal horizons of consciousness which, though non-intuitively given, are nevertheless given in a "horizon-consciousness" (H VIII 82–86, 132, 146, 165).

But just as one can exercise the reduction on one's own acts and their sense accomplishments that are intentionally implied, so too is one opened to other modes of presentification that transcend the immediate ego. One such mode is intropathy (H VIII 135). By exposing my entire life to the reduction, others become problematic and the experience of others becomes an explicit phenomenological theme:

> For I do not only gain myself as transcendental ego in this [second] way (I who am the subject of phenomenological reducing)—by also integrating alien subjectivity in the [second] method, I gain transcendental *intersubjectivity* or, as we can also say, the transcendental universe of egos, as the transcendental community of single egos transcendentally apprehended. (H VIII 129)

The Other and the Alien

Unlike the Cartesian way—which focused too narrowly and too quickly on a present ego cogito and which hypothesized the possible non-being of the world in spite of universal world belief—Husserl's new way purports to gain an expanded transcendental life by including from the start the entire wealth of natural experience; accepted in the natural attitude is not only the immediately present ego, but a horizon of intertwining intentional implications, a horizon of acceptances, an unthematic background that ultimately includes presentifying acts that involve the sense "other subjectivity" (H VIII 126, 144 f.).

Transcendental phenomenology, in Husserl's view, is no longer limited to my ego, but can accommodate an intersubjective nexus. The alien human subjectivity, transcendentally clarified, is a "second transcendental life" (H VIII 181). It is unrealized and unrealizable originally in my life and is not a unity of actual or possible perceptions. Instead, it is a presentified subjectivity, another constituting subjectivity (H VIII 188 f.). This second transcendental subjectivity is indicative of transcendence in the "genuine" sense. But let us be clear about what this "genuine" transcendence means in the context of intersubjective theory by examining the significance of a "second" transcendental subjectivity.

I would like to make and maintain a strict distinction between two terms in what follows: "the other" and "the alien." Let me concede from the very start: Husserl does not offer such a distinction and tends rather to use these expressions interchangeably. There are nevertheless patterns of usage, which once identified, can elucidate both the senses of "other" and "alien," as well as their respective import for different themes in intersubjective theory.

Let me begin with an etymological look at the expression "other," not to decide its phenomenological significance, but to help describe its internal sense. Like the English term "other," and the French "*autre*," the German "*andere*" (from "*ander*") has a *numerical* function. As the expression of an ordinal number, both terms *ander* and *autre* used to mean and can still mean "*second*."

In German, it was not until the fourteenth century that "*ander*" was replaced by the term "*zweite*." One still hears today, for example, the German expression "*anderthalb*," meaning "one and one half" (actually "the second half") with the remnant "t" indicative of ordinal numbers in late middle high German.[10] Or, one says today, "*zu zweit*" meaning "in twos," which replaced the middle high German "*selbander*" (self-other). "*Zweite*" also translates nicely at times into the English "other" when, for example, one says "*wie kein zweiter*"—"like no other."

In English, too, "other" meant "that which follows the first" or "the second of two or more." Thus, when one said "the other day," it originally meant "the second day," "the following," or "next day." English speakers constantly use the expression "on the *one* hand . . . on the *other* hand," that is, on the *second* hand, retaining the synonymy of the "second" and the "other."

Similarly, according to *Petit Robert*, one could say "*C'est un autre Versailles*" ("It is an other Versailles") and mean "it is a second Versailles"; or one could say "*C'est un autre moi-même*" ("It is an other self") and mean "it is a second self."

Let me now turn to the concept of the "alien." I believe it is safe to say without too much qualification that Husserl tends to use the term "alien" (*das Fremde* and its cognates) when he stresses the novelty of transcendence, its inaccessibility, its unfamiliarity or strangeness; he also uses "alien" when he wants to emphasize a cultural and historical phenomenon. It is also significant to note that when articulating the theory of intersubjectivity in terms of homeworld/alienworld [*Fremdwelt*], Husserl invariably uses the expression "alien" and refrains from the expression "other" (he does not write, for example, "*Anderwelt*").

The German expression *fremd* has an essentially different sense than that of *andere*. Etymologically, *fremd* is derived from the adverb *fram*, meaning, forward, onward, on the way, away, and accordingly, being at a distance, eventually, not belonging to, unacquainted or unfamiliar. It is the root of our English preposition "from." Although *fremd* could be translated as strange or foreign, I will render it as alien because it can be used more consistently in the context of the present work.[11]

How does *fremd* compare with *andere*? Are they interchangeable? A "*Fremdzimmer*," a "guest room," is not just "*ein anderes Zimmer*," "another room." When I ask for another plate of pasta (perhaps I am still hungry and I want "seconds") or even "the other plate of pasta" (perhaps the plate I have is chipped and I want a new one), I do not mean I want a "strange plate," a "foreign plate," or even a "novel plate."

In the context of intersubjectivity I will insist that the "other" is a *logical* concept, whereas the "alien" is an *axiological* one. I want to argue, for example, that a "*Fremdsprache*," a "foreign language," cannot be reduced to an other language, a "second language," as we commonly assert. Or again, an alien culture is not a second culture.

To characterize the alien as the other or as the second is to juxtapose the other to myself in a linear fashion. The second language or culture is one that follows mine in order of dependence and importance: The second is dependent upon the first and grounded in the first, while the first can remain independent of the second. But changing this linear, numerical view does not entail asserting, for instance, that cultures or languages are interchangeable. In order to understand the intersubjective nexus generatively, much will depend upon being able to understand that there can be an axiological priority of a homeworld without this privilege becoming a foundation, which is to say, without it being reduced to a numerical priority or a "first" world. As we will see in the next section, the world as horizon cannot be conceived numerically, and in part 2 it will become more clear that, fundamentally, the homeworld is not a first world and the alienworld not a second world.

This initial approach to the sense of the other gives us a clue to its significance in a philosophy of intersubjectivity. The other is the second; the other I is the second I, in Latin, the *alter* ego. The expression other, I contend, belongs to a first philosophy where it conceives the other I as a *second* subjectivity. Is it any coincidence that the reduction peculiar to intentional phenomenological psychology—as Husserl writes in his lectures on first philosophy—"delivers over a *second* transcendental life" [*ein zweites transzendentales Leben*] (H VIII 189, my emphasis), or that the mundane alien human subject, transcendentally clarified, is "a *second* transcendental subject" [*ein zweites transzendentales Subjekt*] (H VIII 188, my emphasis)? In first philosophy, "the other" can just as easily and just as consistently be rendered, as Husserl does at times, "the second" [(*der*) *Zweite*] (cf. H VIII 137).

The other is always second in first philosophy; it is a second transcendence when compared to the original transcendence of the first sphere. The other is preceded by the first, it "follows" the first, comes "after" the first, as an "alter-native" to the first; it is always, as second, founded on the self, the first original sphere. First philosophy remains a philosophy of my subjectivity, the first subjectivity, and the other, which it attempted to make problematic, turns out to be incidental, a "second" thought, an "after" thought. Here, the self and other exist in a one-sided relation of foundation. The problem with both the Cartesian account and the second way in first philosophy is that they make the mistake of equating myself or my ownness with the first self, equating myself as transcendental subjectivity with the first transcendental subjectivity and reducing alien transcendental subjectivity to an "other," a second transcendental life. Describing the intersubjective nexus numerically and linearly, "First" Philosophy is literally the "second" way.

These conclusions I state here regarding the method of first philosophy are not based on the etymological significance of the term other, but are borne out by the treatment of the other as a second transcendence. This will become clearer under the next heading and in the final chapter of this section.[12]

First Philosophy, First Subjectivity, and the Cartesian Way

First philosophy, I maintain, is a philosophy of first subjectivity and asserts a one-sided relation of foundation, beginning with what is hypostatized first: Myself. For first philosophy, the other is merely second.

It may sound contradictory to hold that first philosophy—which expressly began to take seriously the implied temporal and horizonal life, if not in direct opposition to, then at least as an alternative to the Cartesian way—should be classified as a method within the Cartesian framework. In brief, is it not inconsistent to assert that the "second way" the way of the other is essentially the Cartesian way, an egology?

I want to argue that the second way remains rooted in the first way primarily for four interrelated reasons: (1) the epistemic contingency of the world in relation to the necessity of the ego, (2) the tacit assumption of the world as a thing, (3) the notion of the horizon as a potential present, and (4) the second way's adherence to an intuitive reflective procedure.

1. The path of intentional phenomenological psychology as the second way is a highly unstable and ambiguous method. On the one hand, Husserl begins by asserting that "the world is" and puts this assertion on a par with the proposition "I am." In some ways, the world is even privileged because it is constantly there in our experience in a unique way (H VIII 40 f.). These novel attempts, however, give way under the scrutiny of indubitability: "*It appears*," writes Husserl, "that the general rubric '*The World is*' contains in itself . . . *the universe of all ultimate,* namely, *immediate epistemic principles,* that is, the universe of all necessary experience for a

universal science. *I . . . am* certainly *co-contained in this universe.*" And as what can only be interpreted as a tenacious riposte to his bold assertion in *Ideen I* §49 concerning the perseverance of the ego in the negation of the world, he writes: "With the negation or actual destruction of the world, I myself would be negated or destroyed" (H VIII 42).

But this is only a provisional gesture. For the significance of the world is bludgeoned by the Cartesian maxim of indubitability and apodicticity. No matter how illuminating or instructive these other reflections may appear, continues Husserl, the world cannot withstand the test of genuine apodicticity and indubitability: "*rather the proposition 'I am'* must be *the true principle of all principles* and the first principle of all true philosophy" (H VIII 42). In the end, the world is relegated in first philosophy to the sphere of epistemic contingency, mere "relative necessity," and the ego, because of its immediate givenness in evidence (the insight into the temporal duration of the I seems to be repressed), is raised to the realm of absolute necessity.[13]

2. One could object that, even if *Husserl* does not take the world seriously, certainly *we* could salvage and nurture the insights into the world presented in his lectures on first philosophy and eventually exfoliate the second way. However, if one were to look carefully at the contexts in which Husserl speaks of the world, one would notice that the latter rarely, if ever, moves beyond the status of a thing.

When Husserl asserts that the world is inadequately given, not apodictically like the ego, he invokes the example of the perception of a spatial thing [*Wahrnehmung eines Raumdinges*] to support his conviction (H VIII 42, 44). And when ascertaining the "unannullable epistemic contingency of the world," Husserl appeals to the structure of perception as a perception of a thing [*Dingwahrnehmung*] and virtually equates the latter with a perception of the world [*Weltwahrnehmung*] (H VIII 51).

To be sure, Husserl does not equate the world with a single thing; the world is a *universal thing*, a universe or totality of things adequate to a universal perception. Even when Husserl does, at least in one passage, seem to circumvent the characterization of the world as a totality of things, depicting it as a "horizon," the notion of horizon is essentially a correlate of consciousness as a possible perception, and the world, an infinite horizon of possible perceptual experience. Thus, the notion of world in these lectures does not provide a new starting point from which one could move beyond first philosophy. This brings me to my third point.

3. The notion of horizon is undeniably the key insight sported in these lectures. The concept of horizon, that is, a nexus of "intentional implications," is integral to the problem of temporality and the problem of the other as providing an alternative to the Cartesian method. The

difficulty is that the concept of horizon never really gets beyond being a possible present, a possible experience in the original sphere (cf. H VIII 146–48). It is not characterized as "that from which" present things emerge, or as the condition of present things—the status it will reach in the *Krisis 1*, even if in the form of a promissory note. Instead, it is almost determined negatively as an extension of the present; it is an empty horizon [*Leerhorizont*] requiring fulfillment, recognized by virtue of having been or able to become present. Although one consciously intends it non-intuitively in the form of an eventual intuition, this concept of horizon never escapes conscious givenness.[14]

4. Finally, first philosophy, despite its putative new starting point, remains a progressive, intuitive reflective procedure like the Cartesian way. The import of the second way consisted in gaining horizons of acceptances that were not taken into account in the restrictive and hasty reduction of the initial Cartesian way. Rather than mitigating intuitive reflection, however, the second way just tended to strengthen it. For the second way is merely preliminary to and preparatory for a more exacting Cartesian reflection. Not only does Husserl assert the possibility of surveying [*überschauen*] my entire life (H VIII 154), he also maintains the possibility of subjecting intersubjective historical life to a universal reflection, in one stroke: "on the other hand, there is nevertheless a radical means *of putting all acceptances out of action in one blow.*"[15] A universal reflection [*universale Reflexion*] can purportedly make a whole intersubjective life accessible to surveying consciousness, spanning all temporal horizons and their latent acceptances (H VIII 155).

In spite of the many insights won in his reflections on first philosophy and their radical implications, implications that would demand a thoroughly anti-Cartesian account, Husserl remains true to Cartesian principles and their presuppositions. In the final analysis, the second way becomes a ramification of and compatible with the Cartesian way.[16]

In chapter 4, the final chapter of this section, I take up these reflections on first philosophy and the Cartesian way as they are found in the theory of intersubjectivity presented in the Fifth Cartesian Meditation. I do this by taking up Husserl's reply to the objection of solipsism and then by examining his theory of intropathy in the Fifth Meditation. In the conclusion of this chapter, I point out how intersubjectivity on this model is constituted without language and amounts to imagining silence. I take up the Fifth Meditation because it is not only the view of intersubjectivity most widely attributed to Husserl, but also because it will provide an important basis of contrast for generative phenomenology of intersubjectivity.

4

Taking the "Fifth"

> In the monologue words cannot serve the function of indication for the existence of psychic acts, since here such indication would be entirely without purpose. The acts in question are themselves experienced by us in that very moment.
>
> Husserl[1]

> He who imagines nothing senses no one but himself; he is alone among human kind.
>
> Rousseau[2]

What is regarded by most to be Husserl's definitive stance on intersubjectivity is found in his "Fifth Cartesian Meditation." Because many of the presuppositions and consequences of phenomenological method leading to this theory are called into question by a generative phenomenology, I want to take up the Fifth Meditation here. This is a complex piece, too complex to deal with effectively in a single chapter. Since this meditation counts for so many as a paradigm of foundational intersubjective theory, I assume at least some familiarity with its content. I want to focus on the following salient points concerning the constitution of intersubjectivity: The role of intropathy, the thesis of the reversibility of perspectives, and the absence of language in the constitutional account of intersubjectivity.

Let me begin this chapter by recalling Husserl's inquiry into a genuine mode of transcendence I cited in chapter 3. He asks: "How is this true and genuine transcendence possible, and how can my world take on a new sense whereby it itself comes to be the truly transcendent world, the inter-subjective world?" This question is twofold: It concerns (1) a specific mode of *transcendence* as the condition of (2) an *objective world.*

We have seen that the constitution of the "external world," as *my* particular world, is not transcendence in the rigorous sense; its spatial and temporal aspects that are not given to me directly are objects of my possible perception. Accordingly, this world is not objective because even if its essential contingency did not manifest itself in modalizations such as doubt, it would only be valid for me at this time. We have also seen that the inquiry into the transcendence of the past and the constitution of objectivity within my transcendental life in the form of passive temporal syntheses did not resolve the problem of objectivity either because its objectivity was confined to solipsistic experience: Even the synthesis of *all* my possible acts, past, present, and future could not constitute an objective world in the strict sense, valid beyond the sphere of *my* subjectivity.

After raising the question concerning the constitution of the thing in my experience (our initial sense of transcendence) in the Third Cartesian Meditation, and after briefly highlighting the notion of passive genesis and the question concerning primordial constitution as self-constitution (transcendence in the "paradoxical," "chiasmatic" sense peculiar to monadic life) in the Fourth Cartesian Meditation, Husserl broaches in the Fifth Cartesian Meditation another type of transcendence.

Phenomenology through the Fourth Meditation can still be charged as solipsistic and incapable of accounting for objectivity. Husserl attempts to solve this problem—"the transcendental problem of the objective world"—not by invoking a theological guarantor of objectivity, but through a theory of "intropathy" [*Einfühlung*]. The clarification of intropathy in the Fifth Meditation will be a constitutional analysis of a distinct mode of transcendence, what Husserl calls the "alter ego."

Intersubjective Adjudication: The Charge of Solipsism

The *Cartesianische Meditationen* were written as an introduction to transcendental phenomenology. The composition of these meditations was occasioned in 1929 by an invitation from the *Institut d'Etudes germaniques* and the *Société de Philosophie* for Husserl to present an introduction to transcendental phenomenology in Paris.[3]

That Husserl desperately wanted phenomenology to reply to the charge of solipsism with a phenomenology of intersubjectivity can be witnessed merely by the size of the Fifth Meditation; it is nearly as long as all the other four meditations combined. Important, however, is not its length but the place the Fifth Meditation occupies within first philosophy as a Cartesian method. To illustrate this role, let me be clear about the type of solipsism to which Husserl and first philosophy replies.

Husserl's approach to the problem of solipsism differs from our common assumptions about what solipsism might entail.[4] First, the problem of solipsism Husserl faces is not an existential solipsism as if the question would be whether or not other beings existed. That they exist is accepted as something to be clarified. Husserl attempts to do this by addressing the phenomenological sense "other." Second, he is not attempting to prove the other from the apodicticity of the ego, but to describe the constitution of the sense "other" in my intentional life. Third, a phenomenology of intersubjectivity does not set out to illustrate that the other is certain like the ego is for me, but to describe its modes of givenness, how the other is given to me within my experience. Finally, contrary to many pedestrian formulations, the *fil conducteur* of the Fifth Meditation is not (1) to establish objectivity by recourse (2) to a multiplicity of egos. Husserl handles the latter by an eidetic approach to phenomenology. Where the former is concerned, Husserl's goal is to show how objectivity is possible (and not to establish it) by elucidating a mode of transcendence, that is, the sense of an alter ego in relation to me.

Having clarified these possible misunderstandings, the question motivating the Fifth Meditation can be brought into sharper relief: How can phenomenology account for the originality of the other subjectivity that transcends my own experience and yet whose sense as other is constituted in and from my intentional life? How can another ego (transcendence in the true sense) that is not merely intended as an object in my experience be constituted precisely as other? (H I 121, 123 ff.).

Let me stake out my position on Husserl's ability to respond to this question by invoking the distinction I made above between the other and the alien. I contend that if by transcendence Husserl means the alien, he cannot give a phenomenological account of transcendence within the strictures of the Fifth Meditation, and accordingly, cannot properly address the question of objectivity. Despite his persistent and ardent assertions to the contrary, the Fifth Meditation is not and cannot be a clarification of *Fremd-erfahrung*, of the experience of the alien.

The difference between the senses "other" and "alien" will mark an indelible tension in the text of the Fifth Meditation. Assuredly, Husserl wished to address the experience of the alien here; the text itself is laced with the expression. Indeed, at times Husserl does recognize the difference between a second (or other) and an alien (cf. H I 143). Nevertheless, it will remain an irresovable problem, and the tension between the other and the alien will persist because the method employed—his intentions to the contrary—cannot handle the alien; that is, it treats the alien only as other. His method is unable to handle the alien and is internally limited to explicating the sense "other" primarily for the following reasons: (1) his method commences with an abstraction from everything alien; (2) his account of intersubjectivity begins with the apodicticity of the ego; (3) the account begins from the perspective of the individual ego, from the sphere of one's ownness; (4) the question of solipsism is itself formulated in terms of a one-sided relation of foundation and invites a response that will follow suit; (5) the notion of constitution, while taken to a passive embodied level, is not carried out beyond the relation between my body and another's body: It remains within an I-Thou or I-You synchronic relation; (6) it is a static analysis, an account wherein the problem of genesis, and ultimately history, is absent; (7) finally, even when he does reintroduce the cultural notion of alien, he tends to characterize it as a higher-order "other" within the same methodology.

What one *can* account for very well with the Cartesian method is the sense "other," "the second ego" [*das zweite Ego*] (H I 125). The goal of the Fifth Meditation is to account for the sense of the other, the second ego, by grasping the origin of its sense in the ego; the phenomenological sense "alter" is gained through the constitutional process of "mirroring" or "analogy."

True, Husserl does not use "analogy" in an ordinary sense. "Not actually mirroring," he adds, "not an analogue in the usual sense."[5] Husserl's analysis bears on an ego that is not myself. Were the other a mere reflection, the consciousness of the other would be accessible to my immediate intuition, obviating the problem of intersubjectivity. Husserl is concerned, however, with an ego whose possibilities are *not* my own, with a sense of an other's lived-corporeality that can never be realized in my primordial sphere.

In order to elucidate how an ego—which is not myself and which is not merely an intentional object—can belong to an egology, Husserl must examine the explicit and implicit intentionalities in which the sense "alter ego" is constituted in me (H I 122). What are the epistemic conditions under which an other for-itself is for me?

Husserl attempts to make epistemological sense of a constituting subjectivity for itself within an egology, precisely by not renouncing phenomenology's fruitful methodological insight, namely, the inquiry into modes of givenness. Husserl can inquire into the mode of givenness of this curious for-itself because the (other) subject is not merely a consciousness, but an embodied subject. The phenomenological analysis into the mode of givenness of the inaccessible other will move through *bodily experience.* The "inaccessibility" of the "phenomenological in-itself"[6] will be the mode in which the other is given to me. The other is accessible through embodiment *as inaccessible* (H I 144).[7]

The experience through which an inaccessible being-for-itself is given to me, and the means by which the sense "other ego" is constituted in me is articulated by Husserl in a theory of intropathy.

The Problem of Intropathy

I have no pretension here of exhaustively tracing out the sinuous lines of thought sketching Husserl's theory of "*Fremderfahrung*" from the time of the *Logische Untersuchungen* through first philosophy. Tracking this vast trajectory in detail is a project in itself. Instead, let me note that Husserl develops his theories of the experience of the other at first in a confrontation with Lipps's analogy theory of intropathy. In place of Lipps's emphasis on alien externalizations of life and the expression of psychic movements, Husserl makes his main theme the unity of the lived-physical body [*Leibkörperlichkeit*] as given in one's own self-perceiving on an "aesthesiological-kinetic" level (cf. H XIII 50 f., 62–4, 70 ff.). Accordingly, instead of beginning with higher levels of predicative expression, Husserl argues that these are already mediated through the apprehension of the lived-body as lived-body (H XIII 70 and 76).

Later, Husserl modifies his own approach by focusing on the prominent role of phantasy in the experience of an other by framing his own theory of analogy (cf. esp. H XIII 250 ff.), and by considering normality and abnormality in the constitution of intersubjectivity (a discussion I will withhold until part 2; cf. H XIII 360 ff.).

Under the banner of a single meditation Husserl brings to bear a variety of approaches that are not entirely compatible. To uncover the process by which one sphere of immanence is drawn into a relation with a second, Husserl begins his analysis by exercising a reduction, not only by bracketing the naive acceptance of the being of the alien—yielding the noematic sense "alien"—but by carrying out a "novel" epoche, an "abstractive" epoche. The second movement entails *abstracting from everything alien:* From the *geistige* (spiritual, cultural, historical) world of experience, that is, from written and spoken language, from art works, from utensils, from goods and values, even from objectivity.[8] This abstractive epoche is exercised in order to delimit the sphere that is proper-to-me [*das Mir-Eigene*], the sphere of my ownness (H I 126 f.).

To the sphere of my ownness belongs myself as a constituting subjectivity, my psychic being, my lived-body [*Leib*] as an "I can" and my physical-body [*Körper*]. They all belong to my sphere of ownness because they can be given to me, respectively, in immanent or transcendent originary perception: They do not transcend me in a "genuine" sense. The preliminary problem of intersubjectivity in the *Cartesianische Meditationen*—how one original sphere can posit a second—is generated from this sphere of my ownness, from an ownness whose elements are presupposed by the sense-constitution of another lived-body, another psychic being, and another constituting subjectivity. In short, the ego is the source for the sense alter ego.[9]

Belonging to primitive nature, nature peculiar to one's ownness, is not only my physical-body, but all physical-bodies, including the body that will later be understood as the other's physical-body. Because the realm of the physical-body is the same for my body and the body (of the other), they are accessible to me immediately.

Eventually, another "property" will also be the same for both the alter and the ego, namely, the ego: It is constituted not as an I-myself, but as mirroring my own ego, my monad (H I 125). Since the other ego is constituted in and for me, it will be an ego in a derived sense. Husserl will attempt to describe this derivation of sense through intricate and dense analyses peculiar to the phenomenology of association and the analyses of passive synthesis.

Even though Husserl appeals to passive genesis here, he forthrightly maintains that the constitutional account in the Fifth Meditation is *static:* "Here it is not a matter of disclosing a temporally flowing genesis, but rather a matter of a static analysis" (H I 136). And he even seems to admit that the analysis of intersubjectivity remains at an impasse as long as the problem of genesis is not introduced into the account (H XV 15).[10] That this account is static is bolstered by Husserl's own reflections on the problem of intropathy as the "problem of a *fictive genesis*" belonging to a static phenomenology. He writes critically: "I say fictive genesis. For I can *not assert in advance* that the genesis of the appresentation of the alien *presupposes the preceding genesis of an environing-world without alien-subjectivity*, that is, that such an environing-world is already constituted" (H XIV 477, Husserl's emphasis). The account of intersubjectivity can employ genetic laws of motivation and apperception and still remain static because it does not treat intersubjectivity as inter-monadic becoming. Or more precisely, Husserl offers a static examination of phenomena that have already been disclosed genetically, and he tacks on a layer of culture toward the conclusion of the meditation because it is simply the direction he wants to take the analysis, *eventually*.

Finally, the analysis remains over all static because of its point of departure; it entails a double abstraction, that is, an abstraction from historicity, culture, the alien, etc., and from developmental facticity.

It will not be necessary for the present work to enter into a more detailed (albeit important) exegesis on the relation of passive synthesis to intersubjectivity. It will suffice to sketch the movement of the sense constitution of the other in broad strokes. Let me do this by beginning with the following example.

1. I see a woman climbing. According to Husserl's constitutional account, the rock face, the harness, the karabiners, the shoes, the "legs," "torso," "arms," etc., are all physical-bodies [*Körper*]. Were one simply to stay on this level of abstraction, there would be no way of differentiating the hands from the rope, the feet from the shoes or the rock. As physical-bodies, they all "belong to" my primordial sphere because as "immanent transcendences" they are not transcendence in the genuine sense (H I 134 f.). Instead, they belong among my perceptual objects.

In my primordial sphere, my body, my lived-body, my psychophysical ego are always set in relief, prominent, at least pre-reflectively. The climber next to me, in a relevé straining to reach the grip on an overhang, is also now prominent in my perceptual field as a physical-body. Due to the similarity of the body next to me and mine, the bodies undergo (*must* undergo, says Husserl) a relationship of "pairing" [*Paarung*], a primordial form of the passive synthesis of association by which the other body that is given intuitively takes on the same sense as my physical-body (H I § 51).

What happens now, when poised on the rock face in what resembles a frozen *pas de chat* with one arm extended above gripping a piece of granite, she gropes with the other hand behind her back into her pouch to dust her fingers with resin and chalk? What happens when she manipulates one of the things in *my* field of perception as I had done a moment ago? Certainly, this pouch is in my world of perception; but how can her movement toward it take place beyond the sphere of my ownness? "I can-*not*" locate this movement anywhere in my *originally* given world. If it were locatable, it would simply be a moment of my primordial world, immediately accessible; transcendental subjectivity would be transcendental monism.

There is an "I can" that is not my own and that is not a structure of my "*Sinnlichkeit*." It is nonetheless co-present through a type of appresentation (H I 139). Since my lived-body is the only physical-body originally constituted as lived-body, the physical-body (of the climber) is made co-present *as* lived-body by virtue of what Husserl calls an apperceptive transference [*apperzeptive Übertragung*] of sense.

The transfer of sense takes place initially through the exertion of the affective force of a unity on other similar unities, resulting in an "affective communication" (H XI 180). In this case two pre-objective unities or objects come into relief and form a "pair" in the single unity of consciousness. Because the affective force is inseparable from the sense of the object (cf. section 3), the being-sense of the object is also transferred to another. Now, according to Husserl this can occur purely passively within the living-present and is to be distinguished from the transference of sense that can occur through remembering as awakening a past or through expectation. Where the Fifth Meditation is concerned, Husserl presupposes the static co-existence of co-present objects in a living present. This is important for the Fifth Meditation because Husserl has to explain how a unity is constituted through two *present* objects given in the original.

On the basis of a "binding similarity" between that body there in my primordial sphere, and my own physical-body constituted as lived-body, there is a motivational basis for constituting the other body as another lived-body. The other body takes on the sense "lived-body" through an analogizing apprehension (H I 140).[11] According to Husserl, everyday experience is permeated with such a passive analogizing transference of sense: Even though I have never seen this particular rope before, I am familiar with it through its style, a style that ultimately points back to a "primordial institution" of sense by which an object with a similar sense was constituted for the first time.[12]

As intropathy, analogizing apperception of course goes further than the constitution of the sense lived-body.[13] The other climber is given to me in a founded manner as an analogue to my own ego: "Higher psychic occurrences" such as frustration at slipping, joy at making it to the summit, fear when dangling from a rope two hundred meters above the ground, in short, the other's *Erlebnisse* are indicated to me corporally. They are appresented analogously on the basis of my own comportment under similar circumstances, exhibiting a similar type.

How can the lived-experiences of the other, the psychic determinations that are appresented, be those that belong to the same physical-body given to me originally? Through the concordance of comportment, the psychic life of the other, which is appresented, is confirmed as the other psychic life belonging to the other lived-body, and it continues to do so by the concordant fulfillment of anticipated lived-experiences. Another subjectivity is posited as co-posited, as belonging to another physical-body in my original field but without being accessible to me like my physical-body (cf. H XV 27).

2. The sense lived-body of the other and the other's psychic life are motivated passively. But this is not the full account of the constitution of the other as alter ego. It will involve the intervention of phantasy or imagination. To explicate this next movement, I will draw on Klaus

Held's elucidating distinction between two aspects of the consciousness expressed by the phrase, "as if I were there" [*wie wenn ich dort wäre*] essential for Husserl's analysis.[14] I take up this point because it will have important implications for the thesis of "reversibility" and "symmetry" in this theory of intersubjectivity, and will provide an important contrast for the co-original yet asymmetrical structure of homeworld/alienworld.

Let me continue with my example: Having secured my rope to the last karabiner, arms fatigued, I rest and watch my companion ascend over the top. I am "here" and she is "over there." Still, I am more than just "here"; I am an absolute Here, the center from which the world is oriented up or down, left or right, near or far, even here or there. The Here of my lived-body is the condition of sense for objects in spatial location and orientation.[15] Moreover, by virtue of my kinaesthesis I can freely alter my orientation and thus the system of appearances of my world. I can modify the "there" where my companion is into a "here"; that is, I can ascend to the top (H I 146). According to Held, there are two modes of presentification working together that Husserl must have in order to account for the sense alter ego:[16] a positional and a quasi-positional consciousness "as if I were there."

In a positional presentation, I can remember that I was "over there" at one time (when I finished my previous climb) or I can expect that I will be there later, as soon as I ascend another six meters. Such acts literally "set" (posit) or place the intentional object in a temporal flow and differentiate the present from past or future, and accordingly, a here from a there.[17] In this case, as Held notes, the "*wenn*" in "*wie wenn ich dort wäre*" is ambiguous and has indicative temporal connotations like the English adverb "when." Furthermore, the expression's subjunctive character is not that of an irreality, but that of a potentiality.[18] I can move from here to there, and I can presentify it in such a way that I gain the idea of a Here, over there that will be my own. This present Here, however, is not simultaneous with the Here presentified "over there," precisely because the latter is a Here of a past or a future. I posit a future present or a past present, but not myself as present, "Here" at the same time as a "Present Here" over there. This mode of presentification alone is inadequate to understand the constitution of the other because it is impossible to conceive another Here simultaneous with my Here.

In contrast to but complementing the positional presentification is a "quasi-positional" presentification of *imagination.* In this case, the "*wie wenn* . . ." takes on the imaginative "as if" [*als ob*], and the subjunctive character points beyond potential being in the sense that it no longer posits the reality of something present. Thus, as Held points out, I can imagine the physical-body over there as a psycho-physical being, as I know myself to be, without being at all convinced that it is the case.[19] I need only fictively place myself over there "as if" [*als ob*]. By virtue of presentifying imagination it is possible to imagine a second present, a second original Here—over there—just as if I were there. This second primordial Here would see the same things that I would see, just like I would see them were I there.

By itself this phantasy consciousness, however, cannot clarify the constitution of the sense alter ego, because it does not posit the being of the other and does not prevent me from imagining that it is simply my Here over there.[20] For Husserl, both these types of presentifying consciousness in the form of "as if I were there" function together in the constitution of the sense alter ego; it yields a second absolute Here simultaneously present with my absolute Here whose sense is generated from me.[21] The symmetry of perspectives allows "that which is primordially incompatible in co-existence [to become] compatible" (H I 148).

The other's Here is constituted as having its own primordial world, its own singular spatial nature (H I 146), and I realize that were I in the other's place, its world and its appearances would be the same for me. But rather than having two subjects and two separate worlds, the binding structure of presentation and presentification in intropathy makes possible a special function of co-perception: "Both are so fused that they stand in the functional community *of one* perception" (H XV 29 and H I 150). Intersubjective nature is constituted as an objective world because it is a world that is correlated to a functional community of subjects. Or put in the language with which I began this chapter, it is a world that transcends my actual and possible conscious experience of it (H I § 55).

If the world is objective through the co-constitution of an other ego then, as David Carr rightly observes, the other can never be objective for me in the same way the world is; or it could only be objective "after" the world is.[22] For it is on the basis of the other that there is something constituted that not only transcends (my) *possible* perceptions, but also *my* (possible) perceptions. This is why the physical world with which Husserl begins his analysis—the world that belongs to my primordial sphere—cannot be considered "objective" in the strict sense. More radical than the statement I cited above from the lectures on passive synthesis claiming that without remembering there would be no object, here one would have to say that without the other ego there would be no object, that the experience of the other essentially precedes the experience of the object, or again, that an object can only be experienced as object through the constitution of the sense alter ego.

Imagining Silence

At the time Husserl professed to break with a methodology that was restricted too severely to an egology, he took up basic distinctions with which he opened the second volume of the *Logische Untersuchungen.*

In the First Logical Investigation, Husserl drew a distinction between two types of signs, expression [*Ausdruck*] and indication [*Anzeige*]. In communication, expressive and indicative signs are interwoven [*verflochten*]. There is, however, an essential difference between these two types of signs that can be shown by turning to the "solitary life of the soul." Expression is disclosed as a meaningful sign [*bedeutsame Zeichen*] that can occur without indication in the monologue. The indicative sign, on the other hand, while devoid of meaning [*Bedeutung*], is a significant sign when and where it serves a thinking being as an indication for something else, that is, when it "motivates" the conviction or supposition of the being of the other object, inaccessible to immediate insight (cf. LU II/1 §§ 1–8). Whereas in *expression* there is a referring to objects through meaning and the possibility of interpretation, in *indication* there is an associative tie between two objects. Reflecting back on his *Logische Untersuchungen,* Husserl writes that "the phenomenon of *indication,*" which entails the structure of motivation, already planted the "seed of genetic phenomenology" (EU 78).

In the theory of intersubjectivity sketched in the lectures on *Erste Philosophie* (1923/34) Husserl takes an initial step toward explicating intersubjectivity in terms of the phenomenon of indication, and thus a phenomenology of association.[23] I will have to save a detailed exegesis of this account of intersubjectivity for another time. Let me note only that despite a shift in the role that the lived-body plays in the earlier and later versions,[24] two things remain the same. First, it becomes especially clear in this context that not all indications are linguistic indications. Second, because there is an essential "intertwining" [*Verflectung*] of the psychic life with the lived-body and the latter with the physical-body, intropathy functions as an "indicating intention" through which the other "Self" is mediately appresented as what is purely indicated.[25] Through intropathy I am motivated to posit the being of the other as other. Further, by imagining the indicated other "over there" to be an expressing self "Here," as if I were there, an other is appresented with the possibility of its own monologue. Ultimately an intersubjective nexus emerges among phenomenologically "expressive," that is, essentially silent original spheres. Intersubjectivity is constituted, according to this version, independently of communication and especially linguistic communication.

Having simply sketched this theory of the experience of the other, I want to ask: Has the new reduction made an effect on Husserl's theory of intersubjectivity? Has it significantly propelled his theory beyond a Cartesian account, or stated more dramatically, what does it mean for intersubjective experience to be structured on distinctions utilized within a pure logical grammar? Certainly, Derrida's hallmark work, *La voix et le phénomène,* casts a provocative shadow over this discussion. Is Derrida correct in suspecting that the problems of the reduction and of intersubjectivity are unfolded in a dehiscence between two types of signs?[26]

To be sure, Husserl wishes to eschew the connotations of deduction, drawing logical conclusions or inferences as well as the imputation of causality when characterizing the intersubjective field cast in semiological terminology. In fact, already in the First Investigation, Husserl had a broader view for his semiological theory that would not only be developed in a logical sense, but would be extended to realms of emotional, volitional, and perceptual phenomena; it anticipates a move from predicative experience of judging acts to prepredicative experience of a perceptual sphere, in brief, from active to passive synthesis (cf. LU II/1 28). The question, however, still remains: Is the monological "solitary life of the soul" still a transcendental phenomenological possibility for a philosophy that has purportedly opened up an intersubjective sphere of experience? Does the theory of intropathy open a new path or reinforce old prejudices? If expression and indication are linguistic signs, and if words are in the final analysis bodily gestures, what role is played by language in intersubjectivity? Is the "natural right of indication" of which Husserl writes (H VIII 188) in the last analysis not really just a phenomenological "right to remain silent"? What does the transition from a semiology of meaning to a semiology of sense mean for the role of communication in a phenomenologically described social framework?

In the Fifth Meditation the question of silence entrenches itself because while we may benefit from Husserl's move to the dimension of the lived-body in distinction to, for example, Lipps's theory of intropathy, ultimately, communication plays no constitutive role in the constitution of the other (i.e., in the transcendental experience of the other) or in the constitution of an objective world. The intersubjective nexus is that which occurs between two absolute original spheres who express themselves to themselves, repeating, idealizing silence, "over there," imagining that "over there," there is another *monologue,* self-presence, self-expression, just "as if" I were there. Transcendental experience of the other—through intropathy—is essentially transcendental silence.

Beyond the constitution of the objective world the Fifth Cartesian Meditation boasts, of course, a "higher" level of constitution. The constitution of a cultural community is a stage of analysis whereby Husserl attempts to win back the sense *fremd* in a plural context. His endeavor is basically to conceive cultural communities as parallel to an egological structure, only on a higher level: Just as my primordial sphere is immediately accessible and the source for the sense alter ego, so too is a community of egos (an original We) the constitutive foundation for an other We. Due to the basic structure of the egology present in the Fifth Meditation, the relation of the intersubjective cultural milieus is explicated in terms of a one-sided relation of foundation.[27]

Despite the novel phenomena that Husserl introduces in the concluding pages of the Fifth Meditation such as instinct, the problem of normality, historical constitution, language, etc., it is impossible to address them in the context of an intuitive reflective method. At most, they call into question the Cartesian framework: the apodicticity of the ego as a starting point for a phenomenology of intersubjectivity, the one-sided relation of foundation in the form, ego, and alter ego, the feasibility of a static method for such a task; they challenge the absence of communication and language in a constitutive analysis, as well as the possibility of a reversibility of perspectives. In short, they call into question the status of intropathy as a synonym for *Fremderfahrung*.

Does this mean that one could essentially change the account by introducing the phenomenon of language or culture? "Dialogical" philosophies or philosophies of the "I-Thou," like Theunissen's *Der Andere*, or speech-act theories from Austin to Searle, do not *fundamentally* alter the basic schema, despite their enormous contributions. Merleau-Ponty's insights are instructive in this connection, with the sole qualification that the criticism he levels at the so-called "philosophies of the negative" has a much broader scope:

> Some for others and not only one for the other. The problem of the alien (*d'autrui*) is always posed by the philosophies of the negative under the form of the problem of *the* other [l'*autre*], as if the entire difficulty were to pass from the *one* to the *other*. That is significant. . . . Perhaps it would even be necessary to reverse the customary order of the philosophies of the negative and say that the problem of *the* other is a particular case of *some* others [des *autres*]. . . ."[28]

If, as Merleau-Ponty suggests in this prolonged footnote that the alien is only accessible from the very start within a constellation of some others, the theory of intersubjectivity has been misunderstood as the problem of "the other," it would be necessary to begin a phenomenology of intersubjectivity from the standpoint of such constellations.

These reflections imply that significant advancement cannot be made in philosophies of the social world by simply modifying what is at root an egological account. For phenomenology in particular it means that one must abandon a Cartesian method altogether in all its forms; one can no longer begin a *phenomenology* of intersubjectivity from the intuitive-reflective givenness of consciousness, but must take its bearings from the pregivenness of the world through a regressive procedure, that is, from the difference between static and genetic methods.

In the next section, I address the problem of world in phenomenology as a basis for a new departure for intersubjectivity. This section will function as a transition to the generative formulation of intersubjectivity articulated as the structure homeworld/alienworld.

Section 2

Transcendental Philosophy and the Problem of World

> Ultimately, the entire purport of transcendental philosophy is to go back to those matters that are in principle taken for granted (and all those others that are essentially related to them). . . . It sees in them the most profound and the most difficult problems of the world and cognition of the world. . . .
>
> Husserl[1]

> Between Being in itself and the "interior life" it does not even catch sight of the *problem of the world.* Whereas it is toward that problem that we are making our way. What interests us is not the reasons one can have to consider the existence of the world "uncertain"—as if one already knew what to exist is and as if the whole question were to apply this concept appropriately. For us the essential is to know precisely what the being of the world means.
>
> Merleau-Ponty[2]

The theory of intersubjectivity portrayed in the Fifth Cartesian Meditation relied on results won from a genetic analysis such as the laws of passive synthesis, the concept of monadic ego facticity, even the notion of monadic otherness as a kind of intentional implication. Nevertheless, these matters disclosed by a genetic method were treated in a static constitutional account. While there is no methodological necessity for linking such an approach with an intuitive reflective procedure, Husserl provided a Cartesian account of intersubjectivity by exfoliating the sense of otherness from the standpoint of individual subjectivity. He espouses a foundational account of intersubjectivity on the basis of his abstract progressive point of departure.

But when Husserl examined the relationship *between* static and genetic methods he opened the possibility of a new procedure that does not begin with the intuitive reflective presence of my original sphere. In so doing, he also implicitly prepared a way for a novel formulation of intersubjectivity. By articulating the relationship between ontology and constitutive methods in general and between static and genetic phenomenologies more particularly as relations of leading clue, Husserl initiated a study of transcendental inquiry called "questioning-back" [*Rückfrage*] or what became a type of "regressive" procedure.

A regressive procedure begins with the *problem of world* rather than consciousness. In this section, I introduce briefly the movement of regressive procedure that enables the world to function as a point of departure for transcendental analysis (chapter 5). I then take up the fecund concept of the life-world, first in its provisional senses (chapter 6), and then as the phenomenological notion of "territory" (chapter 7). This will entail explicating the transcendental modalities of the lifeworld-territory as world-horizon and as earth-ground. By approaching intersubjectivity through the concept of territory, it will be possible to broach the geo-historical dimensions of social life.

5

Regressive Procedure

In this chapter I suggest the motives for Husserl's undertaking of regressive procedure and show how it orients phenomenology on the natural world of life. I do this by illustrating how the distinction between ontology and constitutive analyses, especially when this discussion takes place within the context of static and genetic methods, issues in a regressive procedure.

Regressive Approach to the Natural World of Life

In order to sketch the significance of regressive procedure, let me recall the distinctions made in chapter 2 regarding static and genetic analyses. We have seen that a static analysis can be an ontological inquiry that describes structures and essences within the natural attitude, and it can be a constitutive inquiry into how something takes on sense, carried out in the transcendental attitude. I also explained how it is possible for the matters of a static analysis to function as leading clues to the question of the genesis of those matters.

The rudiments for a regressive method are already found in the discussions on ontological and constitutive analyses within a static method, but become articulated more precisely as regressive when Husserl discusses the relation of *Leitfaden* between static and genetic methods. In this very movement from static to genetic matters there is an implicit recasting of phenomenological method. Taking static method as a leading clue to genetic analysis implies a new *order* of procedure for phenomenological investigation (H XI 344; cf. H XV 617).

Rather than beginning straight away with a phenomenological analysis that immediately yields consciousness or subjectivity, and then proceeding from there to eidetic analyses, Husserl proposes to begin with ontology. "It is clear," writes Husserl in 1921, "that one will initially proceed from particular fundamental types . . ." (H XI 344). Types in the sense used here are "vague" essences generated within the natural attitude, for example, "rope," "boulder," "living being," etc.[1] Similar to the organization of phenomenological procedure treated at the conclusion of *Ideen I*, Husserl insists nearly a decade later that matters of static eidetic investigations within the natural attitude can serve as the point of departure for transcendental phenomenological analyses; and here he has genetic constitution particularly in mind: "The question concerns the *leading clues* of the system. As leading clues, we have types of objects, that is, leading clues from the standpoint of *ontology*" (H XI 344, my emphasis).

In another manuscript on the difference between static and genetic phenomenology, written more than a decade after the manuscript just mentioned (1933), Husserl again emphasizes the departure for phenomenology as ontology. Let me call attention once more to the passage I cited above under the heading "Leading Clue." "Thus, that is static phenomenology. I analyze *ontologically* the being-sense world and correlatively I inquire into the certainties of being, specifically, I inquire concretely into the modes of givenness. *Ontological analysis* is the leading clue for the analysis of correlative validities of being" (H XV 616, my emphasis). As Carr succinctly formulates the movement, the question concerning *what* there is and what *kinds* of things there are becomes the point of departure for asking *how* these things and kinds of things are given, or better, pregiven.[2]

That one begins with ontology means that one begins phenomenological analysis by starting within the natural attitude. From here one can proceed to constitutional questions of a static and then a genetic kind. It is with this recognition that the natural concept of the world becomes the new point of departure for phenomenology. In the manuscript on static and genetic methods from 1921 Husserl writes: "*Beginning with the natural attitude*, one can also take as leading clue the 'natural concept of the world' ['*natürlichen Weltbegriff*']" (H XI 344, my emphasis).[3] From here "one raises the natural world into the Eidetic, classifies it, extracts types of constituting objects, and describes (without regard to genesis) constituting consciousness and finally the constitution of this type, world" (H XI 344 f.). In the *Krisis 1* text, Husserl calls this initial stage an "ontology of the lifeworld" (H VI § 51).[4] It starts by grasping both material and formal invariant structures of the "*onta*" or lifeworld beings. After a static constitutive analysis is engaged, however, one can inquire into the genetic and then generative constitution.[5]

Regressive phenomenology designates the order of procedure from the natural world of life experience, to eidetic types, to constitutive questions that yield questions of genesis. The reason this "regressive" movement surfaces in the discussion of static and genetic methods is due to the fact that Husserl initially understands the process of questioning back [*Rückfrage*] to genesis as an inquiry into genesis from the standpoint of ontology. It is a reflecting back [*Rückbesinnung*] from founding layers of validity to developmental genesis: "Obviously, questioning back is a constant inquiry into the founding layers of validity and therefore a questioning back into genesis" (H XV 614). The ontological structure peculiar to a static phenomenology functions accordingly as a "leading clue of questioning back" into genesis (H XV 617).

It is also in this context that Husserl explicitly details a movement for a inquiry into phenomenological genesis that he ties to a regressive procedure. Summing up the results of some reflections in 1933 Husserl labels the theme of his work: " 'Static' phenomenology as opposed to genetic phenomenology." He then enumerates the various stages of investigation as follows: "(1) Ontological structure = structure of the being-sense world in its founding relations of being." This he tells us functions as "(2) [the] leading clue of questioning back: The founding relations of possible experience of the mundane and of world correspond correlatively to the founding relations of being." Finally, (3) this structure of the possibility of world-experience, he continues, is only grasped "abstractly" in the mere transformation of founding relations of being into validity of being: "These mere 'theses'—as I constantly insisted earlier—lie in the modes of givenness (the ontic in the How of the mode of givenness, originally in the way of appearance). Thus, the question into the conditions of the possibility of experience leads to the problem of multiplicities and unities—but then to the problems of originality as primordiality etc." Ultimately, he asserts, within a certain level of genetic phenomenology this leads to the "primordial present" [*urtümliche Gegenwart*] (H XV 617).

Such a regressive movement was already sketched in his well known article "Kant und die Idee der Transzendental-philosophie" from 1924. This piece, also known as the "Kant-Rede" or "Kant Speech" (H VIII 312), is significant for three reasons. First, it occurs during the general period of Husserl's lectures on passive synthesis and on the heels of his thematization of static and genetic phenomenologies. Second, it occurs at the time of the lectures on first philosophy (1923/24); as I noted above, first philosophy is ambiguous, making gestures, on the one hand, to a new methodology that takes its departure from the world, and on the other, reinforcing the apodicticity of the ego as the starting point for philosophy.

The Kant Speech champions the former. Third, this panegyric presented on the occasion of the bicentennial celebration of Kant's birth follows out the methodological order of a regressive style of analysis in promulgating the idea of phenomenology. Although Husserl will continue to court the Cartesian way, "Kant und die Idee der Transzendental-philosophie" outlines a departure from Cartesianism and delineates a procedure endorsed with more conviction in, for example, the later *Krisis* writings.

For the purpose of this chapter, I want to go no further than to point out that by sketching a formal ontology of nature, that is, by asking under which forms of concept and law an objective world (a nature) must stand in general, Husserl considers Kant to be the first to regard science not merely as a theory of objective actualities and possibilities, but as an objective cognitive accomplishment that can be attained by anyone. For Husserl a regressive procedure requires questioning back systematically precisely to those presuppositions [*Selbstverständlichkeiten*] that form a concealed basis of their cognitive accomplishments.

Adapting this formulation of the transcendental problematic, Husserl does indeed endorse a qualified regressive procedure intimated by Kant "in the form of an original regressive formulation." Yet this original regressive formulation points to a "fundamentally different regressive method," one that does not rest on unquestioned presuppositions (H VI 118).

An initial indication that a shift in transcendental method has occurred for Husserl around the period of the Kant Speech is suggested by Husserl's reappropriation of the theme of presupposition from the *Logische Untersuchungen*, both in the sense of *Voraussetzung* and *Selbstverständlichkeit.*[6] His preoccupation with presuppositions in the Kant Speech stands in striking contrast to his otherwise persistent refrain of Husserl's self-acknowledged Cartesian maxim of indubitability. Presupposition, notes Husserl, rather than meaning "premise" indicates the general notion of this or that thing lying in concrete particularity, as already there and continuing to be there in every act of natural life. It means literally positing [*setzen*] something in advance [*im voraus*], hence taking it for granted: "Thus, under the rubric 'presupposition', we describe the general sense of natural life which, as such, it continually carries in itself—as a form of all its convictions, without it ever being [thematically] disclosed [*herausgestellt*]" (H VII 246 n.).

In the Kant Speech the principle of presuppositionlessness becomes an attempt to disclose critically the world of life that is taken for granted in principle and used in prereflective and reflective "natural living." Philosophy is transcendental not because it can uncover an absolute starting point, but because it inquires back into unthematic convictions peculiar to scientific as well as non-scientific life, and into the conditions for the possibility of experience as such.

The process of questioning back displaces the emphasis in phenomenology from an inquiry into *modes of givenness*, which assumes that there can be a simple starting point, to an inquiry into *modes of pregivenness*.[7] The use of the expression "pregivenness," especially in relation to the notion of lifeworld, is significant because it reflects an awareness, implicit or explicit, that the world is always already there, meaningfully, when we reflectively or intuitively turn toward it.[8]

Questioning back into modes of pregivenness entails a unique sort of reflection. This distinctive type of reflection is called "*Besinnung*." *Besinnung* is to be contrasted with an immanent intuitive reflection in the sense of *Reflexion* or *Überschau*.[9] The expression, "*Besinnung*" (occurring in the Kant Speech and figuring prominently in the *Krisis 1* and *Krisis 2*), suggests a twofold distinction between Cartesian and Kantian styles of reflection. First, *Besinnung* is not a reflection in the narrow sense of a self-perception that feigns to grasp in one stroke the entire privileged sphere of subjective being. Rather than a movement in which the ego grasps itself in evidence as ego, *Besinnung* intimates a mediating reflection, a thoughtful or mindful inquiry that takes the criteria of clarity and distinctness as its goal rather than as the starting point of reflection. *Besinnung* is a type of reflection that recognizes how implications of intentional life and forms of pregivenness are also constitutive of phenomena (cf. VII 255, 262–65).

Second, regressive *Besinnung* is not a reflection that wins its object once and for all; instead, it is a reflection as reflecting back [*Rückbesinnung*], as leading back [*Rückführen*] to the world taken for granted in experience, even by intuitive reflection [*Reflexion*]. Since the former process is an inquiry back [*Rückfragen*] into modes of pregivenness, the theme of its reflection becomes gradually clarified as one proceeds.[10]

Orienting transcendental method from the problem of presuppositions (rather than from indubitability) and understanding transcendental thought as a reflective inquiry back (rather than as an immanent intuitive reflection), the overall procedure for transcendental method is decisively transformed. More precisely, the procedure of transcendental method in the Cartesian way is inverted.

Let us recall that transcendental method in the Cartesian way began by bracketing existence to focus on presence in an effort to identify immediately the transcendental dimension as my transcendental subjectivity. This first stage in the progression toward the transcendental dimension became the subject of Husserl's self-censure in *Krisis 1* (§ 43) and to a more ambiguous extent in lectures in *Erste Philosophie*. The second step in his progression entailed raising the transcendental fact of my consciousness to an eidetic level, undertaking an eidetic science of pure consciousness and gaining the transcendental ego as such. Thus, the order of progression entailed, first, a constitutive analysis, and then an eidetic investigation, or what Husserl also calls a phenomenological and an eidetic reduction (H I 106, and see H IX 290).

By contrast, a regressive approach in general, and the procedure actually carried out in the Kant Speech in particular, moves in just the opposite manner. Here, one begins with the natural concept of the world, the world as lived in the natural attitude: "the most presupposed of all presuppositions," that which is "absolutely taken for granted" (H VI 112; H VIII 243 f.). Remaining in the natural attitude, one then raises the dimension of factual existence to the eidetic level. Finally, when phenomenology is raised to a transcendental register phenomenological philosophy is called "to interpret" [*deuten*] the world of natural life;[11] one assesses the naïveté with which reflective and prereflective life accepts the world, questioning back to the constitutive conditions of world-experience. This is a procedure that actively employs the empirical sciences (such as biology, psychology, anthropology) that serves as guides to phenonenological analyses, a procedure sketched out in Husserl's *Krisis 2* writings.[12]

If the world of life is presupposed in all our activities—even reflective intuitive ones—and used by them; if the world of life is the world that is taken for granted, an "unquestioned fact," a "'presupposition' [that is] never formulated," then regressive phenomenology has to be a clarification of what takes place in "natural living" without the overly hasty abstractive leap to consciousness. This is why transcendental phenomenology is also designated as a "constitutive phenomenology *of the natural attitude*" (H V 158, my emphasis).

This departure has important implications for the status of transcendental subjectivity. Provisionally we can say that in regressive procedure transcendental subjectivity is understood as the subject of the natural attitude brought out of its anonymous functioning (who accepts or "has" the world), and described with respect to the multifarious ways in which this subjectivity contributes to the sense of the world, including itself (H VI § 29). For Merleau-Ponty this world constituting subject is primarily the "lived-body," for Scheler, "person," for Heidegger, "Dasein." For Husserl it is "transcendental subjectivity" and eventually what he calls "transcendental intersubjectivity."[13]

Regressive procedure, I have argued, is derived from the difference between ontological and constitutive inquiries that are brought into sharper relief for Husserl in the difference between static and genetic methods. One of the results of these observations is that the natural world of life serves as a positive point of departure for phenomenology. In the following chapter I address in more detail this world of natural experience under the rubric of the "lifeworld." I then explicate the systematic interrelations obtaining between the provisional concepts of the lifeworld.

6

The Lifeworld Problematic

The Place of the Lifeworld

Hesitant to identify his own regressive procedure with that of Kant's, Husserl charges that Kant failed to inquire into the presuppositions of the objective sciences.[1] The objective sciences Husserl has in mind are the mathematical natural sciences and the naturalistic and psychologistic human sciences, all of which presuppose a mathematized and mathematizable nature (H VII 190). Husserl wants to extricate regressive procedure from dogmatism by scrutinizing what Kant took for granted in the promulgation of his regressive procedure, namely, the mathematization of nature. Such a task especially occupies part 2 of *Krisis 1*[2] as a means to situate the way of "questioning back from the pregiven lifeworld" (part 3 A).

Much exegetic ink has already been devoted to Husserl's well-known thesis concerning the universalization of science through mathematization and the instigation of this project by Galileo. Let me simply remind the reader of the most general demarche of Husserl's interpretation.

A peculiar methodological legacy can be traced to Galileo, writes Husserl in § 9 of *Krisis 1*: The heritage of modern science, or more particularly, objectivism. Galileo's legacy to the modern style of thought was the assumption that "to be" is inherently "to be mathematizable." Husserl contends that what began, understandably enough, as a method to overcome the ambiguity and relativity of everyday experience by exacting objectively valid knowledge through the direct and indirect mathematization of nature engendered the very definition of true being (H VI 52).[3] Hence, the conceptualization of the world in modern science became characterized by the proclivity to construct the world ideally, to truncate being through the mathematization of nature.

Gurwitsch reminds us that despite Husserl's indictment of Galileo, Husserl's critique bears neither directly on science per se nor on the historical Galileo, but rather on the way Galileo's methodological technology had been employed to circumscribe being; that is, it is directed against the way modern rationality has interpreted objectivity exclusively through mathematization, thereby forgetting a more basic experiential sense of being.[4]

Husserl reclaims the experiential sense of being by implicitly including the subject in what is assumed to be objective, namely, the "world" that had been interpreted as objective nature. Taking the lived experience of the subject as an integral component of world, Husserl coins the neologism "world of life" or "lifeworld" [*Lebenswelt*].

The expression "lifeworld" carried systematic import for Husserl's *Krisis* writings. Yet this expression had also gained an ever increasing prominence in the 1920s and occurred in selected contexts prior to 1920.[5] Such contexts concern the relation between nature and spirit or again, the natural and human sciences.[6] To the best of my knowledge, the first occurrence of the expression *Lebenswelt* stems from *Ideen II* in an appendix to § 64 from 1916/17 entitled "Relativität der Natur, Absoluteheit des Geistes" ["Relativity of Nature, Absoluteness of Spirit"].[7] The term lifeworld is used here to characterize the personal communicative world, the natural world, the intuitive world, and the aesthetic world of experience, all of which are placed in contrast to the naturalistic or objective worldview peculiar to the natural sciences. As such, the "lifeworld" is basically interchangeable with the expressions "environing-world" [*Umwelt*], "everyday world" [*Alltagswelt*], "world of experience" [*Erfahrungswelt*], and the "natural concept of the world" [*natürlicher Weltbegriff*], which Husserl borrowed from Richard Avenarius.[8]

It is my contention that the tension between the scientific world and the world of natural experience so prominent in *Krisis 1* creates for Husserl a series of provisional concepts of the lifeworld. They number four: (1) the lifeworld as what is in principle intuitable, (2) the lifeworld as a foundation of sense, (3) the lifeworld as the realm of subjective-relative truths, and (4) the lifeworld as an essential structure, as *the* perceptual world. I call these concepts of the lifeworld "provisional" because they belong either to an ontological as opposed to a transcendental perspective on the lifeworld, or because they belong within a static as opposed to a genetic (and ultimately generative) phenomenology. They are to be distinguished from two transcendental concepts of the lifeworld as horizon and as ground (see chapter 7). Thus, rather than postulating a single unambiguous notion of the lifeworld, then, Husserl describes six: Four preliminary and two which belong, properly speaking, to transcendental phenomenology.

Let me emphasize that these four initial notions of the lifeworld that I focus on in the next section are not assimilable into one coherent, univocal theory of "the" lifeworld. Indeed, most commentators who emphasize one prominent notion of the lifeworld, for example, as a foundation for the sciences, as the cultural world, as the world of everyday experience, etc., are usually led by their careful attention to Husserl's texts to a more complicated view that must take into account the presence of conflicting or at least incongruous concepts.[9] On the other hand, simply admitting an ambiguity or even a plurality of lifeworld concepts does not yet suggest how they are related to one another systematically.[10]

I maintain that the four provisional concepts of the lifeworld are not merely juxtaposed, nor do they randomly appear in the course of a general phenomenological description. Instead, they are systematically related and generated, one by the other through a series of motivations and responses. What I designate as the first sense of the lifeworld—the intuitively present world of experience—is a *substantive* characterization of the lifeworld that demands a further *relational* qualification—the lifeworld as foundational for the sciences. This couplet of concepts generates a problem for which a new substantive definition is provided. This structurally third concept—the subjective-relative lifeworld*s*—motivates a final provisional concept as a resolution to the problem. This resolution is another relational concept, namely, the lifeworld as an a priori structure, *the* lifeworld as *the* perceptual world. Let me now turn to these provisional notions.

Provisional Concepts of the Lifeworld

1. *The Lifeworld as Intuitable.* Husserl begins his reflections on the way into phenomenology through the lifeworld with the criticism that Kant's manner of inquiry left unquestioned presuppositions that undermined his very inquiry. This unthematic presupposition is the everyday environing lifeworld as the original source of evidence (H VI 106). The lifeworld has an epistemological priority because it is in principle *intuitable.* For the Husserl of the twenties, the return back to the intuitable world entailed winning back a preconceptual, prelinguistic, prepredicative experience, one that precedes all explicit conceptualization (cf. H IX § 7). At this stage, the lifeworld was understood as the prescientific, immediately given world.

By characterizing the lifeworld as the prescientific intuitable world, Husserl wanted to evoke a realm of evidence having a "higher dignity" than the epistemological certainty afforded by theoretical-logical substructions and idealizing transformations (H VI 124, 130 f.). The lifeworldly evidence of the straight table edge, for example, has such a perceptual higher dignity over the concept of geometrical straight lines. Accordingly, theoretical idealizations are "in principle *not perceptible*" (H VI 130, my emphasis), although they make use of the prescientific, spatio-temporal world (H VI 125, 127, 132, 139, 142 f.).

This concept of the lifeworld rehabilitates the epistemological contribution of simple intuitive experience. I consider this a substantive characterization because while it denotes what the lifeworld is—namely a source of evidence—it does not specify the relation between it and the world of the sciences (H VI 127). Of course, by stating that the lifeworld inherently has an epistemological priority, one already extends the notion of the lifeworld beyond its mere portrayal as what is in principle intuitable: One is on the way to specifying the relation between the "intuitable" lifeworld and the "non-intuitable" constructions of the objective sciences.

2. *The Lifeworld as a Foundation of Sense.* The second provisional sense of the lifeworld has precisely this *relational* function, with the result that its epistemological import is translated into an ontological priority. Here the lifeworld is portrayed as a *foundation of sense* [*Sinnesfundament*] for the sciences as supplying the intuitive basis for scientific objects and propositions (cf. H VI 49). Husserl further qualifies the relation of founding between the lifeworld and the objective sciences as one of contrast (H VI 127). The "pure" experience of the lifeworld exists in a relationship of contrast with the ideal of objective truth precisely in an order of foundation, where the former is said to be founded [*gründet*] in the latter (H VI 133). Moreover, Husserl considers it part of a genuine scientific task (at this stage at least) not merely to consider the lifeworld as an epistemological source of evidence independently of the sciences or objective logical truths, but to follow "their essential order of foundation" [*ihrer wesenmäßigen Fundierungsordnung folgend*] (H VI 127).[11] Let us recall that following out the order of foundation in this manner is still a project that is confined to a static analysis and does not mean following out the developmental process of genesis. Such a static project might well be called "phenomenological archeology."

In a manuscript from 1931, Husserl qualifies phenomenology as "archeology." Phenomenological archeology, he remarks, "digs up" piecemeal the concealed constitutive structures that lie there *ready-made* for us as the world of experience. Regressive questioning back is further characterized not as "construction" (as in Kant), but as "reconstruction, understanding in zigzag," "as in customary archeology."[12]

Phenomenology as regressive or "archeological" reconstruction, then, belongs to a static phenomenology: It is "phenomenological" inasmuch as it inquires into the accomplishments of sense; but it is static because it questions back and then merely lays out the single sense accomplishments.

Be that as it may, at this conceptual stage, the description of the lifeworld becomes problematic and must undergo considerable revision. Husserl reflects: "At first, as long as one only makes contrasts, is only concerned with oppositions, it could appear that nothing more than or different from objective science is needed, just as everyday practical life undertakes its rational reflections, both particular and general, without needing a science for them."[13] This predicament can be stated as follows: If the lifeworld were limited to the sphere of sensuous perception merely, and if theoretical or logical experience (say, science) were in principle excluded from actual or intuitive experience (as non-perceptible), then there would be an epistemological divide separating lifeworld and science: The objective sciences would go unchecked as universal, and the theme "lifeworld" would be circumscribed as a "partial theme" in the full range of objective science in general (H VI 124 ff.). The expression "lifeworld" would be no more than a clarion call for a retreat to an idyllic life of spurious pure, prepredicative experience.

In short, merely contrasting the lifeworld and science in a relation of foundation would imply a dualism between reflective and prereflective life. At stake is nothing less than the possibility for phenomenology to become a science of the lifeworld and of the lifeworld to become a full-fledged scientific theme. On this truncated model, a science of the lifeworld would have the lifeworld as a theme, but would only examine it unidirectionally, as it were, leading to the objective sciences.

If this were to be accepted as the project surrounding Husserl's *Krisis* reflections, phenomenology would certainly have betrayed its critical inspiration. For if it were to rest with tracing the order of foundation from prereflective life to reflective life *from the perspective of the objective sciences* (which are in principle excluded from perceptual, i.e., lifeworld experience) then the *objective* sciences would *presuppose* themselves as the telos of lifeworld experience. They would still not be submitted to critical examination, and phenomenology would be incapable of putting the objective sciences themselves into question (H VI 125)! Of course, putting the objective sciences into question and not taking them for granted was the catalyst for Husserl's regressive procedure of inquiring back into the lifeworld. Hence, this initial characterization of the lifeworld can only be preliminary.

If one were to survey those already familiar with the concept of the lifeworld it would not be altogether surprising to find that one understands by lifeworld the realm of prepredicative and immediate experience. Yet Husserl cannot and, in fact, does not rest with this definition of the lifeworld, although it is initially and sometimes tacitly endorsed by him. Let me be more specific. Husserl does not retract this portrayal of the lifeworld as intuitable; rather, he mitigates the rigid contrast and order of foundation resulting from these first two substantial and relational descriptions.

Husserl *cannot* restrict the lifeworld as what is in principle intuitable to simple sensuous perception that excludes predicative experience and logical thought because of his novel and pioneering insight in the Sixth Logical Investigation concerning categorial intuition. In chapter 1, I remarked that Husserl broke with the traditional epistemological separation between sensibility and the understanding by extending intuition to cover not just simple perception, but affair-complexes, including propositional and predicative experience in general. If the lifeworld is to be understood as that which is in principle intuitable, it cannot be prejudicative, prelinguistic, prepredicative, and as a consequence, pre- or extra-scientific; it must include propositional, linguistic, and judicative spheres of experience.

Husserl *in fact* does regard the lifeworld as inclusive of science and logical thought already in his lectures on *Natur und Geist* from 1927. In this manuscript, sciences are explained as co-facts [*Mit-Tatsachen*] in the world of experience. He asks anticipating an affirmative response: "Is not science itself then a function of life . . . ? Is it not itself a piece of the unitary lifeworld?"[14] Husserl continues: "Whether the sciences be clear or unclear, completely valid or invalid, like all good or bad human formations, they belong to the store of the world as the world of *pure experience.*"[15]

Predicative, linguistic, and theoretical experience are portrayed as belonging to the field of "pure experience" and as making up the lifeworld. In spite of the ideality peculiar to scientific theories, they have direct validity for subjects of a particular scientific community and are actually experienceable (H VI 125 ff., 132 f., 136, 139, 141; cf. Beilage XIX). Theories, logical constructs are, to be sure, not things like stones, houses or trees. Nevertheless they are human accomplishments, and as such, like literature and religious institutions they belong to the concrete unity of the lifeworld as much as flora and fauna. Where the empty notion of intuition becomes more concrete to include scientific experience, where this more full notion of intuition leads to the problem of the lifeworld, there occurs a great transformation in epistemology, contends Husserl, such that now science becomes a partial theme in a general lifeworld problematic (H VI 137 f.; 467).

The concrete unity of the lifeworld extends beyond mere sensuously given things to include theoretical results, ideas, etc., in its general composition. This process of "being added to" its general composition Husserl captures with the term "*einströmen*" or "flowing into." According to Husserl, scientific interests, professional vocations, and so forth are purposeful accomplishments that occur within the world that is constantly accepted by us as valid; they lie in the universal framework of the lifeworld "into which all accomplishments flow and to which all human accomplishing activities and capabilities constantly belong" (H VI fn. 141; 214, and Beilage III; see also H VIII 259 f.).

By taking this characterization of the lifeworld seriously—the lifeworld as itself encompassing the sciences—the lifeworld cannot remain a partial theme of the objective sciences. As formative of the lifeworld, science itself contributes to the pregiven basis of action and cannot be presupposed. What Husserl objected to, Carr points out, was not that science belongs to the lifeworld, but rather that the lifeworld cannot be the world described by objective scientific theory.[16]

We find ourselves now precariously perched in what Husserl labels an "uncomfortable situation," or more drastically stated, a "paradox" (H VI 133 f.; H XXIX 214). On the one hand, Husserl conceives the lifeworld as the founding basis in *contrast* to the scientifically true world. Put simply, he wants to maintain the difference between the search after logical truths and, say, mountain climbing. On the other hand, just like buildings are built on the earth and thus belong to it, so too do objective theories which are rooted in the lifeworld also belong to it (H XXIX 214). Accordingly, Husserl wants to insist on the *unity* of "science" and "lifeworld." This unity is itself the lifeworld that encompasses science "in its own universal concreteness," forming an "insoluble unity" (H VI 134). "So our concept of the lifeworld is beginning to totter. And not also our concept of intuition, our concept of evidence?" (H XXIX 214).

Husserl attempts to resolve this paradox *within* the natural attitude as a "mundane" scientist. In so doing, two further concepts of the lifeworld are generated. This brings me to an explication of the third sense of the lifeworld.

3. *The Subjective-Relative Lifeworlds.* To show the import of the final two provisional concepts of the lifeworld, let me retrace the movement of exposition thus far. I began with the epistemological priority of the lifeworld as that which is in principle intuitable, and then qualified the

lifeworld in terms of a contrast between objective science and the lifeworld. This yielded the second concept of the lifeworld in its ontological priority as a foundation of sense. Having revised the concept of the lifeworld by expanding the notion of intuitive or perceptual experience to span both "science" and "lifeworld" (i.e., lifeworld in the first sense), a third provisional concept was already intimated: the subjective-relative lifeworld.

Gurwitsch has argued that when the scientifically determinate world is methodologically stripped of reference to possible ideal scientific explanation, the world to which we gain access is the lifeworld interpreted and apprehended in a specific subjective-relative way.[17] The world and things take on a peculiar cultural sense as they appear in the context of plans, projects, or communal interactions. Because the world is apprehended in many different ways, the lifeworld is understood as a world unique to particular socio-historical groups. Seen positively, by harkening to the subjective aspect of truth, Husserl advances a conception of the lifeworld that allows for diverse cultural worlds.

This positive implication, however, draws a difficulty in its wake. Once the objective sciences are integrated into the lifeworld, Husserl finds it trying to speak either of science or of lifeworld per se. It impels him, in fact, to write "objective truth" and "lifeworld" in quotes, bracketing them so to speak, since their senses are now implicitly in question (H VI 134). The lifeworld is no longer the lifeworld in the first two senses, and objective truth no longer has validity outside of, but only within lifeworld experience itself. From this situation, Husserl draws the disturbing conclusion (disturbing for science) that the very notion of objective truth has become relativized. He writes (as if forecasting impending doom) that the whole of science is pushed into the "merely subjective-relative" lifeworld (H VI 133).

Importantly, Husserl qualifies the subjective-relative feature of the lifeworld with the adverb "merely." For here there is no *possibility of discriminating between lifeworlds* either in terms of a priority of sense or by virtue of some necessary common feature they all share; instead, they are simply juxtaposed in their differences. My objective truths make sense within my lifeworld, and others' objective truths make sense within theirs. We all have our objective truths for our own lifeworld, but there is no way of scientifically adjudicating between them. The result is that each lifeworld would legitimately have its own science proper to it, and what we mean by a "true" world becomes enigmatic (H VI 134). Our particular lifeworld appears as just *one* particular lifeworld *among many* other lifeworlds (H VI 141 f.). Here the concept of lifeworld means an indiscriminate random *plurality* of lifeworld*s*.

The notion of the lifeworld introduced in this context of *Krisis 1* is seemingly radical because it not only suggests a pluralist view of the lifeworld, but also gestures toward a non-hierarchical conception of the lifeworlds as "cultural worlds" (H VI 141 f.). There are, however, at least two points of clarification that I should like to introduce at this point.

First, the notion of the lifeworld is not introduced by Husserl for the purposes of presenting or advancing a theory of intersubjectivity, despite the fact that many readings take him in this manner. This is not to say that one could not employ this third sense of the lifeworld to inform such a theory, or that one could not work out the implications of a latent theory of intersubjectivity on the basis of these texts. My point is that this third conception of the lifeworld (1) is fundamentally inadequate for intersubjective theory, and (2) is not the only resource for an alternative theory of intersubjectivity in Husserl (alternative, for example, to the Fifth Meditation). Despite certain similarities, the lifeworld as the plural cultural worlds intimated in *Krisis 1* must be rigorously distinguished from the structure and exposition of a theory of the lifeworld and of intersubjectivity that I broach in the conclusion of this section, and in more depth in part 2 of this work, when I address the concepts of homeworld and alienworld.

Second, Husserl does not propose a theory of intersubjectivity with this notion of plural cultural lifeworlds because it is employed as a methodological *springboard* to a final provisional sense of the lifeworld that is necessary for the progress of a regressive procedure. In other words, the problem of relative cultural lifeworlds is not fortuitous; it is one which Husserl was not only aware of, but wanted to provoke because it sets up a difficulty that Husserl *wants* to resolve in a particular manner. Well before the troubling discussion of relativism, Husserl anticipates that many paradoxes will surface, forecasting as well their imminent resolution (H VI 126). The preliminary systematic motivations, cut on the bias of the lifeworld, have their import in an *eidetic method* or an *ontology* of the lifeworld (see H VI § 51). A *lifeworld ontology* serves as a provisional, albeit necessary, stage in a general phenomenological regressive analysis that, ultimately, is submitted to a transcendental clarification.[18]

In this context, one of the motivating circumstances for the task of a lifeworld ontology is the predicament of historical relativism instigated by the dissolution of objective or scientific truths into the multiplicity of factual or situational truths peculiar to merely subjective-relative life-worlds.[19]

Now, one way to overcome a cultural relativism would be to sound a retreat back to the methodological innovations inaugurated by Galileo; this would amount to idealizing or mathematizing the lifeworld in order to gain univocal truths that are the same for everyone. Needless to say, Husserl does not opt for such a path. Not only was objective-logical theory supposed to have already overcome mere subjective-relativism, but it was exposed as belonging to the subjective-relative itself (H VI 135 f.). Moreover, calling into question the methodology of the objective sciences and the mathematization of nature was in the first place one of the central procedural issues of *Krisis 1* (H VI 135, 142).

With this type of overcoming precluded, Husserl didactically asserts that we find ourselves in an embarrassing situation as to what can be undertaken *scientifically*. Is there any sense to asserting intersubjective validity, that is, objectivity common to us all?

4. *The Lifeworld as an Essential Structure: The Eidos of the Perceptual World.* Husserl attempts to surpass mere relativism in this context by means of a scientific venture that is anathema to the procedure inculcated by the objective sciences. The embarrassment disappears, asserts Husserl proudly, when we recognize that the lifeworld, in all its relativity, does have its general structure (H VI 142). The lifeworld becomes a universal (and not merely partial) problem, and is disclosed in its "concrete universality" through the process of the *eidetic reduction.*

In this provisional sense of lifeworld, Husserl again returns to a relation of grounding by resorting to an ontological notion of lifeworld. According to Husserl, the objective sciences have the "same" structures that the "prescientific" lifeworld has. But the sciences presuppose them and forget them in their substruction of a "truth in itself." These "same" structures are invariant structures, eidetic structures that can be systematically disclosed through "sciences of the logos," that is, what Husserl calls a priori or eidetic sciences (H VI 142).

Eidetic sciences disclose the invariant εἴδη that emerge from the relative lifeworlds. They remain "bound to" relative being, but are themselves "not relative" (H IV 142). The eidetic structures that are won from the subjective-relative lifeworld yield the "subjective-relative a priori of the lifeworld" or again, the "universal lifeworld a priori" (H VI 143).

A lifeworld ontology will require us to separate in principle a purely universal lifeworld a priori from an objective a priori that has become substituted for the former by the sciences forgetful of the lifeworld. It is then that we can examine, argues Husserl, the status of the objective logical a priori in relation to the lifeworld a priori. It will enable us, furthermore, to see how the former is grounded in the latter.

The relation of founding that obtains between prepredicative and predicative experience that was at issue in the first two concepts of the lifeworld is not at issue here concerning the lifeworld a priori and the objective a priori. In the first instance, we are not speaking of a particular aspect of an experiencable and experienced lifeworld, but of the "pure eidos" lifeworld and its essential structures. As noted, Husserl attempts to arrive at a common structure shared by all diverse cultural worlds by considering the relative worlds solely in terms of their invariant and unchanging structures, irrespective of their layered on cultural senses. He does this by employing the method of eidetic variation. "What remains is a *perceptual world,* that is to say, a world given in . . . pristinely pure perceptual experience."[20]

The perceptual world is the "lifeworld a priori" distinct from the objective-logical a priori of the objective sciences. The relative cultural worlds are all "bound" to the *singular one world.* But as an eidetic structure it is a world in which no one actually lives. Just as this eidos "perceptual world" is that to which everything relative is bound, but is not itself relative (H VI 142), so too it is that to which everything experiencable is bound, but is not itself experiencable. Here the lifeworld a priori functions in relation to the diverse cultural lifeworlds as an eidos does in relation to its particular instances. In this function, the conception of the lifeworld moves once again from a substantial characterization to a more nuanced relational one.

Let us not forget that the reason Husserl introduces the pure eidos of the lifeworld in *Krisis 1* is to ground the objective-logical sciences. It is not his goal at this stage, for instance, to pursue the more complicated task of describing a *genesis* of the objective sciences, for example, the genesis of logic (H VI 144). His more basic strategy entails simply distinguishing an objective-logical a priori from the lifeworld a priori, say, logic from the structures of the pure perceptual world. This distinction, Husserl maintains, allows one to develop an eidetic science through which the objective-logical sciences can attain a radical grounding. Such a scientific formulation of the lifeworld a priori is "the great task of a pure *theory of the essence of the lifeworld.*"[21]

A lifeworld ontology is a science that is carried out "*without any transcendental interest, that is, in the 'natural attitude'* (transcendentally-philosophically speaking, in the naive attitude prior to the epoche)" (H VI 176, my emphasis). As such, a lifeworld ontology will have to be distinguished from a *transcendental* analysis of the lifeworld. Having explicated the systematic interrelation between the provisional conceptions of the lifeworld, and having hinted at the project of a lifeworld ontology, in the following chapter I will take up the transcendental concepts of the lifeworld.

7

Transcendental Concepts of the Lifeworld

It is remarkable, given the legion of analyses on the lifeworld, that the unique place of the *transcendental* concepts have not been brought into full view, or at least not been subject to more detailed commentary. One explanation for this is Husserl's roughly hewn texts in which the transition from ontological reflections to a transcendental undertaking is buried and obfuscated. Still, in his sketchy fashion Husserl does alert the reader to an important thematic shift in a lifeworld analysis by contrasting the project of a lifeworld ontology with another project.

After extolling the *great task* of a lifeworld ontology, Husserl casually mentions that it suffices to have simply hinted at an ontology. Why such short shrift for such a grand task? Evidently, he has a greater project in mind: "Rather than dwelling [on the lifeworld ontology] we prefer to proceed—as will soon be seen—to a very much greater task, namely towards one that encompasses *it* [scil., a lifeworld ontology]" (H VI 145).

The much greater task to which Husserl alludes is undertaken with transcendental interest in the form of a transcendental phenomenology of the lifeworld: It encompasses the project of a lifeworld ontology insofar as the latter sets up and then is submitted to transcendental clarification. Such a transcendental phenomenology "likewise essentially concerns the lifeworld, but nevertheless *not* as an ontological theme" (H VI 145, my emphasis).

In this, the final chapter of section 2, I explicate the transcendental concepts of the lifeworld. I call this transcendental characterization, in general, the lifeworld as "territory." The lifeworld as territory is designated more particularly in two modalities as "world-horizon" (A) and as "earth-ground" (B). But to grasp the novelty of the lifeworld as territory in its two modalities as world-horizon and earth-ground, I first contrast it briefly with the Cartesian transcendental approach to the notion of the lifeworld as a phenomenon and the world as totality.

The Lifeworld as Phenomenon and the World as Totality

When Husserl approaches the transcendental concept of the lifeworld regressively, he describes it in two coeval modalities, as world-horizon and as earth-ground. When he regards the lifeworld transcendentally from a Cartesian perspective, however, the lifeworld is essentially equated with one modality, the world, which is in turn treated as totality. As I note in the next chapter, the role of "ground" [*Boden*] is virtually absent in any positive sense from the *Krisis 1* reflections (i.e., parts I–III), and only plays a role insofar as it is something to be *over*come, literally *above* which to stand.

In § 51 of *Krisis 1* Husserl signals unequivocally the modification of a lifeworld ontology into a transcendental phenomenology of the lifeworld. Here Husserl shows his Cartesian colors. If we turn back from an ontology of the lifeworld as a science of the essential lifeworldly structures—a scientific posture that remains ensconced in the natural attitude—to the transcendental attitude, then "the *lifeworld* is transformed into the mere transcendental '*phenomenon*' in our transcendental-philosophical framework" (H VI 177, my emphasis). He contends, further, that the lifeworld remains what it essentially was, but is now exposed as a mere component in concrete transcendental subjectivity.

This same contention that the lifeworld is reduced transcendentally to a *cogitatum* writ large is echoed again toward the end of Part III B of *Krisis 1.* There Husserl maintains that when we submit the world as a universe of things to the epoche, the world is transformed into a pure intentional phenomenon.[1] And just as there is one universal nature as a self-enclosed unitary framework, so too is there only one psychic framework, a total framework of all psyches (H VI 258 f.). All particular worlds are the appearances of *the* world for all, as the enduring intentional unity, as the correlate of the intersubjective framework. Moreover, when the lifeworld is equated with *the* single world, Husserl asserts that the world is a "synthetic *totality*" precisely as a correlate of a "universality of synthetically connected accomplishments" (H VI 148, my emphasis; cf. 155 f.).

In order for Husserl to understand the lifeworld as a phenomenon, and hence the world as a synthetic totality, he must assume that the world has the same structure as an "object" or as he sometimes writes, as a physical-body [*Körper*]. There are two reasons Husserl reduces the world to a totality in a Cartesian framework. The first is metaphysical/epistemological, the second is phenomenological.[2]

1. Like Aristotle who asserted that metaphysics is a science that studies being *qua* being,[3] so too does Husserl contend that in order for phenomenology to be philosophy, it must concern itself with the being of beings or "world" (H III 10). The historical role of phenomenology is ultimately to renew philosophy's original self-understanding as it was primordially instituted by the Greeks in philosophy's self-awareness as ἐπιστήμη in distinction to δόξα; as ἐπιστήμη or θεωρία, philosophy is the openness to *the one* world as a whole.[4]

Iso Kern alludes to a passage in *Ideen I* that attests to Husserl's plaguing concern with treating not just regions of the world, within the world, but the *world as world.*[5] In Beilage VI from 1927, Husserl writes: "Can I know that all being whatsoever fits into such a regional distribution, that sciences are to be grounded upon it? Are not regions the universal world-structures, while the concept of the world-structure (since the world is not propounded as a unitary universe) is however not mentioned at all?" (H III 390). Here Husserl is concerned with taking into account the whole of "being," the "world" in its totality in order to be philosophical. For it is only by suspending the mundane world as a whole through the phenomenologist's free will that the world in its totality can become the theme of phenomenological philosophy.[6] In the final analysis, it is such a move that motivates the Cartesian reduction as the negation of the world (H III § 49).

2. Related to this point, but based on phenomenological motives, Husserl treats the whole of the world with transcendental interest as if it were an object. Let us recall that when the results of an empirical or even an ontological analysis are reinterpreted phenomenologically, the "object" is placed in phenomenological brackets and investigated according to its modes of givenness correlated to "subjective" acts, reflective or prereflective. Phenomenologically Husserl expresses this structure as noesis:noema (H III § 114). The noesis is the subjective pole of the correlational whole; it is a process of intending or meaning, in general, the pole of experiencing. The noema is most generally what is intended or meant, that is, experienced in the intentional act.[7]

The noematic sense or "full noema" differs according to the particular lived-experiences. In a phenomenological regard, when I perceive the limestone rock face I have something "perceived as such"; when I remember it, I have a noema whose sense is remembered; I can also imagine it, anticipate it, doubt it, etc., and in each case corresponding to the different modes of intentionality, I have a different noematic sense correlate. Just as there are different and separate acts, for example, now one perception and later another, or now a remembering and before a wishing, so too are there separate and different noemas (cf. H III 321). Although the senses vary according to the noetic quality of the act, it remains nevertheless the same limestone rock face as perceived, remembered, imagined, anticipated or doubted. There is, in other words, an *identical sense* that runs through all the different noemas. For this reason, Husserl insists that within the full noema, there are essentially different levels of the object that can be distinguished.

One level he brings into relief is the "objective sense" [*gegenständlicher Sinn*] (H III 227). The objective sense is the meant objectivity as such, the object simplicter (H III 227, 232); it is the core of sense [*Sinneskern*] that remains identical throughout its multiple modes of givenness.[8]

The terminological shifts and further refinements of "core" and "sense" pursued in the fourth division of *Ideen I* need not concern us here (cf. §§ 131 and 132). Is is important to note that in order to account for identity in a manifold of difference, Husserl makes a systematic distinction between that modality of the object that remains identical—the core or objective sense—and those aspects that vary, the modes of determinate givenness (see also H XI 330, 332).

The objective sense is not only constituted; it also has a constitutive role. Not only are my kinaestheses functional in bringing about a unity of sense, but in being simultaneously directed toward that which is "identical," the latter in turn solicits my kinaesthetic movements. Thus, as the object is more and more determined as to its identical sense, the aspects that are already fulfilled (and that sketch out new intentions) draw in their wake a general framework of sense, prefiguring the path toward further concordant determinability. In this way, the objective sense does not merely "await" richer epistemic contents, but directs them, steadily arousing and steadily fulfilling expectations, *ad infinitum* (H XI 12 f., 19 f., 21). The objective sense co-directs the flow of appearances, but in such a way that it never gains final determination (cf. H XI 22 f.).

On the one hand, an object achieves its sense through motivating kinaestheses and their interlocking appearances. On the other hand, the appearances only gain their sense, and accordingly, action is meaningful, in relation to the objective sense itself, the identical core.[9] In our example, this means that the manifestations of the boulder are meaningful precisely as appearances *of* the "boulder"; in this constitutive regard "the boulder" precedes its moments. Accordingly, the objective sense guides the striving of kinaestheses toward the object as futural, which is to say, it functions teleologically.[10] As teleological, the objective sense becomes constitutive for my very constitutive kinaestheses; as *telos* it becomes *arche* as well.

Now that I have given a brief introduction to the notion of objective sense on the level of objects, I want to turn to Husserl's characterization of the world itself, as a "phenomenon," as an objective sense, and as a telos. It is such an understanding that treats the world as a totality.

The world is treated as a totality because as philosophy, Cartesian phenomenology is concerned with the epistemological problem of reflectively grasping the whole of objects thematically (not just individual objects within the world) and with accounting for their constitutive coherence and continuity. Just as objective sense is itself single and identical, manifested in manifold aspects or profiles (providing the means by which profiles can be related to one another concordantly as profiles), so, too, objects have an intelligible coherence with each other by virtue of their constitutive ties to a single, identical world. In this way, the world becomes the totality [*All, Universum*] of all beings.

What I take issue with is not Husserl's lucid portrayal of the constitutive features of an objective sense. Rather, it is his tacit assumption that the world can function like an objective sense and thus can be clarified like a thing or object.[11] He does this because he conflates the function of an objective sense with the function of a horizon, namely, the process of pointing beyond and guiding perceptions. Of course, neither the objective sense nor a horizon are things or objects. But, when Husserl characterizes the world as an objective sense rather than horizon, he slips, as it were, and tends to treat the world on the model of an object. That is, the analysis of constitution by which Husserl examines the world tends to be the same analysis by which he elucidates an object *as* object. Hence, in order for the world as a universe of things to be no longer presupposed, it is converted into a "phenomenon." The world itself becomes the "One" world, a *cogitatum* writ large as a correlate of experiences, or more precisely as a correlate of intersubjective accomplishments (H VII 252 and 276).

This move enables Husserl to assert that the world-phenomenon *qua* objective sense is both *unified* through individual and collective acts of intention and fulfillment, and functions as *unifying* subjective and intersubjective actions. Consequently, not only are intersubjectively communalized acts correlated to the world-sense, but the latter functions like a Kantian idea, a "telos lying in infinity" (see H VII 274, 276; H III §143). This entire process of fulfillment resolves all occasional disappointments into an overarching concordance, and with the force of progressing experiential verification, resolves all conflicts into a higher harmony.[12]

The world is a universal concordance and the persistent restitution of true being.

We might ask: What has become of the detailed analyses of a lifeworld ontology? What is the point of going through this arduous work of regressive procedure if the only result is to grasp the world as a phenomenon, once again relative to and dependent upon absolute and independent subjectivity (whether individual or collective) in the same way it was a phenomenon in a Cartesian analysis?

My purpose in emphasizing these passages is not to reduce Husserlian phenomenology of the lifeworld to this conservative treatment of the world, but to highlight some implications of this totalizing tendency and to contrast it with a transcendental regressive analysis of the lifeworld as world-horizon and earth-ground. With this in mind, let me summarize the transcendental characterization of the world as totality.

1. The world is presupposed as having the same structure as an object.
2. Phenomenologically, this means that the world becomes a mere correlate of intentional life, bearing all the accessory problems that a Cartesian analysis of the world has.
3. The world becomes an overarching unity, which as *telos* and *arche*, forms one single constitutive force.
4. Precisely as *the* futural world, it guides the development of the unitary sense for all objects, communities, and cultures. This means that all conflicts are implicitly and ultimately overcome.
5. *Ultimately*, there is no possibility of a world encountering a radically different world; it signals the impossibility of an irreducible encounter of a *home*world with an *alien*world.

In the following section I would like to open up the possibility of a different transcendental analysis suggested by Husserl. Here, I follow out Husserl's clue of interpreting the lifeworld transcendentally both as horizon and as ground. These two modalities describe the lifeworld as "territory."

The Lifeworld as Territory

A transcendental analysis of the lifeworld that portrays the world as totality is one but not the *only* possibility for a transcendental consideration of the lifeworld. In the important section of *Krisis I* (§37), which makes explicit the distinction between a lifeworld ontology and the lifeworld treated with transcendental interest, the lifeworld is depicted in such a way that it breaks with a lifeworld ontology, and offers for us an alternative to the concept of world as totality. In this instance, the lifeworld is described in two modalities, as "horizon" and as "ground."[13]

There are two clues within the space of a few lines in Husserl's *Krisis 1* suggesting that we are moving into a transcendental treatment of the lifeworld as horizon and as ground. First, the portrayal of the lifeworld as horizon and as ground directly follows the announcement that we are leaving a lifeworld ontology, and that the "ontic Universe" of the natural attitude will be interpreted with transcendental interest *as* presupposed or pregiven, examining not *what* the lifeworld is, but *how as* lifeworld it is always already in play. Second, the notion of *pregivenness* itself is inevitably employed by Husserl when he characterizes the world of life in a regressive transcendental analysis. An inquiry into modes of pregivenness distinguishes a transcendental investigation from an ontology insofar as it inquires into the *ways in which* the lifeworld is pregiven. And it distinguishes a regressive procedure from a progressive method inasmuch as it inquires back into the lifeworld in terms of modes of *pregivenness* rather than its modes of *givenness*.

Let me quote from this key transitional section concerning the lifeworld (§37):

> Reminding ourselves of what has been said repeatedly, for us who live wakefully in it, the lifeworld is *always already there*, being for us in advance, "*ground*" for everyone, whether in theoretical or extra-theoretical praxis. The world is pregiven to us, the waking, to us who are always in some way practically interested subjects, not occasionally, but always and necessarily; it is pregiven as the universal field of all actual and possible praxis, *pregiven as horizon* [*Horizont*]. (H VI 145, my emphasis)[14]

Horizon and ground are two transcendental concepts belonging to a transcendental analysis of the lifeworld that depart from a description of the world of experience as totality.[15] As a prelude to an exposition that will detail how these two conceptions depart from notions of totality, let me enumerate some basic reasons for this suggestive departure: (1) horizon and ground are neither objects nor physical-bodies [*Körper*]; (2) they are essentially never "given"; (3) one cannot take perspectives on them; (4) they are both "unique," being predicated neither of singularity nor of plurality like objects are; (5) they cannot become "phenomena" in the sense of objective being; (6) accordingly, they do not admit of identity in the same way an object does and likewise are not overarching unities or totalities; (7) finally, both horizon and ground are constitutive conditions for experience.

Listed above are some traits that both horizon and ground share; other traits peculiar to each are taken up below. Together, these two modalities make up the transcendental structure of the lifeworld as territory. In some of Husserl's later manuscripts, the lifeworld as territory [*Territorium*] is introduced as a distinctive type of lifeworldly *openness* in contrast to the world in the ideality of infinity. It is defined as a spatio-temporal or geo-historical lifeworld that has limits or borders [*Grenzen*].[16] The precise nature of these limits will be taken up in part 2. At this juncture let me describe these two transcendental modalities, each in their turn. This entails interpreting the lifeworld in the first instance as world-horizon (A) and in the second, the lifeworld as earth-ground (B).

A. Lifeworld: World-as-Horizon

Husserl's first provocative clue in the *Krisis 1* that, transcendentally, the lifeworld cannot be regarded as an object originates from the simple but neglected claim that *as horizon,* the world has a fully different structure than an object has: "world '*is*' not like a being, not like an object" (H VI 146). Phenomenologically, the difference consists in how the object is given, or respectively, *how* the horizon is *not* given, being constitutive of givenness. While the talk of "consciousness" might be inappropriate where horizon is concerned, we can nevertheless follow the subtle distinctions elicited by Husserl's assertion that "there exists . . . a *fundamental difference* between the manner of being conscious of world, and the manner of being conscious of thing, conscious of object (in the broadest but purely lifeworldly sense)" (H VI 146, my emphasis).

Things or objects, Husserl specifies, are "given" [*gegeben*], but not the "*world-horizon.*" World-horizon is the condition for the appearance of things. Some-thing is always given *from* the world-horizon, while the world-horizon itself is in principle never given (H VI 146).

Likewise, in an attempt to evoke the way in which the being of the horizon is distinct from that of an object, Husserl advances the striking claim that the world-horizon is neither singular nor plural; to predicate plurality or singularity of the world-horizon would be meaningless, he asserts. Rather, the way of being of the world-horizon is "uniqueness" [*Einzigkeit*]. It is *presupposed* by every plural and every singular extracted from the latter.[17] Simply from these statements, which I read as pointers to a deeper analysis, one can already begin to highlight the distinctiveness of the transcendental concept of the lifeworld as world-horizon in relation to the four provisional concepts of the lifeworld delineated above.

In the first instance, the lifeworld as world-horizon is *not given* and hence is in principle *not* intuitable. It is not present like a thing in the natural or phenomenological attitudes. As horizon, it retracts in favor of the presence of the object.

Second, the lifeworld as horizon is *not a foundation of sense;* it is not a basis upon which everything else builds. Instead, as horizon, it is responsible for the way beings, founded or founding, come into being determinately.

Third, the lifeworld as horizon is *not the merely subjective-relative lifeworlds* that exist essentially in the plural. Husserl even goes so far as to say that a predication of plurality makes no sense when applied to the lifeworld as horizon. The lifeworld as world-horizon is "unique."

Finally, uniqueness as non-plurality does not mean conversely, that the lifeworld is singular, as if there would be "the one lifeworld." The lifeworld as horizon is *not the one perceptual world* won for example by eidetic reduction; it is not, as Husserl writes, the "singular extracted from it [scil., the plural]." Not only is the lifeworld not a being or many beings, it is not a genus or essence of *onta* either. The uniqueness of the lifeworld as world-horizon is independent of singularity and plurality such that both the singular and plural presuppose the lifeworld world-horizon.

Having distinguished the modality of the lifeworld as horizon, let me note that there are three ways in which Husserl treats the concept of horizon. The first is perceptual/psychological in nature; the second is a mixture of "modal" and "substantial" perspectives, and the third is modal and transcendental. Let me attempt to tease these approaches apart.

1. *Perceptual/Psychological Determination of Horizon.* Husserl's early notion of horizon, at least as it is portrayed in *Ideen I,* takes its bearings from the primacy of visual experience. In this case the horizon is not only conceived as a spatial halo, but also as a temporal court [*Hof*] or fringe projected by the object. Husserl writes: "That which is currently perceived, that which is more or less clearly co-present and determined (or at least determined to some extent) is partly permeated, partly surrounded by a *horizon of indeterminate actuality of which I am dimly conscious*" (H III 58). This vague penumbra lies at the periphery of givenness but in such a way that it can become given: "that which is given presently is for the most part surrounded by a halo of indeterminate determination" (H III 160; cf. H XI 6). Accordingly, the horizon is treated as that which "belongs to" and is dependent upon the consciously intended object surrounding a central present, as merely a sphere of possible perceptions.[18]

2. *Substantializing the Horizon.* The second view of horizon is a mixture of "modal" and "substantial" perspectives. In this case, Husserl treats the horizon modally as a nexus of referential implications (H XI 5, 19, and passim), but then assumes the horizon to be a thematic object, a field of fields. As a result he assumes that a horizon can point to another horizon, "inner horizons" indicating "outer horizons," leading finally to an all encompassing totality or universal horizon.[19]

It is one thing, however, to say that one aspect or one theme indicatively points to another by means of the horizon, but quite another to say that a horizon is itself an object that is indicated. The problem with this clarification is that Husserl equates themes with parts and horizons with wholes.[20] In this manner of speaking, the inner horizon could imply an outer horizon. While this would have to be explicated in more intricate stages, the result would be the same: The "boulder" would be said to imply a "forest," the forest, a "countryside," the countryside, a "state", etc. And in each case, that "in" which the theme would be said to be "situated" or "imply" would be counted as a "horizon." In so doing, however, a modal operation, that is, horizon as a nexus of referential implications, has become substantialized as a theme or a thematic whole.

Thus, Husserl's mistake at times is to conceive the lifeworld in a transcendental register as something that can become *gegenständlich;* or again, it is to assume that givenness *points to a horizon* and that a horizon is a theme only as yet not thematic. In this instance, the horizon is no longer phenomenologically described modally *as* pregiven, but "falsified," captured *in* its pregivenness.[21]

3. *Transcendental/Modal Description of Horizon.* Finally, the third treatment of horizon is strictly modal and transcendental. If we remain true to Husserl's qualification of the horizon "genetically" as a nexus of referential implication,[22] then we are concerned with the mode of givenness of the thematic object as givenness in a horizon (cf. H VI 267).

Understanding the lifeworld as world-horizon requires, first, studying the "'pregivenness of the world as such'" exclusively in a modal inquiry (H VI 151). Second, it demands pursuing seriously Husserl's assertions on the transcendental characterization of the lifeworld *as* pregiven that are expressive of a modal determination. These assertions once again are that the lifeworld as horizon is that *from which* we are conscious of something as something given; that the lifeworld as horizon is itself never given as a theme (if it becomes "forest" or "the totality" it is already lost modally as horizon); that it is not a being like an object (it is not a thing that could be clarified as a "noema"), or being like an eidos (such that it could be grasped eidetically); and finally, that it is "unique" in its function as horizon, indifferent to numerical designations such as plurality or singularity and indifferent to comparison between horizons.

By staying attuned to a transcendental characterization of the lifeworld *as* pregiven, the horizon character of the lifeworld cannot be objectified as a thing, a topic, or an object. Nor can it be treated ontologically as an essence. To ask *what* the lifeworld is, is to inquire into its *Quidditas;* it is to have already misconstrued the horizonal character. The response to such a question would of necessity be something static; for example, it will be something that all lifeworlds share (i.e., the fourth provisional sense of lifeworld).

However, describing the lifeworld transcendentally/modally, as that from which an object is given as thematic, yields a different response. Here the horizon is a *way of revealing,* a feature of the process of how something comes into being as present. In this regard, to take up the phenomenological mandate "back to the things themselves" means inquiring back into the mode of pregivenness of the horizonal character of the lifeworld, for horizons are constitutive of our experience of the things themselves. Their validity presupposes the horizon-character by virtue of which something having present validity can refer back to past validity which, in turn, can be reactivated (H VI 152).

Visually, we say that the horizon retreats or recedes in the sense that the horizon is what moves away from us to the extent that we move toward it. Transcendentally, one could also say that it retreats or recedes, but in this instance the meaning would be different. The horizon recedes in the sense that, as that from which the object is given, the horizon withdraws *in favor of the object being given.* Something (and not the horizon itself) is thematic for us because, as a way of revealing, the horizon escapes substantial thematization.

In keeping with the modal style of questioning, we can ask, *how* does the horizon reveal objects in its retreating? Here we can follow Husserl by maintaining that the being-sense of objects is revealed in the way of *referential implications.* The horizon leads us from one aspect to another so that things become determinate, become given, but in such a way that it is essentially open, leaving room for surprise or the unexpected (H XI 22). By being the way in which one thing points toward another, or the way in which sense is implied, the horizon reveals by pointing away from itself. Still, as the process of implying referentially, the horizon itself is never given, never determinate. As indicatively pointing away from itself in the process of receding from givenness, the lifeworld as horizon is indeed "the most presupposed of all presuppositions."

Accordingly, I would argue that the movement of totalizing the world results not from understanding the horizon as a nexus of referential implications, but from slipping into a substantializing attitude when describing the modal function of horizons. It is only then that the horizon becomes a total thing implied by something else, ultimately referring to " 'the' single or universal field." But described modally, using the field of what is present as our starting point, there is nothing peculiar to the horizon that would necessitate it becoming a field of all fields. After having suggested the novelty of the lifeworld as world-horizon, Husserl's error, as suggested, was to have attempted to grasp pregivenness in its wholeness, transforming it thematically into an object-like structure. "The decisive mistake in this understanding . . . ," Held sums up cogently, "lies in the reinterpretation of preintentional nonrelational worldliness as an intentional relation to the world."[23]

As the how of sense revelation the horizon retreats, and in retreating, referentially implies being-sense for a subject or subjects. Thus, not only is an object inseparable from a horizon, but the subject too. Implied by the lifeworld as horizon, in other words, is also the subject for whom the object is relevant, uncertain, disruptive, concordant, enjoyable, displeasing, etc.

The lifeworld as horizon is not to be mistaken for the background of a foreground; for the horizon is beyond even the background.[24] Thus, the horizon is not the "forest" in which the "boulder" is situated, for there is only a foreground and a background, which is to say, a "field" in relation to subjects for whom it is at all meaningful. As the pregiven horizon for praxis, the lifeworld transcendentally understood is the mode of meaningful interaction as implied reciprocal revelation for "subject" and "object," or rather, for "praxis" and "sense" or "meaning." Again, the danger here would be to conceive the horizon as a third term, as some *thing* between praxis and field. The lifeworld as world-horizon *as* pregiven is the structure of their interaction, and only in this sense does it "encompass" them.

With this in mind it is easier to see how the horizon does not "belong to" objects, is not merely an "excess" [*plus ultra*] (H XI 11, 21) of determinate presence or "dependent upon" objective givenness. Instead, we—determinate/latent sense and praxical subjects—"belong to" the pregiven world-horizon whereby meaningful or even senseless action takes shape.

Finally, the horizon is indeterminate and open. The horizon is indeterminate in the sense that it is not itself something waiting to become definite, thematic, or present. Rather, it is a process of revealing, as implying latent and prominent themes in a significant manner.

This type of indeterminacy implies "openness" as opposed to "infinity." If the horizon were something thematic, the world-horizon could become infinite in the sense of *unendlich*. It would become an infinite series of possible things. But such a world-infinity, Husserl contends, is peculiar to "astronomical-physicalistic" infinity, the infinity [*Unendlichkeit*] of endlessness [*Endlosigkeit*], that is, the infinity of a continuum that could be merely thought and proven by the "sciences of the infinity of nature."[25] Such a horizon would be a "world existing in the ideality of infinity."[26]

In contrast, for the world-horizon to be unique means that there can be different modes of revealing, different ways for praxis to be relevant, appropriate or inappropriate without one being reducible to another. These styles of appropriateness are articulated by the peculiar way in which sense-determination is revealed, becoming meaningful for *this* type of interaction or for *that* future action. In this respect, the pregiven lifeworld horizon is a mode of delimiting styles of interaction, of life and of sense. (Let us recall that the early Greek sense of horizon [ὅϱος] was verbal [hence ὁϱίζειν] and not substantive, and meant the process of limiting off or distinguishing.)[27] The world-horizon opens out to new possibilities *by* limiting off the *Spielraum* or "leeway" of possibilities. This is the sense of speaking of the "open" character of the horizon.

Moreover, uniqueness also means that a horizon cannot be regarded in a relation of comparison. To compare would presuppose that a horizon could be identified by its *Quidditas* and eventually be resolved into a higher unity. Uniqueness does not mean singularity.

Nevertheless, as suggested, a world-horizon as a way of revealing does have a peculiar style that can be encountered. Any further specification of this style or of this encounter requires both genetic and generative analyses that I reserve for part 2. Here my goal is simply to articulate the conceptual framework of a transcendental characterization of lifeworld as pregiven. To do this, however, demands not only interpreting the lifeworld as world-horizon, but also in its other modality as earth-ground.

B. Lifeworld: Earth-as-Ground

> I thought only of the Earth. It was the Earth that caused each of us to be that someone he was rather than someone else; up there, wrested from the Earth, it was as if I were no longer that I, nor she that She, for me. I was eager to return to the Earth, and I trembled at the fear of having lost it. The fulfillment of my dream of love had lasted only that instant when we had been united, spinning between Earth and Moon; torn from its earthly soil, my love now knew only the heart-rending nostalgia for what it lacked: a where, a surrounding, a before, an after.
>
> Calvino[28]

It is only with a certain hesitance that I have translated "*Boden*" as ground up to this point. There are basically two German terms that can be rendered accurately in English as ground. The first expression is "*Grund*" and means both ground in the sense of a piece of land or earth, and ground in the sense of "reason," as in giving reasons. More commonly in colloquial and academic German, one hears, for example, "*aus diesem Grund*" (for this reason) or "*im Grunde*" (fundamentally), or even "*auf Grund von*" (and "*aufgrund* . . ."), meaning "on the basis of . . . ," "by reason of . . . ," or still, "because of . . .".

It has already been emphasized above that the lifeworld in a transcendental analysis is not a foundation in the sense of a basis, a set of reasons, or a causal nexus. Had Husserl wanted to convey the sense of a rational foundation or causal connections, he could have selected the much more appropriate term *Grund.* Of course, Husserl does not use the expression *Grund,* but rather *Boden* to express the transcendental character of lifeworld pregivenness.

The term *Boden* can also be rendered in English as ground, if by ground one means earthy-ground, the ground beneath our feet, soil, land. Certainly, *Boden* has a figurative sense as "foundation," when one says, for example, "*auf dem Boden der Wirklichkeit*" (to be planted firmly in reality); but even here *Boden* does not have the strict sense of a rational grounding. More commonly one hears "*auf deutschem Boden*" (on German soil), or "*auf festem Boden*" (on terra firma), etc.

I mention these semantic divergences between *Grund* and *Boden* only as a preliminary indicator that the translation of the term *Boden* as ground for the modality of the lifeworld transcendentally interpreted is not to be taken as a rational foundation of sense, that is, as a *Sinnesfundament* peculiar to the second provisional concept of lifeworld. But even this should not be the measure for determining Husserl's usage of the term. To understand Husserl's sense of *Boden* as a qualification of lifeworld pregivenness, it will be necessary to examine the various contexts in which he uses this expression.

It is my contention that *Krisis 1* only braves a step toward, but does not break into, full stride in developing the transcendental meaning of ground. Ground is often characterized by Husserl as an expression of the prescientific lifeworld that has constant validity for us (H VI 150), as that which objective validity always already presupposes (H VI 151), or as the pregivenness upon which actual and possible experience relies (H VI 156). But there is a less restrictive sense to ground. Let me bring the relevant lines once again to our attention: "the lifeworld is always already there, being for us in advance, 'ground' for everyone, whether in theoretical or extra-theoretical praxis" (H VI 145).

The role of "ground" in *Krisis 1* is not unambiguous; its meaning depends upon whether it is understood within a Cartesian progressive or a regressive procedure.

In the Cartesian approach, the ground is something to be recognized and removed, "stood above" so that the lifeworld as ground, too, can be regarded phenomenologically as a "phenomenon." We read: "I have freed myself precisely from this ground through the epoche; I stand *above* the [life]world, which now has become for me a *phenomenon*" (H VI 155, Husserl's emphasis). The Cartesian transcendental attitude, which allows one to put the lifeworld out of play "in one blow," (H VI 153) is also an attitude that perches

> *above* the pregivenness of the validity of the world, *above* the infinite network of concealed relations of foundation [*Fundierungen*] whereby the world's validities are continually founded on validities, *above* the entire stream of synthetically unified manifolds in which the world has and gains anew the sense-content and validity of being. In other words, we have here an attitude *above* the universal life of consciousness . . . in which the world is "there" for those naively and straightforwardly living in it." (H VI 153, Husserl's emphasis)

Not only do we stand *above* the lifeworld as *ground*, which is now reduced to a phenomenon, but this very ground is to be *removed;* we are to proceed groundless at first, establishing our own, un-natural, un-earthly ground. Husserl contends that instead of having a ground that is taken for granted in advance, we must exclude in principle this ground or any similar one: "Thus, it [phenomenological-transcendental philosophy] must initially begin groundless [*bodenlos*]. But it immediately gains the possibility—from its own power—to fashion itself a ground, namely by seizing in original self-reflection the naive world transformed into a phenomenon, i.e., a universe of phenomena" (H VI 185). The Cartesian mandate requires that we forsake the pregiven lifeworld as ground, that we raise ourselves above it, remove ourselves from it, and create—out of our own mastery and free will—our own ground.

I summarize this Cartesian movement because of its sharp contrast to a regressive-transcendental approach to the lifeworld as ground. Let me recall that the style of questioning conducive to handling the lifeworld *modally* as pregiven ground, as well as its special treatment as earth-ground, is nonetheless found in *Krisis 1.* While some of his statements on ground turn on a refractory assimilation of the lifeworld into a Cartesian framework, Husserl still evokes a "new" non-Cartesian methodology that inquires into the lifeworld *as* pregiven in its determination as ground.

Such an alternative tendency, decisive for a more subtle consideration of ground, is expressed in the following passage of *Krisis 1*: "Let us begin our new way by fostering now an exclusive, consistently theoretical interest in the 'lifeworld' *as* the general 'ground' of human world-life, and precisely in the very *way in which* it carries out this general 'ground' function" (my emphasis).[29]

In well-known manuscripts surrounding the *Krisis* period (to which I will turn shortly), Husserl describes ground under the title of a transcendental investigation of spatiality and lived-bodily kinaestheses. In the final analysis, the lifeworld as ground in the *Krisis 1* functions precisely as a place holder for the theme of ground in these other investigations; here ground is elaborated as "earth-ground" [*Erdboden*]. In fact, *Krisis 2* shows Husserl using precisely this term, "*Erdboden*," in a generative context.[30]

It will become clear in these investigations that speaking figuratively of placing oneself *above* the lifeworld earth-ground, going "groundless," or even establishing a new ground, itself requires the earth-ground that is constitutive of spatio-temporal sense in the first place. The earth-ground is that *from* which being "above" has any sense at all; it is that *from* which an ego or a community of egos are sense-giving. The earth-ground, like the world-horizon, is transcendentally understood insofar as it is not merely a correlate, but a modality in which the lifeworld is *constitutive of* our experience. Thus, it is a strict impossibility especially for phenomenological-transcendental thinking (which discloses the earth-ground regressively) to raise itself *above* the lifeworld as ground, to proceed groundless, even initially, and to treat the earth-ground as just another physical-body or object, which in turn can be regarded as phenomenon. In fact, it is such an attempt that Husserl will criticize as being peculiar to the objective thought of "Modern" rationality—something that Husserl deems inappropriate for transcendental phenomenology.

The exact way in which the lifeworld carries out its ground function for all our practices—whether they be restful, playful, serious and scientific, abstract or concrete—is as earth-ground. Husserl shows how the lifeworld functions as earth-ground especially in two working essays published posthumously: "Grundlegende Untersuchungen zum phänomenologischen Ursprung der Räumlichkeit der Natur" ["Fundamental Investigations into the Phenomenological Origin of the Spatiality of Nature"] (Ms. D 17, from May 7–9, 1934) and "Notizen zur Raumkonstitution" ["Notes on the Constitution of Space"] (Ms. D 18, from May 10, 1934).[31]

In light of Husserl's wavering Cartesian commitments creeping back furtively into his analyses, promoting totalizing perspectives on horizon and ground, one is struck by a most revealing and instructive feature in these writings: Husserl takes phenomenological pains to counter a totalizing perspective that would place the philosopher "over" the earth-ground. Such endeavors of totalizing objectivity that have sustained our contemporary view of world and earth Husserl attributes to the view instigated by "we Copernicans, we Moderns."

The Modern conceit that Husserl strives to overturn in these brief working essays is the egregious treatment of the earth-ground as a mere ball-shaped body [*Körper*], a physical-body among other bodies, a "total-body" [*Totalkörper*]. By describing his pursuit as an "overturning of the Copernican doctrine" ["*Umsturz der kopernikanischen Lehre*"] Husserl is not arguing for a Ptolemaic geocentric overthrow of a heliocentric view of the universe. Nor is he advocating a return to late medieval ad hoc and piecemeal assumptions to explain planetary movements. Still less does he wish to move from planetary kinematic theories to modern astrophysics. Rather, in investigating the constitution of spatiality and kinaesthesis, Husserl is led to challenge the homogenization of the earth-ground into a stellar body (Ursprung, 317, 320, 323), and supports the thesis that the earth-ground is constitutive of our experience of space and movement; in this sense the earth-ground is privileged and is that in relation to which there is both movement and rest (Ursprung, 321).

We know from our own contemporary uncanny photographs taken from the moon not only that the Modern conceit is still with us today, but that it exists in an exacerbated form. We need not only imagine, as Husserl did, that if we could view the earth from a towering perspective, it too could appear as a ball (Ursprung, 317). Our technology effects this for us. But even if it were not possible to take such a singularly explicit, circumspective view of the earth, Husserl contends, it would be enough to totalize the earth-ground through another conception. For the Modern conception is not that the earth is perceived in its entirety, all at once. It can be reduced to a mere physical-body all the same by being the unitary product of concordant syntheses. Even conceived as being perceptible "in a primordial synthesis, as a unity of single experiences connected to one another . . . the earth is still a physical-body!" (Ursprung, 308). The earth-ground, then, should not be taken phenomenologically as a universal concordant synthesis, as a totality, as a physical-body.

Through the objectifying flight from the earth-ground, allowing us to stand above the ground, the earth is transformed into "the giant block" [*der große Klotz*], the "total-body," the resource of physical-bodies that can be broken off and divided up into yet smaller physical-bodies (Ursprung, 308).

Systematically, there are three steps by which Husserl shows how the earth-ground functions modally as constitutive of experience, and in what sense it is not originally constituted as a physical-body or mere phenomenon. This entails (1) a description of the traits peculiar to a physical-body; (2) the constitutive role of the lived-body [*Leib*] for the spatiality, directionality, and kinetics of a physical-body; and (3) the extension of the constitutive role of the lived-body to earth-ground, which in turn is understood as constitutive even of our lived-bodily experience of a physical-body. Let me explicate these points in the order just listed.

1. A physical-body is primarily that which has spatial extension and is often used by Husserl synonymously with the expression "spatial-body" [*Raumkörper*].[32] Husserl maintains that such a body is inconceivable without sensuous qualities (cf. H IV esp. 37 ff.) and has an explicable *quale*, a "what" that can be brought to possible or actual intuitive givenness (Notizen, 27, 28, 31; Ursprung, 310). A physical-body, furthermore, occupies space in a "position" [*Ort*]; it is here or there, above or below, left or right (Notizen, 27, 30 f., 33, 35).[33]

Not only does a physical-body have a self-same identity through unitary concordant syntheses, but numerical predicates apply to such bodies; they are *among* other actual or possible bodies, they coexist in a plurality, they can enter into a larger configuration or affair-complex, they can be divided up into pieces, and they can be compared to one another as similar or different (Notizen, 32; Ursprung, 309–11, 312). Finally, physical-bodies are spatial objects that exhibit motion or rest (Notizen, 34; Ursprung, 309). Let this brief tally of traits suffice for an explanation of what Husserl means by physical-body in the essays in question, and let me turn now to the peculiar role of the lived-body.

2. The lived-body [*Leib*] is not experienced as just another physical-body, but experiences, is not simply localized in space, but spatializes, it is not simply in motion, but moves itself. This strange confluence of being constituted and constituting is more than a mere admixture of nature and spirit, or of the Cartesian components, body and soul.

Rather than asking what the lived-body is (an ontological perspective) or how the lived-body is given as a phenomenon to an external observer (a Cartesian perspective), Husserl inquires into how the lived-body is given—or better, always already pregiven—to itself *as* lived-body, *as* constituting-constituted; how does the lived-body come to itself *as* lived-body?

Husserl responds with the neoteric idiom, "*Empfindniße*." *Empfindniße* are lived-sensations that attest to the reflective-reversible quality of the lived-body, being between "subject" and "object." It would not be time or energy idly spent to develop Husserl's theory of the lived-body as presented in *Ideen II*, its contributions made to the phenomenology of the lived-body, or even its pitfalls. For the purposes of this work, however,

I focus on the way in which Husserl draws on the lived-body and goes beyond it in a constitutional analysis of earth-ground. To do this, let me first show how the fact that the lived-body is revealed to itself as such (and is thus constituted as lived-body and not as a mere physical-body), points to how the lived-body is absolutely "Here" for the relative position of physical-bodies.

The example of *Empfindnisse* in the constitutive relation of touching-touched is Husserl's example par excellence of the lived-body's relation with the natural world of life. It also points to the peculiar privilege the lived-body has in the constitution of things. Generally speaking, the lived-body is constitutive of objects through its bodily movement, its kinaesthesis: By something apparently as simple as eye-movement, touch, smell, etc., or through ostensibly more complex gestures such as walking around an object or climbing on it, my kinaestheses motivate a course of concordant or even discordant appearances of an object, having this or that sense for me.[34]

In relation to my own lived-body, however, I cannot freely or randomly change my position in order to motivate an infinite flow of appearances. Inasmuch as it perceives, it is not perceived: "The same lived-body that serves me as a means for all perception, stands in my way when perceiving itself, and is a *curiously, incompletely* constituted thing" (H IV 159, my emphasis).

Incompletely constituted: Because while it is the very means by which things take on sense and is constituted as such through this process and through its *Empfindnisse,* it is nevertheless not a thing *among* things. Curiously constituted: because as *constituting* it escapes from itself in a perpetual chiasmatic relationship expressed in the movement of touching-touched. There is, then, an incomplete constitution, and perception can only have the pretension of adequacy because the absolute "Hereness" of the lived-body, in relation to which all other bodies are situated, limits the lived-body's take on objects to the same extent that it opens it up to them.[35]

The lived-body, Husserl claims, has the unique distinction of being the "zero-point" of all orientation. All things are necessarily perceived in a certain orientation (H IV 158), and as Merleau-Ponty reminds us, the thing's orientation [*sens*] is intimately bound up with its sense [*sens*].[36] In each mode of appearance, there is an irrevocable relation to a Here; all spatial being necessarily appears in relation to my lived-body as near or far, above or below, left or right. "The 'Far' is far from me, from my lived-body, the 'Right' refers back to the right side of my lived-body, to my right hand for instance" (H IV 158). Wherever the lived-body moves, it is always "Here" in relation to which all physical-bodies are there.

In the same way that the lived-body is absolutely "Here" for the relative position of objects, so too—contends Husserl—is my lived-body in a type of "Rest" that is neither the motion nor rest of physical-bodies. Since Husserl is attempting to think along with the physical sciences as a type of internal critique, he means by motion a variation of position [*Ortsveränderung*], while rest is conceived as a modification of motion (cf. Notizen, 27, 34). Thus, while each part of my lived-body can appear to be in motion or at rest, my lived-body as a whole does not undergo motion or rest of this type; instead, my lived-body is a center in relation to which physical-bodies are in motion and rest (cf. Ursprung, 315). "And my lived-body? My lived-body does not have this [type of] rest and motion—of which we have just spoken—[namely rest and motion in the space of orientation]: It does not move away (as a whole), it rests: this resting, however, is not such that it ever goes over into motion" (Notizen, 27).[37]

The lived-body is a system of kinaesthetic movements that does not move itself away from itself, or from position to position ["*Ich habe keine Fortbewegung* . . ."], but occupies a spatiality of location [*Stelle*].[38] The lived-body is a privileged "Here" as a kinaesthetic locus of orientation (Notizen, 34), which is to say, a privileged "Rest" that is not founded on the motion of physical-bodies nor reducible to their rest.

Nevertheless, for Husserl, not only is my lived-body identified with a "ground-body" [*Bodenkörper*] in relation to which motion and rest is relative and constituted (Ursprung, 311), but my lived-body itself as a constituting bodily-subjectivity is itself constituted in relation to another ground. Put differently, not only do physical-bodies have sense in relation to my lived-body, but my own lived-corporeality as constituting-constituted gains its sense in relation to the earth-ground [*Erdboden*] (cf. Ursprung, 317). In methodological terms, Husserl moves deeper from the aesthetic dimension of the lived-body to the aesthetic dimension of the earth-ground. It is to an exposition of earth-ground that I now turn.

3. Let us return to the conception of the earth Husserl attributes to Modern rationality and to what he called the sciences of infinity of nature, that is, Modern physics, astrophysics, atomicphysics, etc. Lived-bodies, it is asserted, are only kinds of physical-bodies, coincidentally and accidentally occurring on earth. In this view, a total nature could be conceived that would not suffer any loss should all types of organisms and species, including humans be omitted. Furthermore, for scientific rationality, the earth is one physical body *among* other bodies, a star among stars; the earth has a position in a system of stellar positions, undergoing rest and motion like all physical-bodies; it is a total-body, a giant block, a resource of body-pieces. Where this conception of the

earth predominates, it would be ridiculous "to want to think that the earth—'merely because we accidently live on it'—would be the middle point of the world, that it would be privileged precisely because of its 'rest', in relation to which everything moved is moved" (Ursprung, 321).[39] Nevertheless, this is Husserl's position, phenomenologically.

Imperative to any assessment of Husserl's portrayal of the Modern predicament is recognizing that his criticism is not just a remiss and hasty dismissal of assertions propounded by Modern rationality; he takes them seriously in the same diligent manner that he does, for example, geometry. As a component of his "historical critique," Husserl is interested in following out the genesis of experience in which bodies and ultimately the earth are constituted in the way they are today. He wants (1) to show how Modern notions of the physical-body come to supplant a more original experience of spatial bodies through a callous forgetfulness, (2) to call us back to more primordial senses of the lived-body and earth that have been taken for granted in the conception of a physical-body, and (3) to show, in the final analysis, how this more original sense of earth is itself constitutive of the Modern conceptions of physical-body and earth.[40] The same way that Husserl attempted to meet the challenge of inversion and forgetfulness, say, in the "Origin of Geometry," he meets under the rubric of the "Origin of the Spatiality of Nature."

For a transcendental analysis trained on how the earth functions *as* pregiven for lived-bodily beings and for "we Copernicans, we Moderns," the original experiential sense of earth is *Boden*, ground. This ground, Husserl contends, is not initially experienced as a physical-body; only in higher levels of constitution does it become just like any other physical-body that only coincidentally functions like a ground. When this transition occurs, it "removes its original ground-form" leaving us "*bodenlos*," groundless, above-ground (Ursprung, 308).

As we saw, the lived-bodily kinaestheses are in rest [*ruhend*] in relation to physical-bodies. When "I walk" (when "*Ich gehe*"), when "I move myself" (when "*Ich bewege mich*"), I am neither in motion nor in rest (where, of course, the latter is treated as a modification of the motion of physical-bodies); my lived-body-ground is absolute for relative motion and rest. Physical-bodies, on the other hand, undergo rest and motion [*Ruhe und Bewegung*], but do not "move" themselves [*(sie) 'bewegen sich nicht'*] (Ursprung, 314). Moreover, when I move myself, I move through space as I constitute it, or to borrow Merleau-Ponty's expression, I inhabit space; when a physical-body is in motion, it changes position; when it is in rest, it remains unchanged in the same position (Ursprung, 315).

Still, observes Husserl, when "I move myself" as a system of constituting kinaestheses, I still have something else in relation to which I move, to which *I am relative*—something else that is *not* experienced originally as a physical-body: the earth-ground.

Unlike the physical-body and like the lived-body, the earth-ground is not in motion or rest [*Bewegung und Ruhe*] (Ursprung, 315); but unlike the lived-body and like the physical-body, the earth-ground *does not move itself* either [*und bewegt sich nicht der ganze Erdboden*] (Ursprung, 314). *Physical-bodies are in motion, but do not move themselves; I move myself, but am not in motion; the earth is neither in motion nor moves itself:* "In the original shape of its presentation the earth itself does not move itself and does not rest; only in relation to it do rest and motion first have sense" (Ursprung, 309).

Yet insofar as the earth-ground is that in relation to which my lived-body-ground can be said to move, Husserl hazards a designation of what we experience in relation to the earth-ground as a type of primordial Rest, provided that by rest we mean (1) what constitutively precedes movement and motion, as well as rest in a Newtonian sense, (2) what is not a modification of movement or motion, and (3) what is not a quality of physical-bodies. It is explicitly the latter case of physical-bodies, and by implication the lived-body as constituting kinaesthesis that Husserl has in mind when he reaffirms the earth-ground as the condition of the possibility of kinaesthetic and spatial sense. In Husserl's words, it is the earth-ground "that first makes possible the sense of all motion and all rest as a mode of motion. Its resting, however, is not a mode of motion" (Ursprung, 324; see also 313, and cf. Notizen, 32).

It is only for sciences of the infinity of nature that the earth can be said to be in motion or rest, that the earth is homogenized as an earth-body among bodies such that there are no longer any constitutive differences between the earth, the lived-body, and all other types, shapes, and sizes of physical-bodies, from basketballs to stars.

There are basically two ways in which Husserl confronts the homogenization of the earth. In the first instance, he assumes a kind of relative ground-body as a substitute for the earth-ground. To this type of homogeneity, Husserl counters with *temporal* considerations. In the second case he assumes substitutions and sense-reproductions of the earth-ground itself. To these thought-experiments he responds with *historical* considerations. In the first case Husserl takes the example of riding in a moving vehicle, imputing to it the function of a ground-body. In the final analysis, due to lived-body memory, such ground-bodies are only "relative," that is they are themselves relative to the earth-ground.[41] The second case is more dramatic. Here the moving vehicle ostensibly replaces the earth *qua* "flying ark," where my habitual body would have no direct experience of any other earth-ground.

I do not wish to get entangled in the details of Husserl's various examples confronting the problem of homogenization that open, unproductively, a morass of difficulties. Let me rather proceed to the real problem of homogenization that is characterized by the assertion that the earth itself is said to be a mere physical-body upon which we organisms, animals, and humans coincidentally reside and wander about.[42] So, addressing the problem of the flying ark, what brings us "down to earth"?

Similar to the example of a moving vehicle that is more immediately earth-bound, Husserl introduces the thought experiment of a flying ark. Such a flying ark can be a space ship with travelers who journey from the earth over an unspecified amount of time, without ever experiencing another ground or "primordial home" [*Urheimat*]. At this juncture mere temporal-genetic features will not suffice to explain how the earth functions as ground, and historical-generative considerations are called upon to respond to the problem of homogenizing the earth. Whatever the length of time we may have spent away from the earth, there are still stories and traditions, myths and rituals that have been handed down to me, perhaps through me, that give a narrative, historical structure to my earthly "*Stamm.*" They do not merely tell of my earth-ground, but structure my very comportment as an earthly being. Even in changing homesteads [*Heimstätte*], Husserl contends, I have a primordial home that belongs to every people. Having come from the earth, every people share a unique "primordial history" and are ultimately "at home" on the earth-ground.[43]

The earth-ground is that primordial-ground [*Urboden*]. Take the case where stories were in fact not passed on or where I forgot the stories or rituals, etc. Even then, according to Husserl, I would still be tied to the earth and earthly constituted; my body, our bodies, would bear the densities and modulations of the earth, generation after generation. Even if I had been kidnapped alone by "extraterrestrials," my historicity would be structured by the rhythms of my body: my heart beat, my breathing; I would live in or through a specific earthly atmosphere; I would have these kinds of legs and arms because they are born of earthly gravity and walk upon a earthly ground; I would be an emotional, rational being who, not accidentally, has an opposing thumb, is bipedal and featherless.

This is not to say, as Merleau-Ponty observes, that human earthly existence is an unconditioned possession that is guaranteed through some essence at birth.[44] It is to recognize along with Husserl that the earth is privileged as the ground of our being, and that plant life, human life, bacteria and animal life, even stellar bodies gain their *constitutive* sense *from the earth.*[45]

Accordingly, the lifeworld as earth-ground is not a *Sinnesfundament*, a sphere of immediate experience in which something else is founded [*gegründet*]. Nor is it a mere correlate of experience. The earth belongs not *merely* in a biological, psychological, or ecological register for Husserl, but in a *transcendental* register, since it is a condition for the possibility of sense-giving; it functions as the pregiven ground, as that from which things ultimately take on sense; it gives sense even to my lived-corporeality, my lived-subjectivity that is itself and in its own way sense-giving. Ultimately, the earth is not even an origin or a *primordial*-ground [Ur*boden*]. It is a "Stamm*boden*": That from which sense "stems" and is rooted, that to which one "returns" in order for our world to have sense.[46] As *Stamm*, the earth-ground is an enduring process in generation.

In a telling passage, Husserl challenges the Modern worldview that would consider animal and human life as simply arbitrary features on a spherical body, and that would regard the earth as interchangeable with other physical-bodies. We read:

> One must not commit the absurdity, indeed the absurdity [*Verkehrtheit*], of presupposing in the history of humanity, unwittingly and in advance, the dominating naturalistic, and then the anthropological and psychologistic world view; one must not commit the absurdity of regarding the history of the species, within the development of individuals and peoples, the cultivation of science and the interpretation of the world, as a self-evident [*selbstverständlich*], arbitrary occurrence on the Earth that could have taken place just as well on Venus or on Mars. (Ursprung, 323)

The role of the earth-as-ground is irreversible in terms of sense-constitution. In this regard, it is "unique." For the earth to be unique and indifferent to numerical predicates (even if we maintain that there is only "one" earth) means that even if all but one planetary body were destroyed, it would not necessarily function as earth-ground. In fact, this uniqueness is the more profound sense in which Husserl could entertain the possibility that "two" planetary bodies together function as a unique earth-ground (cf. Ursprung, 317 f.).

Admittedly, Husserl seems at times to argue at odds with himself concerning the constitutive role of the earth. On one occasion, the "apodictic ego" leaps onto the page quite unannounced (Ursprung, 323). But comparatively, the constitutive role of the earth, and the implications it has for refining, if not revising the constitutive role of "subjectivity," is by far the more prominent theme in these reflections on the earth-ground.[47]

In this manuscript in particular, Husserl's phenomenological descriptions lead him to assert the *earthly precedence of constitution*. Certainly,

Husserl adds, I can conceive of animal, plant, and human life on stellar bodies, and I can imagine myself flying there, as we would say today, in a space shuttle. But this does not acquit me of posing the historical constitutional questions concerning not only how we got there, but what history we are bearing, what type of directionality, what gait in our walk, what modes of spatiality and temporality we have in relation to which all other things will have sense.[48]

It is the earth-as-ground that is constitutive of sense for both subject and object. Strictly speaking, the expression "flying ark" for the earth is inappropriate, since to be flying, it has to be flying in relation to a ground, which for us is the earth-ground. This criticism holds *mutatis mutandis* for the locution "primordial ark" [*Ur-Arche*]. Even if we were to live on a moon in space stations from which our photographs expose the earth as just another variegated blue marble-shaped sphere, our earthly historicity would bring us "down to earth." The earth is not something we can ever fully "stand above." It is all the more pernicious for phenomenologists to speak in this manner, even figuratively, for it is also phenomenology, as transcendental philosophy that inquires into how the pregiven lifeworld functions constitutively as ground, from which spatial and kinetic signifiers have any sense at all. Furthermore, the earth-ground is not something that belongs to us; it does not function constitutively as a "resource" or "possession." Like the so-called "pieces" that break off from the earth—ranging from the moon, to iceflows, to mineral deposits—and like the birds who fly ostensibly detached from the earth-ground, Husserl's analyses show that, on the contrary, it is to the earth-ground that we belong (Notizen, 35; Ursprung, 315, 319, 324).

Let me conclude this second section by retracing its steps. I opened this section describing a regressive procedure of phenomenology by examining the difference between ontological and constitutive analysis in the framework of static and genetic methods. The starting point for a regressive procedure was said to be the natural world of life or the lifeworld. I then took up the lifeworld problematic by delineating four provisional senses of the lifeworld, distinguishing them from a transcendental analysis of the lifeworld. Within a transcendental analysis I distinguished further between the possibility of regarding the world as a totality and the lifeworld as territory. The lifeworld viewed transcendentally in a regressive procedure has two modalities: world-horizon and earth-ground. Both horizon and ground are constitutive conditions for experience and express two transcendental elaborations of how the lifeworld functions *as* pregiven. Together they make up the concept of the lifeworld as territory, as a geo-historical delimited sphere.

The full explication of the lifeworld as territory will have to await the final section. For ultimately a territory can never be just one spatio-cultural setting among others, one lifeworld indiscriminately juxtaposed to others. It is delimited as *our* historical, cultural territory; it is *normatively* significant as "homeworld" [*Heimwelt*] in a co-constitutive and co-generative relationship with an alienworld [*Fremdwelt*]. In order to take up such generative matters, I have to explicate the problem of normality and abnormality within a genetic methodology. It is then that these matters can function as leading clues to generative phenomenological ones, and to the formulation of a generative phenomenology.

PART 2

NORMALITY, ABNORMALITY, AND NORMATIVE TERRITORIES: TOWARD A GENERATIVE PHENOMENOLOGY

The primary leading clues of part 1 that have guided the study to this point include the distinction between static and genetic methods and matters, the delineation of a regressive procedure (in contrast to a progressive Cartesian one), and the phenomenological treatment of the lifeworld as territory, which is to say, as world-horizon and earth-ground. The matters of genetic phenomenology that I explicate in section 3 of this second part will function as leading clues to a generative phenomenology. They include the problems of normality and abnormality addressed from a genetic perspective.

Once I have defined normality and abnormality within a genetic phenomenology, I will be able to take up the generative phenomena of normative territories through the configurations of homeworld and alienworld. It is only after showing how home-world and alienworld are co-relative and co-generative in an axiological asymmetry that it will be possible to show how generative phenomenology can contribute to a transcendental, non-foundational approach to the problem of the social world. After explicating and relating systematically diverse generative matters found in Husserl's manuscripts, I will formulate the significance of a generative phenomenology.

Section 3

A Genetic Phenomenology of Normality and Abnormality

Introductory Remarks

Like many concepts that form part of our everyday discourse, the notions of "normality" and "abnormality" are evoked in a wide range of contexts that bear on our everyday lives. These concepts in particular are not only vague, but are laden with presuppositions. For example, we often assume clarity of purpose and understanding when characterizing behavior, actions, a body, a person, a lifestyle, or a community as normal or abnormal. In such circumstances the normal is associated with what occurs usually, conventionally, naturally, or originally, the abnormal with what is unusual, exceptional, unconventional, or unnatural; the normal with what is conforming, the abnormal with what is deviant.

Certainly, there have been attempts at gaining *scientific* clarity of the normal and abnormal. Some of the earlier scientific efforts undertaken by figures like J-.F.-V. Broussais and Auguste Comte, Xavier Bichat, and Claude Bernard of the late eighteenth and ninetheenth centuries asserted the continuity of the normal and abnormal by reducing them to mere quantitative variations. That is, in an attempt to overcome "ontological" and "evaluative" conceptions of health and sickness, the physiological and the pathological were interpreted from a theoretical and metrical point of view. Thus, just as the experiential sense of colors in their qualitative uniqueness is reduced to the scientifically measurable variation of wavelengths, so, too, the normal and abnormal, the physiological and pathological, were interpreted from a theoretical and metrical point of view as essentially homogenous, differing only in degree.[1]

In the sphere of psychology, Freud maintains at times that the limits between the normal and pathological are not strictly defined, and holds at other times that the normal and abnormal are qualitatively different.[2] Where sociology is concerned, Émile Durkheim takes a different approach. He attempts to advance a scientific view of normal and pathological phenomena while nonetheless qualifying them through practical value and interpreting the normal as what occurs most often.[3]

These and other "scientific" approaches do us the service of calling into question a transcendent dimension (e.g., "God," "Nature," etc.) as legitimating what is normal and abnormal. They do this by integrating the transcendent sphere into a field of immanence, that is, into society, humanity, and so forth. Helpful as these more traditional endeavors can be in certain respects, however, I take a different approach. In order to elucidate the problem of normality and abnormality, I offer a *phenomenological* interpretation by using Husserl's analyses as a guide. This approach is both curious and novel in two respects.

First, Husserl is not known to be a philosopher concerned with the problems of normality and abnormality. However, these problems permeated his research and appeared already prior to his celebrated work, the *Logische Untersuchungen* (1900–1901), and extended to reflections surrounding his *Krisis* manuscripts. For this division, I draw primarily on relatively obscure but quite abundant unpublished manuscripts concerning the phenomenology of *Urkonstitution* or "primordial constitution" found in the D 13 manuscript series (ca. 1916–21). While Husserl repeatedly set as a project the systematic clarification of fundamental kinds and levels of normality and abnormality, he did not undertake this project in a systematic manner.[4] I argue, however, that among Husserl's persistent albeit scattered occupation with the problems of normality and abnormality, one can articulate a cogent theory of these notions.

Second, Husserl's approach to the normal and abnormal is motivated by *constitutional* concerns rather than medicinal, diagnostic, or therapeutic ones.[5] Once again, by a constitutional account I mean an investigation into how something takes on sense or meaning, initially in relation to the activity of perceiving and knowing. Thus, my analysis will be an account of the normality and the abnormality of experience and not, for instance, of something like "objective nature." This phenomenological perspective has the advantage of taking into consideration the role of the perceiver as constitutive of normality and abnormality rather than taking these notions as given eternally or nondevelopmentally. It also has the advantage of not viewing the perceiver merely as a natural scientific object, measured against presupposed standards of what is normal. For these reasons I will be able to set the discussion of normality and abnormality in a very different context than usual, that is, in a constitutive context as a philosophical problem that has at least as much content as psychological or statistical endeavors.

From the constitutional or phenomenological problematic, Husserl's work and its results challenge many traditional conceptions of normality and abnormality assumed by the theory and practice of physiology, psychology, and therapeutics, and is suggestive for fields as diverse as somatic pathology and normative sociology. As we will see, Husserl's notions are not governed by theories of quantitative variation, statistical frequency, or averageness; nor are they restricted to the contrasts between the natural and the artificial or the original and the acquired.

One further clarification is in order. Following Husserl's lead, I treat normality and abnormality in this division from a *genetic* perspective. This means that these concepts will be described simply with respect to the individual living-being and its environing-world, and not yet with respect to an interpersonal community. Despite certain methodological difficulties, taking up the problem of normality and abnormality within a so-called "solipsistic attitude" has the advantage of disclosing these matters developmentally and relationally.[6] This abstractive standpoint however requires us to take the results of the genetic analysis as provisional and as leading clues to a generative analysis.

Finally, due to the prolific and unorganized state of Husserl's reflections, I will have to interpret at the same time as I explicate Husserl's insights. In this section I distinguish and collate Husserl's phenomenological concept of normality and abnormality in four ways. First, I explicate normality and abnormality in terms of concordance and discordance (chapter 8). Second, I advance Husserl's provocative claim that the normal is the optimal (chapter 9). The optimal enables us to understand how through experience norms are instituted and can take on a normative sense. Chapter 10 is an effort to highlight the process of normalization as the principle of selection and exclusion, and to advance a phenomenological notion of "terrain" as the concordantly optimal environing-world. It is in this chapter that I also take up the third and fourth senses of normality, namely, as typicality and familiarity.

8

Concordance and Discordance

As an introduction to and as a point of contrast with his genetic theory of normality and abnormality, I will begin this chapter by mentioning Husserl's earliest concept of normality and abnormality. Belonging to his genetic theory of normality, I will then discuss the first modality of normality as concordance and will interpret discordance as anomaly.

The Earliest Version

Husserl's earliest theory of normality and abnormality can be found in beginning reflections on perception from August 1898, reflections that are taken up again in his 1904/1905 lectures on perception.[1] Unlike Freud, who in his 1905 treatise "*Drei Abhandlungen über Sexualtheorie*" treated normality, inversion, perversion, and neurosis as psycho-sexual issues,[2] Husserl regarded normality in 1898 and 1905 in the context of the experience of perceptual truth as adequation.

Assuming the distinction between sensation and apprehension, Husserl insists that the difference between a normal and an abnormal perception need not only be seen with respect to external circumstances, but can also be assessed "purely phenomenologically," that is, strictly within the structure of perception itself and independently of notions like stimulation or intensity, sickness, or health.

At this time, Husserl described a perception as normal when the presenting complex of sensation was "similar to" or an "appropriate portrayal of" the directly presented appearance—in other words, when it presented the object or the side of the object "as it actually looks."[3]

Husserl's point seemed to be that I have a normal perception when, for example, an appearance of the stick that I touch *coincides* with the appearance of the stick that I see. In this instance, the stick appears normally as straight when the appearance of straight in the visual sphere coincides with the appearance of straight in the tactile sphere.[4] When, however, the stick is partially submerged in water and appears bent or broken (while when I touch the stick it appears straight) I have an "abnormal perception" due to a certain *conflict*. This conflict, according to Husserl, was not due to the sense-contents themselves, say, the tactile and visual sensations. Instead, the conflict took place between the interpretations or apprehensions.[5]

I do not wish to pursue this notion of normality in any more detail, save for noting that even by the early 1920s, Husserl never really abandoned this characterization of a conflict in a perceptual situation. In fact, he modifies the example sometimes by restricting his analysis to a single sense domain, that is, to the visual one. In the case of a perceptual conflict between a wax figure and a person we have one and the same store of hyletic data or sensations as the general substratum of two conflictual apprehensions: either as a dressed up wax figure or as flesh and blood (H XI 34).

What does change by this time, significantly, is the fact that the notions of coincidence and conflict no longer qualify a perception, respectively, as normal or abnormal. Rather, phenomena such as disappointment, hallucination, illusion, conflict, doubt, etc., are simply termed in general "modalizations" of perception (cf. H XI 25–64). On the other hand, what now qualifies normality is "concordance" [*Einstimmigkeit*], and abnormality, "discordance" [*Unstimmigkeit*].[6]

Two moves occasion this change especially during the period from 1917 to 1921. First, Husserl describes normality and abnormality from a genetic perspective. Rather than understanding normality in a simple slice of time, statically, normality becomes a way of clarifying how differences interact in the formation of identical sense: namely, concordantly or discordantly. Thus, normality is the way in which sense unities (e.g., aspects, perspectives of things, etc.) fit or pass together in the concordant formation and confirmation of sense. Since the notion of normality is developed in the context of analyses concerning passive synthesis, *Einstimmigkeit* is the process of synthetic unity constitution in and through differences; accordingly, *Un-stimmigkeit* is that which does not initially pass into the synthetic constitution of unity.[7]

Second, normality is defined not in terms of the lived-body or subject-pole merely, but as a *relation* between the lived-body and its environing-world. This can be seen through Husserl's critique of the natural sciences.

On Husserl's account, the world of the natural sciences does away with abnormality as a qualitative issue by advancing an idea of normal phenomena that would be exactly the same for all subjects independently of the subject's sensuous make-up.[8] This is the reason Husserl can maintain that a community of physicists *qua* physicists (and not *qua* human or perceptual beings) "see" exactly the same things, in the same way, from all angles without encountering the problem of abnormality.

Since the lived-body, too, is taken as just another physical thing, natural phenomena bear no relation to a lived-body as *constituting*.[9] The fact that I may have bad eyes, that I may have injured my finger, that I may be colorblind, etc.—all this is excluded by the natural scientist who wants to explain the formation of an objective world.[10] For Husserl, however, a communal physics that would never get to know abnormalities of the lived-body is a fiction and cannot be carried out. The very attempt to carry out the fiction, asserts Husserl, does show instead that abnormality and any reference of nature to lived-corporeality is excluded from the physicists' field of investigation; they operate with a closed thematic of physicalistic nature.[11] In Husserl's words, the physicist has a "purely objective orientation," and merely

> takes the given world in normal, concordant experience as reality, and is not interested *in how the sensuous things given hang together with the functioning of lived-corporeality*. He is not interested in the fact that a certain lived-corporeality in certain circumstances, with a certain make-up is required in order for the subject of experience to have particular experiences that are *now normal, now abnormal.*

Instead, the physicist regards the lived-body as an object of normal experience rather than as constituting this normal (or abnormal) experience itself.[12]

In concert with Husserl's view, Georges Canguilhem asserts within the context of somatic pathology that "the laws of physics and chemistry do not vary according to health or sickness."[13] Indeed, it is not the quantitative differences of bodily changes, but the *indifference itself* on the part of the living being to its conditions of life and to the quality of its exchanges with its milieu that is "profoundly abnormal."[14] Husserl's own analyses of normality and abnormality suggest that even a science of nature must not overlook the relation of kinaestheses to nature, but must examine the direct and indirect relations of the lived-body to its environing-world.

Normality and Anomaly

Let me offer a simple illustration of the constitution of normality via concordance. When I touch, say, a boulder, running my finger over its surface, or when I look at such an object from a certain vantage point, I have a normal perception with respect to the appearances if the appearances form a continuity and progressively confirm one another coherently as the experience continues. The concordantly connected appearances need not yield the full sense "boulder"; sense unity can be something as simple as "gritty" or "gray."

In general, when normality is characterized as concordance, Husserl's concept of "*Anomalität*" is understood as discordance. Discordance is essentially an alteration or modification in the constitutional process that Husserl calls either an "inhibition" on the part of the lived-body, or a "rupture" with respect to the world being experienced. Discordance can range from sleep or unconsciousness to a mere alteration in the process of constitution through injury or bodily modifications. Thus, for example, when I suddenly get a blister on my finger, or when a bright flash momentarily blinds me, there is a "break" in the temporal unfolding of appearances, a "rupture" in the constitution of sense. In relation to this concordance, the new appearance is discordant: The old and the new appearances no longer hang together concordantly.

Let me explicate the nature of this discordance. When we characterize something as discordant (as in the example given above), discordance has merely a descriptive or normatively insignificant quality. It is not yet normatively significant as "abnormal," but rather "anomalous."

The terms Husserl uses as contrasts to the expressions "*normal*" and "*Normalität*" are the adjectival forms of "*anomal*" and the substantive "*Anomalität.*" It is fairly well known that the terms "*anomal,*" and in English "anomalous," have been incorrectly traced to the negation of the Greek "νόμος" and the Latin "*norma*" (meaning "rule" or "law"). Instead, *anomal* is a construction of the Greek "ἀν-ὁμᾰλός" (meaning literally "unevenness," "not level," or "not smooth"). Contemporary usage notwithstanding, anomaly (from *anomalia*) was merely a *descriptive* term and did not express the *normative* negation of "normal," namely, "abnormal."[15]

In distinction to Freud, who does use the expressions "*Abnormalität*" and "*abnormal,*"[16] Husserl almost exclusively uses the etymologically descriptive expressions "*anomal*" and "*Anomalität.*" By making this observation, I am in no way claiming that Husserl made a conscious choice between these terms, or that he even distinguished between their older semantic values. In fact, because he only uses "*anomal,*" etc., as a contrast to the normal, we can comfortably assume his employment of the term bears both descriptive and normative connotations.[17]

Still, this etymological distinction can be instructive, especially where Husserl's analyses are concerned. When I experience something as discordant, I do not necessarily experience a negation of a norm as if it would issue in a new normality; rather, I have a rupture within a normal experience. Although I have let the term "abnormality" function ambiguously as a rendition of Husserl's *Anomalität,* in what follows I use the term "anomaly" and its cognates to express a normatively insignificant negation of normality as concordance (i.e., discordance) and reserve the term "abnormality" for a normatively significant negation of the normal. Let me flesh out these distinctions I just made.

When Husserl wants to portray the active aspect of discordance, that is, how a concordant situation becomes discordant, he depicts anomaly as an interruption [*Durchbruch*] or as a rupture or break [*Bruch*] in concordance.[18] In the case of a bright flash to the eyes, the rupture of appearances would not be anomalous because the light was more extreme or intense, as if this anomaly could be assessed as a quantitative variation of light; nor would it be anomalous because I do not "customarily" see things this bright, as if normality and anomaly could be determined by statistical frequency (indeed, this would fail to express how the continuities or discontinuities were related to one another). For Husserl, this event would be anomalous because it breaks the internal coherence of the experience.

Moreover, since the appearances are discordant, the appearances themselves are anomalous. The intrusive after-image of the flash significantly modifies the concordant appearances either of the object all together, or simply the sense unity "gray" of the rock. In either case, the old and new appearances themselves no longer hang together concordantly.

I have chosen this example of the flash to illustrate an initial relation between normality and anomaly because it coincides nicely with Husserl's examples of *Anomalität* as a sudden change, and because it presents anomaly as an intrusive, isolated event.[19] Still, this example has only sketched the idea of anomaly from the side of the object, as it were. Anomaly as discordance also has a correlative characterization on the side of the lived-body.

Where the lived-body is concerned, Husserl presents two kinds of anomaly: inhibition and injury. Let me touch only briefly the first one before proceeding to the next. Nearly four years prior to Freud's influential opusculum *Hemmung, Symptom und Angst* (1926),[20] Husserl interpreted *Anomalität* with respect to the lived-body as "inhibition" [*Hemmung*]. For Freud, an inhibition arises when the exercise of a function would issue in anxiety or when energy is diverted to a particular psychical process. Here, inhibitions restrict ego functions, especially where the ego would conflict with the id or with the superego. According to the *Drei Abhandlungen*, inhibitory functions include pain, shame, and disgust. Finally, although Freud does treat inhibitions on occasion as abnormal, he is also clear that they are not necessarily abnormal, and very often are not.

For Husserl, at one stage of analysis at least, an inhibition is always anomalous. It is anomalous insofar as it interrupts—from the side of the lived-body—the concordant process of sense endowment. This process of sense endowment is the aesthetic principle of the "I can."[21]

Let me recall that Husserl's general concepts of normality and abnormality are tied to the very constitution of sense. As a consequence, normality is questioned "in its *constitutive* significance" and anomaly as the basic discordance of this constitutive experience.[22] Accordingly, the lived-body for Husserl is normal when the "I can" is uninhibited, and anomalous when inhibitions arise with respect to the whole lived-body or at least particular organ functions.[23]

Since the concordance of the aesthetic "I can" and the interruption of experience concern, in somatic pathology, the very constitution of a world of sense, phenomena like shame, pain, or disgust do not function for Husserl as leading examples of inhibition like they do for Freud.[24] Instead, during the writings spanning from 1917 to 1921, Husserl is concerned with what I call "genetic disruptions." I use this expression because they regard the individual simply and are disruptions in a temporal *qua* factical process. Such inhibitions include phenomena like closing one's eyes, sleep, and general powerlessness such as fainting or unconsciousness.[25] Because of their highly problematic nature and inconsistent development, I will not treat them further in this work.[26] I do wish to mention them as one type of anomaly, however, because the concerns motivating their discussion point nicely to a deeper development of discordance in the intersubjective constitution of the world. Similar to the genetic inhibitions of the lived-body, birth and death will be cited by Husserl as generative "pauses" or interruptions of intersubjective and historical sense constitution, and will not be interpreted as mere breaks in sense constitution, but as "essential features" in the constitution of the world.

There are two ways in which an experience can proceed after discordance has occurred. In the first instance, discordance can be integrated into a more encompassing concordance. After the appearances emerge that are again concordant with the previous ones and align themselves according to the earlier anticipations, the anomaly is experienced *as* unusual, *as* an exception. In this instance, a particular experience is revealed through further experience as an isolated event that lacks a determinate ordered relation to the surrounding circumstances.[27] Discordance can be integrated into a more encompassing concordance—thus avoiding a mere juxtaposition of normality and anomaly—because experiential sense is not static, but *genetically developed;* it is genetic concordance in the formation of sense unity that overcomes a possible relativism of the anomalous and the normal.[28]

So, after my injured finger heals or after the blinding flash goes away, I have a series of experiences that cohere with the earlier ones. It is through this contrast with an anomaly that I have an experience of "normal." Moreover, I simultaneously experience the discordance *as* anomalous. It is from this larger genetic context that we can initially speak of an experience as constitutionally normal and of a deviation as an intentional modification of normality.[29]

Because concordance is experienced through discordance in this instance, concordance is experienced not as weakened, but as "expanded" such that overall the experiences accord with one another and incorporate breaks.[30] What is given as a whole through different concordant aspects is the "thing itself," say, the perceptual sense "boulder."

In the second instance, an experience that was initially discordant might itself issue in a *new concordance.* For example, as I continue to touch the rock surface with my left, injured hand, the appearances remain different and modified in relation to the flow of appearances I had previously of the same rock and in relation to those given by my right hand. The surface appears to be quite smooth and not gritty; the rock is much warmer to the touch and not cool. Nevertheless, because the subsequent experiences of the object themselves internally cohere, they issue in a new concordance, what Husserl understands here as a new normality and a new "ortho-aesthetic" system.[31] Now we have the case of anomaly instigating a new concordance, and thus the possibility of a new normative sense. In a similar vein, René Leriche (the former Distinguished Professor of Medicine at the Collège de France) has suggested that disease or injury can be less a matter of a deviant normality than the creation of a new normality, a new way of life "where many things pitched in a new key find unusual resonance."[32] As Durkheim recognized perceptively, anomalies or discordances can be productive: Vaccinations and disease are ways in which new bodily norms are created and produce new normalities.[33]

By way of summary, let me suggest both the advantages of and the difficulties I find with depicting the concepts of normality and abnormality as concordance and discordance. On the one hand, in the tradition of physiology and pathology discordance is a significant notion because it implies a departure from the scientific-theoretical explanation of normality and abnormality. The notion of discordance points to a *qualitative* variation of anomalous phenomena in relation to normal phenomena. If, as Claude Bernard asserts, the renal mechanism of urinary secretion is considered in itself, then disease (e.g., diabetes) is merely a *quantitative* variation of normal phenomena: Glycosuria would only be an excess of glycemia, differing by degree, but qualitatively the same as the normal phenomenon of glucose. On this view, diabetes would not be qualitatively original, but would exist on a measurable continuum of excess and deficiency. The concept of discordance, however, introduces the originality and the experiential uniqueness of an anomaly that is not, on the other hand, simply a symmetrical inversion of the normal. To cite Lagache, the well-known French physician and psychologist, there may be no negative equivalent of the pathological to the normal: "and a curious peculiarity of psychopathological vocabulary is its accommodation of negative expressions without equivalent in normal psychology; how can we not recognize the new light cast upon our knowledge of the human being by notions like those of discordance?"[34]

Moreover, the concept of concordance forces us to examine the problem of normality developmentally. It has the advantage of eschewing certain prejudices, notably, that norms are static and imposed from outside and that what is normal can be ascertained by comparative physiology or psychology. Durkheim is a good case in point. Although he seems to treat the abnormal as what is discordant with the past,[35] he nevertheless defines the normal as the "average" or that which is most generally distributed; what falls outside these parameters is the "morbid" or pathological. This also enables him to define a norm as what can be observed in the greatest number of cases.[36]

But by beginning with the phenomenon of concordance, one is obligated to take normality as something that is instituted though its development over time. In the framework of concordance and discordance, we would not be able to gauge normality by making comparisons or by measuring experiences against external standards that are assumed ready-made; rather, evaluating the normal would demand an internal critique of sorts, according to how experience progresses concordantly. More will be said on this later.

On the other hand, the difficulty I find with defining normality *simply* as concordance is the following: It leaves no room for the qualitative differentiation between concordant orders. Suppose, for example, I have two concordant lasting experiences, one of health, one of sickness. What makes injury or disease less desirable than health? On the model of concordance alone, would mere duration be sufficient to distinguish a normal from an abnormal experience? In the case of competing concordant orders, how is one order actually privileged over another in experience, even though both are or were concordant? Is it something that could be decided presumably only after death? Moreover, must discordance always be viewed negatively, as merely disruptive? What makes discordance more desirable at times, even though it violates concordance? These and similar questions will be addressed in the next chapter. To do this, I will leave aside the terminology of concordance and discordance or anomaly, and speak now of normality and abnormality as optimality and non-optimality. It is within this new context of normality that I will be in a position to reintroduce the concept of anomaly in its positive significance.

9

The Normal as the Optimal and Optimalizing Comportment

By introducing the normal as optimal, it is possible to clarify how we live differences in concordance qualitatively and normatively. In the dimension of optimality, the distinction between the normal and abnormal is not due to the "natural" lived-body as opposed to "artificial" accoutrements, "original" conditions as opposed to "acquired" ones, or even to "conventional" circumstances as opposed to "unusual" features. The "descriptive" qualities of normality and anomaly (as concordance or discordance) are themselves "normatively" normal or abnormal depending upon whether or not they are *optimal* for experience.

We will see that with the characterization of normality as optimality Husserl is sensitive to the genetic production of norms that develop from experience. We will also see how what was anomalous within the sphere of concordance can also become normal, not simply by becoming concordant, but now as being optimal, instituting new norms. The "normal" lived-body in this case will not only be understood as optimal, but as *optimalizing*.

The Optimal as Normative

Missing in the account of normality as concordance is a deeper analysis of how the lived-body is involved with the world from a certain perspective. If the lived-body is intermeshed in a network of phenomena, as Husserl's analyses point out, then there will be a perspective or a situation that will be *preferred* as *better* or *best* for experiencing. As Husserl maintains, lived-corporeality is a system of good and bad presentations; and to this system, in turn, belongs the idea of *optimal* modes of givenness (H XIV 121).

Husserl tends to understand the notion of optimality in two ways. First, a system of appearances is optimal insofar as it presents the *most* of the *same* thing with the greatest *richness* and *differentiation*. Here, the optimal is the greatest unity with greatest differentiation and not mere differentiation. In this instance, one does not understand experience as concordant or discordant; rather, one speaks now of normal experiences being "better," "richer," and abnormal ones as "diminished" or "worse."[1]

It is not uncommon for Husserl to invoke daylight or nearness as examples of optimal circumstances that we perceptual beings normally prefer.[2] In this context, I understand such affirmations less a testament to simple identity thought, than to the preference for an epistemological situation in which the thing and its characteristics come most richly and differentiated to the fore.[3] By contrast, shadows tend to obfuscate the differences compelling Husserl to assert that what is brighter or "lit-up" counts as "the better" or "the norm."[4]

To say that we "prefer" such a situation means that "normally" we tend toward the "maximum" of richness or maximum of focus in which the object is both sharp and differentiated, that we are aesthetically uncomfortable or unbalanced when the light or distance is excessive or deficient. Thus, to see something up close or in bright light does not necessarily mean that we see it optimally. (The same could be said of hearing notes sharply or chrisply, and hearing things "too loudly.")[5]

The normal as optimal is what enriches experiences: The abnormal is not necessarily anomaly, for example, it can be a concordant diminishing of differences. An abnormal perception, according to Husserl, is one that not only gives the perceived object unusually, but *worse*, with less abundance of material differences. Implied in this description is that the concept of abnormality is not merely a factual or normatively insignificant concept; it is a *normatively significant* one. This leads me to the second characterization of the optimal.

Second, for Husserl, the optimal counts as "the thing itself" in practical contexts specific to action and interests. Since the normal *qua* optimal counts as the thing itself, the optimal functions as a norm for abnormal appearances.[6] So, to play on one of Husserl's examples, the sandstone boulder with an arête, a sharp angled vertical ridge, small horizontal ribs, scoops lower in front, pitted out pockets, honed out recesses, and ledges a few centimeters wide—that boulder is experienced as optimal or "complete" by me when I regard it as a climber. For the clear-cutter or hunter, the physicist or the chemist, such ways of experience would seem completely superficial and could not be further from its true being.[7]

With this experience, which may be my very first encounter of such a boulder, its sense is instituted and accepted as "the boulder itself"—at least provisionally; as such it organizes my further perceptions and anticipations of it, my movements around it, and even adumbrates what will count as a "disappointed" perception. Thus, when I look around the boulder to discover an adequate place to begin my climb, and anticipate a side and a top that I do not (yet) feel or see, I accept this whole system of appearances in its givenness; I perceive—in the full sense of the term—the boulder itself.

In the course of experience, appearances that are not as rich in differentiation or that do not reveal the object most fully in this context, then, point back to the optimal *qua* norm as "the best," ordering themselves according to the optimal. Facing the right, I reach now blindly to the left above a sun-baked ledge grasping for a ridge in order to advance a bit higher. The piece of sandstone, curiously, is soft to the touch, and wriggles between my fingers. It is indeed a peculiar feature of the boulder, one that does not offer a point of stability. It is not a rock at all, I discover, but the tail of a lizard who has now skirmished off, sacrificing its tail as a diversion. I reach again for the ridge to secure my balance. I am confident, again, that it is the boulder that I am touching and climbing upon, and continue my ascent.

Abnormal appearances are initially constituted as modifications of or as "deviations" [*Abweichungen*] from a norm only because they implicitly refer back to appearances that function as the optimal and precisely as *their* norm.[8] On this view, something is abnormal not only because it is anomalous or unusual with respect to concordant experiences, but because it is worse for particular conditions of experience. Hence, in the sphere of factual normality, Husserl also detects a normative *teleology*.[9] By teleology, Husserl means that what counts as the thing itself, its "objective sense," guides or organizes my intentions, solicits further perceptions in the direction of the optimal.

This teleology inherent in the optimal means, more simply, that I can have a "normal color" even though by objective standards it continually changes according to the various background lighting, or oscillates between daylight and nightfall. But, argues Husserl, if the optimal, say the optimal color, were not *both* a telos *and* an actual, appearing color, the color seen in poor lighting would have no similarity to the optimal as the "color itself."[10] The appearing colors that are not optimal simultaneously play their chromatic role in their general surroundings as indexes for the normal, that is, optimal colors.[11]

Now, it may be objected that this talk of norms, optima, etc., is itself abstract and bears no relation to the lived-body or to a genetic, developmental process, and further, that an optimal posited as a teleological ideal could never be attained in fact, with the embarrassing consequence that all actual experience would ipso facto be abnormal. On the basis of Husserl's analyses, let me reply to these objections in two stages.

First, the optimal is itself something experienced and experiencable.[12] This is due to the fact that the optimal as norm is instituted and generated genetically from within experience.[13] Optima are instituted within experience by the very fact that we take a perspective on things and are embedded in our surroundings, and that as perspectives on the world, we can be more open to the givenness of objects or more closed to them.

Optimal modes of givenness, moreover, are related to modulations in orientation: A pen viewed across a large room is not given in the same way it is at arms length, just as a human face turned upside down does not have the same value as it does right side up. This is more than mere convention. The reason I sense that I see the object from "too great" a distance or from "too close up" (and that I do not say that I see something else entirely, for example, a fake boulder rather than a real lizard); the reason that I experience a certain disequilibrium telling me that something is "not quite right," concerns the fact that the various perspectives and distances from the object converge upon an optimal orientation.[14] So, Merleau-Ponty writes that "[f]or each object as for each painting in a gallery, there is an *optimal* distance from which it demands being viewed, an orientation through which it gives the most of itself. . . . The distance from me to the object is not a size which increases or decreases, but a tension that oscillates around a norm."[15] Since we interact with a world as perceptual beings, and are not merely spectators, optima are not only produced, but reappropriated as the "best" for the lived-body. By being optimal for experience, a perspective, a color, a shape or certain circumstances *become* privileged.[16]

Again, in a vein quite similar to Husserl, Merleau-Ponty explains:

> I have visual objects because I have a visual field, where *richness and distinctness* are in inverse proportion to one another, and because these two demands—which taken separately would go to infinity—once reunited determine a certain *point of maturity* and *maximum* in the perceptual process. In the same manner, I call experience of the thing or of reality . . . my full coexistence with the phenomenon, at the moment when it would be at its *maximum articulation* in all its relations, and when the "givens [*données*] of different senses" are oriented towards

> this unique pole like my intentions [*visées*] in the microscope oscillate around a *privileged* intended object [*visée privilégiée*].[17]

While Husserl does initiate many of his analyses of normality and abnormality in terms of single organ functions such as seeing or touching, he also moves beyond these investigations, broadening the context to the whole lived-body in its practical tasks. While each of my fingers have their own kinaesthetic systems as fingers of a hand, they take part in the kinaesthetic system as parts of the whole hand. Similarly, my hand, for instance, is only a partial kinaesthetic system in the kinaesthetic system of the orthoaesthetic body.[18] Not only can my right hand "correct" my left hand should the latter be injured, but should the latter be missing, it is possible for the right to accomplish the same sense constitution and same tasks as the left.[19] For this reason complete and absolute uninhibited concordance is not necessary for the normal constitution of a world. Moreover, because my finger, my hand, my eyes, etc., are part of a whole kinaesthetic system of lived-corporeality, I can still live normally and have a orthoaesthetic system should I injure them or lose them, depending on the context of action.[20] The density of concordance of the lived-body is more than what I do or think in this moment; it runs through closing my eyes, stopping up my ears, or even sleeping. For on Husserl's account, abnormality does not lodge in parts of the body; what may appear anomalous in relation to a previous concordance can still be normatively significant, that is, normal in relation to the life lived. This does not rule out the possibility, however, that it could also become normatively less significant, and hence abnormal.

Let us take the example cited by Canguilhem of a man whose arm was nearly severed in an accident, but "saved." Despite what would be considered certain functional and therapeutic abnormalities in relation to the other arm or in relation to the injured arm's previous functioning, the individual as a whole is considered normal as long as the man can continue to act in ways that give meaning to his life, for example, being a carpenter. This certainly goes against the physiologist's view of normality. The fact that inhibitions of flexion and extension motivated the man to acquire new gesticulations to achieve the same technical results as before, allowing him to resume his trade, is not normatively significant in the same way that functional constants of neuromuscular adaptation are for the physiologist examining the arm. This does not mean, on the other hand, that the workers body is the normal body of the gymnast. For Canguilhem as for Husserl, normality concerns lived-experiential normativity and is not a matter of average characteristics or functional constants established in advance and out of context.[21]

When Husserl speaks of the lived-body taken as a whole, he does not mean that the normal lived-body is a mere collocation of ears, eyes, and tactile organs. The lived-body is normal if the different organs accord with one another in a project, if they "*stimmen zusammen.*"[22] There is an implicit unity of the sensuous object as an "*aistheton koinon*" (Ms. D 13 I, 217a) correlative to the internal unity of the perceiving body so that the normal lived-body is one that functions *syn-aesthetically.*[23]

Let us now examine a case where mere differentiation is not optimal. Take for instance a patient's report cited by Minkowski in his *Lived Time.* The patient relates:

> and then sometimes everything is so fragmented, when it should be so unified. A bird in the garden chirps, for example. I heard the bird, and I know that he chirps; but that it is a bird and that he chirps, these two things are separated from each other. There is an abyss. Here I am afraid because I cannot put them back together again. . . . In reality there is no time . . . ; it is as if (helpless he puts his head in his hands)—it is my own fault, I cannot believe that the bird sings any differently than usual. But, as I have said, this is not what counts.[24]

It is clear from this person's description that the separation or fragmentation occurs not on a theoretical, but on a perceptual level, affecting the "orthoaesthetic" or normal perceptual body. Even though the patient *knows* that the bird he *sees* is the one that he *hears* chirping, he himself points out that it is not a question of judgment, but a matter of temporal and spatial lived-bodily experience. From Husserl's explanation of normality we would say that this experience is abnormal, not because everyone else puts the bird and the chirping together, etc., but because the lived-body is not working syn-aesthetically.[25] This designation also allows us to account for the instance of abnormality where all the particular organs function in an uninhibited manner, but where the lived-body itself is not functioning optimally in the sense of experiencing diversity in unity, and not mere differentiation.

This brings me to my second observation, namely, that the optimal as normal also implies optimalizing experience.

Normal Comportment as Optimalizing

As actually instituted in experience and as experiencable, the optimal norm is a maximum of richness and unity in relation to which my other perceptions are abnormal, non-optimal. My burned finger is abnormal not merely because the appearances are discordant, but because given my earlier experiences that established a particular norm, I feel things poorly. Rather than Husserl's notion of normality as optimality reinstating a conservative relation of the normal to the abnormal—where any change or modification of the lived-body or appearances means abnormality—it tends to take the "normal" beyond distinctions of the "original" and the "secondary," or the "natural" and the "artificial," and opens the possibility of *new optimal* modes of givenness and thus of the constitution of a new normality.

On the axis of concordant normality, my vision could be "normal" in the sense that it yields concordant appearances, whether or not I see poorly or well. They are the eyes I was born with, and this is the vision to which I am accustomed. In this respect, anything that disrupts this concordance is anomalous. Anyone who tries on someone else's glasses or gets prescription lenses for the first time experiences such an interruption and anomaly.

On the axis of optimality, however, the anomalous *qua* discordant can become normal. Let us take Husserl's examples of undergoing optical surgery or getting prescription glasses. Husserl's point is not that surgery or glasses return vision to a previous "original" state or make vision conform to an average or preset standard of 20/20 vision.[26] His point is that making vision normal *qua* optimal enhances my ability "*to enrich the content of the world so that it has more determinations than I knew before*" (H XIV 121). In fact, when one puts on glasses for the first time, one does not feel that "this is the way I used to see" or that "now I see like everyone else"; rather, one notices more differentiation in color; that the leaves on the trees have fine contours, that the borders on street signs are sharp, that there are cracks between boards, spaces between written words, etc. Vision is normal not in the sense that it is original, but maximal. Wittgenstein seems to make a similar observation. If we can distinguish between color-sightedness and color-blindness as two different language-games, what would make the former normal and the latter abnormal would not be a matter of the majority; rather, it lies in the ability to differentiate colors, that is, between red and green.[27]

Moreover, in opposition both to the Greeks who essentially equated the normal with the natural (the normal was understood as operating τὰ κατά φύσις), and to nineteenth- and twentieth-century psychopathology, which equated human normality with *homo natura*, the normal in Husserl's works is not identified with the natural. Instead, it cuts across the natural/artificial and natural/cultural distinction. This is best seen when new optima are created by so-called "artificial" means (e.g., glasses).

The normal *qua* optimal cuts across an original/secondary distinction as well insofar as new optima and thus new norms can be generated and surpassed in experience.[28] Here the "original" is overcome by the so-called "secondary."

Finally, the normal as optimal is not necessarily what is functional or average. Here we might take as an example the case of "The Twins" reported by Oliver Sacks.[29] These autistic twins were extraordinary contemplators of number, especially primes, as they lived their lives in communion with each other. When the twins were separated "for their own good" in order to function "in an appropriate, socially acceptable way" they lost the personal and emotional center of their lives as well as their remarkable numerical powers. Here the creation of average or so-called "normal" functioning eclipses a particular realm of optimal ability.

What I find particularly striking and clearly original in Husserl's work on normality and abnormality is not only the fact that he attempts to account for the internal development and institution of norms; more provocatively, he accounts for the possibility of *transcending* those norms and instituting new ones, *despite the presence of a norm that already functions teleologically* for anomalies. This is to say both that the lived-body is normal in transcending norms when it is optimalizing or creating new norms, and that anomaly can function innovatively in the institution of norms. It is not given a priori that the anomalies will be simply incorporated into a "higher," overarching teleological or concordant unity. All of this becomes problematic in the positive sense if we no longer accept the simplistic notions of the normal and norm. Let me explain this with two points of clarification.

First, in order for the institution of norms to be the transcending of norms, the normal lived-body cannot be simply the concordant lived-body. Even as optimal, the normal lived-body cannot simply be one that perceives more differences or has a "richer" or "better" sensuous make-up [*Sinnlichkeit*] (H XIII 383). Rather, the *normal* lived-body as optimal must be *optimalizing* in the sense of creating norms and optimal experiences.[30] As optimalizing, so writes Husserl, normal lived-corporeality is that which *produces* or *makes possible* a circle of optima.[31] Normality, then, is the process of creating norms, the ability to survive new norms of life, and the possibility of tolerating infractions of the habitual norm, instituting new norms in new situations.[32] Thus, what we call a "norm" occurs through optimalizing, which is to say, action can be normative even if it is not according to a set norm.

So, for example, for some black populations in areas of Africa subject to many forms of malaria, the sickle cell trait—an abnormality or "blood disease" by some standards—functions as a resistance to some of the most deadly forms of malaria.[33] This so-called "abnormality" has also led to a new style of life that is optimal, at least physiologically, for that environment—despite the "majority," the "average," or the "statistical frequency" of its occurrence on a broader scale. Of course, the role of context here is extremely important; if, for example, a Western doctor administers barbiturates to these people, a sickle crisis ensues that can lead to brain damage or death; and without the context of these life-threatening malarias, the sickle trait could indeed be seen as "unhealthy." But in and of itself, the sickle-cell trait cannot be seen a priori as normal or abnormal. For taken separately, the living being and the environing-world are not normal or abnormal; it is their relationship that makes them such.[34]

I now come to my second point concerning the nature of norm-transcendence. Since normal lived-corporeality is not just optimal but optimalizing, since it not only lives according to norms, but institutes them in normalizing comportment, it is *possible to transcend* the previous norms *qua* norms. Instituting new norms in new situations is only possible if the teleological character of norms is not fixed and eternal. I have mentioned above that once a norm as the best is instituted through experience, anomalies are either drawn to the norm, like when vague images on a screen are out of focus and serve as indexes for a clear figure, or are seen as approximations of or deviations from the thing itself. They refer back—as abnormal—to the optimal as *their* norm.

Even though a new vision can be understood as discordant in relation to the previous one (like in the example of optical surgery given above where the lived-body itself is modified), an optimal vision can supplant the earlier one in a kind of re-valuation: The new one *becomes* normal and the old one now refers to the new optimal as *its* norm.[35] Thus, it is possible for new optima to be formed, and although a normal system must be constituted originally, it remains a question, observes Husserl, to what extent it is necessary for an originally instituted normal system to maintain perpetually its teleological system of reference![36]

Since a normal system is not guaranteed in advance and for all time, then what was seen previously only as a discordance, as a deviance, or as a modification can also function creatively as instituting new norms. It can only do this, however, by *transcending* the previous norms. In order to transcend the norm, the fact that the deviation refers back to the norm teleologically cannot be decisive. Such new optima and new norms are constituted, Husserl asserts, "*in spite of the reference back to the earlier norm.*"[37]

From one perspective experiences are ordered according to the previous norm; from another, they actually surpass it such that the old order refers to the new as the norm; the former as abnormal, the newer as normal. Where norms are instituted as particularly engaging for action, what is practically non-optimal is excluded by its self-subordination to what is practically optimal. And this takes place *in and through the very kind of givenness or pregivenness* it is, and not by way of a choice made from what is already fixed or determined. It presents itself as an attenuated or a faint "value-relief" for action. In this way, norms can be "de-valued" before they are eliminated and ineffective.[38] As a result, the new experiences do not get completely incorporated into the previous order, even though they did function or may continue to function in other respects as indexes of an earlier norm. By instituting a new norm, the norm to which the event referred can become precisely the "former" norm; the established order the "old" order. This, in turn, results in a kind of conflict of norms and orders.

Such a conflict of orders is open to what might be called a "transvaluation" of the normal and abnormal. In a striking passage Husserl suggests this transvaluation. We have seen that from a perspective in which the present norms are lived, a new perception or a new sense could be counted as abnormal. If, however, this discordant perspective were more than simply "new," but also "a 'finer' organization of sense"; if the so-called disruptive, "unusual," or exceptional features of vision or touch were modes of "increased accomplishments," they would not simply be anomalous or abnormal. The new optimal "would not be abnormal, *but more normal than ever, increased normality,* and what was previously called normal would be abnormal."[39] Husserl's statement implies a twofold transvaluation. On the one hand, he accounts for the possibility that what is considered anomalous or abnormal on the axis of concordance may issue in a new normality as optimal, and on the other, what was at one time instituted as a norm can be disclosed as "not as normal" or even as abnormal on the axis of optimality.[40]

If we were to brave a glimpse into the intersubjective sphere of normality on the basis of what has been discussed, we would see similar implications. The greatest number of cases, the majority of instances, the average could not make up a normal society because it may not be optimal in its context; indeed, the average could be abnormal. On the other hand, the view of optimality is not elitist because the overwhelming majority could express the optimal mode of life for that environing-world. The optimal is not associated with the "few" any more than the abnormal is expressive of so-called "deviant behavior." As I show in the next chapter, there is nevertheless a certain justification for a coincidence of normality with a great number of instances. But this is not due to an abstract and hasty identification of the two. It is rooted in the very genesis of normality in a specific environing-world. Grasping this point, however, will entail examining the confluence of concordant and optimal modes of normality. In the next chapter I take up the integration of the normal *qua* concordance and *qua* optimal under the title of "normalization."

10

Normalization and Terrain

We have seen that from a phenomenological perspective normality and abnormality can be understood in two ways. These two ways differ considerably from more traditional assessments that portray the normal as what is given in advance as natural, original, usual, or average, and the abnormal as what is merely unnatural, derivative, exceptional, or deviant. In a constitutional account, on the contrary, the normal can be characterized genetically as concordance, and abnormality or anomaly as discordance. In yet another respect, normality is what is optimal and abnormality what is non-optimal.

Seen as a whole, normal experience is neither completely concordant nor merely optimal. Recognizing this means that when normality and abnormality are understood simply in terms of concordance and optimality we already have the possibility of normative conflicts and of the transvaluation of norms where some norms become subordinate to or surpass others, developmentally, through experience.

The combination of concordant and optimalizing comportment gives rise to an overall process of normalization that I take up more concretely as a process of "discriminating experience." Discriminating experience as normative experience is only possible because the normative field simultaneously exerts an "affective force." The process of selecting and excluding optima in concordant comportment establishes a "genetic density" of the optimal, namely the typical. The typical in normalizing comportment, furthermore, issues in a normal *qua* typically familiar environing-world or "terrain." By way of transition to a generative phenomenology and the problematic of homeworld/alienworld, I conclude by distinguishing between the phenomenological concepts of terrain and territory.

Normalization as Discriminating Experience

On the one hand, the optimal emerges in and through its relation to an experiencing being, and on the other, normal experience prefers the optimal and thus tends toward it. I would like to describe this preference and emergence further as the process of selection and exclusion.

Husserl describes the "tendency toward the optimum" as "the *principle of selection* of practical possibilities."[1] The implications of Husserl's statement are far reaching, especially for the theory of intersubjective constitution. Let me sketch the rudiments of this principle here.

Most basically, the "principle of selection" calls into question a theory of constitution forged by a progressive method in which sense is given independently of temporal and spatial horizons. The principle of selection, in contrast, is a process of sense constitution that takes up *pregiven* sense and transforms it in an orientation toward further sense emergence. Such a "*reprise*"—to borrow Merleau-Ponty's expression—is formative as trans-formative of sense.

Yet, the tendency toward the optimum as selecting the optimal is not the selection of everything that offers itself as possibly best, but best in this specific context for this specific action. Selection entails at the same time an *exclusion* in which other possible optima become or remain latent possibilities.

By Husserl's expression "principle of selection" as directed toward the optimum, then, I understand a constitutive duet of "taking up" and "leaving out," as it were. Husserl's principle means simply that experience is *not indifferent*, but *responsive to* or engaged in the conditions of its very experiencing. Because selection and exclusion are two aspects of a discretionary process directed toward what is best for experience, two modes of the same movement of discriminating among optima, I also refer to this experience as discriminating experience.[2]

The terms selection and exclusion or simply discriminating experience can be misleading by connoting judicative or reflective operations. One could, for example, imagine selection to be something like shopping for ripe tomatoes splayed out on shelf at a supermarket, or like picking out options in a multiple choice exam, or even something quite arbitrary like selecting "heads" or "tails" at the toss of a coin. In these instances there would be *no practical involvement in the very appearance* of what is selected and *no essential ties to the context.* The movement I am attempting to elicit, however, is co-determinative of its appearance as something to be selected. Let me explain.

First, Husserl writes explicitly that the tendency toward the optimum is the principle of selection of *practical* possibilities. This means that normative experience is the discrimination of the optimal as relevant for comportment. What is practical does not necessarily stand in opposition to what is theoretical, if by theoretical we understand the praxis peculiar to, say, the mathematician or the chemist who also operate within a field of practical motivations and interests. By using the expression "practical," Husserl implies that what counts as optimal is *specific to action* and *to context:* "What suffices as practical counts as the Self. Thus the house itself and its true being, and specifically with respect to its pure bodily thingliness, is quickly given optimally, that is, experienced as complete for that person who regards it as a buyer or a seller. For the physicist and the chemist, such ways of experience would seem completely superficial and could still not be further from its true being."[3]

Second, the appearance of the optima does not occur prior to selection but only *through* selection. The optima self-emerge as such by virtue of their modes of disclosure, in their inextricable relation to discriminating experience. They emerge without further ado, as it were, insofar as they present themselves prominently as particularly engaging for action. This emergence of norms through discriminating experience is what I mean by the institution [*Stiftung*] of norms. Accordingly, this is why I mentioned above that the optimal emerges *in and through the very kind of givenness or pregivenness* it is, while what is non-optimal is excluded by its self-subordination to what is optimal, without having recourse to a reflective choice of possibilities that are determined in advance.[4]

When Husserl speaks of the selection and exclusion of practical *possibilities,* these possibilities are not things determined in advance: The optima are seen as eclipsing other possibilities only retrospectively. The mention of practical possibilities, then, indicate a future dimension such that optima are not only significant for the present, but relevant for a future orientation as the openness of comportment.

In short, the process of selection and exclusion is discriminating experience as the constitution of sense. Optima, for their part, are sense-unities constituted as such through their very modes of presentation as practically significant for a specific context of future comportment.

In the sphere of physiology, the principle of selection and exclusion has become a particularly suitable concept employed for articulating the normative experience of life. On Canguilhem's view, the process of selection and exclusion refers to the "dynamic polarity of life," that is, to the fact that life is "biologically normative." In the evaluative experience of norms, organic life is not "detached" in relation to its conditions of life and does not merely assess a "fact" in relation to a "norm." Canguilhem writes:

> The most simple biological nutritive organization of assimilation and excretion expresses a [dynamic] polarity. When the wastes of assimilation are no longer excreted by an organism and congests or poisons the interior milieu—all that is, in effect, according to law (physical, chemical, etc.); *but nothing of that is according to the norm, which is the activity of the organism itself.* That is the simple fact we want to designate by speaking of biological normativity.[5]

Even an amoeba, Canguilhem asserts, is biologically normative by "preferring" and "excluding."[6]

By preferring and excluding different aspects of its environment, an organism begins to define, out of experience itself, a normal way of being. Here, of course, normal does not mean in the first instance what is average, but a privileged mode of comportment especially suited to the organism. Drawing on Goldstein, Canguilhem understands privileged comportment [*comportement privilégié*] as preferred comportment of which an organism is particularly capable under specific conditions: "This way of life, which is characterized by an ensemble of privileged reactions, is that in which the living being responds best to the demands of its surroundings and lives in harmony with its milieu."[7]

Where Husserl is lax is his systematic delineation of the normative formation of a milieu in the principle of selection and exclusion by referring simply to practical possibilities or interests, Max Scheler significantly clarifies this process by sketching the foundational order of intentional experience that is formative of a "milieu." Beginning with intentional experience that is dependent upon others in an order of foundation, he distinguishes between "attention," "interest," "perception," and "experienced efficacy." It is the latter concept that bears on what Canguilhem terms "normative experience" or what I have called normalization, and that is especially pertinent to Husserl's theory of "affective relief." As an instructive preface to the notion of affective relief, let me offer a brief synopsis of the different experiences distinguished by Scheler as they relate to the formation of a milieu.

Mere attention cannot account for the structuring of a milieu since, according to Scheler, I turn my attention to something only *after* it is effectively given in a milieu. That is, I can be "attentive to" things without comprehending any values in them or without their being normatively effective on me one way or another.[8] Distinguishing between attention and interest, Scheler writes sardonically: "Let's have none of those absurd pedagogical theories that hold that one could awaken the *interest* of a student in an object by increasing his *attention!* Rather, one must awaken interest in the object; attention will then increase by itself!"[9]

Interest, however, already presupposes that things are experienced in their efficacy. For two farmers negotiating over a farm, the same milieu is given in their consideration of the land, the buildings, the stables and barns, etc.; the same milieu-things will become alive and effective on them in their dealings; in addition, these milieu-things will be quite different for someone who is painting a picture of the farm.[10] While the milieu is the same for the farmers, their interests can nonetheless be different depending upon whether one is the buyer or seller; while these differences in interest will yield various emphasizes and importances they can only do so on the basis of the pregiven milieu effectively experienced.

Moreover, although active perception also encompasses interest, it too presupposes experienced efficacy. For example, we can effectively experience changes in our milieu without knowing what has changed in the perceived object, just like we can experience the efficacy of something that we, nonetheless, do not perceive.[11] In the first instance, we can think of the times we have immediately recognized a change in the appearance of acquaintances or close friends (say, by shaving a beard). Often we implicitly recognize a difference, but are all the same at a loss to specify what that change was. More often than not, if we do specify something, we find that we have "falsely" identified the change, for example, by citing a haircut or new glasses. In the second instance, we might think, as Scheler suggests, of the removal of a familiar painting from a room in which we live. Here we experience a change in the setting as, say, comfortable, drab, or spacious, but without necessarily perceiving any particular object, especially since that object effecting the change has been removed.

For Scheler, a milieu is that which I experience as effective and is efficaciously relative to my existence [*daseinsrelativ*]. Lived-experience and milieu undergo co-relative modifications, whether or not these modifications can be identified in "founded acts." Hence Scheler writes that something is efficaciously experienced [*wirksam erlebt*] when an orientation varies with my experiencing [*Erleben*]. This takes place whether or not I can specify this variation as a variation of a determinate thing and the variation of my experiencing as the variation of a determinate experience. This also holds whether or not that which is "experienced as effective" is "perceived" in any form.[12] Hence, it is not far-fetched to assert that a die for the gambler does not have six equal sides.[13]

Scheler's analysis of a milieu has the distinct advantage of explicitly tying the formation of a milieu to an efficacy in experience that occurs prior to our interest in it or to our attention turning toward it. In order for my attention to be directed toward my milieu or to my "milieu-things," in order that I take an interest in them or even perceive them, the milieu must already be pregiven as experienced in its efficacy on me. To grasp this experienced efficacy of a milieu still more specifically in relation to the discriminating experience of optima, I will turn to Husserl's descriptions of "affection," particularly as it applies to something coming into "relief."

I turn to these notions of affection and relief because they intimate in what way the *milieu itself* is "active," "imposing," and effective in the normative discrimination of optima. Not just anything can be selected or excluded because contextually the milieu itself provokes the optimal such that lived-experience is as much responsive as it is initiatory.

Affective Relief and the Provocation of Norms

Husserl's primary contribution to the theory of "relief" [*Relief*] or prominence [*Abgehobenheit*] is not that there is always a figure which stands out from a background (something that Gestalt psychology has also worked out in extraordinary detail); rather, it lies in his contention that what comes into relief is always *charged* with significance, effective in the sense of exerting an "affective force" [*affektiver Kraft*], and further, that this affective force of something prominent is linked to the discriminating experience of optima.

A good part of the Third Division of *Analysen zur Passiven Synthesis* (on "association") is devoted to the phenomenon of "affection." His guiding question can be stated as follows: When something becomes prominent for me, is it there in its prominence, awaiting, "neutrally," my affirmation or selection; or does it already exercise some influence on me, luring me to take it up? Or again, are there unities of sense that could come into being independently of affection if the "relevant conditions" of becoming a unity are fulfilled (e.g., concrescence, contrast, etc.); or does a unity of sense, even the most elementary phase of the living present, *co-originate* with affection *in order to be* precisely this sense-unity? Put more simply, does affective force presuppose prominence, or does prominence presuppose affective force (H XI 149, 153, 161, 165)?

Husserl's examples of something becoming a prominent unity of sense range anywhere from hearing an explosion, to listening to mellifluous notes played on a piano, to seeing flashes of light in the sky. A sound may exercise a greater affective force if its contrast with its surroundings is sharper, and a lesser force the more its richly defined contours become muddled or disappear. Furthermore, something that is unfavorably [*ungünstig*] prominent, such as a softly played note in the background, can acquire a more affective force than it would have by itself by virtue of its concordance with other notes that come into sharp, optimal relief; the former notes undergo a "transference of affection" in the direction of the past and delineate a future affective efficacy for the whole melody (H XI 152 ff.).

In all cases, responds Husserl, a unity of sense is only shaped or constituted as such by being *affective!* He writes: "Affective unities must be constituted in order for a world of objects to be constituted in subjectivity at all" (H XI 162). Affective unities are constituted by being simultaneously affective on us. But how can a sense-unity *be* affective in order to be constituted by the ego? Aren't we just turning around in circles? If sense constitution did presuppose affection, would not the very constitution of sense somehow presuppose, paradoxically, that sense was already constituted so that it could exert an affective force on me in order to be constituted?

Indeed, if we were able to maintain a Cartesian interpretation of sense constitution that relied solely on the initiating activity of the ego giving sense, or on the overlay of interpretation on hyletic data, it would be absurd to hold that something could be affective, enticing constitution before it was constituted by the ego as a sense-unity.

But in the analyses of passive synthesis Husserl is concerned—similar to Scheler—with an affective efficacy that operates within the pregivenness of spatial and temporal horizons, irreducible to the levels of interest and attention, but that nevertheless can stimulate interest or awaken attention (H XI 150, 153, 166, 168). To differentiate between these levels, and to hone in on the phenomenon of affective force, Husserl summons the distinction between pregivenness and givenness, a difference I have tied to the procedural differences of regressive and progressive phenomenological approaches. Sometimes this distinction is played out in the following way for Husserl: Something constituted is *pregiven* insofar as it exercises an affective force; it is *given* when the ego turns toward the object in an attitude of interest or in an attentive manner (H XI 162). Husserl is concerned here not merely with the constitution by an ego, but also with a "primordial"-constitution that is called "passive" (for want of a more appropriate term) in relation to the activity of the ego. (H XI 76). Accordingly, when the transcendental reduction is understood regressively, it "leads the naive being of the world *back* to *pregiving* . . . subjectivity" and to the "world as *pregivenness*," to the world as an "*habitual acquisition*" (H XV 149, my emphasis).

Such a formulation, like the one given above, would only be paradoxical were we to disavow the possibility of temporal dimensions inhering in the formation of sense-unity itself so that it would be without past, without future—if, that is, a theory of constitution would remain informed by the notion static givenness rather than genetic pregivenness. Taking its point of departure from the latter notion, Husserl's analyses of passive synthesis and affection shatter the Cartesian logic of sense constitution. In fact, what we learn from genetic phenomenology and throughout these lectures is that *primordial* constitution [*Ur-konstitution*] must presuppose a *past* temporal dimension in order for sense to be constituted in the present! Eventually, this *"Ur"-konstitution* peculiar to a genetic phenomenology will be ensconced within a *"Stamm"-konstitution* peculiar to a generative phenomenology (cf. chapter 13).

Staying, in this section, within the field of primordial constitution, we can say that the latter is not simply the intentional directedness on the part of the subject, but coevally the affective force on the part of the "object" or "object phase" that *solicits* the subject. " 'What is there' is decided upon from the standpoint of the matter [*Sache*], issuing from the matter itself, and in making a decision, the ego follows the resoluteness on the part of the matter itself. The ego finds itself governed by it, and then merely establishes itself subjectively on its ground" (H XI 51).

There are no sense-unities, to say nothing of objects, that are merely neutral, simply "for themselves." They are at the same time for the subject, affecting the subject, as propulsive or repulsive. If a unity of sense is neglected, excluded, it is not because it is "a pure affective nothing" (H XI 163). To say that something exercises a feeble force is not the same as saying that there is no force functioning in an enticing manner at all. There exists, rather, a gradation of affection, depending on context, "favorable conditions," and privileged comportment in which it can become prominent and optimal.[14]

Accordingly, there can be many affective forces soliciting our affirmation and our turning toward them [*Zuwendung*], but we can never turn to them all at once or with indiscriminate interest. Of necessity, we are discriminating, and correlatively the field of experience organizes itself hierarchically remaining nonetheless open. The object-pole does not simply dictate its own affective prominence, for what becomes affectively prominent depends on a context of practice. From the side of the object, it is a suggestion, a proposal, or as Whitehead would say, a "lure." Norms become normative initially by guiding or soliciting experience without the normal determining what is to be selected or excluded in advance.

Absolutely no affective force, which is to say correlatively, no discrimination of sense is equivalent to the death of sense or meaning. For without any affective force, even indirectly through the "transference of affection," there is no exclusion, no discrimination, no "normality." The normative sense diminishes, and the affective force of norms decline; they no longer function motivationally in the constitution of individual and collective practices. Even though the "material conditions" of institutions may long survive, their provocative, normative character becomes hollow, lacking an affective internal sense. (It will be in this way that we will be able to understand in a generative context the phenomenological significance of a "dead culture.")

On this theory of discriminating experience and affective relief, primordial constitution is itself the process of selection and exclusion. It is not the reflective activity on the part of an abstract ego overlaying interpretation on sense data. Even if one were to view the process of subjective constitution more generously as lived-bodily perception, one would still have to say that constitution of sense is not merely a process originating on the part of the subject as something I initiate. It is the taking-up and rejection of that which offers itself in its pregiven affective force of prominence that becomes indeed prominent *for me in my taking it up* as part of my living present or my perceptual field, as part of my basic comportment or part of my life. Thus, there is sense constitution through the taking-up/rejection of sense as exerting an affective force.

Since there is no neutral constitution, and in fact, no constitution of objects at all without affection, even the elemental living present is, as primordially constituted, essentially an "affective unity." This is a point on which Husserl insists: "affection already plays its *essential* role in the *constitution* of *all* matters having the character of an object, such that *without it* there would be no objects at all and no present organized with objects."[15] The fact that something comes into relief or prominence is not separated from the affective force it exerts on the subject to incorporate it into its perceptual process. If something is there for me at all, it is because it is charged with significance. Hence, claims Husserl, "the perspective is an *affective* perspective," and a relief is always already an "*affective* relief."[16]

The concepts of affective relief or affective perspective suggest that if something is prominent in our field of comportment, it is prominent because it "says" something to us in a way that *makes a difference;* it exerts an affective efficacy on us in a specific context and does not achieve prominence in an indiscriminate manner. This means, further, that a relief or perspective is *better* or more *favorable* than others, that an affective relief can be optimal and function as a norm for normal life. In this way the optimal as a norm becomes normative for experience through experience and not speculatively and in principle.

The normal is a kind of structure that develops within experience which functions teleologically to guide experience. And although our various perceptions at least implicitly refer to a norm, they can simultaneously transcend it with the institution of new normative optima even though previously the latter may not have been optimal: The optimum is a relative maximum.[17] Here we have the case of modulations in the fields of experience, the transition from affective reliefs from worse to better or from better to worse, the struggle or rivalry [*Widerstreit*] between affective prominences, and their emergence as normative optima.[18]

Of course, something like an explosion is affectively prominent and not necessarily optimal. It may only be anomalous. But when a perspective is better or more favorable, when a way of life is optimal, the optima are especially affective and exercise a pull on us to be taken up again and again as normal.

Moreover, optima need not be admitted or affirmed in our actual experience. If we say that norms are "binding," they are not binding in the sense of necessitating action indiscriminately. Rather, they are "compelling," as particularly relevant or advantageous for an optimal mode of comportment or for a normal life. For normalizing life, not all norms are equal in all contexts. Some are privileged by the style of the life being lived and the mode of disclosure of the norm itself, exerting more or less force. As I mentioned above, this does not happen in principle. When these norms are affirmed, it does not take place by exercising our "free will," out of "respect" or "duty." This recognition of norms however is evaluative. According to Scheler, an artist is "controlled" by the norms or laws of her art without having "to apply" them or act out of respect for them. Nor does she realize their fulfillment, their surpassing, or their shortcomings only in the result, that is, the work of art as a product. There is a practical "obeying" and a "disobeying" of norms, observes Scheler, as they are expressed in the action, experienced as fulfilled or broken, and given only in and through these experiences.[19] A normal life, and ultimately an ethical life, is not merely descriptive, but evaluative, normative.

This is certainly not the place to engage in an explicit debate with Kantian ethics. I do want to suggest for the purposes of this section that while norms are not context independent, they are not for that matter simply relative, nor is our living according to them arbitrary. Norms are generated in and through living as optimal for that life. As affective, norms function efficaciously in experience, soliciting comportment, and are "binding" for normal experience to this extent.

In the following section, I will sketch how these norms are contextual without being merely relative, and in addition, how they become normative without being abstract or a-historical. I do this by explaining how, within this schema, norms acquire a "genetic density" and further, how this structures a normatively significant environing-world or a "terrain."

Genetic Density of the Optimal as the Typical

On Husserl's account of normality we have seen that the normal is not the usual or the average, but rather what is concordant and optimal. The question I take up now concerns how the normal in the senses sketched above *becomes* typical and familiar in experience (without presupposing simply that the normal is typical or familiar). I do this first by describing how an optimum becomes "typical" and how the normal takes on a normative character such that it is binding for that experience.

The optimal emerges in an affective prominence as a solicitation for taking-up and integration into that particular life experience. That is, the process of taking-up becomes the normal (*qua* optimal) interrelation between the "subject" and its environing-world as what is best for it. When comportment does take up the enticement of the norm (*qua* optimal) and *repeats* it (concordantly), this reappropriation of what is optimal begins to *stylize* the life according to that norm: The optimal is integrated into a way of life that is *concordantly optimal*.

The importance of concordance as a modality of the normal lies in the institution of a relation that facilitates the continued, futural appropriation of the optimal. In other words, if there is a concordant occurrence of the optimal, it is more likely the case that what emerges will be optimal for that experience, and further, that this experience will be able to sustain the optimal mode of life over time.

Concordance, then, is the capacity to take up the optimal and to repeat it in an internally coherent manner. When the optimal is taken up concordantly, the normal acquires a density that is developed over time, that is, it acquires a *genetic density*. This genetic density of the optimal is a patterned density that predisposes action for the normal *qua* optima. Thus, while the concordant repetition of the optimal gives rise to a genetic density, genetic density in turn becomes a predisposition for the optimal. The fact that certain species of shrub (like mint and sagebrush) grow in soil that becomes toxic (abnormal) to many grassland species, and actually contributes to the (normal/optimal) toxic levels for their privileged reproduction by secreting the toxins that reduce the germination or growth of grasses, is a case in point.[20]

Genetic density is the stylization of interaction between the subject and the environing-world such that the latter, in which the subject coheres, is not *just any* environing-world. Correlatively, the comportment of the subject, while open, is not arbitrary, but guided or oriented by its milieu. A specific milieu is normative for a specific context of action and distinguishes itself from other such contexts. If solicitation and continued affirmation build up a genetic density of and predisposition for what is optimal, the interaction that is generated becomes a *privileged* basis and context for those forms of life living in this way.

If not directly from Husserl, then at least through the works of Alfred Schutz, it is well known that type [*Typus*], the typical, and typicality [*Typik, das Typische*] are notions consistently associated with the normal and the optimal. Just how they are related seems somewhat more ambiguous. Taking Husserl's association of the concepts normal, optima, and typical, I would like to explicate their systematic rapport. In so doing, I inquire into how the optimal becomes a type, how the normal *qua* optimal becomes the normal *qua* typical. Taking this pursuit one step further, I propose how we *usually* come to affirm the optimal, that is, how the normal can be said to be not merely typical but even "familiar."

Let me define the typical as the optimal in its genetic density.[21] The optimal becomes a type when it is repeated concordantly and integrated into the rapport of lived-experience with the environing-world. Or put differently, a system of affective tendencies toward the optimal that are developed through concordant iteration is constitutive of typicality.

Whereas the norm *can* be instituted in a single experience and achieve a kind of "ideal" status as in-itself or as an objective sense that allows it to function teleologically, a "type" is the concordant repetition of the optimal; consequently, the latter's "ideality" develops from the "ideality" of the optimal insofar as the optimal's ideality acquires genetic density. Concretely, the genetic density of optimal comportment in this or that instance can lead to the formation of what we call a "body type." Here we might want to think of the sense behind the assertion that a marathon runner has a different "body type" than a sprinter, or that a free climber has a different "body type" than an alpinist. In Husserl's words, normality would be understood as "a certain *typical* constancy in the comportment of lived-corporeality" (H XIV 121, my emphasis).

I am reluctant to speak of body types as mere "physiological norms," as if rhythms of life such as pulse, respiration, and even longevity, height, or urine were not also inextricably related to social normativity, economic productivity, and religious values. Having expressed this reservation, let me say that human physiological norms express the typical stylization of human life rather than reflecting an already fixed "human nature."

The process of constituting a normal *qua* typical life or world is called *typification*, analogous to the process of optimalization. Typification is the process by which I render typical that which is unknown according to a certain style. Like optimalization, it is selective and exclusive. Even though we have not yet experienced diverse aspects of a thing in its particularity, typification prefigures similar concordant features, making precisely those (and not other) aspects that are foreshadowed particularly prominent, affective as expected; even though we have never been in this particular situation before, we can anticipate a "typical way" of acting. Thus, I can recognize something I have never seen before as "typical." This is one way in which I am able to etch out a familiar world.

Some of the implications of typification will be seen in section 4. Here let me emphasize that the typical is not a mere repetition of the optimal; rather, it is generative because a *future* dimension is also implied in typical experience. In this regard typification and typical experience can be seen as guiding experience, in this way, sketching a style of a normal world. For Husserl one mode of world experience is the typical world (EU, 398 f.).

While it is tempting to think of typicality straightaway as "average," we must remember that only because the optimal is carried out in its temporal density can the typical become average. In fact, in relation to an arithmetical average, the normal as typical might well be extreme and even find no relation to factual existence.[22]

At issue here is the peculiar trait of ideality and the normative status of a typical norm. The very temporal genesis of the optimal that yields the typical produces an enduring typical norm. As typical, the optimal is expressed not just in this instance, but again and again in a concordant, constant manner so that ipso facto the type becomes valid over time. Practical "constants," to invoke the language of Goldstein,[23] imply typical constants that institute orders and express the enduring efficacy of a type. The type acquires the idealization of the "again and again" so that "typically" the normal "I can" becomes a typical "I can . . . again and again." Accordingly, if "I cannot" do such and such in relation to this environing-world, then that relation is "atypical" and thus "abnormal." This is the sense, I believe, of speaking of practical constants as "habitual norms": The typical "I can" expresses the practical constants of "I am repeatedly able to." Practical constants are experientially *expected* to last through discordances with the result that the discordances, for their part, are expected to refer back to the typical or become "mere" anomalies from the standpoint of this typical norm. The fact that anomalies emerge in a typical and not merely a concordant context is one reason why anomalies do not institute new norms so frequently, and are experienced instead as simply exceptional.

But just because the typical has the characteristic of being valid over time does not mean that its ideality is eternal and a-temporal. It is only its inveteracy and persistently possible relevance for future action that makes it seem natural in the sense of eternal. As patterned through comportment, the typical also patterns and stylizes comportment. Its internal sense and its ability to be provocative makes the optimal worthy of repetition and allows it to maintain its normative status. Whether it be in the sphere of "physiological" norms like body weight, or "social" norms on the order of justice, the normal as the typical also structures needs and demands, and exerts a force to guide future action in the direction of the norm. By simply asserting that the normal is typical, familiar, or usual, by asserting that a norm is ideal, one conceals the very precariousness of norms' coming into being, and the acquired resilience and stability that norms so readily exhibit. One also fails to see how so much that ruptures the genetic density of the optimal is "merely" anomalous, and why it is so difficult for an anomaly to take root normatively and supersede a norm.

Simply beginning on the level of the typical encourages one to take its ideality as ready-made. The danger is that one too readily characterizes action one-sidedly under the form of the typical without being attentive to how action, as concordantly optimal, serves in the genesis of typicality. In short, one fails to appreciate the acquired imperturbability and reliability of the norm, and loses a sense for the malleability of the ideal.

I concur with Alfred Schutz that the typical must have occurred concretely in some form in order to function as an ideal-type.[24] At times, however, Schutz seems to understand a type statically, as a "cross section" of our experience as if "freezing it into a slide."[25] The difficulty is that such an analysis, which is primarily concerned with the social sphere, emerges *via* my *mere* contemporaries.[26] That is, his discussion of an ideal-type deals with others merely synchronically in a *static* phenomenological analysis. Staying within the confines of a static phenomenology, he can define a type as a "fixed concept."[27]

On the view that I am expounding, the ideal-type would not be understood through "abstraction from the subjective context of meaning,"[28] but by taking the latter seriously in its genesis. Because of the difficulties of understanding the notion of ideal-type from a static method, I prefer Schutz's dynamic point of view on the formation of typicality.[29]

Drawing on Husserl's phenomenology of association, Schutz connects the formation of typicality to experiences that become "sedimented" and called forth, "awakened" from their latency in the past to bond as the same type in the present: "Thus the apperception of an objectivity in its horizon calls forth the recollection of other objectivities similar to or even like the former, and constitutes therewith a typicality on the ground of which by apperceptive transference [*Apperzeptive Übertragung*] other objectivities of a similar kind are also apperceived from the outset as objectivities of the same type, that is, of a pregiven more or less specific familiarity."[30]

Although Schutz evokes the language of passive synthesis to explain the constitution of typicality, what I find conspicuously lacking in this account is any explicit connection of typicality to the optimal and in this way linking the typical to the normal. Only implicitly does Schutz gesture toward the relation of the typical to the optimal by citing a text from Husserl that points to the principle of selection at work in the formation of typicality. Asking why certain characteristics are "paired" with others as typically similar, while others are disregarded at least for the time being, Schutz cites a passage from Husserl's *Erfahrung und Urteil.* Let me cite this text from Husserl in full: "Our interest is thereby *not indifferently* parcelled out to all the characteristics that become prominent; rather, our gaze is directed towards especially impressive properties, through which the object of precisely this type or of this individual object distinguishes itself from other objects of an equal or similar type."[31]

It only requires one small, but important connection for us to realize that the apperceptive transference of sense operative in the formation of a *type* is simultaneously the transference of the *optimal's affective force* (the "transference of affection" encountered above) in the constitution of a type. Correlative to the process of selection and exclusion, a type also exercises an *affective force in its ideality* and as such is affectively typical.

The genetic density of the optimal in the formation of a type is the vantage point from which I have attempted to elicit normality—in its various configurations—coming into being. It is also the perspective from which I address the "familiar" context for lived-experience and different forms of life. Such a normatively significant environing-world I call a "terrain."

A Phenomenological Notion of Terrain

The term terrain is used in physiology and pathology to designate the organism's resistance to or disposition for pathogenic agents. I use the term for the discriminating overtones it has for comportment, for its suggestive geological and environmental allusions, and for its resonance with the notion of territory as the lifeworld in its two modalities as earth-ground and world-horizon.

A terrain is not an area cut out from a preestablished whole; it is not that which we subjectively "create" or that to which we must unilaterally adapt. Rather, a terrain is the typically familiar milieu, affective in experience and constituted as privileged through the genetic density of the optimal.

Adeptly bridging anthropology, geography, and ecology Max Sorre, a proponent of "human geography," defines an inhabited space or an "*oekoumène*" as an optimal zone for optimal comportment. Summarizing his work, *Les fondements biologiques de la géographie humaine*, Sorre writes: "The central notion of this whole book is that of the optimum,—the value of each of the elements of the surroundings for which a specific [*déterminée*] function is accomplished the best. The general optimum is the result of all the functional optima."[32] Sorre continues to explain that these optima do not correspond to fixed and immutable values, but achieve a flexible stability expressive of what I have referred to as the stability of a typical environing-world. Thus, the "physiological constants" of a terrain are not "constants in the absolute sense of the term. . . . There is rather for each function and for the ensemble of functions an optimal zone. . . . [T]his zone corresponds to the amplitude of normal [sic] variations, to the interior of the *oekoumène*."[33]

While Sorre's work on human geography is particularly lucid in the interpretation of empirical data for disclosing "the fundamental conditions of the constitution of the *oekoumène*" and particularly trenchant in seeing the interconnections with and necessity for a "geography of shelter," a "geography of clothing," a "geography of habitat," etc.,[34] his work requires some embellishment to bring his insights on "optimal zones" to accord with the phenomenological meaning of normality I have been discussing here.

Let me now advance a phenomenological understanding of what I call a "terrain." Terrain is not simply an optimal zone or an ensemble of functional optima since it is optimal in a genetic density, that is, typical and, as it were, a habitat of types. As a typical environment for a certain action, group, or species, as "constantly" there throughout various divergences and discordances, a terrain becomes the milieu we especially *count on*. It is precisely in this sense that one is justified in speaking of the terrain as "familiar" [*vertraut*] or as that to which one is accustomed [*gewöhnt*].

If there is any sense in speaking of the normal as the familiar—as Husserl does inded do—it is not because the normal can be abstractly identified with the familiar. Rather, the familiar is an expression of the typical that, in turn, is an expression of the optimal in its genetically dense concordance.[35] Through the stylized repetition and responsive comportment to the norm *qua* optimum, a structure of normal comportment emerges that becomes typically familiar of the experience.

Being typically familiar of experience does not suggest a statistical average represented now by a bell curve in contrast to a "flat" arithmetical average. With a bell curve, the greatest statistical frequency is normal when it determines that the greatest divergences are at the same time the most rare. However, the normal as normative is neither a matter of numerical distribution nor of statistical frequency, nor even determined by laws of chance. If one wished to hazard the proposition that the normal is average, one would only be justified in doing so inasmuch as the average could be recognized as derivative from and expressive of the normal *qua* optimal, and not the other way around. Something is not normal because it is frequent; it is frequent because it is normal.[36]

Furthermore, if we mean by the quasi-phenomenological, quasi-existentialist locution "everdayness" something like familiarity or typicality, then it is fully inaccurate to speak of an "*average* everydayness"; the everyday [*das Alltägliche*], as what is familiar to us through types and upon which we rely for the efficacy of action, is not average. It is in the first instance, however, optimal or typical. Only insofar as the average is typically constant and hence familiar can one claim that the everyday is average.

Our familiarity with a terrain is the prereflective and pregiven familiarity of types. Since the terrain is pregiven in experience as familiar through its typical affective force, a terrain is always a *privileged* terrain, and not simply one among others. The familiar terrain is privileged not merely because we prefer it for some reason or by chance; rather, we actually *carry with us the structure of our terrain* in the structure of our lived-bodies, in our typical comportment and in our practices.

Having noted *that* a terrain is privileged insofar as it is typically familiar, it remains to specify the scope of a terrain. In its broadest parameters, a terrain is species specific. This assertion complies with Husserl's contention that normality is unique to each species.[37] Let us define a species as a gathering of individuals, diverging in various degrees, but whose typical unity allows them to reproduce and at least to repeat themselves, and to express concordant normalizing relations with an affective environment.[38] Defining species this way in terms of normalization, one can account for Husserl's observation that "*[a] priori*, no one, no species can say that they have the optimal experience in their system of experience" (H XIV 135). In other words, different species will have different functional optima, different typicalities, and different familiar terrains. The terrain of an eagle is normatively different from the terrain of a dog, which moreover is different from the terrain of a human.[39]

Cutting across this species specific definition are the lower parameters of a terrain. Here, a terrain can apply to a practice, a lifestyle, or a function. For instance, a hunting dog chasing down game might be said to share the same terrain as a hunter. Nevertheless, the terrain of the latter two would be different from a hiker on a walk through the same landscape.

These delimiting comments are cursory and require further explication. Let me do this by noting the three following aspects of a terrain.

1. A terrain is distinct from its "material" or "physical" location, let us say, from its environing-world [*Umwelt*]. For example, the terrain of the climber is not the same as the terrain as a hiker or the terrain of an artist, even though they may share the same forest. Similarly, what is typically relevant for the logger is not for the spotted owl. This is, in the first instance, not a matter of shared or diverging "interests." As that from which there are perceptual contents, thematic interests or the possibilities of picking out things attentively, the normative pregivenness of a terrain is "more" than what we perceive, are attentive to, or interested in. The familiarity of a terrain has more to do with the way things in the terrain typically behave, which in turn efficaciously sketches out a range of future comportment, prefiguring this rather than that, highlighting one practice, dimming down another.

The normative pull of affectively familiar types, or "terrain-types," on the organism do not function like causes. The privileged conditions for living and the affectively familiar objects themselves call for different practices of taking-up and rejection, preferring and excluding; accordingly, these practices and conditions motivationally differentiate themselves as normal from one terrain to another. Thus, the very direction of functions or of a life in a terrain is structured differently according to the normative values they exhibit. This is why, for instance, certain primates, birds, and flora may occupy the same environing-world, while normatively speaking, they do not occupy the same terrain.

2. There is no terrain in-itself. That is, one cannot simply "relocate" a terrain. Because the material and physical surroundings are saturated with normative significance in a terrain, a terrain cannot be geographically or geologically indifferent. One of the interesting implications of the school of human geography for this study is that the mere change of location cannot be sufficient to constitute a terrain as the optimally and typically familiar milieu. Thus, an individual or a group can change locations and still not have a terrain. On our understanding, this would be interpreted as an inability to sustain their norms there. From this perspective we might want to say that *the lived-body attaches to a terrain.*

Put somewhat differently, since normality is not defined in isolation from the living beings and the terrain is but the very relation between living beings and their environing-world, a new location may be normatively atypical or unfamiliar, that is, abnormal. And it may be abnormal to such an extent that it cannot be integrated into a new normality. Because a terrain is the concordantly optimal environing-world as typically familiar for normative experience, this new environing-world would be abnormal, and not a new terrain.

Nevertheless, where objects encountered are typically familiar, and the conditions normatively significant, an environing-world could become a terrain. This is possible, in part, because normal experience is not simply a matter of adaptation to fixed norms. It is also optimalizing: It can transcend previous norms, and in transcending them concordantly, fashion new norms. The same reason why a new terrain can be etched out is the same reason why the existence of the same terrain in not guaranteed in advance.

3. A terrain is never simply abandoned. My concern in this point is similar to the former, but approached from a different perspective. Here my emphasis is on our inability simply to forsake a terrain. This can be addressed in two ways. First, when a place is fixed and a terrain changes, and second, when one moves to a different location.

In the first case, we can take the example of a radical defoliation of the upper canopy of a forest: Even though it remains the "same place," and the floor of the forest—initially—remains virtually unchanged, it is not the same terrain for life forms on the floor of the forest. It is a different terrain because it radially changes the optimal light absorption by plants, the rhythm of nocturnal life, the wind velocity and humidity for the floor life, etc. In other words, just because an individual or group loses a terrain does not mean that the terrain is simply left behind. It is integrated into the life forms themselves to such an extent that a sudden change like radical defoliation can result in the death of many forms of plant life or in the introduction of different species with different physiological norms. This brings me to my second approach to this problem.

When we "change places" or take up residence elsewhere, we do not simply leave the terrain behind.[40] Here we might want to invert the claim made under the former point by saying that from this perspective *the terrain attaches to the lived-body*. We have already encountered a variation of this principle above in relation to the transcendental function of the earth-as-ground. The typicality of the terrain is inscribed in the typicality of comportment. By changing location, the terrain does not necessarily change. The normal terrain is not simply abandoned since the norms guiding our comportment are carried with us; they are an integral part of the terrain "of" which we are formative and "in" which we inhere.

With this discussion of terrain as the normal environing-world in the sense of being optimal as typically familiar, we are on the verge of describing normality and abnormality in relation to a "territory" and thus broaching the problematic of homeworld/alienworld. Let me now compare and contrast the concepts of terrain and territory in order open up the dimension of generative intersubjectivity in the following section.

Terrain and Territory

Under the last heading, I advanced the notion of a terrain as a normatively significant environing-world that ranges anywhere from functions to species. Peculiar to the formation of a terrain is the process of normalization as normatively discriminating experience. The notion of territory was defined in chapter 7 as a transcendental concept of the lifeworld in its modalities as earth-ground and as world-horizon. It was further understood as a geographical and historical constitutive condition for intersubjective experience.

The notion of territory was evoked at that time simply as a descriptive concept. That is, it is not yet clarified in its normative significance for the constitution of intersubjective relations. Accordingly, I have not yet explained how a territory is privileged as normatively familiar. To do this requires a discussion of homeworld and alienworld.

I would like to initiate a clarification of the normative significance of territory, first by distinguishing a territory from a terrain. I understand terrain and territory as modal determinations that do not follow the strict divisions between, say, "nature" and "culture" or "animal" and "human." A territory, for example, is not to be identified with or restricted to a "humanized" world, as Husserl tends to do (cf. H XV 206). On the other hand, I would contend that phenomenologically, human beings are essential to the formation of a territory without exhausting other possibilities, and to this extent a territory can be called, as Husserl writes, a humanized environing-world.

A terrain is marked by the primacy of affectivity in the process of discriminating experience or normalization. In a territory the dimension of affectivity in the provocation of norms is still present, but is overshadowed by an active thematic or pre-thematic *delimitation* as the emergence of "limits" [*Grenzen*].[41] In other words, there is a "self-relating integrity," as Waldenfels might call it,[42] where the emergence of limits are concerned and that are not so easily identifiable in the discrimination of a terrain. For this reason, I find it difficult to speak of a terrain as having "limits."

A territory is the most general sense of geological and historical delimitation for a community as *ground* and *horizon*. That is, for Husserl a territory is a *geo-historical* formation as the inscription of "symbolic" historical limits, as it were, on the global earth. As a result, he contends that "nature is divided into territories" in such a way that nature cannot be conceived concretely outside of culture and language (H XV 391). Indeed, Husserl insists that "in transcendental interpretation *nature itself becomes a creation [Gebilde] of transcendental history*" (H XV 391 f.).

At this point of analysis we merely have the possibility of many possible "different worlds," which might suggest a kind of abstract relativism (cf. H IX 497 f.). This stance will be shown to be deficient, for it is not yet at the level of a generative analysis of generative phenomena such as homeworld and alienworld. Here, however, I simply want to compare and contrast the notion of terrain with the provisional, descriptive notion of territory.

A territory can take on many forms: a yard, a village, a house, a ship, a nation, a province and the flexible borders belonging to nomadic people (H XV 206).

Territories and terrains are related in three ways. First, a terrain and a territory may overlap or coincide. In this instance we could think of the different terrains for various species belonging, for example, to the north and south exposures of mountains on either side of the Columbia River, and the territorial frontiers of the states, Oregon and Washington. Or we might take the example of a rain forest as a specific terrain becoming a "nature preserve." Both these examples show the fallacy of calling something like a river a "natural frontier" or "natural border," and of trying to maintain a division between "nature" and "culture." The fact that a "nature preserve" is a territory already calls into question these antiquated categories.

Second, several terrains may coexist in a single territory. While a climber and a hunter may occupy different terrains, they may both share the same territory, say, the village of Berdorf in Luxembourg.

Third, it is possible to have different territories in the same terrain. Here we might think of the "reservations" of Native Americans. The formation of a reservation may create different geographical and horizonal delimited territories in an otherwise shared terrain. Or to cite a positive example, we could think of the recent creation of the Nunavut Territory in Canada that is inhabited and governed by the Inuit. Nunavut cuts through various terrains extending from the Saskatchewan-Manitoba border practically to the North Pole.

Finally, let me add that there is no territory that is not somehow related to a terrain. While my particular territory may not be at all related to another living being's terrain, there is always some coexistence of a terrain and a territory in one of the three ways named above. (I can think of only one exception to this. The moon, for example, might be called a territory. But the moon is in no way a terrain, at least not yet. That is, it is not normatively significant as affectively provocative of norms for any living beings.)

Territories, however, can be normatively significant or privileged as normatively familiar, and concretely understood, limits are actually normative limits. When we move to this level of analysis, a territory is understood generatively as "homeworld," and as normatively non-familiar and inaccessible as "alienworld." Clarifying the normative dimensions of homeworld and alienworld will be the task of the fourth and final section of this work.

Section 4

Generativity as the Matter of Generative Phenomenology

RADIX MATRIX

As one speaks to stone, like
you,
from the chasm, from
a home become a
sister to me, hurled
towards me, you,
you that long ago
you in the nothingness of a night,
you in the multi-night, en-
countered, you
multi-you—:

At that time, when I was not there,
at that time when you
paced the ploughed field, alone:

Who,
who was it, that
lineage, the murdered, that looms
black into the sky:
rod and bulb—?

(Root.
Abraham's root. Jesse's root. No
one's
root-O
ours.)

Yes,
as one speaks to stone, as
you
with the hands grope into there,
and into nothing, such
is what is here:
this fertile
soil too gapes,
this
going down
is one of the
crests growing wild.

Celan[1]

The matters, *die Sachen selbst*, of this section are generative. The previous matters that have functioned as leading clues to generativity can be summarized as follows. The static matter of consciousness and the structural components relating to sense constitution led to the discussion of the so-called genuine absolute: self-temporalizing monadic facticity. Despite various advances proffered by an analysis of monadic facticity, Husserl's analyses promulgated, for the most part, a foundational theory of intersubjectivity tied to the problem of "the other."

Nevertheless, attention to genetic matters prompted the formulation of the difference between static structural and static constitutive analyses, and between static method as a whole and genetic method. The difference between ontology and constitutive analyses within the context of static and genetic phenomenologies enabled us to adumbrate a regressive procedure of transcendental analysis in contrast to a progressive Cartesian one.

In a regressive procedure, one begins from the natural world of life or the lifeworld. Having distinguished between the provisional senses of the lifeworld and the regressive-transcendental features as world-horizon and earth-ground—which made up the concept of the lifeworld as territory—I then examined Husserl's copious manuscripts on primordial constitution that treat normality and abnormality within a genetic phenomenological perspective. This study yielded four systematically interrelated notions of normality: concordance, optimality, typicality, and familiarity. I then advanced a phenomenological notion of terrain as a normatively effective milieu that is typically familiar.

Whereas normality and abnormality were regarded from a genetic perspective insofar as normality was defined in terms of the relation between individual life and its terrain, now I take up normality and abnormality from the standpoint of the lifeworld as territory. This entails viewing a normatively significant lifeworld as an intersubjectively typically familiar territory in which we are "at home." Accordingly, alienness will not be in the first instance an alien subject, but an intersubjective geo-historical world that is normatively alien, that is, an *alienworld.* As a geo-historical process of becoming through the cogeneration of homeworld and alienworld, the general intersubjective framework will be understood as "generative." After describing the non-foundational or co-constitutive structure of "homeworld/alienworld," I will be in a position to flesh out other "generative phenomena."

The leading generative matter of a generative phenomenology that I take up in this section is the phenomenological co-generation and axiological asymmetry of homeworld and alienworld. The other generative matters that I address—such as appropriation, transgression, tradition, the constitutive roles of birth and death, communication and narrative, homecomrades, renewal, responsivity, etc.—all these serve in explicating the matter of generative phenomenology. Ultimately, these matters can be captured by Husserl's expression "generativity" [*Generativität*]. Generativity is both the process of becoming, hence the process of "generation," and a process that occurs over the "generations," hence specifically the process of *historical* and *social* movement. Like the matters of the previous section, because these generative phenomena are scattered throughout Husserl's later writings and not developed systematically, I will have to interpret them at the same time that I explicate them and illustrate their systematic interrelation. Because the generative dimension is new to most, to those both within and outside of the phenomenological tradition, and because this study is the first presentation of the generative matters as such, I will explicate the generative "things themselves" in some detail. These matters, further, will then serve as leading clues to the formulation of a "generative phenomenology."[2]

This will be the order of exposition for the final section of this study: In chapter 11, I illustrate the uniqueness of the structure of homeworld and alienworld as a "liminal" structure and advance two modes of "liminal experiencing": appropriation and transgression. Chapters 12 and 13 deal specifically with liminal experience as appropriation, and chapter 14 takes up liminal experience as transgression. Together, these latter three chapters will describe generativity through the co-generative and axiologically asymmetrical framework of homeworld/alienworld that is co-constituted through the processes of appropriation and transgression. In the concluding chapter of this work (chapter 15), I will formulate the role, significance, and import of a generative phenomenology.

11

Introduction to the Problematic of Homeworld/Alienworld

I would like to take my cue for this chapter from the pioneering work of Richard Grathoff and Maurice Natanson on the problem of normality and abnormality in the constitution of intersubjectivity. I do this because they suggest two possible approaches to the problem of intersubjectivity—in reference to Husserl's work—through the problem of normality and abnormality. Comparing and contrasting their approaches with the approach undertaken in this study, I frame, in a preliminary fashion, the significance of the point of departure for transcendental intersubjectivity from the structure homeworld/alienworld.

After illustrating in what way both present foundational accounts of intersubjectivity, I show in what sense the structure homeworld/alienworld is co-generative and co-relative. To do this I define the structure homeworld/alienworld as a "liminal" structure, co-constituted through "liminal experiencing."

Toward Intersubjective Normality and Abnormality

As common ground, it is fair to say that both Natanson and Grathoff share these four basic presuppositions: Husserl's phenomenology, some understanding of the relationship between typicality and normality, Schutz's early presentation of this relationship, and the problem of intersubjectivity vis-à-vis normality and abnormality. Beyond this common ground, however, one encounters important fissures. It is precisely in the interstices of these two approaches that I wish to sketch the import of the generative problematic, homeworld/alienworld.

First, Natanson. In his incisive contribution, Maurice Natanson begins with the problem of abnormality as the phenomenon of morbidity and points to the necessity of grappling with this problem by returning to the everyday lifeworld of the patient.[1] His question concerns how the typical everyday life of the individual can imply those "types" with which others establish their hold on their world.[2]

Natanson notes that what is *typical* for myself is immediately *familiar* to me, that is, it has its roots in my lifeworld in "silent familiarity."[3] The worlds of others are in the first instance those that are familiar to the respective others. Thus, the typical is identified with what is familiar *to me,* which is *immediately* and silently given as *my lifeworld:* Each single individual has his or her own lifeworld as a normal lifeworld.[4] It now remains to be seen how this understanding of normality relates to the problem of intersubjectivity.

Formulating the fundamental problem of intersubjectivity, Natanson contends that my world is a typically familiar world; from the perspective of familiarity this world becomes a common world by my ability to typify a world of "others." In a secondary sense, the typicality of my lifeworld relates to that of the friend, the neighbor, or the complete stranger. In short, the integration of multiple lifeworlds is explained by an inherent typifying ability.[5] Natanson characterizes the ability to typify as the ability to typify the alien in a style of what is already familiar to me.

Even if only indirectly, Natanson seems to refer here to Husserl's contention in the context of a genetic phenomenology that a normal community is formed out of the genesis of a normal self. In order to understand how we come to a normal community "*von mir aus,*" from the standpoint of my primordiality, Husserl interprets the constitution of the "other" as the process of typification. The "other" is constituted as similar to me, as "*meinesgleichen*": "Everyone newly emerging into my circle is apperceived according to my likeness [*Ebenbild*], and now he is called *normal* when the general prefiguring of the horizon (which he must have for me with the onset of perceptual intropathy precisely as similar to me [*meinesgleichen*]) accords to me [*mit mir stimmt*] in the general structural style." If all further experience runs concordantly, "the other is then a normal other" (H XV 136). As a result of this analysis I gain an "abstractively reduced" other, a "first other," a "normal other" as a personal thou for whom I too can become, reciprocally, a thou. Through reciprocal intropathy, contends Husserl, a common, familiar, that is, normal world of experience is constituted (H XV 136–38).

Staying within the context of normality and abnormality that is essentially circumscribed by the project of the Fifth Cartesian Meditation, Natanson will go so far as to say that it is by virtue of my original grasp of familiarity that I can recognize the unfamiliar, the alien: The ability to typify is the essential means of human normality to ensure against the existential shock of having to the see the world the way it is.[6] Those who have lost the ability to typify the world, he maintains, are abnormal, pathological, or "morbid."[7]

Because the typical is equated with the normal, a morbid lifeworld is posited that is fully different from an "everyday" type. Everyday communication and intersubjective understanding exist only within the normal lifeworld that is accessible to everyone, immediately and directly. In contrast, the morbid lifeworld, the world of morbid phantasies, is accessible only *mediately* through "world-stories" [*Weltberichte*] from the patients.[8] Thus, what distinguishes the relation of normal worlds to each other, and the relation of normal worlds to abnormal ones is the necessity of so-called world-stories. Nevertheless, to account for the intersubjective nexus of familiar and non-familiar, the unity of the normal and the pathological, Natanson bypasses the phenomenological question of familiarity and attributes community to a *silently taken sociality* that is an *ontological given.*[9] This ontological given is the unitary basis for the sociality of the familiar and the non-familiar.

To summarize the essential points: For Natanson, (1) the typical is what is familiar to me; (2) there is a direct equation of the typically familiar with the normal; (3) the first normal lifeworld is *my* lifeworld, that is, each individual has her or his own lifeworld; (4) other lifeworlds are initially those that are familiar to the respective others; nonetheless, "normally" they can be integrated into my lifeworld through typification; (5) intersubjective mediation such as world-stories is peculiar to the relationship of morbid worlds (i.e., abnormal worlds) to normal worlds; and finally, (6) co-being is posited as the ontological ground subtending the familiar and the non-familiar.

Grathoff takes issue with nearly all of these points. Most notably, he objects to the "existentialist interpretation of the lifeworld" as an individualized world restricted to the actions of a single individual. Second, he challenges the simple identification of the normal with familiar.[10] Not only is there no textual justification for this assertion in either Husserl or Schutz, Grathoff continues, but such an interpretation even effaces the wide range of familiarity peculiar to the lifeworld that is implicit in Husserl's concept of the typical. For Grathoff, this familiarity is the constitutive basis [*Grund*] for the experience of the alien and of what is unknown [*Unbekannt*].

Perceptively, Grathoff notes that Husserl not only recognizes different levels of being *familiar,* but also different grades of being *acquainted* [*Bekanntsein*]. On this view, there would never be the un-familiar, which in Natanson's scheme would be the abnormal, but rather only the un-acquainted [*Unbekannt*]. These realms of acquaintance and non-acquaintance are said to be "embedded in" an "encompassing and universal familiarity" that is the pregiven lifeworld, *accessible* to everyone. Thus rather than simply presupposing a communal world as an ontological given, as Natanson does, Grathoff accounts for a shared world through the very notion of familiarity.[11]

Emphatically opposing Natanson's position, Grathoff asserts: "There is not even a non-familiarity [*Nicht-Vertrautsein*]," just as there are no "entirely other lifeworlds." As witness to his position Grathoff recalls Husserl's insight from *Krisis 1* that the lifeworld does not admit of a plural, and reassures the reader that his analysis need not touch on the "Husserlian thesis of the singularity of the lifeworld." Further exacerbating the problem of the plurality of lifeworlds, on his view, is the fact that Natanson ultimately reduces the lifeworld to the particular individual actor.[12]

At all events, the lifeworld for Grathoff is "an intentional correlate" that has the all encompassing character of familiarity. As a consequence, we can encounter the unacquainted without abandoning the sphere of the familiar. That normality also includes the problem of the acquainted and unacquainted is the simple experiential reason why Grathoff contends that the typical (and the typically familiar) cannot be identified with the normal. Hence, in place of Natanson's concept of lifeworld, Grathoff introduces the Schelerian concept of milieu as developed by Gurwitsch.[13]

Let this suffice as a summary of these two positions, both of which enterprisingly tackle the problem of intersubjectivity through the concepts of normality and abnormality. Now I would like to explain how, despite their differences, or more precisely, because of the kind of differences they have, they both miss the mark of a unique theory of intersubjectivity approached both regressively through the lifeworld and in terms of normality and abnormality.

1. Natanson's inspiration for approaching the problem of intersubjectivity through Husserl's concept of the lifeworld and as tied to the problem of normality is certainly a pioneering undertaking. The problem is that the lifeworld in the first instance is *my lifeworld,* making normality, despite his protests, into an individual affair. In other words, he restricts the problem of normality and abnormality to a genetic perspective. But as we will see later in this division, the *first* sphere of normality for Husserl is the *intersubjective* lifeworld, the homeworld.

2. The threat that Grathoff perceives in Natanson's alleged egology of the lifeworld does not justify Grathoff's assertion of "a single all encompassing" lifeworld interpreted as the normal lifeworld of familiarity. Indeed, we have seen that the transcendental concept of the lifeworld is not a totality; as unique it does not admit of plurality just as it does not admit of a singularity! Here the difficulty is that in place of Natanson's putative plurality of individual lifeworlds and ontological unity, Grathoff actually substitutes a new *Grund*, a total basis of familiarity on which he can distinguish differences of acquaintance. There is no non-familiarity, essentially no "alien," only "others."[14] Whereas for Natanson the individual familiar lifeworld becomes an egological foundation, on Grathoff's account, the total familiar lifeworld becomes an all encompassing foundation. In both camps we are left with a foundational theory of intersubjectivity: Either as an egology of the lifeworld or the lifeworld as an all-encompassing *Grund*, neither can do justice to the generative matters of home or alien.

3. Natanson has the advantage of being able to account for the non-familiar. Yet in so doing he identifies the alien with one modality of alienness: morbidity. We might ask: How do we characterize experiences that are typically different from my own, not optimal for me, and nevertheless coherent? What is the phenomenological status of an alienworld that resists being integrated into our world? Must we presuppose, further, that "I" am already familiar to myself? Finally, is morbidity simply a result of not reducing ("typifying") the alien to the other?

4. Grathoff seemingly handles such problems within intersubjective normality by distinguishing the sphere of familiarity from that of acquaintance [*Bekanntheit*]. But here the "alien" disappears altogether; there are only "others" on the ground of familiarity, no aliens. For him, there is no longer abnormality from the point of view of normality, and in Husserl's words, no "alienworld" that stretches beyond our familiar comprehension. Thus, Grathoff is off the mark when he asserts that there is structurally no non-familiar.

5. If we are to join Natanson's persuasion that there is indeed a non-familiar, we must nevertheless challenge his assumption that a morbid world is somehow constituted through *Weltberichte* differently than a normal world. I will explicate in more detail below how even the normal lifeworld as homeworld is constituted mediately through world-stories, narrative, myth, etc. By itself, this mediation and world-story telling is not sufficient to distinguish a homeworld from an alienworld.

6. Finally, when Natanson does approach the intersubjective relation of the normal to the abnormal, he abandons the dimension of familiarity and posits instead an ontological given that subtends the two.

In presupposing this ontological basis, he relinquishes a transcendental perspective by no longer inquiring into *how* intersubjectivity is constituted, and simply posits in his own way an underlying totality.

In sum, both Grathoff's and Natanson's approaches present two ways of formulating the problem of intersubjectivity through the concepts of normality and abnormality. My point is that they both miss much that is still rich in a phenomenology of intersubjectivity when approached through the phenomena of normality and abnormality, a phenomenology that I elicit through a generative analysis of homeworld/alienworld.

My cursory criticism of both their positions ultimately amounts to understanding how we could have different lifeworlds, as Natanson seems to imply, without it meaning a fragmentation into individual lifeworlds, as Grathoff justifiably counters. How we can have a unity of unique intersubjective lifeworlds, not as grounding, founding, encompassing, or subtending differences, but in and through difference as an intersubjective encounter?

Liminal Experience as the Co-Generation of Home/Alien

In distinction to a genetic analysis that is restricted to the becoming of individual subjectivity, a synchronic field of contemporary individuals, and intersubjectivity as founded in an egology, generative phenomenology treats phenomena that are *historical, geological, cultural, intersubjective, and normative* from the very start.

It is in the context of the *Cartesianische Meditationen*—and in the Fifth Meditation to be exact—that Husserl not only explicitly introduces the concept of "generative" problems, but also hints at the project of a generative phenomenology as going beyond a genetic phenomenology. In a passage that has been overlooked in a myriad of commentaries on Husserl's theory of intersubjectivity, Husserl provides the following clue to a generative phenomenology. He writes:

> To be sure, to a large extent genetic problems [*genetische Probleme*]—and naturally those of the first and most fundamental level—have already entered into actual phenomenological work. . . . The constitution of internal time-consciousness and the entire phenomenological theory of association belong here. . . . But thereby the *generative problems* [*generativen Probleme*] pointed to above concerning birth and death and the nexus of the generation of psycho-physical being [*Generationszusammenhang der Animalität*] have certainly not been touched upon yet. Obviously they belong to a higher dimension and

> presuppose such immense interpretive work of the lower spheres that they will not be able to become problems of [phenomenological] work for a long time to come. (H I 169)[15]

In this passage we see Husserl beginning to differentiate the projects of genetic and generative phenomenological methods, phenomenological methods whose scopes are co-determined by their problems and matters. Generative problems entail the dimension of sense constitution that takes place historically, geologically, and intersubjectively. The starting point of many of his generative reflections is the constitution of normatively significant lifeworlds, that is, the co-constitutive relation of homeworld and alienworld.

Homeworld and alienworld are co-constituted through the process of normalization and issue in what are normal and abnormal lifeworlds. Once again, by normal and abnormal, Husserl does not mean medicinal or psychological normality, but rather modalities of sense constitution.

The fact that home and alien are co-constituted marks an extremely important divergence both from a foundational theory of intersubjectivity and from Husserl's initial formulation of normality and abnormality. In his early genetic presentation of normality and abnormality, Husserl tended to treat the abnormal as an intentional modification of the normal. As such, the abnormal was constitutively and one-sidedly dependent upon the normal. What I find suggestive when normality and abnormality are expressed in generative terms is that Husserl is led to break with a one-sided foundational description of intersubjectivity. Normal and abnormal, home and alien, become "liminal" notions. By liminal I mean not merely that home and alien are formed by positing limits, but that they are *mutually delimited* as home and as alien, as normal and as abnormal. For this reason they are *co-relative* and *co-constitutive.*

I discuss the structure of home and alien by describing the process of normalization as "liminal experiencing." There are two modes of liminal experiencing: "appropriation" and "transgression." This constitutive duet unfolds as the *co-constitution of the alien through appropriative experience of the home, and as the co-constitution of the home through the transgressive experience of the alien.* Here neither homeworld nor alienworld can be regarded as the "original sphere" since they are in a continual historical becoming as delimited from one another. This is the sense in which home and alien are co-generative.

Let me begin to show the significance and novelty of the structure homeworld/alienworld for a phenomenology of intersubjectivity by portraying this delimitation from the side of the liminal experience of appropriation.

Appropriation is a form of sense constitution that takes up pregiven sense as stemming from a homeworld and its unique tradition. This form of sense constitution is described in Husserl's works as historical and intersubjective, and issues in the co-constitution *qua* reconstitution of the homeworld.

On the one hand, by developing the homeworld through various modes of appropriation (such as repeating, ritual, communication, narrative, renewal, etc.) an alienworld is simultaneously co-constituted and delimited as such. Put differently, through the process of co-constituting a homeworld as normal or as typically familiar, a "world" is simultaneously co-constituted as not belonging to our conceptual systems, our normality, our values, norms, traditions, etc., which is to say, it is constituted *as* alien, unfamiliar, atypical, "abnormal." In short, an alienworld is co-constituted through the constitution of a homeworld as not normatively significant in the same way that a homeworld is for homecomrades (see chapter 13).

Let me caution that describing the constitution and reconstitution of the home does not presuppose that there is somehow already a home existing prior to the co-constitution of the alien. Likewise, describing the constitution of the alien through the development of the home does not presuppose the existence of alienness as somehow already created in advance. As Foucault suggests, it is not a matter of inquiring into how one circumscribes a pre-fabricated alienness, but of understanding how alienness itself is constituted.[16] The co-constitution of a homeworld by homecomrades gives rise to the sense of an alienworld by developing and appropriating the sense of a *NORMAL* lifeworld. As a result, even where the alien is not explicitly present, even when we are not explicitly cognizant of the alien, the constitution of the alien is already underway through liminal co-constitution. This takes place independently of the "reciprocal relation" of intropathy in which the body of the other must be presented in order for the sense "other" to be appresented.[17]

Husserl sometimes describes this aspect of the liminal process of co-constitution as a limiting-off [*Umgrenzen*]. He writes, for example, that if humans are constituted in a historically enduring community as normal, then their homeworld that is constituted concretely for them is "limited-off" [*umgrenzt*] as a particular historical community from normatively different historical communities.[18] Limits of a home emerge through the appropriation of a home, and the alien is liminally encountered as such by being delimited from the home *as* alien.

Our homeworld is a liminal normal world and not "the" total world since it is limited off as familiar from an unfamiliar "outside" (cf. H XV 430). Where this movement is concerned, the latter is not constituted "before" the familiar is constituted; through what is relevant for our practical life it is constituted as "generally irrelevant," or "unfamiliar." Through normalization a world is constituted specifically as our normal lifeworld; at the same time an alienworld is constituted as not belonging to our conceptual systems, our normality, our values, norms, traditions, etc. For this reason, Husserl can write that the normality of existence is the "normality for the limiting-off of 'the' world" (H XV 431). Since this normality is always in relation to an alienworld as not normal for us, the alienworld is designated as an "outside."

Describing in more detail the normal "inside," Husserl writes that "[t]he *normal* life as *generative* has now *its* historicity and initially its own life-temporality and world-temporality peculiar to every generation, which itself has its horizons of familiarity and unfamiliarity" (my emphasis).[19] Generative constitution develops the sense of a homeworld and alienworld; we exist in such a way that our world takes on a privileged sense as "home," which may be thought of as being inside, near, accessible, etc. Because this inside is privileged as being normatively relevant for us, inside and outside, home and alien cannot be understood as being merely relative in the sense of reversible or exchangeable.

In a heuristic retort Waldenfels asks rhetorically: Is the fish inside or the bird outside the water? Is the bird inside or the fish outside the air?[20] An attempt to provide answers to these questions would be misleading because the questions themselves are abstract; they presuppose a homogenous space and time, surveyed by an anonymous, extracampine observer, feigning non-participation in spatiality and temporality.

It is not enough to be merely located in space or time in order to experience the differentiation of inner and outer, Waldenfels explains; things that occur this way in space stand merely in a "relation of neighbors," so to speak; in the strict sense they do not have limits [*Grenzen*]. A limit first emerges when a being comports itself to space and time *as its spatio-temporal field.*[21] Hence, if the so-called "inside" *were not normatively significant, there would be no limits.*

By developing our life, our temporality, our historicity, we are always already in a liminal encounter with the alienworld, co-constituting the alienworld *by* reconstituting the home as a normatively significant lifeworld. *Because we are home* we "belong to" the alienworld in the process of co-constitution, but again, precisely by not belonging to the alien as being "home."

Thus far I have only touched on *one* aspect of this co-constitutive structure of homeworld/alienworld. Whereas the first to be mentioned was a co-constitution of the alien through the appropriation of the home, the other movement is a co-constitution of the home through the *transgressive* encounter with the alien.

If the co-constitution of the alien through the home were the only movement described by Husserl in the generation of home and alien, we might fail to see the uniqueness of this new approach. It would resemble too closely a one-sided foundational approach to the constitution of intersubjectivity. This would be reminiscent of the style of constitution in play in the Fifth Cartesian Meditation in which the self was said to have sense as the "sphere of ownness" shorn of any contact with the alien. In distinction to this one-sided movement, the liminal experience of appropriation is essentially complemented by another liminal experience, transgression.

The home is not a one-sided original sphere, but understood as being co-constituted *as* home by encountering an alienworld, and thus through a transgressive liminal encounter there is a *becoming alien of the home.* Recognizing that home and alien are constituted as a liminal structure means that the limits themselves are never encountered directly (which would already be to objectify them); rather, they arise through liminal encounters. This is another way of saying that the home can neither constitutively precede the alien, nor the alien precede the home; they are co-constituted as a co-relative structure.

This being the case, one would also have to reevaluate the structure of normality and abnormality from the generative structure of homeworld/alienworld. This is one reason why I cautioned earlier in section 3 that the reader should not accept all the results of normality and abnormality as final, and further that the normal and abnormal would have to be reexamined through the generative analysis of homeworld/alienworld.

Were the normal to precede the abnormal as an intentional modification of the former, then not only would the home have to precede the alien, but as "abnormal" the alien would have to be a mere intentional modification of the home. This however clearly contradicts the insight into the co-relative, non-foundational, co-constitutive structure peculiar to homeworld/alienworld. The conservative consequence of a foundational structure for normality and abnormality is challenged by Husserl when he portrays the *homeworld as being co-constituted through the alienworld.* Husserl writes, for example: "There is constituted an alien humankind, an alien humanity, an alien people, for instance. *Precisely thereby* there is constituted for me and for us '*our own*' community of homecomrades, community of a people in relation to our cultural environing-world as the world of our human validities, our particular ones."[22] Thus, the homeworld comes into relief as such through the encounter of an alienworld: "[the] homeworld *only comes into relief* when other homeworlds, other peoples are already there along with the homeworld in the horizon. The lived-environing-world in the horizon of alien lived-environing-worlds, my people surrounded by alien peoples" (my emphasis).[23] By following out the implications for normality and abnormality given the mutually constitutive structure of homeworld/alienworld, Husserl is forced to admit that normality similarly is co-constituted through the co-occurrence of abnormality: "*The distinguishing trait situated in the We and in everyone is normality* which, however, *first comes into relief as such* through the co-occurrence of the abnormal" (my emphasis).[24]

One provisional but important point to be extracted from these texts at this initial stage of analysis is that the home cannot be viewed as a mere parallel to the ego in a Cartesian account, mirrored only on a "higher level."[25] The home is not one-sidedly absolute, independent, or original; the alienworld is not one-sidedly relative or dependent. By the same token, the alien does not precede the constitution of the home. Insisting on this co-relativity for the emergence of home and alien, Husserl asserts that home and alien belong together in a permanent relativity: "Indeed, the contrast of homey or familiar and alien belongs to the permanent structure of every world, and precisely in a permanent relativity."[26] Such a permanent relativity means, further, that homeworld and alienworld are co-dependent in being uniquely what they are: "We are only, and for us the world exists only in the relativity of normalities and abnormalities."[27]

Unlike the prospect of relativism mentioned above in the third provisional concept of the lifeworld as "merely subjective-relative" (chapter 6), and in contrast to the specter of a mere plurality of territories intimated at the conclusion of the last section, the structure homeworld/alienworld is distinct from a mere plurality of lifeworlds. It is a co-relativity, a co-generation, a co-dependence in a mutual independence. Being essentially relative to one another, homeworld and alienworld are constituted in their uniqueness by being delimited from one another in a mutual relativity as home and as alien. This is why it is appropriate to write the intersubjective structure as "homeworld/alienworld."

Moreover, if the homeworld were equivalent to a mere lifeworld in the third provisional sense adumbrated above, it would be just one particular lifeworld among many others, and there would be no possibility of discriminating between lifeworlds as normatively significant or insignificant, that is, of understanding how our lifeworld as our homeworld is privileged for us *as* home, as normal, as familiar, as *our* world. There would also be no possibility for clarifying how there can be alienness in relation to our home, how its independence and integrity cannot be reduced to our world or to just any other lifeworld.

The privilege that I have attributed to the homeworld will be worked out in greater detail in the following two chapters. Let me note here that it is not a structural priority, that in turn would make the alienworld one-sidedly dependent upon a homeworld in a foundational relation of dependence. A homeworld is privileged because it develops with a coherence internal to it. A homeworld is normal because *qua* typically familiar in the generative density of a tradition, it is that through which our experiences coalesce as our own and in such a way that our world structures our experience itself.

It is from the perspective of the home as a normal lifeworld that the alienworld is experienced *as not normal, not home for us.* The home remains in relation to the alien by experiencing the *inaccessibility* through the integrity of the limits of the alien. To be sure, the alien is somehow experiencable, accessible to the home. But that the alienworld is somehow experiencable does not mean that it is experienced in the mode of accessibility like the home is for us. This aspect of the co-relativity of home and alien that I am evoking here will be described as an "axiological asymmetry" such that home and alien are irreducible and irreversible.

The ethical dimension of this co-constitutive relativity and asymmetry will be taken up especially in chapters 12 and 14. Let me mention at this point that when I speak about the constitutive maintenance of the homeworld through appropriation, it must be understood that it is also essential to the constitutive, liminal maintenance of the alienworld. This implies a peculiar self-responsibility that goes beyond a self-interest. For even the destruction of the homeworld would mean, constitutively, the destruction of the alienworld. Accordingly, since the constitution of the homeworld is co-constituted through the encounter with the alienworld, the destruction of the alienworld would be simultaneously the destruction of the homeworld. This, of course, is much different than holding, as Husserl did in *Ideen I,* that the self as the absolute sphere of being could survive the annihilation of the world without affecting its full foundational integrity (§ 49). In distinction, the homeworld is not at all a "first" world that would be absolutely and one-sidedly foundational for the alienworld as a "second" world. Instead, the home and the alien exist essentially in a co-relative structure.

This implies an unconventional logic of (1) self-responsibility and (2) responsibility toward the alien.

(1) Conventionally, self-responsibility entails looking out for oneself, taking charge of one's own life, answering for one's actions to others, or accepting praise or blame for what one has undertaken or failed to do. But here, not only would self-responsibility entail being responsible for the home, it would simultaneously mean being responsible toward the alien. Being responsible toward the alien would be implied

in *self*-responsibility because the home becomes home in and through our encounters with aliens; the well-being of home co-develops with the well-being of aliens of an alienworld, letting them be and become precisely alien.

(2) Conventionally, being responsible toward the alien is interpreted as being responsible *for* the other in the sense that one takes over a project in place of the other. This often leads to a patronizing relationship that can easily develop into a pattern of domination or one-sided dependency. Such a responsibility also tends to mean that if I am responsible "for" the other, then the other is also responsible for me, too. In other words, the same type of responsibility that holds for me is said to hold reciprocally for the alien and from the perspective of the alien.

But co-participation in the generative structure does not lie in creating an overarching synthesis or reducing the alien to the home or even the home to the alien, but *in responding to the alien from the perspective of the home.* That is, response is a way in which the transgressive encounter unfolds in a *non-symmetrical* or *non-reciprocal* affinity as *responsivity.* Ultimately, it is through the transgressive encounter of the alien, taken up responsibly as responsivity, that motivates the critique of the home as a mode of self-responsibility.

Finally, the liminal structure of home and alien takes place on many levels of intersubjective experience: as home family/alien family, home town/alien town, homeland/alienland, etc. As such, they crisscross, intersect, and intertwine in various respects and do not englobe each other like Russian matryoshka dolls. To understand this co-constitutive structure home/alien phenomenologically, I will take Husserl's lead and inquire into "*how* this continuity in the relativity of familiarity and alien is maintained; or *how* it is maintained in the relativity of different levels of homeland and the alien, village and alien village, homeland and alien land with the alien community of homecomrades, of own people and alien people" without, however, positing—as Husserl sometimes feels compelled to do—an overarching totality.[28]

Certainly, there are tensions in Husserl's account of generative matters. Rather than denying them, I prefer to keep them in play, reading them as important and instructive differences in a transcendental phenomenology of intersubjectivity. In particular, I develop a perspective suggested by Husserl that animates many of his analyses, reflections on and descriptions of generativity, one that suggests a generative phenomenology of intersubjectivity.

Let me begin doing this in the next two chapters by examining the process of appropriation in the constitution of the structure homeworld/alienworld as it relates expressly to the homeworld.

12

Liminal Experience as Appropriation: Making Ourselves at Home

> "There is still one of which you never speak."
> Marco Polo bowed his head.
> "Venice," the Khan said.
> Marco smiled. "What else do you believe I have been talking to you about?"
> The emperor did not turn a hair. "And yet I have never heard you mention that name."
> And Polo said: "Every time I describe a city I am saying something about Venice."
> "When I ask you about other cities, I want to hear about them. And about Venice, when I ask you about Venice."
> "To distinguish the other cities' qualities, I must speak of a first city that remains implicit. For me it is Venice."
> "You should then begin each tale of your travels from the departure, describing Venice as it is, all of it, not omitting anything you remember of it."
>
> Calvino[1]

My intention in this chapter and in the next is to describe the generative dimension of constitution as co-constitution starting with the homeworld. Having said this, it is important not to lose sight of the fact that while I will be discussing the constitution of the homeworld in some detail as a kind of co-constitution and re-constitution, there is always already a delimitation as co-generation of the alienworld in and through the very development of the homeworld. Thus, when describing the constitution of the homeworld, I will also be implicitly describing the co-constitution of the alienworld *as* alien.

To portray this modality of constitution I will begin by explicating the notion of home and the fundamental changes that the concept of constitution undergoes when grasped generatively. After describing the significance of home and home constitution, I will then address the process of ethical renewal and critique of this appropriation of a home. Following this, I will take up the role of language *qua* expressive communication that Husserl attributes to the constitution of a homeworld.

Home and Home Constitution

As a concept belonging to everyday discourse, "home" is so overburdened with cultural, political, sociological, and economic meanings, to say nothing of feelings of sentimentality it evokes, that it seems to resist a concerted and systematic analysis. To counter this resistance, a brief survey of the unusual ways Husserl uses the notion of home in his later writings might be helpful. *Heim* or home is at the root of many common and novel locutions: *Heimsphäre* [homesphere], *Heimrahmen* [homeframework], *Heimat, Heimatland,* and *Heimland* [homeland], *Heimstätte* [homestead] as well as *Heim-Umwelt* [home-environing-world], *Heimterritorium* [hometerritory], *Heimweltlichkeit* [homeworldliness], and of course *Heimwelt* [homeworld].

Further, he qualifies one who lives a homelife [*Heimleben*] in a *Heimhorizont* [homehorizon] as a *Heimgenosse* [homecomrade] who, in turn, makes up a *Heimgenossenschaft* [community of homecomrades] or *Heimorganization* [home organization]. Those who are *beheimatet* or residents of a homeworld are *Heimmenschen* [homehumans] or a *Heimvolk* [homepeople] of a *Heimmenschlichkeit* or *Heimmenschheit* [homehumanity]. Concordant optima or types in the homesphere are identified according to a home-type [*heimatlicher Typus*]. Moreover, there are *heimische Pflanzen* [home plants], *heimische Tiere,* or *Heimtiere* [home animals] along with peculiar *heimische Dinge* [home things].

Finally, that which falls outside of the home is *das Außerheimische* and belongs either to a *heimlose Gebiet* [homeless region] (or what he calls a *Niemandsland* [no-man's-land] or to an *unheimische Welt,* that is, a *fremde Heimwelt* [alien homeworld]. This broad array of expressions, as unorthodox as they may seem, jar loose our accustomed concepts of home for a unique analysis of intersubjectivity. They certainly challenge any equation of a home with something like an ego. Subjects do not "own" a home; rather, we as homecomrades appropriate a home as belonging to a homeworld. Similarly, while we can say that "I" belong to a home, or that I am at home, we cannot say that I am "a" home. What Husserl is sometimes wont to call the "lowest level" is not the ego at all, but the home to which the "ego" belongs.[2]

To the best of my knowledge, the expressions "home" and "homeworld" occur in Husserl's writings in a manuscript dated approximately 1920.[3] This is a good example of how Husserl takes up phenomena (e.g., homeworld and alienworld) that exceed the boundaries of one method (in this case, genetic) and demand the formulation of a new method (i.e., a generative one), a method that must have been in play in order to take up the matters he did. In this early manuscript Husserl simply distinguishes between a static and a genetic method, with no mention of generativity. But when the notion of home is taken up in full force a decade later, it is with a burgeoning distinction between genetic and generative matters.

The significance of Husserl's turn to the generative theme of homeworld can be summarized as a turn to that situation, that concrete lifeworld wherein we are typically familiar, normal, or "at home." When the notion of home and homeworld is first introduced, Husserl explains that our world is the world constituted for us in which we are homey or familiar—*heimisch*—in widest sense. It is the world that we shape or would like to shape *as home,* a home that evolves with ever new content and an ever new "face."[4]

A home is a "geo-historical horizon" (H XV 411 f.) that exists not only synchronically, but endures diachronically through a unity of descendants who constitute a "generative unity" (H XV 179 f., 391). The home is a normal framework that is always already intersubjective from the very start. It is within a home framework that "I" can be said to be normal. The homeworld and not the ego, according to Husserl, is the first sphere of normality, subverting the contention that the ego-subjectivity is an original sphere.[5]

By introducing a normal home as an irreducible intersubjective theme, Husserl implicitly calls into question a mere genetic perspective on normality as the starting point for phenomenological analysis. One cannot begin with a solipsistically reduced individual in order then to build up to a normal lifeworld. On the contrary, Husserl asserts that "[t]he normal individual is normal in and by virtue of the normal community."[6] Likewise, in order to determine the meaning of normality, one cannot remain within an account of the genesis of normal senses or of a normal individual; one must proceed to a "transcendental sociology."[7]

A normal intersubjective community, however, might be taken simply as the world of my contemporaries such that the homeworld would be understood as the sphere of synchronic normal individuals, that is, a temporal dimension designated by the co-presence of homecomrades. But Husserl is emphatic that generativity goes beyond intersubjectivity in the sense of co-presence: The generativity of the home runs through the normal human community as a community of generations (cf. H XV 207–9). Home constitution is a mode of constitution in which the individual participates; it is a mode of constitution that occurs "through" and "beyond" the ego, and does not simply begin with egological subjectivity. This is one reason why Husserl sees the necessity of going beyond a genetic phenomenology, and why the phenomena of "birth" and "death" become integrated into a constitutive generative phenomenology.

Let me now examine Husserl's implicit revisions of sense constitution as this process is viewed generatively. I do this in four stages, first by describing the world constitutive roles of birth and death, second by noting the modifications that take place when a genetic phenomenology of association is transformed into a generative one, third by suggesting generative sense constitution to be not a "primordial" constitution but a "stamm" constitution, and finally by describing specifically the process of appropriation and repeating.

1. As noted in the text cited from the Fifth Meditation concerning the distinction between genetic and generative problems, generative matters like birth and death are excluded from transcendental analysis in a genetic context. Genetic phenomenology is as yet too abstract. It is well known that during the period of passive synthesis, in the early 1920s, Husserl asserted that transcendental subjectivity neither is born nor dies.[8] In other words, methodologically, in "first genesis" everything that lies prior to human childhood or after adulthood remains unquestioned (cf. H XV 619). Birth and death cannot become problems of constitutive analyses because a genetic analysis remains within the strictures of internal time-consciousness, internal to the becoming of the individual; it is still rooted in "egological primordiality" and centered on the question of "original" or "primordial" constitution. Whereas sleep is a constitutional discordance that can be integrated into individual sense constitution, for genetic phenomenology birth and death present profound hiatus that egological constitution cannot overcome. They are precisely the limits of subjective sense constitution. The "*Historie*" of the individual within these bounds remains confined to "constitutive genesis."[9]

In an extremely rich manuscript from 1931, we see Husserl still struggling precisely with the roles of sleep, birth, and death. He is unable to understand just how birth and death belong essentially to world constitution. He reflects: "To be sure, sleep, birth, death—are problems as occurrences in the factical world. . . ." And it is questionable, he continues, "whether they must belong *essentially* at all to a world, whether they must have their ways of *original* constitution" (my emphasis).[10] In a similar vein, he questions: "Can intersubjective spatio-temporality and world be constituted without all that [scil., birth and death]; are death, etc., coincidental factual occurrences of the world? Curious facts!"[11] Finally he asks: "Can transcendental subjectivity, which is constituted in the world with birth and death, begin and end in its absoluteness?" Then he replies: "But death and after death [—] that is being for no one and likewise being-prior-to-birth, not-being. . . . But I have constituted pauses of sleep, primordially and intersubjectively; I have not constituted being-prior-to-birth primordially and intersubjectively."[12]

From these remarks, we see that the complex of issues Husserl has in mind are circumscribed either by the individual subject or by an intersubjective nexus that is contemporaneous at most. That is, he grapples with the constitutive features of sleep, birth, and death within the confines of a *genetic* phenomenology. Unlike sleep, birth and death cannot yet be investigated as essential features in the constitution of the world because they signal for a genetic phenomenology a decisive break with the concordance of world constitution. It can only treat "inhibitions" such as sleep or fainting because they figure as phases within a concordant life or within a synchronic intersubjective temporal segment. Since a genetic analysis begins and ends with the individual or a contemporaneous community—in either passive or active synthesis—birth and death escape the parameters of a genetic transcendental phenomenology.

But by taking up the homeworld as generative Husserl is obliged to describe birth and death in generative phenomenology as "*essential occurrences for world-constitution.*"[13] Generative world constitution extends before me and after me, before us and after us in a community of generations (H XV 199 f., 207 f.). Accordingly, the concordant normality of which Husserl writes is not the concordance of an individual life, but a concordance of a historical community. When the homeworld acquires a historically and typically familiar style, its concordance becomes a tradition. Let me define a tradition, then, as the normal homeworld in its *generative density*.

In the same manuscript I cited above concerning birth and death in a genetic context, Husserl raises the same problems in a generative one. The problem of constitution extends now historically, diachronically. He writes that transcendentally the world is a constitutive product of subjects with one another "in a *unity of tradition*, this tradition that is constituted in the world itself "*beyond the 'pauses' [of the] birth and death of the individual.*"[14] With the introduction of the dimension of history and the unity of a tradition—and not just of the unity of a life—we have an intersubjective nexus that is constituted generatively; birth and death are now figured into intersubjective and world constitution. In stark contrast to Heidegger who never really sees birth as a world or temporal constitutive feature, Husserl will emphasize that, generatively speaking, every new birth is not only a *mundane* occurrence, but also indeed a *transcendental* occurrence.[15]

2. I have noted that the theory of passive synthesis as the phenomenology of association is related to a genetic phenomenology by treating the process of individual self-temporalization. In the 1930s Husserl intimates a shift of the phenomenology of association onto a new axis. The configurations of sense constitution—"co-existence and succession" [*Ko-existenz und Sukzession*], "coincidence by distance" [*Deckung par distance*], "fusion in distance" [*Verschmelzung in Distanz*], "similarity in and through distance" [*Ähnlichkeit unter Abstand*], "concrescence and discretion" [*Konkretion und Diskretion*][16] (all extremely dynamic formulations)—take on a historical and intersubjective significance. Now, rather than writing of the sedimentation of retention, we have the sedimentation of a tradition; rather than reawakening and reactivating a mere temporal past, Husserl writes of reawakening and reactivating a historical past;[17] rather than a personal memory or *Erinnerung*, Husserl introduces a communal generative remembrance or *Gedächtnis*.[18] A historical tradition becomes characterized as a living, productive formation of sense that integrates the sedimented layers of earlier productive formations. Thus, Husserl defines history as "from the very beginning nothing other than the living movement of the coexistence [*Miteinander*] and intertwining [*Ineinander*] of original sense formation and sedimentation of sense" (H VI 380).

The historical problem of association is not peculiar merely to the sciences and a scientific community (H VI 378), but is a basic problem of intersubjective historicity. When the same terms used for the description of the association of sense are employed for sense formation in an intersubjective and historical tradition, the phenomenology of association begins to break loose from the model of intropathy and the primacy of individual subjectivity. This direction of Husserl's thought can be gleaned from this rather cryptic passage: "thus bequeathing originally, generatively and bequeathing the customary tradition, historically. Everything is association. Coincidence is transference of sense. Here we encounter curiosities."[19]

The curiosities to which Husserl alludes concern the transcendental unity of a history through the transmission and transference of sense as a modality of generative sense constitution. As phenomenologists we are still inquiring after the "sources of validity" [*Geltungsquellen*] in experience; but these generative "sources" of sense are not premised on the self, conceived statically or genetically. Sense constitution does not simply begin with an individual subject, but extends beyond me and "stems" from a tradition. The genetic associative "transference of sense" [*Sinnübertragung*] takes on a new dimension as the "heritage of sense" [*Sinnerbschaft*] in a generative context.[20] Sense is "propagated" by being handed down through a tradition.[21]

When phenomenology takes up the phenomenon of intersubjectivity outside of the question of generation (as it did in the Fifth Cartesian Meditation), then this phenomenology of the social world would have to remain abstract. But as Husserl himself recognizes, if we engage the question of generativity, then the problem of the social world becomes concrete, and we have a generatively constituted temporality, that is, historicity [*Geschichtlichkeit*].

The distinction between facticity and historicity, between genesis and generation is portrayed by Husserl in a passage worth citing in full. He writes:

> The constitution of an abiding co-humanity, of a general sociality referring co-relatively to a practical environing-world, can be treated *abstractly* already *prior to generation*; and, thus, by virtue of the type of temporalization of this practical environing-world as *personally* significant, there already exists *an abstract historicity* enclosed within it. If we put into play *generation*, then this progression in terms of *concretion* is also a *concretization* of the remaining co-humanity, mother, i.e., parents and child, etc.; and at the same time we have a *more concrete, generatively* formed temporalization and *historical* environing-world.[22]

Husserl sketches two distinct dimensions of phenomena here. On the one hand, we have genetic matters that are referred to as phenomena "prior to generation," that is, a field of synchronic contemporaries that are in the process of becoming through "personal" or individual "self"-temporalization; this is the dimension of "abstract historicity." On the other hand, Husserl describes generative matters that are in the process of becoming over the generations. These matters include intersubjective and cultural temporalization, a concrete, generatively formed temporality or historicity.

An "initial" analysis that is concerned with the temporality of life and world temporality is peculiar to each generation taken by itself, that is, a contemporaneous interpersonal field; however, a "generative" analysis is one in which "normal life as generative life has *now* its *historicity* [*Geschichtlichkeit*]";[23] it spans the historical nexus of generations in a tradition. Accordingly, we belong to a homeworld "in the unity of generatively bounded history" (H XV 219 and cf. n. 160). No longer is there merely a genesis of sense, but a *generation of sense*; no longer is temporality merely self-temporalization, but generatively formed intersubjective historicity; no longer is there merely a question of intropathy (for it cannot take place with our dead or unborn homecomrades, with our ancestors, with those unknown while nevertheless familiar), but a problem of sense constitution through sense propagation and inheritance.[24]

Let me note furthermore that in a genetic phenomenology where birth and death fall outside of phenomenology's parameters, "unending" temporality had to be posited *within* the life of a transcendental ego.[25] But because the temporality of the home is seen in terms of generation, a home is constitutively what I am "born into" and "die out of" (H XV 138 f.); likewise, the so-called generative endlessness is described in terms of the historical endlessness of generations (H XV 169, 172, 179). "I understand," writes Husserl, "human beings in the world altogether *generatively* in open endlessness on both sides" (H XV 168). Whereas the Cartesian subject has no transcendental relatives, the generative constitution of sense includes the contribution of ancestors and descendents, predecessors and successors in the formation of a generative historicity. A generative phenomenology opens up the temporal context historically and inquires into the constitution of sense for intersubjective historicity that is pregiven in the normal homeworld for me and for us.

While Husserl sometimes considers "mother and child" as "the generative as such,"[26] for him the community of generations is not restricted to biological generations or to generations of a bloodline. With the transcendental question of generation "comes the transcendental clarification of the generative heritage, *not the biophysical*, but the psychic and thus also the transcendental."[27] Steering us away from biologically rooted conceptions of generation, home, and, by implication, race, Husserl will maintain that generative connections arise by participating in a community or in a tradition; it concerns various styles of a homelife, taking up or rejecting the values of a homeworld, repeating or criticizing life and culture through past and future generations.

Because generativity is inextricably bound to historicity, culture, tradition, language, systems of values and norms, etc., an adopted child can participate and be born into the generativity of a "family home"; an incoming class at a university can make up a new generation that participates in a tradition preceding it and following it; a family that moves into a new town can participate in the generational continuity of a hometown, homecomrades of a homeworld can participate in generativity without "knowing" the other homecomrades, etc.

3. A generative phenomenology moves beyond a genetic phenomenology by not being a description "origins," in the usual sense anyway. For the home in the structure homeworld/alienworld does not function as an "*Ursprung*," but as a "*Stamm*."

"*Stamm*" is an expression Husserl employs frequently in his later writings in order to describe various facets of homeworld co-constitution, whether the home be considered a family home or the earth as a homestead.

For example, *Stämmen* is used as a synonym for homepeoples (H XV 206), and *Nomandenstamm* for a homehumanity without a fixed homeland (H XV 411). Further, Husserl coins the neologism *stammheitlich* as an equivalent of *heimatlich*, and qualifies *fremd* or alien as *fremdstämmisch*. Accordingly, a community of homecomrades who are tied to one another by virtue of their home is called a *Stammverwandtschaft* or a *Stammesgenossenschaft* (H XV 432 n.; H XXIX 37–38, 201). Even the earth-ground as a *Heimstätte* (homestead) is called a *Stammboden*.

The German expression, *Stamm*, can be translated into English in a variety of ways, depending on the context. It can mean a "stem" of a plant, a "trunk" of a tree, a "strain" of bacteria. Similarly, *Stamm* can mean "root," in the sense of the Latin "*radix*." If a word, for example, were said to be "*stammverwandt*," it would be a cognate, derived from the same root: A "*Stammsilbe*" is a radical, a root syllable, a "*Stammvokal*," a root vowel.

Not unrelated to the former sense, *Stamm* can also be understood genealogically as "stock" or "lineage" in a bloodline. A "*Stammbaum*" is a "family tree," a "*Stammhaus*" is a "parent branch" or "company," and a "*Stammburg*" is an ancestral castle. Moreover, *Stammkunden* are "regulars" in a restaurant or a café; a *Stammtisch* is a table frequented by and reserved for regulars; a *Stammlokal* is a familiar or favorite café. Finally, a "*Stammmutter*" is a progenitrix, a "*Stammvater*," a progenitor, and a "*Stammland*," a "place of origin."

Thus, we come across the sense of *Stamm* as that of an origin. This origin, however, is not that of an "*Ur*" of a primordial beginning; it is not a point from which I progress; it is not a "first." Rather, it is a "from whence" of emergence, beyond the powers of my subjectivity and a from whence which is perhaps beyond the reach of my cognition. For this reason, a *Besinnung* on the *Stamm* of a homepeople may require narrative myth to articulate their so-called "origin":[28] a homehumanity is "the normal form of a mythical *Stamm*people" [*die normale Form mythischer Stammvölker*] (H XV 432 n).[29]

Unlike origin [*Ursprung*], stamm is not unidirectional. A phenomenology of origins or of *primordial* constitution [*Ur-konstitution*] traces a movement that goes out from an origin; it is a genesis of self-temporalization, from past to future, as it were. A stamm, however, is not only a past "from which," but a "from which" that bears *repeating* in the form of a "toward which." *Stamm* entails a normal familiarity that is built up by actively repeating as appropriating and coming back to. Here we can understand the sense in which children in grade-school or high-school have a "homeroom"; they have a communal "stamm"-room where pupils of the same grade meet everyday at the same time of the day. It serves as both a place of departure and a place of return. We can also see in the example not only the temporal, but also the spatial, significance of the home as stamm.

Generatively speaking, a stamm is where we generationally repeat ourselves, where we come into being and pass away, where we pick up and take up where other generations left off, and where future generations take up our contribution. Perhaps, then, it is no coincidence that in the context of generativity Husserl will not simply write of sense originating from individual activity or passivity, but will write of sense constitution as sense "stemming" from a familiar world, or again, that validities "stem" from a tradition.[30]

As opposed to an origin, a stamm endures as generating.[31] If we understand home not as a sphere of primordiality but as stamm, we will be able to understand the phenomenon of *Heimweh* or homesickness. Scheler explains, for example, that when in a foreign place [*in der Fremde*], one may suddenly be overtaken by stirrings of love for our homeland without having any "idea" of home in mind. Here we experience a powerful longing and are overcome with a tenderness for something that is familiar and homey. We may even endure this longing for a considerable time without realizing that it is our home for which we yearn.[32] On the account proposed here, this so-called nostalgia for home may be rooted in an "inhibition" of our *normal* ability "to go back home," to return to the stamm. This inhibition of returning would be abnormal in the sense of a disruption in the process of stamm constitution.

Phenomenology as a philosophy of primordial constitution cannot account for the phenomenon of homesickness. For lacking is precisely a repeatability, a returning to, that would move primordiality beyond originality. This is why a generative phenomenology demands a transition from primordial-constitution to stamm-constitution. Likewise, rather than referring to the process of constitution as "origination," it is more accurate to understand it as "generation." Phenomenology as a clarification of stamm constitution would have to take into account this repeatability in generation; it would not be an analysis of a primordial or original self-temporalization, but of a generational intersubjective historicity, constitutive of and constituted in a homeworld. Only then would it be in a position to clarify the dimension of the individual. Genetic phenomenology as a philosophy of primordial constitution is to be undertaken within the context of a generative phenomenology as a philosophy of stamm constitution.

4. The sense stemming from a tradition, the bequeathing of a heritage, a transference of cultural sense, all are expressions of only one aspect of generative sense constitution. Not only is sense handed down, but it is also taken up, appropriated.

Following out the lines of constitution generatively, I already find myself as a personal member of a homehumanity: For as long as I have accepted a world, asserts Husserl, this world has always already been a world whose sense and validities stem from a tradition.[33] Generative phenomenology takes into account the constitution of the homeworld by describing the constitution of sense as co-constitution. Specifically, this co-constitution is clarified as the appropriation or re-constitution of sense stemming from a tradition.

Appropriation [*Übernahme*] and taking-up [*Aufnehmen*] are ways in which the *individual* being participates in the co-constitution of a homeworld, with those both contemporaneous to me, and with those generatively preceding and surviving me. It is, as it were, a type of genesis *within* historicity, and not abstracted from it. Thus, belonging to the generative phenomenology of association, appropriating sense is the process of "reawakening" sedimented sense or "reactivating" previous acquisitions. Husserl contends that when I "carry out" the ways of comportment of others "along with" an other, when I accept the positions and the validities of others, I do so in a way that is constitutively more dense that the quasi-positional "as if" they were mine. Instead, I take them over and make them my own in a "co-position-taking" [*Mitstellungnehmen*]: "*I appropriate,* as it were, that which is actually valid as such for him, as my validity, his judgments as mine."[34]

Because we appropriate a tradition, the sense that was not our "own," so to speak, transforms our own being-sense, *we become other through others.* The ego as the ostensible original sphere is not at all so "original." In Husserl's words: "We stand in the tradition; we become other through others, taking up in us what is personal to them, necessarily transformed in us. Generatively: Not only is the empty-formal structure, the monadic-ego-like structure bequeathed, but [also] the bequeathed characteristics; how does that happen? With the awakening of a new monad, the parental habituality is awoken or pre-awoken; but the new monad has a new *hyle* and the parental monad, its own habituality . . . all of that in sedimented overlapping and being 'commingled', being fused. A different, albeit related question is the question of birth and death."[35]

While I do in some sense become other in the appropriation of sense, I do not become self-less; rather, I become myself as a homecomrade. The will of an other is not immediately my will; the other's decisions or resolutions are not immediately my own; co-living and co-accepting do not mean that the works of the homecomrades can be reductively regarded as my works, even if they are not, on the other hand, solipsistically engendered (H XV 364).

One reason that appropriation is not simply identity-formation is due to the fact that appropriation is simultaneously "disappropriation" [*Nichtübernehmen*] (H XV 464). Let me remind the reader that I am presently concerned with how the communal sense of a tradition concordantly coheres to constitute a typically familiar homeworld. It is beyond the task of this undertaking to explore how disappropriating sense can be reformative or revolutionary, or to suggest how sense is creatively rejected, although I do hint at some possibilities below. My point is that even for appropriation to function as appropriation, there is an implicit distancing in identity formation. This distancing may take place through such commonplace acts ranging from performing different functions to forgetting. For example, if ritual is the process of communally repeating the sense of a tradition, it is simultaneously the process of distancing oneself from certain aspects of it. Edward Casey cogently remarks that rituals serve not only to remember, but also to forget, not only to make sense accessible, but also inaccessible. For example, in ritual one forgets the past that intervenes between ritualistic enactments or how one learned the ritual; one can even forget oneself as an individual.[36]

To cite another instructive example, Scheler will distinguish between mere identity formation and the process of appropriating the same sense in which difference is necessarily implicated. He does this by making a lucid distinction between the "leader" and the "exemplar." A leader, according to Scheler, is limited to a specific present space-time nexus and is trained on doing some*thing*, on the "what" of action. Accordingly, essential to a leader is a follower who copies or imitates this "what." The exemplar, on the other hand, is not restricted to this historical present, does not require followers, obedience, imitation, and does not need to issue commands in order to be an exemplar. Those who do take after the exemplar become *as* [*wie*] the exemplar; they do not become what [*was*] the person is.[37]

Employing this helpful distinction in our terminology, it is possible to understand how we can appropriate the *sense* of the tradition or action, which is indissolubly tied to the type of action we perform, without this appropriation being reducible to doing *what* the action is, as in mere repetition, obedience, or imitation. Because appropriation is a mode of co-constitution of sense and not mere imitation, I need not do exactly the same things or perform exactly the same acts in order to appropriate the same sense. I become *as* my homecomrades are without becoming *what* they are. Moreover, I *need* not do exactly the same *things* in order to appropriate the common sense or historical meaning of past events that are significant to my homeworld, although it may often occur by these means as in ritual. But as we have seen, even ritual includes a distancing.

Finally, the homecomrades with whom I co-live and co-constitute our homeworld need not be the homecomrades that are actually present. They can be my ancestors or other homecomrades who lived generations before me and whom I know only indirectly through, say, world-stories. In fact, I can still participate in a homeworld and become a homecomrade in the community of a homeworld with other homecomrades whom I do not even know at all. In short, my homeworld has sense and is a sphere of validity out of intersubjective appropriation which links me not only with the present but with the past and prepares world-acceptances for the future.

Let me introduce one further distinction implied by Husserl in the constitution of a homeworld, namely, that between repeating and repetition. Every animal generation, on Husserl's view, merely repeats [*repetiert*] its specific environing-world with the peculiar typicality of its particular species. It does not create a system of spiritual acquisitions in the unity of their life that they experience *as development.*[38] A human cultural world, Husserl contends, does experience this development as historical time that spans the generations. Hence, while animals reproduce, they are said not to live historically in a generative world.[39] Whereas animals are considered to be subjects of an environing-world, human sociality is characterized by personal subjects who are bound to one another in a historico-cultural world.[40] "The human being is an historical being and lives in a 'humanity' that is in historical becoming, a becoming that fashions history" (H XV 180). One way in which this development is experienced according to Husserl is in world-story-telling, that is, in various narrative accounts.[41]

Finally, because humans live in a lifeworld that is formed in a relatively steady normality that extends generationally and generatively in an open community, the structure homeworld/alienworld is peculiarly human (H XV 169 n. 1).

What are ways in which a homeworld is generated and appropriated? Husserl does provide some clues as to how the homeworld is appropriated and reconstituted as the homeworld, and how one becomes a homecomrade in such a home. His examples stem from a communal, everyday homelife: From the constitutive function of the length and structure of a workday to practical goals and intentions; from shared modes of orientation (say, orienting oneself from the East—as the word suggests—or from the North) to methods of counting (e.g., the adding machine and the abacus); from social habits and customs, table manners and dietary regiments to personal events such as anniversaries and birthdays; from religious rituals such as bar mitzvahs, marriages, and funerals to secular rituals such as independence day celebrations, annual parades, and town fairs; from stories passed down by elders to memorials that literally reawaken the sedimented past in order to bring us together to reevaluate our common heritage or our common suffering.

What we have here is not a "reproduction" of the lifeworld that is modeled on a Marxian conception of "production,"[42] but manifold ways in which the lifeworld or homeworld is constituted in normatively significant ways as co-constituted and re-constituted. The constitution and reconstitution of a homeworld is something that constantly goes on, but not something we can take for granted. Its sense does not remain fixed since its normal, typical structure is *modified in the repeating*, that is, it is generated. Husserl maintains that the concrete typicality of a homeworld is transformed through reconstitution; many concrete types "fall out," but in such a way that the general type of a homeworld as a homeworld is maintained (H XV 181). Because the sense of a tradition is undergoing constant transformation, central to appropriation is an attentiveness to the becoming of the homeworld. The expressions "freedom" and "choice" are persistently employed by Husserl when describing active participation in a homeworld to convey the sense of a critical distance from our tradition, our generativity, our culture, our history. It is what he calls by the name of "renewal" and "critique." Let me turn now to these two modalities of appropriation that find their genuine place in the framework of a generative phenomenology.

Renewal and Critique

Taking up and actively repeating sense that stems from a tradition, we accept a tradition as valid in many respects. Even though appropriation can be simultaneously disappropriation as selective and exclusive, appropriation is not necessarily a *critical* appropriation of a home; even though active repeating is distinct from mere repetition on Husserl's account, repeating a home may become the stagnation of a home life; it may signal the inertia and degeneracy of its *generative force*. In order for a homeworld to become a homeworld, a homeworld demands what Husserl calls "continual *renewal*" of its generative force (H XXVII 4 f., 43).

"Renewal" [*Erneuerung*] is the expression Husserl used in a series of articles appearing in the early 1920s for the process of *social, political, and ethical* transformation of human culture (1922–24). Renewal is an "absolute *ethical* demand" consisting in the struggle toward a "better humanity" and a "genuine human culture." At the invitation of a Japanese periodical, *The Kaizo* (meaning "renewal"), Husserl drafted five articles, only the first three of which were actually published.[43] A complete review of these essays and an appraisal of their full thematic content is beyond the scope of this work. However, I would like to entertain the concept of renewal and its place in the generative becoming of a home.

The *Kaizo* articles were written against the backdrop of what Husserl perceived as a crisis haunting European culture after the First World War. The crisis concerned a troubled faith and skeptical pessimism: not on a mere cognitive or epistemological plane—usually at the forefront of Husserl's work. Rather, it concerned the entire sphere of culture, and specifically, European culture (H XXVII 4 f.).[44]

By culture, Husserl understands the ensemble of human accomplishments that come together in the continuing activities of communal life and that have their existence in the abiding tradition of a community (H XXVII 21). But culture is not a mere unity of given communal accomplishments, say, intellectual, artistic, political, or religious: In the first place, it is human beings who bring these norms into being that in turn define the essence of a culture; in the second, culture is most fundamentally an ethical domain. It is a "normal" culture (normal in the full sense of the word), brought about through human accomplishments that I have refered to above as the process of normalization.

Husserl calls for renewal not because we are failing to create culture and cultural values; this takes place through the appropriation of norms and values by new generations, repeating them in ritual, work habits, storytelling, etc. His challenge instead is to do this reasonably, that is, critically. We read: "We are human beings, freely willing subjects who together actively intervene in our[45] [own] environing-world, constantly shaping it along with others. We do so whether we want to or not, whether for better or worse. Can we not also do it *reasonably*; is reasonability and excellence of ability not within our power?" (H XXVII 4).

Whether in the guise of an eidetic science (i.e., an ontology) or as a transcendental rigorous science, phenomenology is conceived in these essays primarily as an ethical task.[46] Husserl portrays science not only as a trait in the development of humanity, but as influencing and guiding the self-development of humanity of which it is conscious (H XXVII 56). The purpose, however, is not absolute knowledge, but the ethical becoming of humanity from within the development of human culture.

With at least the distinction between static and genetic phenomenology clearly in hand, and emphasizing the dynamic movement of science that functions guidingly, but that also remains embedded within the life of humanity, Husserl asserts with a sense of urgency: "we must recognize at once that all this is not to be understood statically, but dynamically genetically [*sic*]. Rigorous science is not objective being, but the becoming [*Werden*] of an ideal objectivity; and if it is essentially only in becoming, then the idea of genuine humanity and its method of self-formation is also only in becoming" (H XXVII 55).

The renewal of human culture must be understood in the "genesis of renewal" as the science of a humanity developing reciprocally with the advent of an ethical humanity. What Husserl describes as a process of self-development is most rigorously a process of the self-realization of human culture (H XXVII 56). The ethical dimension belongs to culture as a "highest" value.

Yet the lifeform of the ethical human being, contends Husserl, is not only relatively of the highest value, that is, one culture domain relative to another, say, to the artistic life, but "singly" and "absolutely." Again, Husserl is emphatic: "The genuine artist, for example, is as such not yet a genuine human being in the highest sense. But the genuine human being can be a genuine artist, and *can* only be so *if* ethical self-regulation *demands* this of him" (H XXVII 29).

It follows from such a characterization of the ethical life that *ethically* one cannot become human and cultural in just any way one likes, since becoming human is an ethical prospect. On the other hand, it would be inaccurate to say that a particular mode of life is somehow grounded in ethics. Husserl's position is more nuanced. His point is that "normally" cultural life can be anything *as* an ethical life. As a result, the artistic life is, of course, undertaken as an artistic life, but not *merely* as an artistic life since "normally" for this person or this community it is undertaken as an ethical task. Thus Husserl would say that an ethical human being is not simply an artist because she writes, dances, paints, etc., but rather that she becomes an artist insofar as this style of life is "required" for the co-realization of the moral tenor of the self and community. And we could say the same of the teacher, the carpenter, the politician, or the lawyer.

Here we find a striking spin on Plato's notion of the Good that transcends Being. For later in this same article Husserl concludes that ethical justice becomes the ultimate form of justice, and implies that the "good in itself" is only good insofar as it is morally good. We read: "*Only ethical justice is ultimate justice.* What is otherwise called simply valuable or good in itself only receives this name because it fulfills certain essential conditions that demand considering it in the framework of an ethical life a priori as a positive factor of value in taking account of value, rather than excluding it *a limine*" (H XXVII 42). This does not mean, as some would contend, that "moral reason" replaces "speculative reason," or that "moral philosophy" becomes now "first philosophy." Instead, philosophy or reason, as moral or speculative, receives its value in the context of an ethical life, according to the demands of an ethical individual and communal self-regulation.[47]

The normative idea of reason as responsibility is an ethical reason that imbues variegated areas of culture, from logic to aesthetics. It is an "ethical conscience" (H XXVII 29). Culture then is axiological, not in the sense of being a doctrine of value, but in the sense that all of culture's domains are guided ultimately by ethical norms that come into being through human action, and more specifically through the ethical human life (H XXVII 32, 42, 63).

The ethical human life is normal because it is bound to norms and lives in them (H XXVII 59); an ethical norm is neither an a-historical principle to which one must slavishly conform, nor a mere historical fact, a being [*Sein*]; it is rather a binding should-be [*Seinsollen*] that itself arises out of the framework of human communal normality, that is, from the framework of the "*Sittlichen*," of the "καθῆκον" (H XV 44; cf. 184).

In a work that follows on the heels of a description of normality in terms of optimality, it is not surprising to discover Husserl appealing to the notion of optimality in order to portray the bindingness of norms generated from within a normal cultural framework. But instead of describing it on a *perceptually* constitutive level, the normal is understood in the *Kaizo* articles on an *ethically* constitutive level as optimal, as "the best possible" [*das Bestmögliche*]. One important difference, as will become clearer below, is that Husserl's description of the perceptual/epistemological optimal tends to stress *discovering* richness and diversity given in a perceptual object in varying contexts. The cultural/ethical best possible, however, suggests a richness and diversity that is *to be generated*.[48]

What type of normativity do we gain with such a characterization? Husserl admits that the expression, "the best possible," is general and formal, and that its content is incompletely determined (H XXVII 33). The reason for this, I would argue, is that the normal *qua* optimal is conceived generatively, and as a result is evolving in its content along with ethical action. Or more precisely put, the vagueness of this formulation is due to the historicity and generativity of the homeworld itself and cannot be specified speculatively in advance. Its characterization is necessarily "incompletely determined" because the norm is tied to the process by which it is achieved such that the content of the norm arises in the context of process.[49]

In the preceding section of this work, I examined the norms of a normal life as more or less habitual. Culturally, of course, we can live a certain way simply because it has always been done that way by our parents, our ancestors, etc. (H XV 144). While the habitual character does give a clue to the bindingness of norms as internally developing from a homeworld, norms are not binding simply by having been repeated, but as a practical, reasonable possibility of *renewing* our life (H XXVII 33). In order to function as norms, they have to be made normal through renewal.

Husserl writes that the extent to which the practical possibility of renewing one's entire life is open, becoming ethically the best possible is set in contrast not only to an "organic passivity of repetition," but also to the merely theoretical absolute ideal of completeness imposed on an ethical life from the outside (H XXVII 34, 42, 44). Thus "against the idea of absolute completeness out of absolute reason" it belongs essentially to the "practical imperative" "to do that which is the *best possible* at a given time [*das zur Zeit Bestmögliche*] and in this way to become better and better according to the present [*zeitiger*] possibility" (H XXVII 36). Such a contextual, "relative" best possible life for the subject is demanded absolutely; that is, through human ethical experience it becomes a kind of "absolute imperative."[50]

I have also mentioned above that the optimal or best possible is realized in experience at the same time that it functions teleologically as a norm in order to become optimal and guide experience. The best possible peculiar to the ethical life functions in the same way. On the one hand, the normal ethical life must be a historical or contextual life, realized and realizable in particular human circumstances in order for this way of life to be the best possible. On the other hand, this relative ideal also functions teleologically and "bears the stamp of infinity" (H XXVII 34). This understanding has two consequences.

First, an action that is not the best possible for human culture necessarily refers back to the best possible in carrying it out: "[The 'unethical' life] refers back to the *pregnant concept of an ethical life*." The ethical life includes the unethical life because the former is developing the continuity of a generative density and is not simply contained in an instantaneous act. Likewise, the ethical life according to Husserl is made up of various levels of norm realization, "among them the ideal *optimal form* of a consistent life according to 'the best', namely, the respective best possible 'knowledge and conscience' for the ethical subject in question" (H XXVII 39 f.).

Second, because the best possible is a kind of concrete absolute, the present enthical optimum can be superseded, instituting a new ethical best possible *despite* its teleological reference back to the previous norm (cf. chapter 9). In a specific ethical context, an act or an ethical life can appear as an ethical "anomaly"; but this anomaly may at the same time point beyond the current ethical norms that define the culture and institute a new normality, a new best possible. Ethical norms that develop dynamically in the process of human life and culture make it impossible to specify the content of these optima in advance.

Applying our earlier exposition of the optimal to this discussion, it is possible, if not to specify its content, then at least to give sharper contours to its formality. We can say that living the best possible life in terms of the practical possibility of renewal is the *affirmation and realization of the highest differentiation and richness of generativity.*

A new form of human being emerges in the self-regulation of a life according to the best possible, as the necessary form of the "true human": "Self-humanization" is a "constant genesis of self-formation" (H XV 391). But, asserts Husserl, this type of ethical human being "is not yet the best possible as such" (H XXVII 45).

Why is ethical self-regulation not the best possible "as such"? Why is it not fully ethical? Is Husserl resorting to an abstract norm or to an imperative that one can never attain due to human finitude? At first glance, it would appear that Husserl has in mind an absolute best possible that human life would be incapable of realizing in an ethical life. Upon closer inspection, however, he is not becoming more abstract, but more concrete. Living according to an ethical self-regulation is not fully ethical because it is still based on the *contemporary individual,* on a "self." Ethically, I am responsible not only for my own becoming but for the *generation* of a ethical context that I take up and in which I am inextricably involved. Accordingly, Husserl hedges his remarks on *self*-regulation because his own analyses remain up to this point merely *genetic.* The dimension lacking is the *generative* dimension as *communal* and *historical* (cf. H XXVII 45 f.).

Although Husserl had not yet distinguished between genetic and generative dimensions in this early work, he nonetheless points toward the generative dimension by evoking the historico-cultural character of communal ethical life. Husserl explains that the inclusion of the human being in a human community and the fact that this life is integrated into a communal life has consequences that "*determine ethical comportment from the very start,*" giving to the categorical imperative a closer formal determination (H XXVII 45). Belonging to my own being, will, and realization is also being, willing, and realizing this best possible of the other; self-responsibility is responsibility *before the other* (H XXVII 46 f.; H XV 422). Moreover, realizing the optimal in the ethical life means renewing the cultural community in its *historical* self-transformation, its institutions, organizations, and cultural goods of every kind: In short, realizing the best possible of the homeworld is the *renewal of its generative force.*

The social and ethical degeneracy of a culture is no more intrinsic to the unfolding of a homeworld than its possible flourishing. What is certain is that viewed generatively, the homeworld undergoes constant historical transformation (H XV 181). Given this configuration, namely, that the homeworld is undergoing constant normative transformation through active (but not necessarily reasonable) repeating, and the fact that homecomrades have an ethical responsibility for the historically generative force of the homeworld, the ethical becoming of a homeworld requires a persistent attentiveness to its normative generation, a "continual renewal" that Husserl clarifies under the process of "critique."

Most of us are familiar with the notion of historical critique in Husserl primarily from his *Krisis 1* work.[51] There Husserl describes "continual critique" as an "inquiry back" [*Rückfrage*] into *our* historical framework in an effort to discern our unique historical task—not from the outside, externally, "but rather *from within*" (H VI 72). A critical understanding of our history entails examining our surviving values and goals that have been handed down to us and sedimented, linking us as well to future generations. Such an "historical inquiry back" is not portrayed as a private task of an isolated philosopher in the present, but as an intersubjective task, a *generative* task through the "exchange of critique" with those present and with the past tradition (H VI 73).

Significantly—and here we touch base with the project of renewal—the *Krisis 1* understands historical critique is a "responsible critique" that is undertaken not merely as an attempt to make explicit what is latent or sedimented as if to free ourselves from prejudices and presuppositions simply; rather it is an effort to revitalize and to carry on the sedimented system of values and goals *as* taken for granted—even in the form of a "radical transformation"—reawakening a generative community. Such a process Husserl calls a genuine or most profound self-reflection [*Selbstbesinnung*].

We realize from the publication of the *Kaizo* articles that the notion of historical critique was also prominent about a decade earlier in the fifth and final draft of Husserl's contribution to *The Kaizo.*[52] Critique here is a mode of historical inquiry that indicates a transformation from passive to ethically active comportment, from an "unfree" historical naïveté to a "free" position-taking (H XXVII 62). The extent to which Husserl's use of "free" and "unfree" is appropriate or ultimately misleading given the historical embeddedness of the individual in a generative tradition is open to question. In spite of this questionable usage I believe that the central import of his invocation of critique can still be ascertained.

Husserl seems to distinguish between two senses of critique. The first sense is the "faculty of critique" [*Vermögen der Kritik*] that is endemic to human life. We exercise it in everyday practical affairs, albeit incompletely, by considering whether or not our goals and means are actually correct, and without simply casting aside our convictions.

This faculty of critique, however, is not ultimate, for we can transform it into a "critical attitude," by placing our pregiven convictions, our appropriations in question, considering to what extent they deserve credit (H XXVII 63 f.).

Interestingly, Husserl uses the expression "critical attitude" [*kritische Einstellung*] and not the expression "transcendental attitude," or "phenomenological attitude," etc., as a way of describing the process of freeing oneself from a potentially naive appropriation and complacent repeating of a tradition. The fact that Husserl uses "critical" rather than "transcendental" in this context is suggestive. It implies a way of taking a distance from the tradition "within" the tradition, a "slackening" of the intentional threads, as Merleau-Ponty would say, rather than completely severing them. It suggests a generative transcendental attitude that must explicate the essential normality present in the actual and possible movement from one cultural complex to another as it itself embodies them.[53]

By the critique of tradition and the present world, Husserl has in mind the function of preparing a new rational formation, that is, a new shape of responsible humanity. Moreover, such a rational life Husserl considers to be the "philosophical life." But this subject of reason, he clarifies, cannot be the isolated single-ego, who as isolated cannot exist; rather he or she is the communal subject.[54] Because the ethical organization of society through rational willing is the reshaping of a new humanity, the philosopher can be said to be the "functionary" of humanity.

Certainly, Husserl's posture of critique is a far cry from what critical theory has called "immanent critique." Nevertheless we can see certain affinities between the two. In particular, the critical attitude is fundamentally a critique of the normative dimension of a homeworld *from within* a developing homeworld in order to evaluate its own contradictions and inconsistencies; it neither presupposes that the normative content of a homeworld can be given in advance, nor that it is imposed outside of its historical generation. Despite its vagueness, or perhaps precisely because of it, at least the early inspiration of the "critique" of critical theory and the "critical attitude" of a generative phenomenology have this much in common. Seyla Benhabib's introduction to the notion of critique can serve as a touchstone. She observes that " . . . [the] unclarity [concerning the normative foundations of critical theory] is not due to a lack of conceptual acuity or to analytical confusion. It is endemic to the mode of inquiry known as 'critique' that, despite its emphatic normative dimension, it considers itself to have transcended the normative naïveté of evaluative theories prescribing an ideal ethics and an ideal politics. . . ."[55]

For a generative phenomenology, evaluating a homeworld's own inconsistencies or contradictions is a delicate point. Certainly, Husserl's emphasis remains on assessing the consistency and deviations of a culture, specifically European culture, according to its primordial institution in ancient Greece. The difficulty is that he tends to expand an immanent ethical reform of this homeworld to an all encompassing world, "one humanity," "one normality," and hence to a ubiquitous homeworld.[56] While I will address this point in more detail below, let me remark provisionally that the cultural expansion of a homeworld over all other homeworlds in the effort to create a "universal ethical humanity" would actually be the destruction of generativity, of the becoming of homeworld/alienworld.

If we take Husserl's insights into the genesis and generation of the optimal seriously, then the ethical best possible need not merely refer back to *a* primordial institution; ethical critique and renewal would not have to be oriented on "the one world." In addition to referring back, the institution of norms and thus the development of a culture can also go beyond the previous best possible, despite its teleology, precisely *as* best possible, and institute new normalities and new optima. Hence, even within the homeworld itself there can be *diverse, conflicting, and rivaling normalities.* The *renewal* of a culture's generative force may even require such diversity and such a transcending.

I would argue that this latter conception is more to the point of Husserl's "continual renewal," a renewal that is in generation. An emphatic urgency for critique or renewal would serve no real purpose were there only a single possibility inherent in the generation of a culture, and not a diversity of possibilities and norms that give shape to the emergence of a homeworld. The ethical demand for renewal would not be literally "imperative" were a critique undertaken from a perspective outside of ethical development and not, instead, undertaken from within a humanity in the process of becoming. There is not a simple choice between the alternatives of either generation or degeneracy; what is required is a critique within a field of competing optima, competing normalities that are oriented toward realizing the generation of a homeworld.[57] All the more reason that our convictions be placed constantly in question in a continual renewal! Critique, most profoundly, would not be "free" in the sense of autonomy or being unconstrained, but in the sense of a freeing up of possibilities, of emancipating present and future best possible ways for generating a homeworld, evaluating them as they are historically emerging.

Just as the homeworld is not simply given once and for all, so too are its ethical norms in constant transformation, demanding the critical attitude and normative renewal. Accordingly, critique must also be open to the transcendence of its best possible, to an evaluation of its own internal contradictions, not simply in light of the past, but in light of its future becoming. Generatively speaking, history would not simply be what has been realized, but what is realizable; ethical justice would have to interpret systems of norms, values, and virtue not simply on the basis of past deeds, but from the perspective of an ambiguous future emergence. Such a critique may entail or require a normality that overcome the previous best possible, even though just what this best possible is can only be determined in the process of its historical emergence, in the particular historical intersubjective situation that is in the process of becoming ethically optimal. This would be an immanent critique that is open to transcendence in a variety of ways.

Ultimately, the self-responsibility for our culture and the critical attitude toward its generativity would not lead to wars of "ethnic purity" or to religious conversions, but would simultaneously be a responsibility for an alien culture. If renewal as becoming ethically the best possible with respect to our homeworld is a self-responsibility toward the historical generative force whose best possible realization remains of necessity ambiguous, then not only does ethical renewal and critique of the generative framework require openness on our part toward other possibilities that realize this generativity, but self-responsibility becomes simultaneously being responsible toward an alien culture that co-generatively becomes what it is in the becoming of the homeworld. Let me emphasize, this being responsible for the home and toward the alien in this way does not mean taking over the responsibility *of* the alien. This is an important point and will be taken up again in the chapter on liminal experience as transgression. Before doing this, however, I will continue explicating liminal experience as appropriation, now by turning to the role of expressive communication in the co-constitution of a home intersubjective nexus.

Language, Expressive Communication, Narrative

I have addressed various ways in which the homeworld is appropriated as reconstituted, generated, and critically renewed. I will now feature a dimension that became prominent in some of Husserl's later reflections, especially those concerning the homeworld. Integral to the modes of appropriation and critique of a generative homeworld is the constitutive role of language.

There are three important implications of Husserl's assessment of language as it relates to the constitution of a homeworld that I will flesh out here. The first concerns the role of language and its challenge to the privileged role of intropathy, the second, the constitutive dimension of "communicative expressions," and the third, the role of narrative in the historical becoming of a homeworld. On the whole, I work from provocative hints found in Husserl's texts and will have to develop some of their implications for a generative phenomenology.

1. It is interesting to note that in the context of the homeworld, linguistic communication [*sprachliche Mitteilung, Kommunikation*] tends to eclipse intropathy [*Einfühlung*] in the constitution of an intersubjective nexus. Examining the function of linguistic communication for the constitution of the homeworld, Husserl writes: "*The homeworld of humans . . . is fundamentally and essentially determined by language.*"[58] Only through language, he continues, does there grow not only a sensuous communal world, a co-living present-world with past and future horizons, but a practical human homeworld (H XV 225). From sensuous experience to practical affairs, our homelife as a communal life is structured and determined by language.

Were intropathy to be primary in the constitution of a social unity, we would expect to find a habitual, sensuous, pre-linguistic social unity at the foundation of a communicative one, since intropathy functions through a genetic process of passive association. Here, communication would be established through intropathy. While touted at times,[59] Husserl does not hold this view consistently in a generative context. In fact, we find just the reverse to be the case, namely, it is *intropathy that is constitutively dependent upon linguistic communication.* Foreshadowing his position on the integral role of communication and community in the constitution of normality, Husserl writes in a manuscript concerning soliloquy and intersubjective normality: "But it is not ruled out that the differences between one's own and alien 'normality' . . . arise *on the basis of a community, first through the establishment of communication.*"[60] Even a sensuous community, one cultivated on the level of the sensuous lived-body, is constituted through language.

The implication here is rich, for it means that the lived-body, my lived-body is not pre-linguistic, even though it may be pre-propositional. My lived-body is imbued with a "multiplicity of own and alien linguistic formations" with their novel types of validity and accessibility (H XV 225), just as the home—the narrowest intersubjective unity—is already linguistic, at some level both own and alien through language. This alone would seem to short-circuit any attempt at an abstractive reduction to reach the putative primordial "sphere of ownness."[61]

Moreover, as if to weigh the significance of language against that of intropathy in a generative framework Husserl asserts that it is by virtue of language and not intropathy that we constitute a social world. Contrary to the assertions made in a genetic approach, he writes that even when intropathy occurs reciprocally, actively and thoroughly, we *still do not have the constitution of a social unity.*[62] Likewise, Husserl deems it necessary to distinguish a "mere collective unity" from a "communicative unity" or personally bound community: Lacking in his previous theory of intersubjectivity based on intropathy is the act of communication that is creative of community.[63]

Of course, there are many types of communication that are creative of diverse communities and that are peculiar to different forms of life, for instance, the communication of bees, of ants, of birds, of whales, etc. But Husserl maintains that for the constitution of a generative community linguistic communication is essential. Communicative unity is the unity of discourse, of addressing [*Anrede, Ansprechen*] and taking up the address [*Aufnahme der Anrede*].[64] This taking-up does not mean that one must reply positively or fulfill a wish; for rejecting the address, turning it down, turning away, or denying it is still a mode of taking up and thus a way of being together in a community. Through this process of addressing and having to respond to the address in some way, a "*first unity,*" is constituted.

Yet the homeworld is not constituted merely by the function of communication; rather, it is constituted through a customary style of communication, that is, through a language that has significance for a group of people generatively. We read: "Every common world and thus every homeworld is already constituted by communication and creates ever new possibilities of communication. The common world, as a familiar, traditional lived-environing-world of a community of persons that is bound to a common life, does not only arise from the function of communication or these bound persons; rather, the common world is an abiding homeworld only because belonging to it [the homeworld] as co-constituted is a custom of communication, a customary style of communication in which everyone is raised—in the widest sense, a language."[65]

2. To be sure, Husserl has never denied that communication, especially linguistic communication, was essential to the formation of community, and specifically, to the formation of a human community. What I find intriguing in Husserl's later assessment is an important qualification concerning the relationship of linguistic communication to intropathy. If the former does not fully supplant the role of intropathy in the

constitutive account of intersubjectivity, then at least, it seems, intropathy and communication are decisively intermingled, enough to challenge seriously the exposition provided in the Fifth Cartesian Meditation.

Still, one could argue that this reassessment of linguistic communication and intropathy is only patchwork and does not yet get at the heart of the problem. That is, the difficultly surrounding Husserl's theory of language, communication, and sociality does not concern so much linguistic communication as it does *expressive* communication. Let me explain this comment by briefly summarizing what has already been presented above.[66]

One might contest that the main difficulty in Husserl's theory of communication for a phenomenology of intersubjectivity stems from the "phenomenological" distinction he already made in the *Logische Untersuchungen* between two types of signs: expression and indication. This is a lesson we have not only learned from Husserl's First Investigation, but one underscored by Derrida's influential work *La voix et le phénomène.*

In the First Investigation—and taken up later directly into the discussion of intersubjectivity—expression was characterized as a voluntary, willful act of manifestation. True, in communication expressions function as indications; but even though expressions do involve indication de facto, essentially and phenomenologically they do not (LU II/1, 32 f.). On the other hand, communication with its indicative relation was described as escaping the intentional control of expression in involuntary association. As a result, communication was deemed by Husserl as structurally extrinsic to expression. Likewise, expression was characterized as a meaningful sign that could occur structurally without indication as a *monologue* taking place in the silent stillness of thought, in the "solitary life of the soul" (LU II/1 35–37).

Particularly striking is the fundamentally new distinction concerning expression drawn along the lines of *normality and abnormality* in his generative descriptions involving the homeworld. In so doing, Husserl suggests a new differentiation between a *normal expression* and an *abnormal expression* (H XV 220 f.). By normal expression Husserl understands a "serious" expression, that is, one wherein the interlocutors attempt to achieve understanding, or at least where I have the expectation that the person I address will understand, even though this expectation may be disappointed (cf. H XV 220, 475).

An *abnormal* expression, conversely, is characterized as being playful [*spielerisch*], or as a phantasy-expression; some examples he gives include lying or intentional dissimulation as in being deceitful (H XV 220 f., 478). Moreover, while distinguishing between normal and abnormal expressions, Husserl makes an obvious critical allusion to his earlier theory of expression presented in the *Logische Untersuchungen.* Provocatively, Husserl writes that "*now*" he considers "*monological* expressions in the silence of thought" to be counted among the *abnormal* modes of expression![67]

Husserl's point is that *normal* expressions are those kinds of signs that are always already intersubjective, essentially communicative, and co-constitutive of a community. Communication would be normal when it constitutes a concordant community of understanding that is optimal, integrating a rich diversity of perspectives in a shared unity. To be sure, he does not discount the possibility and actuality of monological or—what are no doubt structurally different—intentionally dissimulating expressions; he does nevertheless suggest that if expressions are *not essentially communicative,* that is, if they rupture the process of shared understanding, they are *abnormal.*

That is, if we wanted to say from a genetic perspective (which is consistent with the phenomenology of communication) that the abnormal is a modification of the normal, the fact that the monologue or soliloquy is now characterized as an abnormal mode of experience means that it cannot function in a one-sided relation of foundation for communication. For the phenomenologically foundational mode would be communicative expression. Here, it seems to me, Husserl is on the verge of evoking a distinction similar to Habermas's, namely, between "communicative action" and "strategic action," or following Austin, illocutionary and perlocutionary speech-acts.

This is not the place to engage in a comparative analysis of Husserl and Habermas on the role of language, nor to delve into a detailed discussion of the difference between the theory of expression as presented in the *Logische Untersuchungen* and this suggestive text, nor further, to examine at this time the implications of this text in light of Derrida's work. Let me say simply that placing *monological expressions* in the nest with "other" abnormal expressions certainly calls into question some of the distinctions made in the First Logical Investigation. And *if* Derrida is correct in the connection he draws between the soliloquy and the solipsistic self, then this has many implications as well for the method employed in the Fifth Cartesian Meditation.

Now, to the best of my knowledge Husserl neither repeats this assertion regarding the abnormality of monological expressions, nor does he take the occasion to develop explicitly the implications of this statement for a theory of linguistic meaning. It is appropriate, nonetheless, to mention this striking text because it signals an attempt on Husserl's part to reexamine the role of expression in the context of generative phenomena such as normality and abnormality in the constitution of a homeworld.

3. What type of communicative expressions might be involved in the constitution of a homeworld? Certainly, among communicative expressions we would include synchronic dialogue in the sense of contemporaneous writing or speaking.[68] But by normal expressions Husserl also seems to have something else in mind, namely, a tradition of communicative expressions or historical dialogue. In fact, if we think of expression here *generatively*, and if we examine the "*function of language in the chain of generations*" as Husserl proposes to do (H XV 224), then we might grasp communicative expression in another sense that Husserl addressed especially during the 1930s, that is, as historical narrative.

Of lasting importance and of particular interest for Husserl are, of course, *scientific* communicative expressions that contribute to the creation of a science. And not surprisingly, participating in a science, from geometry to philosophy, is Husserl's preeminent model of participating in historically communicative expressions (cf. H VI Beilage III). Science is itself a "system of expressions" that extends temporally *qua* synchronically and historically *qua* diachronically, making up a social sphere or tradition that I, as a scientist, find pregiven and take up expressively (cf. H XV 221).

While science is Husserl's favored example, it is nonetheless a particular and perhaps more refined version of the general historical structure of linguistic co-constitution. When writing of the constitution of a normal communal world, of "our world," Husserl introduces the general role of *Geschichte* that is "awakened" through the telling [*Erzählung*] of the *Geschichte.* Such a history belongs not to any tradition in general, but to a home tradition, a home history, a home story. Accordingly, we participate in the constitution of sense that stems from a tradition through narrative "reawakening" the sedimented historical sense of a tradition bequeathed through generations.

In German "*Geschichte*" has two principle meanings: "narrative" or "story," and "history." When Husserl writes "*Geschichte—Geschichtserzählung*, what the elders and the oldest recount [*erzählen*], as that which their elders recounted, etc." (H XV 145), he is evoking a process of recounting history as narrative storytelling in the homeworld and as constitutive of the homeworld.

The relation between narrative and history has recently been the topic of a plethora of works. Some of the most noteworthy include Ricoeur's three-volume work *Temps et récit*, MacIntyre's *After Virtue* and *Whose Justice? Which Rationality?*, Olafson's *The Dialectic of Action*, and Carr's *Time, Narrative and History.*[69] Working from hints found in Husserl's earlier reflections on temporality and later writings on historicity from *Krisis 1*, and drawing on Heidegger as well as Hegel, David Carr has anticipated many features peculiar to a generative phenomenology with respect to the structure of narrative.[70]

In his reflections on the constitution of a homeworld, we find Husserl himself experimenting in the direction of a phenomenology of narrative and history. His reflections on narration and narrative history—sparing as they may seem—took place in the context of the *communal* experience of the homeworld, and not, for example, within the framework of the genesis of the individual. In focusing on the role of narrative in the reconstitution of the homeworld, and by considering "the function of language through generations," I am not excluding the individual from the narrative structure. Rather, I am attempting to follow out the insight that regards the home as the "narrowest" intersubjective structure, and to view the individual within such a generative context. This implies that even the constitution of the individual as such occurs through a social and historical structure. Remarking on Husserl's evaluation of the individual from the period of *Krisis 1*, Carr observes that even when operating under the paradigm of consciousness, the individual is taken historically and in a narrative structure for its own constitution: "But to the extent that the paradigm of consciousness is the quest for theoretical understanding, and this personal 'story' is linked to the 'history' of that quest, the individual understands himself as *being* essentially the inheritor and continuer of a tradition. Especially in *The Crisis*, this is the individual's 'self-constitution'."[71]

My emphasis here is not on the narrative structure of the individual and its peculiar mode of self-constitution.[72] I want to illustrate with this brief remark that the genesis of the individual is implicated in the generative dimension of history. Having acknowledged this status of self-constitution, my emphasis will be on the communal, historical experience of the homeworld and its generation through narrative. I would like to do this by delineating six points concerning how narrative serves in the constitution and reconstitution of the homeworld.

1. Narrative functions in the reconstitution of the homeworld by making the history of the homeworld normal in the sense of *concordant*. Against Ricoeur who maintains that narratives are essentially external to the experience of temporality, I maintain that temporal experience is already structured historically through narrative.[73] In this sense it is possible to assert that narratives engender a concordance internal to the development of a homeworld.

Moreover, it is in view of this internal coherence that other events can be seen as discordances or disruptions in the normal life of the homepeople. Here we would have to agree with MacIntyre who suggests that the unity of a history—personal or communal—is tied up with the internal coherence of a narrative, knitting together a development of the past, present, and future along a concordant storyline.[74] Thus, worshiping the golden calf could be interpreted by the people of Israel *as* a qualitative divergence or discordance, as abnormal in the experience of their history bound to Yahweh.

As noted previously, peculiar to a homeworld on Husserl's view is that the homecomrades not only develop, but experience development [*Entwicklung*] *as* development (H XV 181). Narrative, I propose, is an essential way in which the unfolding of historical time is experienced *as development*: Homecomrades experience their temporal development of the homeworld in the structure of *Geschichte*: history/narrative.

2. A narrative structure will include how the past is related to the present, and what the trajectory of the past and the present means for the future, despite discordances. Narrative is one way in which the communal life of a homepeople is elucidated or highlighted.

As the historical narrative is repeated by retelling the history, the historical development is experienced in a certain temporal density. But rather than such a repeating yielding a genetic density, now we would say that it constitutes a *generative density*. One reason historical development is generatively dense is due to the fact that it is a concordance that extends beyond the boundaries of my life and beyond those of my contemporaneous homecomrades. But it is also generative in the sense that it is a repeatable concordance of history.

Such a generative density is not imposed on the homeworld from without; rather, it is internal to the development of the homeworld precisely as a tradition: Tradition has its own generative internal coherence and thus becomes a *normal history of a homeworld.*

In colloquial conversation, we often use the expressions "normally", "traditionally", "usually" in an interchangeable fashion. We say, for example, "traditionally we eat dinner at seven o'clock" or "normally we go for a walk at eight o'clock," etc. It is possible to account for this integration of tradition into normality implied in such usage by understanding *tradition as a typical familiarity that extends historically.* In this instance, the history of a homepeople is normal or usual through the generative density of tradition. Moreover, the institution of a tradition is not the "beginning" of that tradition; rather its institution is the continuing generation of a tradition. Tradition is normal as a generatively dense familiarity; it functions as a stamm.

3. To be sure, there is a certain priority to tradition insofar as it becomes generatively dense through repeating and thus qualifies the developmental sense of a homeworld. Nevertheless, other narrative perspectives can arise that may challenge the concordance or the density

of the predominant narrative expressing the tradition of a homepeople. Despite their reference back to the normal tradition, they may offer different ways of normatively drawing the narrative lines, ways that optimally tell the history of a home in its developmental meaning. Thus we have the case of *competing* narratives for a homepeople.

As an example here we could invoke the precarious position of the Jews as the early Christians and the emergence of Christianity. Working within the same normal *qua* generatively dense tradition, the early Christians literally reconstituted a new history and historical past by emphasizing certain narrative events in the Jewish past as particularly relevant for their present and future. Thus certain psalms and prophetic messages are selected as particularly relevant for and anticipatory of a Christian narrative history; the Tree of Life is paralleled with the Cross, the Garden of Eden with Golgotha, Adam and Moses with Jesus, etc. As a result we do not have one narrative history and its generatively dense tradition giving way to another, but in this case two competing generatively dense normal traditions reconstituted through narrative participation.

4. What becomes especially clear when examining the generative density of a tradition and the possibility of conflicting narratives is the fact that historical narrative is not something that goes through us without us. As suggested in passing under the last point, operative in the constitution of a narrative history, and thus the reconstitution of the homeworld, is the discrimating process. The normal history in its generative density is not given once and for all, but as still in the process of becoming; it requires constant reformulation and critique, in short, what I have called above, renewal.

It goes to Carr's credit to have emphasized the role of the storyteller. Interpreting our role in history as being "caught up" [*verstrickt*] in the historical narrative, Dilthey in particular seems to leave out what Carr calls an "organizing principle" (i.e., our principle of selection and exclusion).[75] In terms of narrative, this principle might be called a "narrator."

When countering narrative as mere anonymity, it is tempting to view such a critique as an attempt to posit someone who stands outside of the historical narrative, who functions as an origin of the narrative, and who manipulates the storyline as some privileged abstract subject. Eventually, we would come up against what Foucault has so trenchantly described as an "author."[76] This, however, would be an uncritical reversal.

If we give to the narrator the status of a principle of selection and exclusion or organizing principle, we are not all the same considering the narrator as a genetic phenomenon. For, there is a difference between the *genetic* origin of a story, an *author*, and a *generative* generator of a narrative, a *narrator.*[77]

Still, just because the narrator is not an author does not mean that the discriminating activity of the narrator is nothing. Narration is not a mere passive handing down. For without the active participation of a narrator—singular or collective, known or unknown, in an oral or written tradition—the narrative would not be realized in its unique manner and capable of reconstituting the homeworld.

This "in between" of anonymous machinations and authorship is the work of the narrator who creatively appropriates the generative historical/narrative tradition as already accomplished in and through the activity of narrating. For what the narrator is narrating is not a static essence, but the developmental essence of a homeworld as it is in generation through narrative. The past has its sense insofar as it takes its bearings toward the future becoming of the historical narrative, that is, the historical development of the homeworld.

Viewed in terms of the reconstitution of the homeworld, it is not decisive who the "author" of a narrative history was. Certainly, it was not important for the narrators of the Old Testament; even the Gospels, which are attributed to individual personages, have many sources. Nor is authorship the essential element for folklorists. Ray Hicks, the master of "Jack Tales" in Appalachia, neither considers storytelling a profession nor understands himself as the stories' author, even though he does refer to himself as a "master" of the tales: He is rather a narrator of Jack Tales that have been handed down to him through eight generations. While coming to him from his European ancestors, by recounting them, the stories *become* through Hicks the narrative of *Appalachian* life and *Appalachia* poverty. His narratives are literally folk-lore, narrating the life of a homepeople. For Hicks these narratives are more than innocent yarns. He understands his responsibility as narrator to tell the *stories* the way scripture is read, as he says, for joy and for wisdom.

In fact, when narration is understood generatively, the author becomes a moot point: Did "the" author ever exist in narrative? Was there ever "an" origin? These questions are eclipsed from the perspective of narrative, for narrative is generated and in generation communally. Should we not say of narration what Merleau-Ponty says in general of all speech, namely, that through it my thoughts are already displaced into the thoughts of others, and others' into mine such that we are guided by a thought of which no particular person is the sole thinker, author, or origin?[78] Through narrative, homepeople are guided by the same thoughts, as it were, and these thoughts give rise to the shared historical narrative.

Although I have emphasized a peculiar responsibility of a narrator insofar as the latter has a grasp on the narration, this grasp is from the inside of the narrative itself. Such a narrative grasp of the narrator is not a leap beyond time, but a way of being in historical time,[79] since the narrator is articulated in the very narrative he or she is articulating. The experience of the homeworld (and, as we will see, of an alienworld), Husserl maintains again and again, is *von uns aus*, from the perspective of and within the homeworld. Such an experience prevents an overview [*Überschau*] both for individuals who are surpassed by the narrative during their lifetime, and for the community whose history they express. A home narrative and home narration is a participation in the history of a homeworld from within the homeworld; it is a creative reconstitution of the homeworld in which we find ourselves already involved.

5. If one meant by narrator the beginning or inventor of the story or history, and if one sought such a beginning in the structure of the reconstitution of the homeworld through narration, then we would indeed land in a type of individualism of constitution. And a one-sided individualism at that. For in this case it would only be the narrator who contributed to the constitution of the homeworld. But since narration is an appropriation of a history that we homecomrades inherit, the narrative structure of history is co-constitutive as co-participatory.

Those co-participants past, present, or future are not just the narrators or the generations of narrators, but include those who are actively attentive to the story. By participating in the retelling of this history/narrative, even by listening, we become integrated into its generative structure of life and thought. In some sense we are already participating in our narrative histories, and by being attentive to them by reciting them, learning them by heart, participating in them, or even listening to them, we actively participate and experience the development of our history as such. Through this co-participation in a narrative, each of us becomes a co-institutor [*Mitstifter*] and co-bearer [*Mitträger*] of our history with those actually contemporaneous, with past generations, and with the future generations of possible participants to whom we hand down the historical narrative.

Furthermore, in the cases of home family stories, in the narratives of a homepeople or in stories handed down in the work place from one generation of employee to another, co-participation also extends to those whose common history we recall and recount in the narrative, whether alive or dead, actual persons or fictional personages. They not only join up with the continuity of our lives, but orientate the repeating of the concordance in the generative density of a tradition.

6. This leads me to my final point. I have designated narrative as a type of "communicative expression" as co-constitutive of intersub-

jectivity. As communicative expression, narrative is both normal and abnormal, that is, both serious and playful, while however never being a monologue.

On the one hand, narratives are serious in the sense that they convey truths about our homelife, our home history. They relate past events and interpret them in a way that is meaningful and in a way that shapes and expresses our self-understanding. Very often they speak of "actual" historical figures, Abraham Lincoln, Mary Wollstonecraft; they tell of "natural" events, floods, earthquakes; they recount trials and tribulations of a people, captivity or slavery.

On the other hand, narration is not the reporting of specious "objective facts" since the events or figures are already experienced and interpreted in light of their meaning for a homelife and a homepeople. Some events will be experienced with special prominence, some figures will become "bigger than life," emphasizing a particular sense that is relevant for the homelife and its future, or as defining its orientation. Characters and their achievements as they relate to our common homeworld may be peculiarly highlighted to emphasize the coherence of the past with the present, or to support the generative density of a tradition and its relevance for our future, while to an outside observer, this may appear as unrealistic or as a gratuitous embellishment.

The fact that "phantasy-expressions" or interpretive imagination are involved in historical narrative means that the historical narrative has a *mythical* element. As an obvious example, we can think here of the Greek myths, the Mahabharata (which means literally "the great story"), the Hebrew "Genesis", the Babylonian "Genesis", *Enûma elish*, etc. One of the principle reasons for such a mythical character of narrative is the fact that in narrative we attempt to give a meaning to a past that extends *beyond* our life or our collective memory, but that nevertheless is interpreted and experienced *in* the life of a homeworld as concordant with our present. Mythical narratives attempt to give an account of a "genesis" that is genetically impossible to know, but generatively possible to experience in the generative density of a tradition and in particular, through narrative. We do not encompass our own origin, not only because we were not there, but because it is still in generation as a stamm. We take up a situation in which we find ourselves and are already involved, connecting that which we inherit with a heritage that makes sense, that is, with a heritage that is concordant and generatively significant with the present and the orientation toward the future. It is no coincidence, then, that Husserl refers to a *home*humanity as the normal form of a mythical *stamm*people.[80]

13

Liminal Experience as Appropriation: Home Economics

"And you?" the Great Khan asked Polo, "you return from lands equally distant and you can tell me only the thoughts that come to a man who sits on his doorstep at evening to enjoy the cool air. What is the use, then, of all your traveling?"

"It is evening. We are seated on the steps of your palace. There is a slight breeze," Marco Polo answered. "Whatever country my words may evoke around you, you will see it from such a vantage point, even if instead of the palace there is a village on pilings and the breeze carries the stench of a muddy estuary."

Calvino[1]

In the last chapter I examined the process of appropriation as the process of co-constituting a home. In so doing I took up various modes of appropriation including ethical renewal and communicative expressions such as narrative. Having discussed these different aspects of appropriation, I will go one step further and characterize the homeworld as "our world." From here it will also be possible to specify *who* belongs to "our" world. Finally, I will indicate the extent to which a homeworld can remain a homeworld.

The Homeworld as Our World

The structure homeworld/alienworld, I have maintained, is a new point of departure for a philosophy of the social world that is most concretely a generative phenomenology.

Investigating the problem of world in Husserl's phenomenology, Klaus Held has emphasized the plural, social sphere in his article on Husserl's concept of homeworld and alienworld. Giving a systematic interpretation to Husserl's later manuscripts on intersubjectivity, Held has done a great service in bringing the problematic of homeworld and alienworld once again to the fore.

The major difficulty with Held's account, as I have already pointed out, concerns his interpretation of the structure of homeworld and alienworld as merely parallel to the foundational account of intersubjectivity found in the Fifth Cartesian Meditation. For Held, the two accounts differ only insofar as the latter is a singular account and the former a plural account, mirroring the ego and alter ego on a higher level.[2] Although Husserl experiments with some facets of the Fifth Meditation in the account of homeworld and alienworld,[3] his descriptions of a foundational account simply do not mesh with those of the homeworld and alienworld. In fact, it should be abundantly clear by this point that the very structure of homeworld/alienworld presents a dramatic *shift* in a phenomenology of intersubjectivity, breaking decisively with the foundational account of the Fifth Meditation.

Allowing one to draw such a parallel of the homeworld to the primordial sphere of the "ego" is the assumption that the homeworld is simply an encompassing plural sphere of egos, a "We" sphere or a "We-world." Plurality conceived in the form of a We alone, however, is not sufficient to distinguish the communal sphere from the "I" as an original sphere or from a one-sided foundation (cf. H I 135–37).

Without appealing to the later manuscripts of Husserl, David Carr is on the right track in approaching the problem of intersubjectivity from the perspective of *community*, and not from a third-person perspective or from the perspective of a singular "ego." Going from individual to individual, it is difficult to see how one could have a communal experience like a demonstration, a ball-game, a wedding, or a barn-raising;[4] we would merely have something on the order of "I built the house," "you built the house," "he built the house," or in writing an article together, "I wrote a line," "you wrote a line," "I had a thought," "you had a thought," etc. Instead, Carr wants to undertake an analysis of community from the point of view of membership and from a phenomenological perspective of the first person. His point of departure is the first-person plural, the "We."[5] Although Carr's actual analysis of communal experience is more sensitive than this formulation would allow, let me state immediately that the homeworld cannot be understood as a We-world.

The designation of the mode of stamm constitution peculiar to a homeworld as the liminal experience of appropriation has contributed to a clarification of *how* the homeworld is to be understood phenomenologically. Although calling the homeworld a We-world is on the right path, it is not yet concrete. What would be the concrete constitutive expression of this sphere?

A homeworld is not an I-world or an expanded I-world, that is, a We-world; moreover, it is not just any communal world as if it were one world among others; rather, as Husserl writes again and again, a homeworld is *our world*, and is clarified from within the homeworld in terms of *our* experience.[6]

"Our world" as opposed to "We-world" expresses the process involved in the constitution and reconstitution of a home, namely, that a home is formed through *appropriation* and *disappropriation*. It is a *possessive* sphere, a sphere of relative intimacy and "accessibility." Through appropriation (not only in the sense of *übernehmen* but also *zueignen*), we take up and adopt the normal generative world and make the home our own, making ourselves at home (H XV 624; cf. 176). Yet there is a twofold relation of possession in our world. Not only do we make the world our own, but more profoundly, as our normal delimited world-horizon and earth-ground, we are possessed by it; that is, we belong to our homeworld. The homeworld is not a plural parallel to an ego because the home is the communal appropriative sphere through which "we" are constituting and constituted.

In a peculiar way, then, the homeworld might be understood as a "sphere of ownness" [*Eigenheitssphäre*]. But if it were, we would have to understand the homeworld as a sphere that is *made our own and that is constantly in the making* through appropriation, and as a unique (home) sphere to which we belong. The homeworld is not just any world, but selectively appropriated with the density of a tradition. It is not only the world we experience, but the world *from which* we experience. The question arises however: Just who belongs to "our" world? If the homeworld is not arbitrary, but delimited as normal, then likewise those who co-constitute the homeworld are not arbitrary. Let me address these considerations in the next section.

Homecomrades

Just as we should refrain from speaking merely of "a" world in a generative phenomenology, as if a homeworld would be merely one world among others, just as the homeworld is neither simply a collection of "I"s nor an indiscriminate We-world, so too is it inaccurate to speak of those who belong to our world and who co-constitute it as "subjects." Although Husserl does speak at times of "co-constituting subjects" [*mitkonstituierende Subjekte*], those who co-constitute the homeworld are not merely "subjects" and do not make up a "we subjectivity" [*Wir Subjektivität*] (H I 137). Rather, those who share our homeworld are "*homecomrades*" [*Heimgenosse*]. Homecomrades are subjects qualified constitutively and intersubjectively in terms of a home; they are "transcendental comrades," "co-bearers of our world" (cf. H XV 161–63).[7]

Since homecomrades are related by a typically familiar home space and time, I want to reappropriate the expression "other" from first philosophy and use it in a generative context. Rather than it referring to a "second ego," the term "other" will mean those homecomrades who share a *typically familiar home* space and home time. The expression "other," however, will still be distinguished from the expression "alien." The latter will be understood as those beings who are generatively and genetically *not typically familiar.*

Seen generatively, the homeworld is a community of homecomrades [*Heimgenossenschaft*]; individuals in a homeworld are simultaneously "made home" [*beheimatet*] in the process of co-constituting a home. As such they are the "*Beheimateten*" (H XV 625, 627). The identity of the individual, then, is revealed as a homecomrade in communal and historical interaction. Who we are is *how* we are as home.

This manner of speaking and these neologisms are, of course, cumbersome. But this is all the more reason to read them as an effort to introduce intersubjective expressions evocative of the home and consequently as an effort to undertake a novel approach to a phenomenology of intersubjectivity.

If we take these new intersubjective concepts seriously, we see a curious dialectic taking shape, one that is peculiar to the generative phenomena of the homeworld. It is true that the homeworld is constituted as co-constituted "by" homecomrades. But just who the homecomrades are is not given in advance. Are they people who already live in a certain location or take up residence there? Are homecomrades present from the very start and then together constitute a homeworld?

On a more dynamic view, we would have to say that a homeworld does not arise independently from homecomrades, and homecomrades are not given outside of or prior to a home. Rather, a homeworld is co-constituted by homecomrades who *become homecomrades* in appropriating and reconstituting the homeworld.

Not everyone participates as a homecomrade in the same way. Since normal and abnormal, home and alien are "operative concepts"—concepts that occur on many levels and whose contents shift depending on the context—there are many ways in which one can be normal and abnormal, familiar and unfamiliar, acquainted and unacquainted, and still be home, other, or alien.[8]

First, in order for someone to be my homecomrade or for us to share the same homeworld, this "other" person need not be someone in my circle of acquaintance. They may be an "unknown homecomrade" [*unbekannte Heimgenosse*], someone with whom I am unacquainted, but who is nevertheless home with me, familiar to me (cf. H XV 204 and 210). By sharing in the same rituals and customs or by undertaking the same work, by bringing to expression our particular generative historicity, we can already participate with others intimately as homecomrades without having to know exactly who each other is. According to Husserl, a homecomrade is still a co-bearer of our world and familiar *even if I have "no inkling" who* my home constituting comrades are (H XV 161; H XXIX 197). Similarly, in the generative dimension of a familiar tradition, the communal experience of our world extends through the chain of generations forming a home or "generative bond"; it extends indirectly from those who are known to those who are not known or present at all.[9] Such a dimension of community would be a structural impossibility on the model of intropathy.

We may recognize another homecomrade on this basis of this or that familiarity. Familiarity can show itself through a particular style of dress, typical smells of food, typically familiar accents. We may recognize a homecomrade in a familiar reaction to a sport event, by the way they cross the street when the light is red, how they handle a knife and fork, by their gait or pace, by the values they hold, etc.

When we are dealing concretely with the intercultural dynamics of homeworld and alienworld, even the very typicality of objects, maintains Husserl, cannot be gained by the process of abstraction or formalization. For merely extracting an essence on the basis of external features is insufficient to determine a type. The typicality of objects emerge in the projects of persons or a community, and in the way in which they typically realize these projects in relation to others in their common world.

Second, not only can I become acquainted with a homecomrade, but I can also become acquainted with an alien (stranger, foreigner) or an alienworld. Whereas in the former instance acquaintance is a possibility within familiarity, here it occurs in the field of non-familiarity. And this takes place without removing the non-familiarity or alienness of the alien.[10] So, even if I become good friends with a foreigner, we need not necessarily become homecomrades. We could, for example, meet each other everyday and remain unfamiliar to each other, never share a typical world, a common political life, the same ideals, etc.

(H XV 408). Indeed, we may *recognize* or even *respect* the integrity of his life or of her commitments. But respect or recognition does not make a homecomrade! Against Hegel, Husserl would have to maintain that the recognition of another being as a self-conscious being (or the failure to do so) is not the basis for the constitution of intersubjectivity or of communal experience. *The constitution of a normal homeworld is essentially prior to co-recognition.*

Finally, we reach a delicate issue in Husserl's description of a home-life and homecomradeship. It concerns his assessment of who belongs to a homeworld as normal and abnormal.

For Husserl, children and animals each in their own way occupy a precarious position as those who co-constitute a homeworld. This precariousness is reflected in his designation of children and animals as "abnormal." Prima facie, many of his comments concerning children and animals seem to be neither flattering nor very sensitive to their contribution to a homeworld. The difficulty stems from his descriptions of constitution, normality, and normalization from the perspective of the "mature" adult and his conception of rational activity (H XV 140 ff.). His descriptions seem all the more troublesome given the historical events during which these reflections were recorded, namely, the rise of National Socialism. Rather than avoid these problems and these sensitive issues, I would like to turn briefly to his examples and attempt to make some sense out of them as they relate to the *generative* constitution of a homeworld.

It is important to recall once again that Husserl's usage of normal and abnormal is not psychological or medicinal, but *constitutional;* it concerns the way in which sense emerges as concordant, optimal, typical, and familiar for our various experiences and comportment. Likewise, the assertion that children or animals are abnormal cannot be due simply to an analytic and tautological definition that they are either not mature adults or not human. This would add nothing to the clarification of *how* a homeworld is co-constituted historically.

I believe that Rudolf Bernet is on the right track when he observes that a child is called abnormal because for Husserl the child does not yet contribute to the rational sense of the world. I also concur with his view that maturation would have to be understood as a process of appropriation or the reconstitution of the world's sense, enabling the child to become normal with us in our world.[11] But this is still too general.

As we have already briefly glimpsed above, animals are said to lack a homeworld, not because they are non-human, but because on Husserl's view they are not generative. Similarly, if children are viewed by Husserl as somehow abnormal in relation to mature adults, it cannot be due to the fact that they are not mature adults.[12] The problem of normality and abnormality of childhood will have to be due for Husserl not merely to the rational, but to the generative appropriation of a homeworld.

That it is possible to make a distinction in normality and abnormality along generative and genetic lines in this instance is suggested by Husserl himself. On the basis of his assertions on the abnormality of children, one might wish to establish some affinity between Husserl's characterization of the child and those, say, of the neurologist Hughlings Jackson who equates the comportment of the child with that of the sick person.[13] But if we regard the question of normality and abnormality in terms of *genetic constitution,* children would have to be understood as normal in the full sense since they too are normalizing and optimalizing in their constitution of a normative world. Given the fact that children constantly integrate new norms, they might even be called above normal [*übernormal*] in their ability to normalize comportment. Here it would be absurd to identify symmetrically the comportment of the child with that of a sick adult: "It fails to understand this eagerness that pushes the child to raise itself constantly to new norms so profoundly opposed to the care of conservation that guides the sick person in the obsessive and often exhausting maintenance of the sole norms of life within which he feels nearly normal."[14] Accordingly, there can be no identity with the delirium of the adult with the mentality of a child or with so-called 'primitive' mentality.[15]

On a genetic level, we would say that in general, the child's comportment is normal. But the question of abnormality of children occurs for Husserl in a *generative* context. To assert that "our" children are normal in relation to alien peoples because they have the same tradition, eat the same meals, have the same habits, or share the same language, is for Husserl to beg the question. The manner in which an alien is unfamiliar with our tradition is different from a child who is unfamiliar with our tradition, just as it is different for children to learn their *home* language than it is for adults to learn a *foreign* language on the basis of an already acquired home language. This is an extremely important difference, one that has to do with the generative density of appropriating a home. If we distinguish between a family home and a cultural home, then a child might be considered home in the former, having learned and participated in its rituals, etc., without being home in a hometown or cultural homeworld. All the same, this does not mean that a child at every stage has already acquired a home tradition; rather, it still remains something to be appropriated, the home language is still to be learned, responsibility for the generation of the homeworld is still to be taken.

Furthermore, Husserl is not concerned merely with a blanket childhood, but with a whole range of stages in the constitution of a homeworld: "The generative framework," he writes, encompasses the "embryo," "new born" [*Neugeborene, Wickelkind*]," the "nursing infant" [*Säugling*]," "early childhood," and later childhood that he calls "actual childhood" (H XV 178, 604 f.).[16] While Husserl does not explicate the role of constitution in these different stages, his basic point seems to be that in a generative context of a normal homeworld, children can be considered abnormal in two respects.

In the first instance, infancy means being literally "without language." As one of the primary modes of appropriating and reconstituting a homeworld, infants who do not (yet) have a language do not yet co-participate in the linguistic community of a homeworld, in a normal communal world. Required of a constitutional analysis of appropriation would be an investigation into the child's acquisition of language.[17] Such an analysis would have to be sensitive to the process of becoming normal in a generative tradition of communicative expressions, and not take normality as a fait accompli.

The second and not unrelated reason concerns the issue of the active appropriation of and participation in an historical tradition. Similar to his point made about animals and generativity, Husserl believes that while children live in a generative framework, they do not *experience* their development *as* generative, they do not experience temporality *as historicity*. He writes, for instance, that "[i]n my childhood, I was still shut off from the *sense of the generative existence of humanity and of a history;* I knew nothing yet of tradition, for me there was no tradition" (H XV 140, my emphasis). It was only others who knew that precisely the very games I played and the fables I listened to and recounted were transmitted to me from a very old tradition through others (H XV 140). Again, emphasizing the lack of generativity in childhood and in the constitution of abnormality, Husserl reflects further: "I had no idea about birth and death, even if I already had words for them. I knew nothing of literature, of science, of art, of historical culture at all, even though I already had an environing-world with pictures and instruments."

On the basis of such statements, I tend to view Husserl's comments on abnormality and children not as the naive rambling of an aging adult, but as reflections into the nature of constitution in a generative framework, a framework with which he was beginning to grapple explicitly at the time of these writings. Making ourselves at home as our world to which we belong entails more than a "sub-liminal" belonging, but an active responsibility for setting limits, for repeating, for renewing the homeworld.

As a testimony to the important role such an appropriation has for the constitution of a homeworld, we need only look at the central place initiation rites or rituals of appropriation have had in the continuing of a tradition, whether they range from confirmation to bungee-jumping, or from patriarchal practices of genital mutilation to foot-binding. It would be a separate task to analyze the ways in which initiation rituals are practiced according to (1) whether they are "freely" taken up or "forced," and (2) how the latter are distributed along gender lines. What I would like to stress is that there are a multitude of initiation rituals that serve as markers for taking up a homeworld, and leaving childhood; in one way or another they serve as an induction into generativity as our ability to be generative, in a biological sense to be sure, but also in an historical cultural sense as the generation or generative becoming of a tradition.

In general, then, Husserl's claim would be that in order to become a homecomrade and *in this sense* to participate in co-constituting a homeworld, one must appropriate (or be induced to appropriate) a tradition and participate in its generativity. Further, if it is possible to interpret Husserl's analysis of the role of children and normality as I have done, namely, in light of generative co-constitution, then I believe that the role of children in a homeworld can highlight the precariousness and contingency of such co-constitution in general.

The example of children as being on the border between home and alien, between normality and abnormality, shows a kind of *transgression within the homeworld itself*, where being born into a homeworld may not necessarily mean that one is automatically at home. Just as Husserl's analyses of being home and the normality of the homeworld for children point to the home as something not to be taken for granted, but rather examined as a process of being acquired, should not his analyses have the same import for adult life? Is this not the significance of renewal and critique? Is there not more of an affinity between adult and childlike co-constitution then at first admitted by Husserl, at least in this respect?

I raise these questions not merely because Husserl admits that a community of mature adults is an abstraction from the very start, (H XV 141; cf. 178), but because being mature does not guarantee the constitution of a homeworld and its appropriation. We find if not the same, then at least a similar precariousness and contingency of co-constitution in adult life, since even the homeworld is not given as ready-made. Maturation would be the process of actively and critically becoming home. For Husserl himself protests: "There is no fixed world for us," and to speak of "another world as the world for us with all its vague single subjective and intersubjective horizons does not have the least sense for us" (H XV 212); our acquisitions that we have already acquired are "*continually in the process of being acquired*" [*immerzu im Erwerben*] (H XV 201, my emphasis). Thus, to acquire a tradition means to acquire it continually, co-constituting it as normal. Accordingly, "the being of the world only has an appearance of fixity; in reality it is a fixity of a normal structure."[18]

What does it mean to have the fixity of a normal structure? On the one hand, Husserl attributes to the homeworld a certain steadiness or stability. As mature adults, we structure a normal community whose style "no longer fundamentally changes" (H XV 140 f.). This steadiness, I would argue, does not accrue from adulthood, but from the sedimentation of a tradition. Just as through the genetic density of the optimal we structure a terrain as typically familiar and hence as a world of experience that we can count on, so too, through the generative repeating of the normal home life, we structure an historical familiarity or a tradition that has a generative steadiness. The stability of the homeworld is acquired, sedimented, as the steadiness of a generative density. But again, this stability is constantly reaffirmed through repeating that is a repeating *as* the same, and hence is not the constitution of a simple identity.

On the other hand, to qualify this steadiness or fixity as a normal structure is to imply that it is structured through normality, or again, that it is a contingent steadiness in the process of becoming, made through the process of normalizing appropriation and disappropriation. Although the homeworld tradition is a steadiness we can count on, it is nonetheless one that is flexible and precarious. Thus, we would have to say of all normal constitution what Husserl explicitly attributes to the process of appropriation of a tradition in childhood, namely, that "the being-sense of the world I had was in *progressive transformation of sense* [*Umbildung des Sinnes*], not a mere expansion of sense through the occupation of horizons" (H XV 140, my emphasis).

The point here, of course, is not to say that children are really adults, that adult life is childhood or still less, to disregard "the unity of life," as MacIntyre calls it, by separating childhood from adulthood.[19] Rather, I wish to insist that home constitution is not a process accomplished once and for all when a putative adulthood is reached. For adulthood itself might not be maturity, understood of course not in a biological but generative register. If home constitution were accomplished once and for all, there would be no cause for generative repeating, renewal, or critique, processes Husserl clearly deems essential to the formation of a homeworld. Instead, would we not have to say that maturity, like an acquisition, is attainted only to the extent that it is constantly *in acquisition*, to the extent that we are constantly becoming "mature" or "normal"? Would we not have to admit, as Husserl hints, that there is normality *in a homeworld in different forms and levels*, from childhood to adulthood (H XV 54)? Indeed, it is within the framework of a generative phenomenology that we can understand the constitutional significance of a "generation gap," as a kind of alienness within a generative home.

Certainly, genetically speaking, every species has its own normality, its own concordantly, typically familiar world of experience. Would we not have to concede, as well, a range of normality and abnormality from new born to mature animals (H XV 173 and 167)? Would we not also have to take account of the ways in which animals contribute to the appropriation and structuring of a homeworld as co-constituting our world? Even on Husserl's prevalent view of historical co-participation as being engaged in a cognitive project, he does toy with the possibility of animals contributing to the constitution of our world. For example, a dog's sense of smell can teach us something of our world that we never knew before, and thus can function as co-constituting our world. Not only would animals be "home animals" in the sense that they are familiar to us or indigenous to our homeland (H XV 623 f.), but they would become homecomrades as co-participants in the constitution of our homeworld as "world co-constitutors."[20]

Just as there are different modalities of appropriating a homeworld, so too are there also diverse forms of disappropriating that same home-world ranging from revolt to negligence. From the perspective of the homeworld, these different modalities can be interpreted as abnormal.

Let me note that critical renewal for Husserl is not a revolution but a reform of a tradition's immanent sense. Nevertheless, in attempting to realize this sense, exercising critique can become a struggle against the very tradition in which one finds oneself involved, its prejudices and presuppositions wittingly or unwittingly appropriated. Such prejudices and presuppositions can be found in the more narrow field of the scientific pursuit of knowledge as well as in a broader social context and general moral de-generation, for example, the feminization of poverty, racial prejudice, etc. In Husserl's formulation, the struggle against a communal situation, that is, a tradition, is a struggle against the meant presuppositions of life-experience. "It is always a struggle, and in the full sense, against the 'situation', against the sedimented acquisitions from highly mediate validities of being, that have become 'taken for granted'."[21] As a result, critical activity (which might occur anywhere from reform in scientific method to civil disobedience) can be interpreted as disappropriating the current normality, and generatively speaking, the tradition, even though its purpose is precisely to realize more fully that very normality and tradition. History is replete with examples, the most famous of which for philosophers is Socrates' trial and death in Athens.

From the perspective of generative normalization—the process of becoming historically normal—history is as yet unfinished and instigates the conflict between the normal and abnormal or between various normalities. Because the critical attitude is not oriented on the past, but toward the future becoming of the homeworld, the meaning of critique is essentially ambiguous and contingent. And because our actions are never merely our own, but belong to the generative framework, whatever we do will involve the risk of being normal or abnormal and of being understood as appropriative or disappropriative.

There are of course other examples of disappropriation that manifest themselves as 'abnormal' in senses other than the attitude of active critique. For example, disappropriation could encompass the refusal of active participation in a homelife, cultural or political apathy, extreme introversion, eating disorders, retirement, or suicide.

Jonathan Kozol, for example, writes of a woman who inherited ten million dollars at the age of twenty-one and who at the same time had worked with mostly battered and ill-nourished children. What she perceived as a profound discrepancy was manifested as bulimia: "The year in Roxbury hit her so hard that it grew into an ordeal for her *to go back home* to her own family 'place'. . . . Each time, then, that she went home—for instance, at Thanksgiving, Christmas or some other holiday—she found it agonizing to sit at the dinner table and digest her food. She began to vomit secretly upstairs, or spit out food into her handkerchief or napkin."[22] In the context of this work, bulimia would not be interpreted as a physiological problem, but as an implicit refusal to appropriate the home, its values and tradition.

Similarly, Merleau-Ponty relates the case of a young woman who was forbidden by her mother to see a young man with whom the young woman was in love. As a result the young woman could not sleep, lost her appetite as well as her ability to speak: Merleau-Ponty interprets:

> what is "fixated" on the mouth is not merely sexual existence; it is, more generally, relations with others of which speech is their vehicle. If emotion elects to express itself by aphonia, it is because of all the bodily functions speech is the most intimately tied to communal existence, or as we will say, to coexistence. Aphonia, then, represents a refusal of co-existence, as in other subjects a nervous breakdown is the means of fleeing a situation.[23]

Finally, let us consider the instance of retirement that Husserl cites as a possible mode of abnormality. This comes as a curious comment made by Husserl (who was emeritus and approximately seventy years old at the time this manuscript was written). Husserl considers retirement to be abnormal *to the extent* that the retiree is no longer "active," that is, actively participating in the generation of a homeworld. His examples of non-participation are as simple as no longer "giving advice," in whatever fashion, to other homecomrades (cf. H XV 178). If we interpret Husserl's comments in a generative context, then a situation like retirement can be considered abnormal only insofar as it means withdrawing from participation in a homelife.[24]

Having distinguished who belongs to a homeworld and the various dimensions of familiarity and non-familiarity, normality and abnormality in the constitution of a homeworld, let me now sketch the parameters of a homeworld.

When Is a Home a Home?

A homeworld, as we have seen, is a normal territory, exists in the generative density of a tradition that functions as a stamm, and is experienced temporally as historical development. It is from the start an intersubjective sphere of ownness, as it were, our world.

The homeworld, moreover, is a privileged world since it is not merely one world among others, and our homecomrades are not simply individuals who happen to occupy the same space. The aerial view of a cartographer who looks down from above on the land and maps out land masses cannot delimit a homeworld. A census taker who might link homecomrades together by the happenstance of their being in the same area cannot constitute homecomrades. All third-person perspectives on the constitution of a homeworld are inadequate: From the perspective of the generative constitution of a home such groupings are arbitrary.[25] For example, the south side of Chicago does not necessarily make up the same homeworld as the north side, even though they both are said to belong to the same territory called "Chicago." In contrast, what I have been describing as a homeworld develops with a coherence internal to the homeworld, from the perspective of a normatively privileged earth-ground and world-horizon. Homeworlds, again, can intersect and overlap on many different levels.[26]

A homeworld is privileged because it is that through which our experiences coalesce as our own and in such a way that our world structures our experience itself. This constitutional privilege of course is indifferent to whether we like it or not, or to whether it makes us happy or miserable. The point is that the norms that guide the homeworld are our norms, our way of life as that to which we have accrued. Even our bodies take on the styles and habitualities of comportment unique to our cultural values. Aesthetically (in the literal sense), it structures our way of seeing, the sounds and tonal ranges we hear, familiar smells and the odors of our bodies. Indeed, this is so much so the case that it might not be too strained to speak of the lived-body precisely as a "home-body."

In characterizing a homeworld, Husserl sometimes writes of it as a "near world" [*Nahwelt*]. This depiction not only resonates with the trait of accessibility Husserl attributes to the home, but also with the geographical or spatial intimacy of a homeworld. But simply being in a particular location for some time and having been born there does not necessarily make a territory a homeworld. Being a prisoner of war or being brought into slavery in another land does not mean that this location, no matter how long I remain in it, is my homeworld. If my family moves into a new house, it may not be home for quite some time: It may be a familiar spot, but not yet have the generative density of a sedimented tradition; perhaps it is not a setting that draws me home, like a stamm. In relating their experiences, Native Americans note that simply remaining on a reservation for generations does not make the reservation home. In this case one is geographically placed in a territory where the territory is not a homeworld and where it may never become literally a "homeland." The phenomenon of the "reservation" points to how the culturally invested homeworld is tightly interdependent with the *geological* aspect of a homeworld, and where the diminution of the one entails a loss of the other: The modulations of the homeland directly modify the generative density of the tradition, cultural lives, and practices.

If we apply these considerations to the contemporary phenomenon of "homelessness," we would have to concur that the homeless—as they are called now—cannot be equated with not having a home. Likewise, sheltering the homeless cannot be equated with giving them a "home." In the first place, a home cannot be "given" from an external perspective. Rather, it is generated developmentally and intersubjectively, and experienced as such from the *perspective of the participants,* as belonging to a home. In addition, putting the so-called homeless into shelters may just be another way of institutionalizing and controlling the poorest of the poor, alcoholics, the so-called "mentally ill," etc., without having to co-participate with them actively in forming a home. In short, premised on an idea of home as an homogenous sphere, impervious to the alien, it may just be an insidious way of covering over a deeper sense of homelessness that intrudes in all our lives such as a perpetual encounter and co-constitution with the alien.[27]

Be that as it may, the home is not restricted to the present place, but can exist in the past and preserved, so to speak, through personal or collective memory or through the co-constitution of narrative. In this instance, the home can be the place of our birth. Husserl seems particularly sensitive to this possibility in his example of the earth as earth-ground. Whether in an airplane, a space shuttle, or a "flying ark" taking us to another planet, the earth functions not only as our *Boden* but as our "primordial homeland" [*Urheimat*] or our "primordial homestead" [*Urheimstätte*].[28] If we take this rather extreme instance or a more common experience like traveling in a foreign land, homesickness would serve as an experiential indication that our world is not this place we are at present. Furthermore, what holds for a terrain also holds for the homeworld: Simply because I move about, leave my geographical location entirely, or change residence does not necessarily mitigate the impact of home, nor does it mean that I simply leave its geology behind. It remains in my daily customs of eating, in the types of foods I prefer, my measure of distances, in my language, etc.

For this reason, it would perhaps be more prudent to call the generative density of a tradition peculiar to a home not merely a density, but a "generative *momentum*." Just because I stop actively thinking about a thought that I have been working on for days does not mean that "I" stop thinking about it; I continue to work on it even when I do not want to, even in my sleep. In the same way the generative momentum of a homeworld works through us even when we ostensibly leave it.

On the other hand, while a homeworld is most often tied to a geographical location of some sort (the place of our birth, our present residence), the homeworld cannot be equated simply with the place of birth.[29] For again this would be to restrict the home to an origin, and to overlook its essential character as a stamm. As a child I may have had several homes, and a later one may be more a home than the "original" one. According to Husserl, I have a homeland as a nomad even though I am not sedentary.[30] In a related manner, the Diaspora did not necessarily imply the loss of the Jewish homeworld. The latter continued to be generated throughout the diaspora in relatively stable, coherent or normal traditions. Likewise, the homeworld, and particularly its geographical dimension can exist in the future, as is the case with the "promised homeland."

Finally, Husserl cites the "peculiar" possibility of a homeworld that is in principle not limited geographically. This is the case with "Europe," he claims, which includes the English dominions, the United States, etc. (H VI 318). Here Europe is understood as a "spiritual formation" that shares the same philosophical and scientific tradition instituted by Ancient Greece (H VI 320 ff.). Consequently, becoming European for him means an eventual planetary solidarity of humanity in a single world.[31] I will take issue with this point in the next chapter. Let me note provisionally that such a universalization of a homeworld would be the demise of the structure homeworld/alienworld.

Thus far I have been occupied with registering the various ways in which a home remains a home through modulations of its temporal and spatial features. But even though a generative density or momentum is integral to a home, a home need not remain a home: The momentum may come to a halt, the density ossify.

The dissolution of a home can be gauged in many respects. A family home can dissolve with the breakup of a family; a home town can lose its character as home when the territory is destroyed by chemicals, fire, radiation, or loss of employment. A home culture can lie dormant for ages and be taken up later as with Ancient Greece and the Renaissance.

Finally, there is the prospect of a dead culture. Here we might think of the Mayan, Aztec, or Incan civilizations. In some way or another, the values that once animated these homeworlds no longer function guidingly or are normatively relevant. Sense constitution no longer stems from a tradition, and the latter's sense is no longer appropriated, generatively repeated, renewed (H XXIX 149). Here disappropriation can range from the forgetting of a tradition (H XV 139) to cultural conquest and the systematic denial of a cultural heritage. Even when we can trace the probable *biological* descendents of a "dead culture," it does not necessarily mean that there still exists a *generative* connection. Calvino's prose makes this case nicely: "At times even the names of the inhabitants remain the same, and their voices' accent, and also the features of the faces; but the gods who live beneath the names and above places have gone off without a word and outsiders have settled in their place."[32]

In short, a home is no longer a home when the sense of the homeworld is no longer appropriated, when it is no longer identifiable as *our* world.

14

Liminal Experience as Transgression

> Marco Polo imagined answering (or Kublai Khan imagined his answer) that the more one was lost in unfamiliar quarters of distant cities, the more one understood the other cities he had crossed to arrive there; and he retraced the stages of his journeys, and he came to know the port from which he had set sail, and the familiar places of his youth, and the surroundings of home, and a little square of Venice where he gamboled as a child.
>
> Calvino[1]

The last two chapters have been an attempt to describe liminal experience in terms of the co-constitution of a homeworld as the delimitation from and co-constitution of an alienworld. By appropriating, repeating, renewing our world, and thereby constituting it as our homeworld, we are already in an encounter situation with an alienworld, co-constituting the alien as alien.

In this chapter, I would like to describe the other dimension of this co-constitution of the liminal structure homeworld/alienworld. Whereas formerly I described the co-constitution of the home and simultaneously the co-constitution of the alien through the appropriation of a home, now I will describe the co-constitution of the alien and simultaneously the co-constitution of the home through a more direct encounter with the alien. My order of description, however, should not be any indication of a precedence in the order of constitution. Both movements of co-constitution are co-generative.

To describe the constitution of homeworld/alienworld through the liminal experience of the alienworld as transgression, I will first describe the irreducibility of the structure home/alien through various modes of inaccessibility. The discussion of inaccessibility will then lead me to portray the structure of homeworld/alienworld as irreversible. I will conclude this chapter with a brief sketch of the dual constitutive movement of appropriation and transgression normatively as one of critique/responsivity.

The Co-Generation and Irreducibility of Home/Alien

I would like to argue for the fundamental irreducibility of the structure homeworld/alienworld. By irreducible, I mean that both practically and ethically the homeworld and alienworld cannot be synthesized into a "higher unity" taking the form of an all encompassing "one world." This is the case for generative reasons.

Husserl conceives the prospect of the one world [*die eine Welt*] on the basis of a quest for scientific objectivity. He does so in two ways. In the first case, the one world is regarded *statically* as a substratum or a totality of which the home and alien are just different interpretations or perspectival adumbrations.[2] Here the world is treated like a thematic object upon which we focus our attention, functioning like an identical pole (H XV 210, 217, 437).

The second way he proposes to grasp the one world is *genetically*. In this case the one world is said to evolve practically through expansion as the one "homeworld" of a higher order, making the alien familiar.[3] Because the world that Husserl has in mind here is Europe and European culture expressed in the teleology of scientific reason primordially instituted by the Greeks, the "practice" involved is the cognitive practice of scientific reason (cf. H VI 318 ff.). As a result, the one world is often conceived as a total rational synthesis of actual and possible homeworlds of lower-order homeworlds (H XV 217, 225 ff.).

While achieving the one world seems to be Husserl's goal, I contend that his generative descriptions of intersubjectivity call this into question: Such a synthesis of homeworld and alienworld generatively examined is impossible. And it is precisely upon *generative* phenomena and not static or genetic that the drive toward the one world stumbles. Let me begin to explicate this point by citing the questions Husserl raises.

Husserl suggests that an alien community of homecomrades and their "alien homeworld" is normatively different for those of us in our homeworld: Their validities are not our own. Because the alienworld has its own generative density of a tradition, Husserl writes that it is a question "to what extent and how far I can *appropriate* in understanding [*im Nachverstehen*] their [the aliens'] experiential validities, that is, how far I can progress in bringing into a synthesis their homeworld with that of mine" (H XV 233–34).

In an ethical register, Husserl poses similar questions. From an ontological perspective he tends to handle the problem of a "universal ethic and religion" in terms of something like a concrete universal. Admitting that human worlds are given in the mode of "homeworldliness" and "alien," with their corresponding ethical lives and religions, Husserl implies that they are united by an abstract universal generality that is purely formal in such a way as to leave open how ethics and religion will be determined or be concrete. Everything concrete is only concrete in its general type.[4]

From a genetic perspective, Husserl poses the problem differently. At the conclusion of the fourth *Kaizo* article Husserl asks (merely rhetorically it seems) whether a "closed-off" world should open itself up toward the "outside"; is it not *ethically* required to let an ethical community grow out over the entire world? He states further that we come to the ultimate idea of a universal ethical humanity, to a true human world-people over all particular peoples and to a over-people encompassing them, to a unitary culture, to a world state over all single systems of states. (H XXVII 58 f.).

Because of the generative dimensions of the home and alien, it is important to guard these questions as questions, and not as assertions. Along with the exposition preceding this chapter, let me respond to these questions by describing the co-generative liminal experience as a transgressive encounter.

The difficulty in describing transgression for a generative phenomenology entails having to speak of the limits of an encounter that only arise in and through the encounter. Or put differently, it is the difficulty of characterizing the generation of a homeworld while it is still becoming what it is through an encounter with an alienworld at the same time that the alienworld is still in generation in this very development and encounter. Thus, when I speak of an encounter of the alien by the home, I am not presupposing the home as a ready-made sphere from which one comfortably departs in order to encounter another sphere that is not in co-generation through this encounter.

Because of the liminal, co-generative character of intersubjective experience, Husserl's occasional metaphors of the homeworld as a ball-shaped or ring-formed sphere that gets larger through types of appropriation, like a tree that puts on one more ring with each passing year, are clearly inadequate (cf. H XV 429 f.). Since the interrelation of various dimensions of homeworld do not englobe each other like ever larger and ever smaller series of concentric circles, it is not the case that "our nation" encompasses "our city" that encompasses "our town" that encompass "our field" that again encompasses "our garden," etc. (cf. H XV 222). We have examined how this conception is an attempt to thematize the world-horzion *in* its pregivenness and not clarify it *as* pregiven (chapter 7). Rather than a model of concentric circles, it would be better to understand the diverse dimensions of homeworlds as overlapping, intersecting in such a way that they do not exactly coincide. Homeworlds and alienworlds, to use Merleau-Ponty's term, are "interworldly" [*intermondes*]: A Jewish home family may not be a homecomrade to a National Socialist home nation even though they share the same territory; the homesphere of a university may only coincide at various intervals with a home town on their communal homelife regarding, say, issues of homosexuality, the military, or economics. The interrelation of homeworlds themselves are much more complex than a movement of expansion; the limits of the homeworld/alienworld also shift, become transformed, and not just in the manner of a more encompassing ripple spreading outwards from a central splash.

Moreover, we have already seen in the last chapter with respect to the co-constitution of our world that the homeworld is not a solid sphere of absolute normality, and that even homecomrades are not homogeneously normal. The co-constitution of the homeworld is the process of becoming normal, which is to say, abnormality is also constitutive of it. The movement from immaturity to maturity itself entails its own type of transgression within the very limits of the homeworld.

Despite Husserl's misleading metaphors, he seems alert to the openness of the homeworld on many accounts. Even when he enlists the metaphors of ball-shaped spheres or rings, he cautions that the homeworld does not have the character of an insular finite space for which no outside is constituted, and further that homecomrades do not comport themselves in the homeworld as if they were born in a prison cell without doors or windows. If it were the case that we were closed off from an alienworld in the homeworld, then indeed, nothing beyond us would be of any concern to us. Instead, just by being home we are already in contact with an alien; likewise, by developing a homeworld "inside," we are already thereby co-constituting an "outside."[5]

Thus, I concur with Holenstein's assertion that the homeworld cannot be conceived of as a homogeneous, compact sphere, centered in on itself, discretely set off from another sphere, but instead as heterogeneous, where cultural worlds are intertwining structures.[6] But for all that, one should not conclude that a homeworld is a bricolage, as Holenstein rhetorically intimates.[7]

Having the density and momentum of a generative tradition, a homeworld is not arbitrary either. The same extent to which our lived-corporeality can venture forth according to typical interactive styles (H XV 430) is the same extent to which our comportment is not arbitrary, enabling us in our particular style to have contact with others of a different style. If we were simply closed in on ourselves, or if we were merely a bricolage, there would indeed be no typically familiar style, no generative density of a tradition, no normality or abnormality, and no possibility of encounter either of the home though the alien or of the alien through the home.

In distinction to the process of appropriation through which the alien is encountered by generating limits that are expanded or narrowed, let me now discuss the experience of transgression [*Überschreitung*] as a mode of encounter with the alien (cf. H XV 139, 232, 429). A transcendental inquiry into the How of this transgression will discriminate between two ways in which such a transgressive encounter takes place. They correspond to what I called in section 3 anomaly and abnormality in their specific senses.

In the first case the alien is experienced as what is *initially incomprehensible.* Husserl writes: "Our first knowledge [*Kenntnisnahme*] of the alien, or what should now be our first knowledge of the alien, is not understandable according to a concrete style without further ado. *The alien is not experiencable without further ado as that which is already familiar. . . . Rather, the alien is initially the incomprehensible alien*" (H XV 432, my emphasis).

Let me follow Husserl one step further in his observation that, in this one aspect of transgressive experience, the incomprehensibility of the alien issues from an experienced "break" or "rupture" in our concordant and typically familiar experience.

The encounter with the alien is experienced as a break because the alien *qua* alien is what cannot be anticipated or known in advance according to a typical style, as *meinesgleichen* or as *unseresgleichen.* Strictly speaking, the alien is only anticipated as "other," but never *as* alien. Resisting typification, the alien disrupts this expectation of encountering an other; the concrete analogy, the entire style of the open outside anticipated by home experience "is *ruptured*" (H XV 431). By virtue of this rupture, and because I do not apperceive the alien according to a "homeworldly type," the alien is not comprehensible according to our familiar style as if she or he were a homecomrade, but rather is "initially incomprehensible."[8]

Within the possibility of a break or a rupture of homeworld or normal experience, Husserl distinguishes between two kinds of breaks. The first of these is a "light" break or slight disruption of normal experience. In this case something in particular does not jive (*stimmt nicht*) with the previous experience, things do not run according to plan, like when one is surprised. But on the whole, this disruption is ordered into and subsumed under a familiar system of experience that remains undisturbed (H XV 210): "Normally human existence remains in this normality despite particular inhibitions, disruptions, breaks of this normality" (H XV 213).

The second kind of break is characterized as a "heavy" break. His examples here tend to be interpersonal and communal breaks. He cites the instance of the death of a child, which can change the entire horizon of interests and thus the mode of life of the parents; the death of a spouse as a co-bearer of a communal life task; the dismissal of coworkers with whom we have committed our communal life goals; a war, which calls into question the entire future of a homepeople or a home nation; natural disasters such as floods or earthquakes, which upset our entire normal and communal homeworld; the break of a tradition as in forgetting, and finally the intervention of others in our lives, which alter the unfolding of our future experience. These are just some examples of the disruption of a homeworld experience that give rise to an explicit "limit-situation" [*Grenzstituation*] that calls into question my power to appropriate (H XV 211; cf. 207).

It would not be a fruitless enterprise to compare the similarities and peculiarities of Husserl's later theory of intersubjectivity with that of Levinas, without, however, reducing the uniqueness or guiding insights of the latter to the former. For Levinas, it is uniquely the face of the Other [*l'Autrui*] that calls me, my power of appropriation into question; it is the very epiphany of Infinity in the face coming from the future, and by which the future is defined, that "paralyzes" the "possessions" of appropriation, ruptures the ontological sphere of solitude or subjectivity, and institutes the intersubjective nexus as a temporal one and as an irreducible and asymmetrical plurality.[9] For Levinas, the *way* in which a plural intersubjective nexus arises is through "separation": I "experience" (as it were) the Other *as inexperiencable.* Such an in-depth comparison concerning the experience of this rupture by the Other or the alien, and the calling into question of my liberty of appropriation, however, cannot become the present task.[10] Instead, I would like to move on to the other dimension of the experience of transgression that, for Husserl, takes us beyond the "anomalous" experience of the alien to the "normatively significant" experience of the alien. In so doing it also takes us beyond a mere I-Thou or I-You relation. The reasons for this concern the generative depth of the alien.

The normative experience of the alien as transgression can be likened to the light break and to the heavy break mentioned above insofar as our normal structure of experience is challenged and restructured. This yields, as Husserl writes, an "initial" incomprehensibility. One might now expect a description of how this initial incomprehensibility is overcome in favor of a rational synthesis. But by examining Husserl's generative analysis of the experience of an alienworld, we find instead that the generative experience of the alien gives rise to a more *profound* incomprehensibility, what I will take up below under the concept of *inaccessibility*. I contend that the break or rupture I have discussed thus far suggests an initial incomprehensibility not because it can be overcome, but because it does not yet capture the depth dimension of the experience of the generative alien.

According to Husserl, I do not simply encounter the alien as an isolated individual or as someone merely contemporaneous to me, but as an alien or aliens *of* an alienworld and alien community. The alien as anomalous is also the alien as *abnormal* in the sense of bearing an alien normativity and generative density that is not my own. Explaining that members of an alienworld have different experiences, different natural surroundings, life goals, convictions, habitualities, practical modes of comportment, traditions, etc., Husserl remarks that they have an alien cultural world "as valid for them, not for us" (H XV 214).

The distinction that Husserl draws between the recognition of a cultural difference that has the integrity of a normal tradition, but is not all the same *experienced by us as normal for us*, is extremely important. It suggests that the alienworld is normatively different, that is, an alien *home*-world. Calling the alienworld [*Fremdwelt*] an alien homeworld [*fremde Heimwelt*] means that the incomprehensibility of the alien and the rupture of normality instigated by the alien do not remain on an initial level of anomalous incomprehensibility, but reaches deeper into an incomprehensibility that has the integrity of another normativity, one that cannot be overcome through a simple appropriation. To be sure, the alienworld is recognized as typical *in some way*, that is, in an alien typicality, as having a certain concordance, as having the generative density of a tradition, but in such a way that it does not have sense for us like it apparently has for the members of an alienworld. Realizing that there is a different world with its own style as an alien "homeworld" does not mean that it can simply be colonized as *our world;* the generative depth of the alienworld forestalls a transgressive experience that would make us home everywhere we go.

To illustrate the generative depth of the alien, Husserl distinguishes between an "authentic" and "inauthentic" alien. By the latter he has in mind unfamiliar things, or animals and plants of an alien territory that might only be recognizable in terms of their regional types: for example, for Americans, a bidet (inanimate object), a tapir (psychophysical being), a eucalyptus tree (organic being) (cf. H XV 432). But included here would also have to be the momentary, or genetically developed alien, abstracted from its generative dimension; it is merely surprising as a rupture in my or our normal experience. By contrast, the proper sense of alien concerns an intrinsic *historical* and *historicizing* dimension that is not peculiar to a bidet, a tapir, a eucalyptus tree, or even the human subject regarded solely in terms of factical self-temporalization. Because this *historical* dimension is essential to the proper sense of alien, Husserl calls the latter the "mythical alien."

By calling an alien mythical, Husserl does not mean that its alienness is invented; rather, he wishes to evoke an alien as having a foreign cultural or historical density. My encounter with an individual alien is simultaneously an encounter with a dense and momentous tradition that is articulated through, for example, myth, narrative, world-stories, etc. It is a dimension that we cannot simply overcome as we would a disappointment or surprise.[11]

When we encounter an alien, we encounter the depth of alien people, an alien tradition, alien world-stories that structure their experiences and worldviews; we encounter "generatively alien humanities," aliens who are structured as alien by virtue of their stamm, being for us *fremdstämmisch.*[12] Likewise, we do not get to know alien people through intropathy or through mere genetic apperception; generatively speaking, we have to get to know their homeworld as alienworld for us; "I would have 'to grow up in' it like a child in the world of adults, finally come to understand [their] history."[13] Accordingly, the alienness of the alien does not come from a structural weakness in the constitution of a homeworld, as if appropriation could take place without delimitation; nor is alienness the result of an intentional implication of sense (as purported in Husserl's "second way"); nor finally is the alienness of the alien due to a mere rupture in our normal experience, no matter how long it may last. Rather, alienness arises *from the generative depth of the alien.* It is precisely generativity that calls a coincidence or synthesis of home and alien into question. But the same generativity that calls a synthesis into question is also the same generative difference through which we are together and encounter one another. This is a generativity to which phenomenology must be sensitive.

At times, Husserl is profoundly sensitive to the irreducibility of homeworld/alienworld through generativity in very provocative formulations. Perhaps one of the most provocative formulations ensues from his analysis of alienness in terms of *inaccessibility.* Husserl often characterizes the homeworld as that which is "accessible" by virtue of its familiarity, its comprehensibility, its geological nearness, and its practical possibilities for comportment. In general, for Husserl, the homeworld is accessible to us in the mode of accessibility.

When inquiring into our mode of experience of the alienworld Husserl also describes it phenomenologically in terms of modes of "accessibility." This is why I mentioned above that to regard the alien *qua* alien as completely external to any sort of encounter would be an impossibility. Waldenfels keenly writes, for example, that if we would understand the alien as constituted merely from within the alien (i.e., as outside of any contact with the home), the latter would remain simply presupposed and not clarified as alien. "Something that were entirely 'alien to experience' ([H] XVII, 240) would not only be an absurdity, it would virtually lose its character of alienness, since there would be nothing from which it could escape. It would simply be there and would lose its offensiveness, its 'punch', like the surprise that becomes the rule."[14]

That the alienworld is somehow "accessible" does not mean that it is experienced in the mode of accessibility. For what prevents alienness from becoming accessible to the homeworld like the homeworld is to itself is both of their respective generative densities. Phenomenologically, we are asking not *what* the alienworld is, not whether it exists; we do not even ask *whether* the alienworld is accessible; rather, we inquire into the *modes* of accessibility, *how* it is accessible. We can read Husserl's following description as a response to such an inquiry. Husserl writes that "normally, we live in our homeworld," in an environing-world that is the familiar world for us. "In mediate horizons there are heterogeneous [*fremdartigen*] humanities and cultures; they belong to them as alien and heterogeneous, *but alienness means accessibility in genuine inaccessibility, in the mode of incomprehensibility*" (my emphasis).[15]

What does Husserl mean by this curious and enigmatic formulation that alienness is accessible in inaccessibility, in the mode of incomprehensibility? How is the alienworld both accessible yet inaccessible and incomprehensible? As mentioned earlier, the structure homeworld/alienworld is such that the alien is not simply barred from the home as if the home were closed off, having no doors or no windows. When one asks *how* the alienworld is accessible or given, the phenomenological reply is in the *mode* of inaccessibility, that is, in a modality different from the way in which the home is accessible to itself. What Husserl suggests here is that in order for the alien to be alien, the alien is somehow *encountered* without it becoming homogeneous with the home or typified according to the home; it is experienced in an encounter precisely *as* alien or *as* heterogeneous. Again, the alien is genuinely alien as a mythical alien, as a generative alien, as an alien of an alien stamm.

Through the mutual co-generation of home and alien, the alienworld is accessible to the home, but accessible precisely *as inaccessible:* The home remains in relation to the alien by experiencing the inaccessibility and integrity of the limits of the alien. Accordingly, an encounter with an alienworld is not an abstraction from its cultural integrity or generative historicity, but as a world accepted by an alienworld, as normal for them and *as not normal, not home for us*. Viewed from the other side of this co-constitutive movement, rather than losing the home in the encounter, we gain the home *as* home, as constituted for us in a more intimate mode of accessibility. To bring the important text once more to our attention, Husserl contends that "[t]here is constituted an alien humankind, an alien humanity, an alien people, for instance. *Precisely thereby* there is constituted for me and for us '*our own*' community of homecomrades, community of a people in relation to our cultural environing-world as the world of our human validities, our particular ones."[16] As a result of this understanding it is possible to make two points regarding the encounter of our homeworld with an alienworld. First, we understand an alienworld not by reducing it to ours, but by understanding it *as* ultimately *incomprehensible in its generativity*. Such an incomprehensibility is more profound than the "initial" incomprehensibility mentioned above. Second, we come to understand our own homeworld by understanding an alienworld in its incomprehensibility or generativity. This establishes what Husserl refers to as a generative bond (H XV 219). Let me clarify these points by explaining how the homeworld and alienworld are in constant transformation through their liminal encounters.

I noted in chapter 13 that there are various kinds of normality and abnormality within the homeworld itself. These levels of normality and abnormality indicate that even for the homecomrades, the homeworld is not fully accessible. Not only is there an inter-worldly inaccessibility, but also an intra-worldly and even intra-subjective inaccessibility and incomprehensibility. Our genetic and generative pasts can also be alien to us in various degrees and not entirely accessible; from my own birth and childhood, to our home ancestors, a type of *alienness permeates home* experience.

One reason why we can be alien to ourselves concerns our own generative past that extends before us and after us through the generations of a homeworld and that we bring to bear in our habitualities and acts. Another reason concerns the very co-generative structure of home/alien. Adapting Waldenfels's formulation and insight in the direction of this work, let me state that since the home only opens up as home from the liminal encounter with the alien, alienness must intrude into the very experience peculiar to the home; just as the perception of temporality implies for Husserl the becoming temporal of perception (H X 22), so too does the experience of the alien imply the becoming alien of home experience.[17]

And Husserl says as much. Not only do we become *other* through the "others" *of our own tradition*,[18] but our own home community and homeworld is co-constituted through a transgressive encounter with the alienworld such that the homeworld itself is transformed in and through the transgressive encounter: "Thus, when I understand this *quasi* or actually genetically [*sic*]-historically, I have *a transformation of my and of our world-experience and [a transformation] of the world itself*" (my emphasis).[19] Through liminal encounters with the alienworld, the typicality of the homeworld itself is transformed, without, however, losing its character as homeworld. Precisely as homeworld, it becomes what it is through liminal encounters.

Again Husserl emphasizes this point:

> The content of the homeworld . . . becomes transformed; new objects emerge newly from the passivity or activity of those experiencing . . . they become known through experience and remain for a time, others disappear, become transformed. *In this way the concrete type of the homeworld* is also transformed in its temporary character. But this mode of transformation *itself belongs to the general type of the being of the homeworld.* (H XV 222, my emphasis)

Generatively understood, the liminal transgressive encounter of the alienworld by the home is simultaneously a co-constitution of the home as home in relation to an alienworld, which is to say, there is a *becoming alien of the home.*[20]

This becoming alien of the home is one way in which the home is never fully accessible to itself. It also expresses a unity of home and alien through their difference, a unity that does not depend upon a resolution in a higher synthesis. Structurally, the homeworld is not "finite"—a misleading expression Husserl uses at times—that implies that it can extend to "infinity"; rather, it is *"delimited"* from the alienworld in order to become homeworld. The home still remains home, and the alien alien, even though the home is transformed in the encounter. Through the liminal transgressive encounter with the alien, homecomrades realize their *own* possibilities. Because home and alien become what they are through appropriative and transgressive encounters co-generatively, the generative structure home/alien is *irreducible.* As Husserl himself is willing to admit at times, there is really no such thing as an all-encompassing homeworld. For it would lose its character of being a homeworld with the advent of the one world.

Why do we see such an ambiguity in Husserl's descriptions of homeworld and alienworld? I maintain that when home and alien is described in a permanent co-relativity, he is addressing their delimitation; when he moves to the level of the one world, he presupposes the homeworld as finite, and thus as able to expand to infinity (cf. H XV 235). But these two approaches are profoundly different with quite different consequences.

I have spoken of homeworld/alienworld as an irreducible structure. This does not mean that such a structure is a-historical or that it rules out the transformation of the content of the homeworld and alienworld. It is a structure that is becoming what it is historically and intersubjectively in the very clarification of its structure, from narrative to historical critique.

Certainly we face attempts to overcome alienness: One can attempt to destroy an alien people by mass genocide, by displacing them from their earth-ground or home-land, by cultural domination, etc. But for all that, one would never gain total access to the alien generativity. Were the homeworld to overcome alienness, the homeworld would no longer be a homeworld since it would cease to be what it is as co-relative to and co-generative with an alienworld. Instead, there would be a destruction of *the entire structure* homeworld/alienworld. This means further that the inaccessibility of the alien that is delimited through the home would remain inaccessible precisely through the destruction of the alien. In this sense the structure homeworld/alienworld is irreducible, and overcoming this structure a generative impossibility. Only by abstracting from generativity is the prospect of the one world conceivable.

In what sense is homeworld/alienworld ethically irreducible? Is it an ethical imperative to attain "the one world"? The attempt to do this, I suggest, would be the attempt to *overcome generativity*, the very generative force that "ethical conscience" was summoned to renew, not destroy. By making a so-called ethical one world, we would not be renewing generativity but negating it, actually making "our" world unethical. It would be to objectify the alien, to make the alien accessible, reifying the generative force, and the alienworld's generative becoming. This does not mean that we cannot become responsive to alien generativity by being responsible to ours, but it does mean that we cannot ethically take over their responsibility. What prevents this, I argue under the next heading, is the fundamental, axiological asymmetry of homeworld/alienworld that is expressed in an ethical impossibility of taking over the responsibility of the alien.

The Axiological Asymmetry of Homeworld/Alienworld

Throughout this section I have explained the constitution of homeworld/alienworld as a co-constitutive and co-generative relation in the form of a mutual delimitation. The home is co-generated (co-constituted) through a transgressive experience of the alien (which is simultaneously constitutive of the alien), and the alien is co-generated (co-constituted) through an appropriative experience of the home (which is simultaneously constitutive of the home).

The structure of this co-constitution is such that homeworld and alienworld are *co-generative* and do not exist in a one-sided relationship of constitutive foundation. So, for example, the homeworld is not an absolute, independent, necessary foundation of a merely relative, dependent, and contingent alienworld. Thus, the structure homeworld/alienworld is a "non-foundational" one with respect to a one-sided relation of foundation. This structure could only be considered "foundational" in a positive sense if we understand by this term the other meaning of foundation explicated in Husserl's *Logische Untersuchungen*, namely, a mutual or reciprocal relation of foundation, a co-foundation.[21]

It may appear, however, that this co-generation and co-relativity as stated here implies a *reversibility* of home and alien. It might indeed be tempting to apply the same assertions regarding the homeworld *mutatis mutandis* to the alienworld, "as if" it were home. But can we simply attribute the same structure of experience so casually to the alien? Is it simply the case that what holds for the homeworld holds for the alienworld in this manner? I would like to explain here how co-generation does not entail such a reversibility—or positively put, how the structure homeworld/alienworld entails an *axiological asymmetry*. This axiological asymmetry is due to generativity, and is not to a constitutive one-sided relation of foundation. As an introduction to this style of understanding, let me emphasize the important difference between the account of intersubjectivity in the Fifth Meditation and in the co-generative account of homeworld/alienworld. I will discuss this difference along the lines of the reversibility thesis.

It would seem that something like the reversibility of perspectives would comply with a non-foundational (or co-foundational) account of intersubjectivity. For reversibility ostensibly challenges a rigid one-sided structure in which the ego has an a priori foundational privilege over an "other" ego.

Yet we find just the opposite to be the case. If we examine Husserl's own theories of intersubjectivity we find that in the Fifth Meditation, a foundational account, the original sphere of the ego is sustained precisely by the reversibility of perspectives in order to gain an intersubjective nexus for the constitution of objectivity. Put differently, the need and utility of reversibility is *based on* or *presupposes* a foundational sphere. In the final analysis, a foundational account and the reversibility thesis are not only compatible with and require one another, but are of the same mettle.

By contrast, the co-generational structure of homeworld/alienworld cannot abide a reversibility of perspectives. Instead, this generative account is compatible with asymmetry of home and alien. Let me explain.

As opposed to "occupation" [*Besetzung*], which pushes out, narrows in, or alters limits in some way, transgression [*Überschreitung*] literally crosses over the limits and thus brings an explicit experience of limits into being.[22] Whereas occupation essentially stays within the limits of the homeworld, keeping the experience of limits implicit by "fulfilling" empty horizons (H XV 232, 236, 429), transgression expresses the liminal character of experience—and thus the limits of experience—by going beyond them.

If we were to examine transgressive experience *abstractly*, we might conclude that it is a process of crossing over that "leaves home." In other words, transgression would be an encounter with the alien that simply abandons the conditions or the limits of the home for the encounter. As opposed to an occupation that remains "within," it would simply cross over. But generatively considered, transgressive experience does not leave home in going beyond; it is a *crossing over from within*.

Crossing over from within means both that we encounter the alien from the integrity of who we are as home, and that the integrity of the alien keeps us at bay; it means that we are insuperably *of* a generative density and momentum, and that the alien brings to bear a generativity that engages us in the encounter. Crossing over from within is a different way of saying that we experience the alien *as* inaccessible, or that the mode of accessibility of the alien is inaccessibility. Thus, even though factually an alien may come to us, say, by entering our home (H XV 205), even though we may encounter the alien through stories told of travels (H XV 437) or by "going outward," traveling to a distant land, a transgressive encounter phenomenologically understood is always one that encounters the alien by crossing over from within. To be otherwise would demand the presumptuous and even patronizing position of *taking the perspective of the alien.* However, feigning the perspective of the alien by the home is precisely what is excluded by the co-generative structure, homeworld/alienworld, as well as by the ethical imperative of critique.

Husserl seems to be sensitive to this process by continually describing the experience of the homeworld and alienworld as a going out from our (or my) perspective: *von uns aus* or *von mir aus* (cf. H XV Text 14, Text 36). World experience, writes Husserl, has the peculiar structure of being oriented *from our situation,* not merely in a spatial fashion, but historically and intersubjectively (H XV 220). This understanding carries with it the insight that I or we cannot experience the alien experiences, that they are not merely accessible to the home or the ego, and that we encounter the alien *from a distance.* The difficulty in Husserl's exposition, as I intimated, is that he tends to compromise this insight by either assuming an "immediate" accessibility of the home by the home, or he restricts encounter to a process of appropriative experience, and then reasons from here at times to a totalizing view.

But certainly, if there is a becoming alien of the home in appropriative and transgressive encounters, then even the "position" from which we encounter the alien is not a fixed and immutable launching point for an encounter. The "position" from which one encounters the alien is in the process of being formulated as a position in the process of the encounter: "This type of transformation itself belongs to the general type of being of the homeworld."[23]

Husserl's occasional slippage should not prevent us from working out the implications of appropriative and transgressive encounters. Taking a step in this direction, let me distinguish transgression from violence. The reason foundational accounts of intersubjectivity and the reversibility of perspectives are compatible is due to the fact that they are two aspects of the same form of violence. According to the view propounded here, transgression is a process of crossing over the limits of the home, encountering the alien, from within the *limits* of the home (even if we go outside the physical strictures of a "home"). Transgressive encounter is essentially responsive to "limit-claims." Violence, by contrast, consists in various ways of denying or occluding "limit-claims."

I use the expression "limit-claims" as a modification of Waldenfels's suggestion of two different types of comportment toward limits: attentiveness to limits [*Grenzachtung*] and injury of limits [*Grenzverletztung*].[24] Strictly speaking, however, limits are neither respected nor injured, only implicit or explicit limit-*claims* by persons peculiar to an intersubjective or interpersonal encounter can be respected or injured.[25]

Violence (in Latin, *violentia*) is literally the violation of limit-claims. The violation of limit-claims can take place in two ways, both of which attempt to make inaccessibility accessible.

The first of these is familiar to us under the rubric of a hierarchical domination. The latter is violent as injurious to limit-claims because it denies the uniqueness of the alien and attempts to subsume the alien under the rule of the "first." It reifies limits by making an axiological asymmetry merely a one-sided relation in which the "first" is *not* responsible for or responsive to the alien in the mode of inaccessibility. An obvious example of this is the fascist relation or what Adorno and many members of the "Frankfurt School" have analyzed as the "authoritarian personality."[26] It is not only observed in modes of totalitarianism such as National Socialism or communism, but also in myriad forms of patriarchy in which women are viewed as essentially *accessible* to men. It can also be seen in colonization and missionary work as in the case of the American missionaries' conversion of the Yaquí Indians of Bolivia, and again in the denial of an alienworld's customs and language as in the case of China's rapport with Tibet.

In this first type of violation of limit-claims not only are the limit-claims of the alien violated, but also those of the home. This is more than saying something on the order of "the aggressor gets hurt too." Rather, the violation occurs because the home is not responded to critically in its limitedness and uniqueness peculiar to its own generativity. That is, it assumes that one's own generativity is purely or immediately accessible. But the violation goes still further. The negation of limit-claims of the alien is simultaneously the negation of limit-claims of the home—whether implicit or explicit and with different import and consequence depending on whether it is home or alien—*because the entire intersubjective and interpersonal structure, home/alien, is violated.* It is essentially a breach of responsiveness to the interpersonal process of co-generation, or put differently, to existence that becomes in and through their co-generative structure.

In another work I have articulated the inner machinations of this type of violence of limit-claims as a "logic of dissimulation."[27] It is a logic of dissimulation because it seeks to conceal the responsiveness endemic to a liminal encounter and to dominate it in a one-sided reification of liminal experience in which it is the alien who is made one-sidedly responsible for and accessible to the "first."

Undertaken as an effort to challenge this type of domination and violence is the contemporary pursuit of the *reversibility* and *symmetry* of perspectives. This is the attempt to erase the limits that are perceived as responsible for hierarchical domination and one-sidedness. It attempts to integrate those who have been "limited-off" or excluded by a "privileged perspective," and to remove potentially harmful distinctions pertaining to an "in-group" and an "out-group," an "inside" and an "outside." Limits themselves are ostensibly razed in an effort to create a nondominating, nonintimidating, nonhierarchical, noncompetitive, equal, interchangeable, in short a so-called non-limiting situation. This has been enacted in social movements, political affinity groups, educational settings, therapy meetings, and in the general attitude of "immediate intimacy"; it is an attitude that edges toward a world *sans frontières.* As a result, we no longer speak today in "politically correct" circles of "foreigners" or "aliens," but of "internationals," a style of speech that indeed suggests that home and alien are interchangeable! Our conviction in such practices are premised on the viability of the *reversibility of perspectives* where home and alien are essentially interchangeable, even if only in the form of a quasi-positional "as if."

The theoretical voice of the reversibility of perspectives can be found, in differing form and content, in Georg Simmel who maintained that society is the sum of the reciprocal effects of its members,[28] in Leopold von Wiese's "doctrine of relation" [*Beziehunglehre*],[29] in Theodor Litt who understood the reciprocity of perspectives as the primordial phenomenon of society,[30] in Howard Becker's *Man in Reciprocity*,[31] and in Bronislaw Malinowski, understanding reciprocity as the basis of the social structure.[32] Particularly relevant expressions of the reversibility thesis also include George Herbert Mead's "taking the role of the other"[33] and the reciprocity of perspectives in Schutz.

Discussing the similarities and differences of these theories as well as their peculiar utilization in contemporary social pragmatics is beyond the scope of this work. Let it suffice to note that among these theories, Schutz's is the most cogent. For it is Schutz who works out how the differences in individual perspectives can be overcome by two "pragmatically motivated fundamental constructions" or idealizations of everyday knowledge: the idealization of the interchangeability of standpoints, and the idealization of the congruence of systems of relevances.[34]

How limit-claims are violated in the first version presented above is obvious, how in the latter, not so clear. The reason it is not clear in this latter case is due to its logic that operates by logic of "self-dissimulation."[35] The reversibility of perspectives is self-dissimulating because it conceals limits by dissimulating its dissimulation of limits. To express this in other terms, the reversibility thesis is effective by ostensibly overcoming the limits that it interprets as being responsible for a dominating relationship. What goes unnoticed, however, is that this is actually a more insidious violation of limit-claims.

If we interpret the assumptions behind the reversibility of perspectives we find that it too violates limit-claims because it presupposes that home and alien are now interchangeable and mutually accessible, that is, symmetrically accessible to the same degree. It too operates by a twofold violation: First, it denies the generative dimension of the home in its phenomenologically privileged status as our world; second, it violates the limit-claims of the alien whose generative density resists such an assumption of mutual accessibility. Whereas in the traditional form of domination the limits are reified and made determinate in a one-sided relation of accessibility to the alien, in the latter the limits are made fully indeterminate to the point of no longer being taken seriously as limit-claims; as a result, the responsibility is made equal and interchangeable. This, however, presupposes in another form that we are able to speak from the perspective of the alien and for the alien; it presupposes that the alien is accessible to us in the same way that we are to ourselves. To treat the home as interchangeable with the alien would be to presuppose that the alien is at my disposal, accessible in the mode of accessibility. It would depreciate the personal and generative inaccessibility of the alien, an alien that is inaccessible precisely because it is *in relation to us at a distance of generativity*. This accounts for the simple fact that an American ethnology of the Japanese culture does not coincide with a Japanese ethnology of the American culture.[36]

But if the co-generative structure of homeworld/alienworld has an axiological asymmetry, we would have to refigure the logic of responsibility. When asked whether the Other [*l'Autrui*] was not also, in turn, responsible for me, Levinas responds in a well-known interview with Philippe Nemo, "perhaps, but that is *his* affair." He continues to explain that because the intersubjective relation is non-symmetrical, I am responsible for the Other without anticipating or attributing to the Other a reciprocal responsibility, even if it costs me my life.[37] This means in effect, following Levinas, that we who are home are responsible asymmetrically toward the alien and for ourselves in our unique way without being able to contest that this responsibility hold equally for the alien or to enforce the same type of response.

As opposed to Kant's autonomy of the will, we have a radical heteronomy; as opposed to morality as founded in the interiority of reason, we have morality as based in exteriority, in the inaccessibility of and responsibility toward the alien. This asymmetrical responsibility toward the alien, however, means more than a mere responsibility for the alien. For the latter is simultaneously a responsibility for the moral generative becoming of the entire co-generative structure, home/alien, *von uns aus*, from the home, such that the alien cannot replace us in this responsibility.

The proposition that community is created or enhanced through the reversibility of perspectives or by "taking the place of the other" is not only a proposition of a certain type of violence, but futile and naive at best. It is *futile* because the generativity of home and alien is not interchangeable. To presuppose that a situation is reversible would be to abstract from the generative and even genetic dimensions of the home and alien, and to posit them in a theoretical and atomistic "*simple location*," to speak with Whitehead.[38] To make home and alien reversible through a spurious exchange of perspectives, one would have to take oneself out of the structure home/alien, positing oneself above it and all generativity, in order then to say that one is like the other, that the alien is like the home, the home like the alien. Yet every comparison of this sort already *presupposes an incomparable or asymmetrical situation*; even if comparisons are made, they are done so as a possible response to the *asymmetry* of home and alien.[39]

The reversibility of perspectives presupposes, then, not only that our own personal or historical past is accessible to us, but also that the generative dimension of the alien is accessible, and accessible in the same way. To raise a poignant question from contemporary practices, do we really "experience homelessness" or understand the homeless by supposedly "becoming like the homeless" as so many newscasters, politicians, and social advocates are wont to do? Instead, should we not begin to understand the implications of *encounter* through an insuperable asymmetry whose irreversibility cannot be mitigated by taking the place of the other?

The attitude of reversibility is *naive* because it fails to recognize that through appropriative and transgressive liminal experiences we are already in an *encounter* situation through co-generativity as a delimitation of home and alien. It forgets that we, as home, are *already becoming alien* through liminal encounters without having to take on "foreign qualities." One does not have to try to become alien, because we are already becoming alien by encountering the alien at a distance, transgressing from within. Because there is an ongoing unity of co-participation in a structure that takes place through the liminal encounters themselves, the need to convert, to expand to the one world, or to self-surrender already takes place after the fact of a unity through generative difference by being home in relation to an alien at a distance. Because it does violence to the limit-claims of the structure homeworld/alienworld, that is, ultimately to the dimension of generativity, the attempt to establish the one world is in the final analysis unethical.

Critique and Responsivity

Let me conclude this chapter with a brief outline of an active responsible co-participation in the irreducible and asymmetrical structure of homeworld/alienworld from the perspective of the homeworld. This is an effort to describe how the unity of home/alien is effected asymmetrically through the co-generative difference of homeworld and alienworld without reaching for an all-encompassing one world. Responsibility for an irreducible and asymmetrical unity of homeworld and alienworld can be found in liminal appropriative and transgressive encounters as *critical* and *responsive* modes of comportment.

Not every encounter yields the same transformations of homeworld and alienworld, and the liminal encounters of appropriation and transgression are not pure or harmless. In fact, because the appropriative and transgressive experiences are *liminal* encounters, there is always a dimension of conflict or encroachment. The point of actively realizing unity, however, is not to rid ourselves of conflict or encroachment, to deny the existence of limit-claims, to eradicate being at a distance, or to approach home and alien through the reversibility of perspectives: These practices only obfuscate the problem of unity and the problem of domination. The point, rather, is to work creatively within these conflicts and encroachments of liminal experiences.[40]

Two ways of doing this are suggested by appropriative and transgressive liminal encounters. The first concerns the process of appropriation and the co-constitution of the homeworld. We have seen in chapter 12 how the responsible constitution of the homeworld is tied to "the problem of *critique* of a homeworld in the horizon of alien homeworlds." We have also understood the attitude of critique as a way in which homecomrades critically comport themselves to their own process of appropriation. It may entail rejecting certain presuppositions of a homeworld, its values and demands; it may entail the renewal of a homeworld's norms, revitalizing and renewing its internal sense; it may even demand going against the prevalent normality, replacing old norms with a new ethical normality in an attempt to realize the homeworld more fully. In any case, the main import of critique would be to deepen the homeworld *as* homeworld in its liminal encounters with an alienworld, and to succor the constant transformations of the homeworld. Thus critique is a way taking a critical attitude toward the process of appropriation.

Exercising critique of the homeworld by the homeworld is one way in which a liminal encounter of appropriation does not become just another form of violence. Nevertheless, it is not an independent mode. To be sure, critique is positive insofar as it is concerned with the becoming of the homeworld. But it only makes sense as critique by being co-relative to the comportment toward the alien. In fact, critique for Husserl is instigated in and through encounters with the alien.[41] This co-relative mode of responsive comportment, which also serves as a motivation for critique of the home, is *being responsive toward* the alien.

We have already encountered some traces of the structure of this responsivity in section 3 concerning the notion of affectivity and affective pull coming from the "matter itself," and in chapter 12 concerning expressive communication as being addressed and taking up the address. Here I would like to understand this responsivity on a more personal level as responsive intersubjective comportment, that is, as the process of co-participation that gives rise to a unity of home and alien through their generative difference.[42]

Husserl gives us a clue here. He contends that in being addressed and in the appropriation of the address, the ego and the alien come to a first unity (H XV 476). Co-participation in the generative structure and the creation of unity do not lie in creating an overarching synthesis, but *in responding to the alien from the perspective of the home.* Such a responsivity is a way in which the transgressive encounter unfolds in a non-symmetrical affinity. Following Levinas and Waldenfels, the alien is accessible as that toward which we respond and have responded. But because we respond to the alien in its inaccessibility, and because the limit-claims come from the dimension of its inaccessibility, the limit-*claims* can never be completely fulfilled or satisfied.[43]

I mentioned that critique is co-relative to responsivity because critique and responsivity by themselves would have no meaning. Through critique, the homeworld is developed as homeworld in relation to an alienworld; accordingly, critique is a way in which the alienworld becomes alien and functions as an implicit way of responding to the alien.

On the other hand, responsivity is a comportment toward the alien that exists with the home in an ineluctable asymmetry. Being responsive to the alien is a participation with the alien *as* alien in its generative depth. Or put differently, our mode of accessibility to the alien as inaccessible is expressed in a transgressive liminal encounter as being responsive toward. Being responsive is an asymmetrical mode of comportment; it expresses the fact that the sense of the alien is not something I merely initiate or is merely an implied intentional sense. I respond from the home toward that which does not simply originate from the home. In being responsive, I go toward that which comes from without—the alien—from within. Being responsive, in turn, is implicitly becoming critical of the home. It is a becoming critical of the home because the home is in a relationship of encounter with the uniqueness and inaccessible depth of the alien. In this way, critique and responsivity are co-generative and co-relative in a relationship of participation that is asymmetrical.

Working out the direct social and political implications of this asymmetry and co-generativity, of critique and responsivity, is beyond the scope of this work and will have to be reserved for a future project. For the purposes of this study, I would like to formulate the consequences and import of a generative phenomenological method. This will be the task of the concluding chapter.

15

Conclusion: Generative Phenomenology

Maurice Merleau-Ponty's preface to the *Phénoménologie de la perception* is an eloquent testimony to the unfinished nature of phenomenology and to the inchoative demeanor distinctive of Husserl's works. At the time of Merleau-Ponty's work, the most dynamic tenets of phenomenology were purported to be a "genetic methodology," the problem of genesis or temporalization, and the concept of the "lifeworld." These novel discoveries seemed to lie at the outermost reaches of phenomenology and were heralded as the vanguard of phenomenology's new direction, nuancing if not recasting the meaning of Husserl's philosophical efforts.

What we have seen in this final section is the evocation of still different matters, *generative* matters that go beyond genesis and more specifically the structure of the homeworld and alienworld that goes beyond the concept of the lifeworld. Let me now regard as leading clues the matters and method of a genetic phenomenology, and let me take the generative matters discussed in the last division as leading clues to the formulation of a "generative phenomenology." Let me emphasize that Husserl himself does not explicitly formulate a dimension of phenomenology *as* generative. But on the basis of the wide rage of texts that discuss "generative problems," problems or matters that we have encountered in this last section, I believe the formulation of this dimension as generative phenomenology is not only justified, but called for.

The generative dimension of phenomenology will not be found by tallying the number of times Husserl uses the expression "generative," pervasive and plentiful as they are, nor will it be evoked by scrutinizing the order of exposition of Husserl's texts. For one set of problems often became apparent to Husserl while working out others, and one avenue of approach often lingered years before receiving direct attention.

Generative phenomenology will open up by following out, interpretatively, "leading clues" that function both as guiding insights and detours, eliciting the various tensions that a style of thought that is still in the process of being formulated—as it has been said—is sure to generate. Moreover, the project of a generative phenomenology transcends the particular philosopher, Edmund Husserl. Let me explain these two qualifications under the following headings. I will first take up the generation of phenomenology and will conclude this work with a discussion on the relation of phenomenology to generativity.

The Generation of Phenomenology

Generativity concerns historical and intersubjective becoming, and in particular the becoming of the diverse co-generative, liminal, and asymmetrical structure, home/alien. How does a philosopher renowned for his assiduous attention to consciousness, egological subjectivity, and punctual presence anticipate a method for handling intersubjective and historical movement? Let me approach this question in terms of the possible historical influences on Husserl, and with respect to the problem of generativity within phenomenology.

I do not think that it would be wrong-headed to seek Husserl's engagement with generativity and generative problems in motivations that lie outside the internal development of Husserl's own work as it was developed prior to the 1930s. In many ways such influences would be consistent with the notion of generativity. After all, Husserl never considered phenomenology to be an undertaking accomplished by a single thinker. As he himself cautioned again and again, phenomenology is a communal enterprise that is learned not merely by studying it, but by actively taking it up. For Husserl, phenomenology as a scientific enterprise consisted in an ongoing historical project in which one participated.

It is well known that Heidegger was Husserl's close assistant from 1919 to 1922, and that even after disappointed attempts at collaboration, Husserl still regarded Heidegger as the only qualified successor to his chair in Freiburg (in 1928).[1] Moreover, because the majority of Husserl's writings on generative themes occur around the years 1930 and following, and because Heidegger's new philosophical perspective was so appealing to many of Husserl's own students, it would not be surprising to cite Heidegger, following the publication of his *Sein und Zeit*, as a motivating factor in Husserl's reflections on the problem of historicity.[2] In fact, in the summer of 1929, Husserl devoted a two-month study to *Sein und Zeit* as well as to some of Heidegger's more recent writings in order to come to grips with Heidegger's philosophy.[3] Particularly relevant here are the occurrences of the expressions "generation" [*Generation*] and "historicity" [*Geschichtlichkeit*] that are found in the second chapter of the second division of Heidegger's *Sein und Zeit.*[4] Given this association, esteem, and even a possible rivalry as a backdrop, it has become almost commonplace to link themes found, for example, in Husserl's *Krisis 1* (which dealt with notions like the lifeworld and history) to Heidegger's monumental work.

But if we are seeking so-called external historical influences on Husserl in this regard, then a much more likely source would be Dilthey.[5] One clue in this direction is Heidegger himself. For precisely at the places where Heidegger uses generation and historicity, Heidegger himself refers to Dilthey.[6]

Certainly, Husserl knew and respected Dilthey long before Heidegger's appropriation of the latter's work. Indeed, a relationship between the two thinkers was already established in the first decade of the twentieth century and became particularly poignant on the touchy question of historicism. A lively and revealing exchange was provoked by Husserl's famous "*Logos*" article from 1911, "Philosophie als strenge Wissenschaft."[7]

Not only was Husserl indirectly occupied with Dilthey in the 1920s through his own students (for example, Landgrebe who received his doctorate under Husserl for a thesis entitled "Wilhelm Diltheys Theorie der Geisteswissenschaften" in 1927),[8] or through Dilthey's students (for example, Georg Misch's *Lebensphilosophie und Phänomenologie* from 1929),[9] but—if Husserl's acquisition of volumes 5 and 6 of Dilthey's *Nachlaß* in July 1924 are any indication—Husserl continued to be occupied directly with Dilthey's work.[10] In particular, we find similar themes occurring in a generative phenomenology that are peculiar to Dilthey, especially the question of historicity and the historico-spiritual movement of intersubjective accomplishments evaluated in terms of the temporal-space [*Zeitraum*] of generations.

The points of convergence between Dilthey and Husserl are simply too vast to be covered in this work.[11] My point in these concluding remarks is simply that in seeking the development of the problem of generativity in Husserl, one should not underestimate the influence that both Dilthey and Heidegger did exert or could have exerted on Husserl's thought by the 1930s.

Be that as it may, it would be misleading to look *only* to external sources for the generation of generative themes in Husserl's reflections.

More precisely, I want to maintain in what follows that the dimension of a generative phenomenology is generated as part of the *self-explication of phenomenology itself.*[12] This disclosure has to do with the style of phenomenological reflection that Husserl instigated.

To the best of my knowledge, neither Dilthey nor Heidegger ever use the expressions "*generativ*" or "*Generativität*," and the theory of constitution as the reconstitution of normatively significant *homeworlds and alienworlds* appears quite unique to Husserl's theory of intersubjectivity. As we have seen, generative notions like home, homeworld, and alienworld can already be found in Husserl's writings around 1920. It was also during this period (1922–24) that Husserl wrote explicitly on the becoming of historically intersubjective phenomena in the Japanese periodical *The Kaizo.* I mention these occurrences to illustrate that while Husserl was concerned with social and historical questions, he did not pursue them methodically because, in his view, phenomenology was not ready for these problems methodologically.

To be sure, Dilthey did analyze ontological categories of society that effect our concrete understanding, as well as the actual structural differences obtaining between generations and life. For Dilthey, one must perform a hermeneutical operation on objectifications of life, a process of "understanding" in which living human historical experience is grasped. But the crucial point at which Husserl's method diverges from Dilthey's hermeneutics is that juncture where the social structures are still presupposed in the interpretation. That is, Dilthey does not inquire into *how* these social and historical structures take on sense or how they are themselves generated. Put still differently, although according to Dilthey the human being does not have a fixed nature and is in the process of becoming historically, the philosopher of the *Geisteswissenschaften* does not investigate the *structure of this becoming* or the *becoming of this structure.*

By contrast, the task of a generative phenomenology is precisely to inquire after how historical and intersubjective structures themselves become meaningful at all, how these structures are and can be generated. Accordingly, not only the past and present dimensions are invoked here, but the future too becomes a "matter" of generative phenomenology.

Having made these initial gestures toward the generation of method, let me advance more explicitly to the generation of phenomenology within phenomenology. The problem of generativity did not arise willy-nilly, as just one phenomenological matter among others. It grew as an historical response to a cultural crisis in a broad sense, not merely a crisis of reason and science, but ultimately of an ethical community. This is to say, generative matters issued from a response to the failure of previous philosophical *and* phenomenological attempts to address a crisis in reason, social violence, and systemic cultural degeneration that could not be responded to by a philosophy of consciousness. What it instigated was nothing less than a series of shifts in paradigms for phenomenology.

More precisely a genetic perspective of "primordial" self-temporalization in a mere contemporaneous context could not speak adequately to problems confronting the "deep" temporality of a culture in a perpetual relationship of encounter with alien cultures. Historicity and generations of communal worlds had to be integrated into a constitutive account of the intersubjective nexus. A cultural crisis that touched the heart of an ethical community, as well as the prospects of social and political hegemony, demanded a normative and generational conception of the lifeworld in order to indicate a possible direction of the generation and generative renewal of norms. Because the intersubjective nexus entailed alienness and alien historicity it also required investigating how these lifeworlds were delimited normatively and generationally.

Enabling phenomenology to overcome its aporetic foundational account is the generative framework, articulated in the liminal notions of homeworld and alienworld. It is a structure I have argued that is generatively and ethically irreducible and is axiologically asymmetrical, essentially calling into question our attempts to feign a universalist perspective on generativity. In the final analysis, historical critique and responsivity from the perspective of the homeworld become the responsible phenomenological posture for participating in the generative structure of homeworld/alienworld.

Explaining more methodically the generation of generative phenomenology entails examining the matters and methods of phenomenology that I explicated above: static, genetic, and generative dimensions. Having already described the relation between static and genetic matters and methods in the first three sections of this work, it remains to describe the relation of leading clue that exists between genetic and generative methods.

Following Husserl's understanding of leading clue as the relation of motivation obtaining between methods and matters, we could say that genetic phenomenology functions as a *leading clue* for generative phenomenology. We find at least three similarities that hold for genetic and generative dimensions that held for static and genetic ones, and one important difference.

First, just as Husserl treated genetic problems sometimes years prior to calling them genetic in their proper sense, or expounding upon a genetic as distinct from a static phenomenology, so, too, Husserl took up generative problems such as homeworld and alienworld, birth and death, sense-constitution through appropriation, social ethics, etc., while still working within the context of a genetic analysis and burgeoning distinction between static and genetic phenomenologies. Second, just as the structure of essence, type, etc., as well as static constitution become the leading clues for genesis, so too does genesis itself become an open structure as a leading clue for generativity. Third, just as static and genetic phenomena stand in a relation of the simple to the complex, so too does Husserl intimate (initially) that genetic and generative phenomena exist in a relation of the simple to the complex: The individual genesis must be worked out prior to intersubjective becoming or generation, self-temporalization and monadic facticity prior to communal historicity, the constitution of the unity of a life prior to the constitution of the unity of a tradition.

Finally, the relation between genetic and generative analyses differ in relation to static and genetic methods in one important respect. Whereas static and genetic matters fall under different rubrics, that is, that which is "structural," and that which is "dynamic," genetic and generative phenomena, on the other hand, both come under the rubric of dynamism and temporalization: Genetic method is concerned with self-temporalization or facticity, and generative method with socio-historical temporalization or historicity. In this respect, there seems to be more of an affinity between genetic and generative phenomena—and hence more occasion for their conflation and ambiguity—than between static and genetic ones. Perhaps this is one reason it took Husserl some time to see the essential differences between genetic and generative phenomena.

This latter assertion, namely, that *there is* a difference between genetic and generative (as well as static) matters, should not be immune to closer scrutiny. The comparison I just made between static, genetic, and generative matters and methods provokes two important and interrelated questions. First, just how *distinct* are these phenomena of static, genetic, and generative methods? That is, in what sense are the "things themselves" irreducible and distinct matters peculiar to the methodology? Second, this same question can be posed dynamically. What is the *directionality* of phenomenological method? Does working by leading clues only function in one direction, from static to generative, or does it also move in the other direction, from generative to static?

1. Distinctions of Matters and Methods. Jacques Derrida, in his well-known essay " 'Genèse et structure' et la phénoménologie," lucidly responds to the first question by asserting that for Husserl there are some given matters [*données*] that must be described in terms of structure and others in terms of genesis. For example, there are layers of signification that appear as systems, complexes, and static configurations that must obey the legality proper to and the functional signification of the structure under consideration. Other layers, he continues, are given in the essential mode of creation and movement, of inaugural origin or becoming, requiring one to speak of them in the language of genesis, "supposing that there is one or that there is only one."[13] To this we might also add—in the style of Derrida's explication—that indeed there are other languages of becoming, that there are still other layers that are given or pregiven in the essential mode of social and historical generation, and these require being addressed in the language of "generativity."

What Derrida recognizes in this brief passage cited above is a fundamental phenomenological insight, namely, that the *way* something gives itself corresponds simultaneously to the manner in which we turn to it.[14] For the matters will give themselves, for example, statically through a static methodology. This is why Derrida's expression "there are *some* given matters" [*il y a* des *données*] "that *must*" [*qui* doivent] be described in such and such a manner, is ambiguous: To the extent that the necessity is internal to the "opening toward" the phenomena, the matters "must" be described in one way or another.

But—proceeding from static toward generative as Husserl is initially wont to do—does "necessity" mean that the phenomena given in one way cannot be described any other way? In order to reply to this question, let us first recall that by static method Husserl means two things: An ontology that describes essences, types, structures, etc., as taken for granted, and a constitutive clarification of those meant objects and essences which, nevertheless, does not raise questions respecting the genesis of the essence or of the subject. I mention this distinction because in accessing this necessity, we do not want to conflate a change in attitude from, say, ontology (natural attitude) to constitutive phenomenology (transcendental attitude)—both of which may remain static—with a change in methodology from static to genetic phenomenology.

Let us begin with some examples. When it comes to phenomena like consciousness, I do not see a necessity of restriction. For instance, once consciousness is regarded statically in terms of the structure of intentionality, it can also be regarded genetically as a process of self-temporalization. Or let us take the example of a musical tone. Certainly a tone can be described statically in terms of a structural field of differentiation. Or again, a tone can be examined according to a static constitutional schema as sensation or "hyle." But even here, the tone as hyle in a static schema can also be taken as a temporal matter and—as Derrida rightly puts it—as "the possibility of genesis itself."[15] It would seem then that this matter of static analysis is also amenable to a novel genetic constitutional account in a theory of passive synthesis or "transcendental aesthetic."

Even numbers, insofar as they belong to systems of numbers, seem to avail themselves to the language of "inaugural origin," creation, and movement. Witness, for example, Husserl's efforts in the "Origin of Geometry"; would we not speak the language of genesis or generativity when describing the constitutional transformations in our self-understanding and the development of non-Euclidean geometries or alternative logics?

I do not want to suggest that static analysis cannot have a certain advantage in relation to other methodological approaches, since it can deal with stable laws and structural relations that provide a certain "clarity and distinctness" that we lack in genetic and generative analyses. In Derrida's words a static analysis can provide an analysis of the very "structure" of opening, "structural a priori's" of genesis itself.[16] This structural aspect, along with constitutional considerations, are certainly integral to what Husserl understands by transcendental phenomenology.

Moreover, certain static *qua* mundane disciplines can serve as leading clues for constitutional analyses. For example, psychology could be understood as an empirical science that guides a constitutional genetic account; anthropology (with which Husserl became more and more interested in the 1930s) could serve as a valuable guide for a generative account.[17] Furthermore, the genetic dimension of phenomenology can be understood to make up a distinctive field of research. There is, for example, an irreducible character peculiar to the events of an individual life as experienced by and as the individual. This irreducibility is highlighted by the fact that we can regard the individual infant from a genetic perspective as constitutionally normal and indeed optimalizing, but perhaps quite differently within a generative dimension of constitution.

But my interest goes much further than asserting that peculiar phenomena are opened up through different methods; this would itself be merely a "structural" view. Rather, it bears directly on the possibility of generativity, both in the sense of the phenomenology of generation and the generation of phenomenology. For I am addressing the movement between the methods and matters. Before avowing his own view, Derrida asserts that for Husserl, the movement from the structural analyses of static constitution to analyses of genetic constitution is "nevertheless . . . a simple progress that does *not imply at all a 'surpassing'* . . . and still less an option and especially not repentance. It is an deepening of a work which *leaves intact* that which has been discovered" (my emphasis).[18] Derrida continues in this vein comparing this movement to Husserl's own metaphors of archeology: One excavates genetic foundations and originary productivity *without* destroying or disturbing any of the more superficial structures already exposed.

It is on these points that we would have to challenge the assumptions that Derrida attributes to Husserl about phenomenological method, and maintain instead—in the spirit of much of Derrida's work on Husserl—that in many if not most cases, static structures *are* surpassed through "deeper" genetic analyses, and genetic matters and methods "rattled" or "ruined" by generative ones.

For example, is it not true that through genetic analyses the hyle/morphe distinction peculiar to a static model of constitution is seriously called into question, implying a surpassing by more nuanced descriptions of constitution: the phenomenology of association, the process of habitualization, sedimentation, reactivation, and the fundamental role of horizons in the constitution of sense? Or to cite a familiar example from section 1,[19] is not the "Absolute" that is defined statically as the "being of consciousness" superseded by the so-called "true Absolute," that is, the process of concrete self-temporalization, facticity or the factical monad?

These examples are sufficient to provoke the following considerations. If the progression from static to genetic phenomenology does not "damage" the earlier results as we proceed, then phenomenology can reach closure; it could not be generative. But if the results of the former analyses can be called into question, then phenomenology cannot and must not only proceed in one direction, from static to generative; it can and must also double back on itself, so to speak, in a critical manner, moving from generative to static dimensions. Would this reevaluation in the very progression of phenomenology not also suggest that static method might lose its privileged role for Husserl as the sole leading clue for phenomenology? Would the dual movement from static to generative and generative to static, etc., not open the possibility for phenomenology itself to become generative? Does it not give new meaning to Husserl's promulgation that the phenomenologist is a "perpetual beginner"? These considerations lead me to my second point under this problematic of leading clues.

2. Directionality. We have seen that when Husserl describes genetic phenomena in relation to static ones, the latter are called abstract, whereas the former are deemed concrete. When Husserl begins to describe generative phenomena in the 1930s, we witness a similar strategy in play. Let me recall a text I have already evoked above. Husserl writes:

> The constitution of an abiding co-humanity, of a general sociality referring co-relatively to a practical environing-world, can be treated *abstractly* already *prior to generation*; and, thus, by virtue of the type of temporalization of this practical environing-world as *personally*

> significant, there already exists *an abstract historicity* enclosed within it. If we put into play *generation*, then this progression in terms of *concretion* is also a *concretization* of the remaining co-humanity, mother, i.e., parents and child, etc.; and at the same time we have a *more concrete, generatively* formed temporalization and *historical* environing-world. (my emphasis)[20]

Here, the movement from genetic to generative dimensions is depicted as a removal of abstraction or a "concretization" of matters. Here the concrete matter of phenomenology is not genesis but *generativity*, that is, the matter of phenomenology as emerging generatively.

What methodological assumptions are in play in order for Husserl to describe genetic and generative matters in this way? First, the "simple," that is, the static, can no longer be the concrete because now the putative "simple" is that which is more abstract.[21] Similarly, "generative problems" cannot be understood as belonging to a "higher" dimension presupposing the "lower" spheres.[22] The case now is just the reverse. Notice in this text, for example, that the individual is not described as a foundation for the community, or self-temporalization as foundational for historicity; rather, self-temporalization is portrayed as an abstraction from and hence "presupposing" concrete historicity. But precisely as concrete, it cannot function as a "foundation" upon which other layers are built. Second, and related to the former point, the genetic sphere does not function merely as a leading clue to the generative domain; rather, the generative becomes implicitly a leading clue for genetic phenomena. This is a more specific way of expressing the general possibility for generative phenomenology: The movement is not from the simple to the complex, but from the concrete to the abstract.

In other words, in order to characterize genetic temporalization as "abstract" historicity, Husserl has to be *already* at a generative level of phenomenology, as concrete, when undertaking, say, genetic analyses. This means, further, that even when one is pursuing static analyses, one is already at the farthest reaches of phenomenology; doing static phenomenology means generativity is already there on the horizon and is implicitly qualifying other endeavors in terms of levels of abstraction *from* generativity. Undertaking static analyses is doing generative phenomenology, only abstractly; or put still differently, static analysis is already situated in generativity.

The various methods and matters of phenomenology would be characterized now in the following way: (1) Generative phenomenology whose matter is generativity is the most concrete dimension of phenomenology; it concerns intersubjective, historical movement. (2) Genetic phenomenology treats generativity shorn of its historical/generational dimension. The movement between levels here would be from generational temporalization or historicity to individual, self-temporalization or facticity. (3) Finally, generativity can be addressed statically through yet another level of abstraction, shorn of all temporal becoming. This would be a static analysis that treats generativity in terms of structure or, again, the structure of generativity. Having outlined this generative movement of phenomenology, let me examine the relation of phenomenology to generativity.

The Relation of Phenomenology to Generativity

The possibility of moving not only from static to generative, but from generative to static matters and methods requires us to examine the relation of phenomenology as a whole to generativity.

If we want to characterize the procedure of phenomenology as a whole we would have to assert that the results of phenomenological analysis, at any stage, are provisional and subject to reevaluation. The reason for this has to do with the very "structure" of generativity as historical and intersubjective becoming.

Let me recall some earlier examples to illustrate how such reevaluation was implied in Husserl's own analyses. When describing the phenomenology of normality and abnormality from a genetic perspective Husserl began within what he called the "solipsistic attitude" in order to move from the simple to the complex. He thus began with particular sense-organs and then moved to the lived-body as a synaesthetic unity. Throughout his descriptions he understood normality and abnormality to stand in a relation of foundation, that is, abnormality was characterized as a "modification" of normality.

But when Husserl turned to generative phenomena nearly a decade later, addressing the problem of normality and abnormality intersubjectively and historically in terms of "homeworld" and "alienworld," he implicitly reinterpreted the concepts of normality and abnormality. They were described as essentially co-relative and co-constitutive, and in this sense were articulated in a relation that might be called non-foundational.

From the disclosure of generative phenomena, what was won through genetic method (namely, a foundational account of normality and abnormality) had to be reexamined, maybe even abandoned or "ruined." Still, due to the structure of generativity, after disclosing the generative dimension, phenomenology can return to the process of genetic development and analyze it in terms of insights gained through generative phenomena. Thus, we do not necessarily loose the significance of individual genetic constitution, but are able to examine it in terms of broader connections. Or, I can go back to a static method after a generative one and "fix" the essential relations of intersubjective and historical becoming, qualifying the earlier ones.[23] This, however, does not mean that the results are definitive, for the sense of generativity is not given completely or adequately. Instead, its sense is determined through its developmental concordance or internal coherence in the process of intersubjective and historical living. Since the matters of phenomenology are generative and hence are matters that are constantly becoming, generative phenomenology would demand a constant going "back and forth" from static to genetic to generative and generative to genetic to static, etc.

But if this is the case, if generativity is a matter in historical becoming, what is phenomenology's and the phenomenologist's relation to generativity?

In the first place, phenomenology cannot be merely *descriptive* or a "reflection on" matters. It is not merely descriptive because the phenomenologist is caught up in generativity. Phenomenology becomes a *participation* in the sense development of an intersubjective historical structure that is in the process of generation as we describe it and as we bring it about. For Husserl this participation was understood essentially as an ethical participation, as a normative undertaking. I mean by normative not that this enterprise prescribes norms, but that the generative phenomenologist is engaged in the critical disclosure and unfolding of homeworld/alienworld, that is, of generativity, and that it makes a difference which way we take it up.[24] For generative phenomenology is conceived as *a* responsible participation in the very becoming of what it is describing. Generative phenomenology is a critical reflection on the historicity of essence whereby the "description" is not only a participation in the development of the "matter," but is also itself transformed in the very process. In other words, it is incumbent upon phenomenology to take account of the constitutive shifts introduced by the phenomenologist into the phenomenon, which in turn modifies the mode of analysis.

Only to the extent that the generative framework is still in transformation and thus beyond total disclosure is the generative framework disclosed for phenomenology. Accordingly, when describing generative matters in the early 1930s, Husserl writes: "*But the phenomenologist and phenomenology themselves stand in this historicity*"![25] Further, he also describes a "mundanization of the transcendental" and a mundanization of "phenomenologizing activities" such that the "transcendental philosopher" him or herself "flows back into the natural world."[26] To express this in a manner with which we are familiar from early French phenomenology, the phenomenological reduction is never complete and cannot exhaust "*die Sachen selbst*"; it is never complete because generativity is also futural, because the phenomenologist has to describe this generative-historical movement *as it is taking place*, and as the phenomenologist is situated in and participates in the constitution of the co-relation homeworld/alienworld co-generatively.

Thus, for a generative phenomenology we might say that there is, too, a kind of "absolute." In its most concrete form this "absolute," however, would be "generativity" itself, that is, the historical, *co*-relative, *co*-generative structure homeworld/alienworld. In this sense, and in this sense alone is the task of generative phenomenology to realize "the absolute": not by achieving absolute knowledge, but by responsibly, that is, *critically* and *responsively* bringing about the intersubjective generative structure. A generative phenomenology does not begin with individual sense consciousness to reach a universal We, but takes as its departure the generative structure homeworld/alienworld *from within* the homeworld. And because the so-called absolute *is* the liminal structure homeworld/alienworld, generative phenomenology remains true to a phenomenology of intersubjectivity by not reducing this interworldly structure to a collective singularity. Ultimately, it is critical of and responsive toward the entire generative structure without the patronizing presumption that we are the entire structure. Hence generative critique is essentially creative, co-participatory, enabling other critiques and responses. Since its historical dimension precludes it from being carried out in the same way by all, it will continue to be a unique and different opportunity for participation.

Finally, what a generative phenomenology will mean or can mean is still open to question. For its meaning is co-determined along with the clarification and realization of a co-generative framework: the liminal becoming of homeworld/alienworld.

If this is the case, if generative phenomenology is to be understood as generative and as a participation in generativity, then it would be impossible to speak of "*Husserl's*" generative phenomenology, or generative phenomenology "*in*" Husserl. Due to the very structure of generativity, Husserl cannot do *generative* phenomenology by himself. Restricting phenomenology to Husserl would entail executing a certain level of abstraction. Because phenomenology would be confined within the strictures of an individual, that is, Husserl, Husserl "by himself" could only be said to do genetic phenomenology. However, as a participation over the generations, generative phenomenology can be realized "through" or "after" Husserl, through or after those to whom Waldenfels, after Ricoeur, has amicably alluded as "Husserl-Heretics":[27] Heidegger, Scheler, Merleau-Ponty, Sartre, Levinas, Derrida, and through those others who also take up phenomenology. Participating in this process is not only the generation of phenomenology, but the phenomenology of generation, that is, a generative phenomenology whose matter is generativity.

Notes

Introduction

1. See Adorno, *Zur Metakritik der Erkenntnistheorie.*

2. Paci, *The Function of the Sciences and the Meaning of Man.* See also Thao, "Marxisme et phénoménologie."

3. Habermas, *Theorie des kommunikativen Handelns. Band 2. Zur Kritik der funktionalistischen Vernunft.*

4. Luhmann, *Soziologische Aufklärung: Aufsätze zur Theorie sozialer Systeme. Band 1*; and *Soziologische Aufklärung. Band 2*; hereafter *Soziologische Aufklärung.*

5. Theunissen, *Der Andere: Studien zur Sozialontologie der Gegenwart.* See also Waldenfels, *Das Zwischenreich des Dialogs*; hereafter *Zwischenreich.*

6. See Giddens, *Central Problems in Social Theory.*

7. Bernstein, *The Restructuring of Social and Political Theory.*

8. Grathoff, *Milieu und Lebenswelt.*

9. See "Selbst-Thematisierungen des Gesellschaftssystems," in *Soziologische Aufklärung Band 2,* 83 and 97 n. 30.

10. The most recent publication of *Krisis* writings contains material that sketches the orientation of parts IV and V of the Krisis. Where the concept of the lifeworld is concerned, the first Krisis publication really only works through parts I–III.

In what follows, I refer to the first Krisis publication as *Krisis 1.* Accordingly, I refer to the new edition of "Crisis" material as *Krisis 2.*

For a critical interpretation of this edition, see my "The New 'Crisis' Contribution"; hereafter "The New 'Crisis'."

11. Those who have made contributions to the problem of normality and abnormality include Maurice Natanson, "Philosophische Grundfragen der Psychiatrie," Richard Grathoff, "Über Typik und Normalität im alltäglichen Milieu," and Gerd Brand, "Die Normalität des und der Anderen." See also R. J. Folter's dissertation *Normaal en abnormaal.* These studies, however, fall short of a systematic examination of the connection between normality and abnormality and do not analyze their generative dimensions.

12. The concepts of homeworld and alienworld have occasionally surfaced in secondary literature on Husserl's phenomenology. The first to have mentioned this theme, I believe, is Jan Patočka in 1936 (translated into French as *Le monde naturel comme problème philosophique*). In 1940, Ludwig Landgrebe also mentioned these notions ("Welt als phänomenologisches Problem," which first

appeared in English translation as "World as Phenomenological Problem"). In 1956 the notion of homeworld was briefly addressed by Alwin Diemer in *Edmund Husserl: Versuch einer systematischen Darstellung seiner Phänomenologie;* hereafter *Edmund Husserl.* René Toulemont, following Landgrebe, treats the pair "*monde familier*" and "*monde étranger*" in *L'essence de la société selon Husserl,* 184 ff.; and Bernhard Waldenfels in 1971 again brings the notion of homeworld into relief (cf. *Zwischenreich*). Homeworld/alienworld is also treated in his "Heimat in der Fremde," in *In den Netzen der Lebenswelt,* 194 ff. More recently, Rudolf Bernet treats homeworld in a piece devoted to the themes of world and subject in his "Le monde et le sujet." Finally, there is Klaus Held's cogent article, "Heimwelt, Fremdwelt, die eine Welt."

13. The relation of the homeworld to normality is suggested by Diemer, *Edmund Husserl,* but is not explicated. On the other hand, the important role of normality is brought out more explicitly by Waldenfels (in his *Ordnung im Zwielicht,* esp. section B), but is not tied to the problem of homeworld and alienworld.

14. See Levinas, *Theorie de l'intuition dans la phénoménologie de Husserl,* 161; hereafter *Theorie de l'intuition.*

15. A non-independent part is called a "moment"; a part that is independent relative to the whole is called a "piece" (LU II/1 § 17). Moments and pieces hang together contextually according to the relation of foundation in encompassing wholes, which themselves can require founding (LU II/1 § 14, Prop. 1).

16. Habermas, *Theorie des kommunikativen Handelns: Band I,* 443 f.; see also 388, 394. Similarly, Husserl contends that an intentional experience that "values"—though founded upon perceiving and judging—is identified according to its "highest" component as a valuing experience.

17. Accordingly, for Husserl perceiving can remain intact should judging or valuing be "stripped off." Nevertheless, Husserl adds, there is a certain phenomenological "modification" of the bottommost layer, the remainder, in the process of this falling away, though he does not specify the phenomenological character of this modification.

18. I follow the 1956 edition by Raymund Schmidt.

19. The notion of phantasy as a 'quasi-positional' act will be important for the Cartesian account of intersubjectivity (see chapter 4).

20. This formulation was already present in the *Logische Untersuchungen.* "In Beziehung auf den als Gegenstand des Aktes verstanden intentionalen Inhalt ist folgendes zu unterscheiden: der *Gegenstand, so wie er intendiert ist,* und schlechthin der *Gegenstand, welcher* intendiert ist" (LU II/1 400; 415 f.). These two perspectives are also expressed in 1905 in *Zur Phänomenologie des inneren Zeitbewußtseins* (H X 25).

See Waldenfels who seems to identify the transcendental perspective with this distinction: "Der transzendentalen Sichtweise bleiben wir insofern verbunden, als wir nicht als selbstverständlich voraussetzen, *daß* es die Welt und die Andern gibt, sondern uns fragen, *wie* es sie gibt." *Zwischenreich,* 59.

21. See Robert Paul Wolff, *Kant's Theory of Mental Activity,* 113 n.

22. See Husserl, *Krisis 2,* esp. text Nr. 28. See also my "The New 'Crisis'," esp. section 4.

Chapter 1

1. From *Cahiers II, Pléiade,* 1398.

2. LU II/1 "Einleitung," 6: "Wir wollen auf die 'Sachen selbst' zurückgehen."

3. Hegel, *Phänomenologie des Geistes,* 11; hereafter *Phänomenologie.* See also 41–43, 49, 58, 64.

4. LU II/1, "Einleitung," 21: "will sie durch Rückgang auf die adäquate erfüllende Anschauung zur Klarheit und Deutlichkeit erheben."

5. *Kritik der reinen Vernunft,* B 350.

6. Evidence in the *Logische Untersuchungen* is defined as the "experience of truth" where truth is understood in two ways: (1) the agreement between the symbolic expression or the "proposition" on the one hand, and the intuitive presentation, on the other (LU I § 51); and (2) the coherence of fulfillments. Here something is true by the fact that the meaning-intentions and meaning-fulfillments internally cohere or are concordant [*einstimmig*] in the unfolding of experience (cf. LU II/2 122 f.). See Tugendhat, *Der Wahrheitsbegriff bei Husserl und Heidegger,* esp. 91–101; hereafter *Wahrheitsbegriff.* See also Louis Dupré, "The Concept of Truth in Husserl's *Logical Investigations,*" and Patzig, "Kritische Bemerkungen zu Husserls Thesen über das Verhältnis von Wahrheit und Evidenz."

The notion of concordance will be taken up in section 3 of this study in relation to the theory of normality and abnormality.

7. See LU II/2 33. For the problem of intuition and evidence in Husserl see Soffer's welcomingly clear exposition of truth and evidence in *Husserl and the Question of Relativism,* especially 66–75 in chapter 3; hereafter *Question.*

8. Levinas, *Théorie de l'intuition,* 126, 133.

9. Cf. in particular H I, First Meditation. And see too H III § 24 and § 141.

10. In *Ideen I* Husserl also distinguishes between a seeing of individuals or facts (assertoric evidence) and an "intellectual" seeing of essences (apodictic evidence). The former applies to the pre-predicative as well as to predicative experience. Intellectual insighting refers in this context to the intuition of essences. It is called apodictic because it is assumed that an essence is given exhaustively in such an intuition (H III 337 f.). At this stage, moreover, adequate and apodictic modes of evidence are identified. But see H I 62 where indubitability need not be tied to adequacy.

11. Within the sphere of objectivating, and by implication, nonobjectivating acts, Husserl distinguishes between original and non-original evidence. Original evidence is a founding mode of evidence in which the object is given in perception, "in the flesh" [*leibhaftig*], and in the mode of presentation [*Gegenwärtigung*]. Original evidence is evidence rooted directly in the present,

hic et nunc, yielding an "immediate evidence" (H III 346 f.). Non-original modes of evidence include modes of presentification [*Vergegenwärtigung*] such as the consciousness of images or pictures, remembering, or intropathy (H III 11, 340 f, 344) and are based mediately in the present. In presentification something absent is rendered present and provides only mediate or derived evidence.

12. For an appropriate clarification of the notion of 'horizon', see section 2, chapter 7, the heading "World-as-Horizon."

13. Within the "Cartesian way" Husserl tries to mitigate this inconsistency distinguishing between two types of indubitability: an empirical and an apodictic indubitability. The world and the ego, Husserl wishes to explain, are both indubitable in an empirical sense. But Husserl's Cartesian maxim does not require a doubt of empirical existence; rather, it is a conceptual possibility [*eine Denkmöglichkeit*]. Even though there are no empirical reasons to doubt the factual existence of the world, it can be doubted in a reflective thought experiment. To preserve a sphere of pure indubitable being, Husserl invokes "another indubitability" won by an "apodictic reduction" (H VIII 125 f.). The ego cogito cannot think itself not thinking, i.e., not existing and is therefore legitimated in a sort of apodictic naïveté.

14. I am indebted to discussions with Donn Welton concerning the relation of the progression of these two moments to transcendental method.

Chapter 2

1. See Boehm, "Das Absolute und die Realität," in *Vom Gesichtspunkt der Phänomenologie*, 72–105. See also Granel, *Le sens du temps et de la perception chez E. Husserl*, esp. 72–92.

2. Thus Husserl claims that it cannot be modalized (H XI 111).

3. H XI 110 n.: "Ich bin damit nicht ganz zufrieden. Das Gegenständliche konstitutiert sich doch von vornherein als Zeitliches, und die momentane Phase ist ein Abstraktion, die wir erst bilden müssen. Die Undurchstreichbarkeit des Moments ist also nicht ein Erstes."

4. See Klaus Held's classic work on the topic, *Lebendige Gegenwart: Die Frage nach der Seinsweise des transzendentalen Ich bei Edmund Husserl;* hereafter *Lebendige Gegenwart.*

5. Ms. A V 10 (1931), 10a: "Die weite, die breite Gegenwart, die gegenwärtige Zeit, etwa die Nachkriegszeit ist für uns reife Menschen lebendige Gegenwart und nicht nur die Minute jetzt, die Stunde, der heutige Tag, das Jahr, sondern diese ganze Reihe von Jahren seit 1914, die ihre individual-typische Geschlossenheit hat, sich für uns kontrastierend in der noch breiteren Gegenwart, auf die wir, die [wir] sie noch erlebt haben, uns einstellen können, die Epoche des neuen Reichs, in der sich uns so scharf Vorkriegsmenschheit und Nachkriegsmenschheit und demnach auch die eine und andere Umweltstypik kontrastiert."

6. See Merleau-Ponty, *Le visible et l'invisible*: "*Ce qu'elle* ne voit pas, c'est pour des raisons de principe qu'elle ne le voit pas, c'est parce qu'elle est conscience qu'elle ne le voit pas," 301. "Il est inévitable que la conscience soit mystifiée,

inversée, indirecte, par principe elle voit les choses *par l'autre bout*," 302; hereafter *Le visible.*

7. See H XIV Beilage I from 1921.

8. Ms. B III 3 (1931), 30b: "Was darüber hinausgeht, in der Weise der konstituierenden Anonymität, [in] der Latenz, ist ein μήὄν; es ist nicht nichts, sondern 'Voraussetzung' des Seins aus einer vergessenen Zeitigung, die noch nicht Zeitigung eines ὄν ist, und so hinterher zu enthüllendes ist, und als notwendig zu erkennende Funktion, zur Ermöglichung für Seiendes (und damit zu einer nachkommenden Zeitigung gebracht)."

9. Aristotle, *Nicomachean Ethics, Book 2,* esp. 1103a–4a.

10. See H I 103, H VI 181, and H XI 341.

11. This becomes clear to Husserl especially in 1930s.

12. H XV 619. Going beyond a "first" genesis is "generativity."

13. I will treat normality and abnormality from this period in section 3.

14. Husserl also refers to static and genetic methods, respectively, as a "descriptive" [*beschreibende*] phenomenology and an "explanatory" [*erklärende*] phenomenology (H XI 340). There are at least two possible precedents for this distinction. The first is Dilthey's well-known article "Ideen über eine beschreibende und zergliedernde Psychologie" (from 1894). The meaning of the distinction, however, is not taken over by Husserl. For Dilthey, "description" is interpretively descriptive, whereas "explanation" is something that the natural sciences do. On the other hand, Husserl takes description here in a much narrower sense and contrasts it with a research perspective that takes an interpretive stand with respect to the teleological genesis of sense. See Dilthey, *Gesammelte Schriften: Band 5. Die Geistige Welt,* 139–240. I would like to thank Bob Scharff for an informative conversation on this matter.

The second is Brentano. For Brentano, the task of ascertaining the basic elements of mental phenomena belongs to a "descriptive psychology," and the task of discerning the regulative manner of their coming into being and passing away belongs to a "genetic" and physiological psychology. See Brentano, *Psychologie vom empirischen Standpunkt.*

15. This is partially reproduced in *Zur Phänomenologie der Intersubjektivität: Zweiter Teil* (H XIV), as Beilage I, and as an appendix to *Analysen zur Passiven Synthesis* (336–45). On June 29, 1918, Husserl wrote to Natorp that he had already overcome—more than a decade before—the level of "static" Platonism and engaged the main theme of phenomenology as the "idea of transcendental genesis." This letter is cited by Iso Kern in his *Husserl und Kant: Eine Untersuchung über Husserls Verhältnis zu Kant und zum Neukantianismus,* 346; hereafter *Husserl und Kant.*

Other explicit indications of a difference in method between a static and genetic phenomenology can be found in Ms. B IV 6, 5a from 1915, *Formale und transzendentale Logik* (H XVII 257, 316), the *Cartesianische Meditationen,* Meditation IV, Ms. B III 3 entitled "Das Problem des Anfangs der (primordialen) Subjektivität," "Anfangende Affektion als instinktive" and "Methode der Rekonstruktion" from 1931, and *Zur Phänomenologie der Intersubjektivität: Dritter*

Teil (H XV), text 35 from 1933 (although the latter text—as we will see in section 4—already goes beyond a genetic method in the direction of a generative one).

On static and genetic method in secondary literature, see Aguirre, *Genetische Phänomenologie und Reduktion;* Holenstein, *Phänomenologie der Assoziation,* hereafter *Assoziation*; Welton, *The Origins of Meaning: A Critical Study of the Thresholds of Husserlian Phenomenology,* hereafter *Origins*; Bernet, Kern, and Marbach, *Edmund Husserl: Darstellung seines Denkens,* 181–89, hereafter *Darstellung*; Kern, *Husserl und Kant,* 348 ff.; and Larrabee, "Husserl's Static and Genetic Phenomenology," hereafter "Genetic Phenomenology."

16. See H III 358 ff, 371 ff.

17. Cf. Merleau-Ponty, *Phénoménologie de la perception,* 374 f.; hereafter *Phénoménologie.*

18. See *Formale und transzendentale Logik,* H XVII 257: "[die] '*statische*' . . . , auf eine schon 'entwickelte' Subjektivität bezogene . . . Konstitution"; and H XI 345.

19. Cf. Welton, *Origins,* esp. 168.

20. H XIV 41, my emphasis: "Der Konstitution nachgehen ist nicht der Genesis nachgehen, die eben Genesis der Konstitution ist und sich als Genesis in einer Monad bewegt." See also H XI 340: "Bei diesen Beschreibungen, den konstitutiven, ist keine Frage nach einer erklärenden Genesis." Note also that in the section of this manuscript appended to the volume on passive synthesis, Husserl explicitly distinguishes between a level of "constitutive phenomenology" and the "phenomenology of genesis" (H XI 340, n. 1), and likewise distinguishes between two modes of constitutive analysis (H XI 345).

21. Cf. Bernet et al., *Darstellung,* 180.

22. See H V 125, 129. See also LU II/2 §§40–52. Cf. Bernet et al., *Darstellung,* 182 f.

23. Cf. Welton, *Origins,* 172.

24. See Holenstein, *Assoziation,* 192 ff.

25. This is the significance, e.g., of his "Origin of Geometry" (H VI Beilage III), which will ultimately transcend the boundaries of a genetic analysis.

26. More will be said about the relationship of static and genetic method to this process of questioning back or a "regressive" approach in section 2.

27. Husserl calls an eidetic science that treats the object whatsoever a formal ontology. A formal ontology contains the forms of all ontologies and prescribes for the material ontologies a formal structure common to them all (H III 27). Put differently, a formal ontology concerns nothing but the empty logical form, comprising formal logic, algebra, the theory of manifolds, the theory of numbers, set theory, etc. (H III 33, 141).

28. Landgrebe, for example, contends that discovering regions of being can only take place by means of a constitutional inquiry. See Landgrebe, *Der Weg der Phänomenologie,* 146 f. In a similar vein Tugendhat asserts: "Therefore, we can in no way arrive at regional fundamental concepts without reflecting on the *modes of givenness*; and only because there are different *ways of givenness* is

there at all the occasion to distinguish between different 'regions'." Tugendhat, *Wahrheitsbegriff,* 179 (my emphasis).

29. Husserl suggests that we can go back and forth between ontology and phenomenology by means of a mere change in perspectives [*eine bloße Blickwendung*]. This results in a methodological "transgression" or a "mixed phenomenological-ontological way of seeing." See H V 81–89, 105. See also H VI 176; H III 364 f., 369, 375 f., 378 ff.

30. HXV 616, my emphasis; and see H III 359 ff., 371 ff.

31. As he did for example with respect to psychology, biology, and anthropology.

32. In Ms. B III 3, 29a, Husserl explains how genesis can be construed from the static correlation of consciousness and thing: "Wir konstruieren dann eine notwendige Genesis zunächst innerhalb der ästhetischen Ding-Bewußtseinsgegebenheiten; die Affektion der abgehobenen hyletischen Daten muß vorangehen und aus genetischen Gründen findet Apperzeption statt und Durchgang durch die Erfassung der hyletischen Daten zu den darin intentionalen, sich abschattenden Einheiten etc. Wir konstruieren nun eine Genesis mit Heranziehung der Weisen, wie überhaupt immer neue Apperzeptionen sich bilden und Wesengesetzlichkeiten der Bildung von sich ablesen lassen."

33. As Larrabee has shown, apperception is a splendid example of a phenomenon that exceeds the boundaries of a static analysis. Cf. "Genetic Phenomenology," 167 f.

34. It is also from the possibility of a genetic analysis that Husserl can explicitly identify his *Ideen* as a piece of static phenomenology (H XIV 41; cf. H XI 345).

35. See above, point 4, p. 48f.

36. H XI 344: "Stellen wir statische und genetische Zusammenhänge gegenüber, so ist es die Frage, ob man eine systematische Phänomenologie der statischen Zusammenhänge wie der von Noesis und Noema zustande bringen kann, ob also Genetisches dabei völlig auszuschalten ist."

37. I am making a critical allusion here to some of Derrida's remarks in *L'écriture et la différence,* 231; hereafter *L'écriture.* See section 4, chapter 15.

Chapter 3

1. Also see Ms. C 5 (1930), 7a: "Im urphänomenalen Strömen der Urpräsenz transzendiert sich dieses Leben selbst, es konstituiert die immanente Zeit, den Erlebnisstrom mit seiner Vergangenheit und Zukunft."

2. By virtue of its temporal dimension, the ego cannot be given in adequate evidence. Whereas Husserl virtually equates adequacy with apodicticity in *Ideen I,* by the *Cartesianische Meditationen* he concedes that adequacy and apodicticity of evidence need not go hand in hand (H I 62). What scientists expect of their principles is absolute indubitability, not adequacy. The Cartesian principle of

indubitability for philosophy, as providing evidence that is "first in itself" and likewise valid for first philosophy, requires a "recognizable apodictic content of being." Such an absolute indubitability, writes Husserl, can be achieved by a "critical reflection" that leaves any imaginable doubt meaningless (H I 56).

3. The relations of immanence and transcendence are difficult to apprehend when Husserl tends to equate transcendent givenness with spatial givenness, and immanent givenness with temporal givenness. For this reason it appears "paradoxical" to assert that consciousness (immanence) is primordial transcendence.

4. See Dastur, "Réduction et intersubjectivité," 61; hereafter "Réduction."

5. H X 237 fn. 1: "Seefelder Manuskripte und ältere über Individuation. Seefeld 1905. Individuation. (Historische Note: In Seefelder Blättern—1905—finde ich schon Begriff und korrekten Gebrauch der 'phänomenologischen Reduktion')."

6. Dastur, "Réduction," 61 f. Supporting this thesis as well is a remark annotated to the title of the text Nr. 6 reading: "Transzendentale Reduktion (Ausschaltung der physischen Natur) ergibt außer dem *ego* auch das andere *ego* und seinen Strom" (H XIII 111).

7. I do not consider the way through "intentional psychology" to be an independent method in the same manner that the Cartesian progressive and the Kantian regressive ways are. Let me simply point out here that the way through intentional psychology embodies in itself the very tension between the regressive critical and the progressive Cartesian procedures.

For a thorough study of phenomenological psychology in Husserl, its historical background and development, see Joseph J. Kockelmans, *Edmund Husserl's Phenomenological Psychology: A Historico-Critical Study.* Concerning the relation between Husserl and Heidegger on transcendental philosophy and phenomenological psychology see Steven Galt Crowell's lucid exposition "Husserl, Heidegger, and Transcendental Philosophy: Another Look at the Encyclopaedia Britannica Article"; hereafter "Another Look."

8. See Crowell, "Another Look," 506 f.

9. H VIII 287 n. 2: "Die Geisteswissenschaften als personale Wissenschaften haben es mit den Personen als handelnden und ihren Handlungen (im weiteren Sinn) zu tun—*nicht mit dem eigentlich konstituierenden Bewußtsein*" (my emphasis).

Thus, what one gains by transcendental phenomenology is not a mundane correlation between subject and object, but a phenomenological correlation between the object as an accomplished structure [*Gebilde*] inseparable from the subject as a process of structuring [*bilden*] (H VIII 290–99). The problem, as I mention below, is that Husserl attempts to carry out this move in a Cartesian framework.

10. See *Duden 7: Das Herkunftswörterbuch* (Mannheim: Dudenverlag, 1963).

11. Even its connotations for politics and science fiction are not too far from Husserl's meaning.

12. I am of course not insisting that every time Husserl writes "other" he is working within a Cartesian framework, or that the term "alien" simply and

of itself evokes a context beyond Cartesian prejudices. But unless I am citing Husserl directly, I will retain these distinctions in the following discussion of intersubjectivity.

13. See H VIII 53, 294; and see H XIV 442.

14. "Horizon" in the sense just sketched is more accurately a "halo" [*Umring* (H III 58) or *Hof* (H III 77)], as suggested in *Ideen I.* In section 2 I will make a distinction between halo, as a psychological notion of horizon, and a transcendental/modal treatment of horizon.

15. H VIII 153; see also H VIII 162; 155–58, 293, 445 f., 461 f.

16. That Husserl saw the way of intentional psychology closely allied with the Cartesian way is also confirmed by marginal notes and insertions made in his copy of *Ideen I* at the time of his First Philosophy lectures. Boehm calls our attention to §§ 33, 34, 38, and 89 of *Ideen I* (cf. his introduction to H VIII, xxxvi n. 5 and xxxvii). One finds the interpretation of consciousness as a theme of psychological phenomenology, the interpretation of human being as psychological ego and a host of other movements to integrate the two approaches.

Chapter 4

1. From LU II/1 § 8.

2. Cited by Derrida, *De la grammatologie,* 265.

3. See H I "Einleitung," xxiii.

4. See David Carr's work, *Interpreting Husserl: Critical and Comparative Studies,* which brings into sharp relief the differences between solipsism in the traditional sense and solipsism at issue in the Fifth Meditation; hereafter *Interpreting Husserl.* See especially 45–69.

5. On Husserl's novel conception of analogy for the constitution of intersubjectivity, see J. François Courtine, "Intersubjectivité et analogie," who places this notion in relation to the tradition of Aristotelian commentary on *analogia entis.* He concludes that the *analogia entis* should be qualified for Husserl corporally as *analogia carnis.* See also his "Différence ontologique et analogie de l'être: Le tournant suarézien."

6. I take this expression "phenomenological in-itself" from Marc Richir and his rich lectures on intersubjectivity and the "en-soi phénoménologique" held at the College International de Philosophie, Paris, Winter, 1989. In this connection see Michel Henry, "Réflexions sur la cinquième méditation cartésienne de Husserl."

7. See H XIV 337 and Husserl's curious use of the "An-sich-sein" of a lived-body that is there for me as a physical thing; it is also an inner-lived-body as a "subjectivity" that cannot be experienced in perception. The other as an an-sich would be precisely "incomprehensible." See H XV 554 f. and 631.

8. Thus, this abstraction goes farther than that of *Ideen II* since the latter treats "mere nature" as the object of the natural scientists and as the "founding sphere." For the *Cartesianische Meditationen,* the abstractive founding sphere is

the nature peculiar to one's ownness [*eigentliche Natur*]. Compare esp. §§ 1–2, 49e of H IV with H I 127.

9. The question I will ask later is whether "I" can have any sense prior to an "alien" or in abstraction from an alien. Does my lived-body have any sense outside of the alien's lived-body?

10. See Yamaguchi's very exacting and subtle work on the relation between passive synthesis and intersubjectivity, *Passive Synthesis und Intersubjectivität bei Husserl*, 83 f.; hereafter *Intersubjektivität*.

11. For a more intricate and detailed analysis of this process see Holenstein, *Assoziation*, Yamaguchi, *Intersubjektivität*, and Theunissen, *Der Andere: Studien zur Sozialontologie der Gegenwart*, esp. chapters 1–3.

12. In the first version of the *Cartesianische Meditationen*, Husserl clarifies this point: "With the first originally instituting apprehension of the teleological sense of a pair of scissors, the child 'sees' scissors without further ado, without [having to] think back to the first pair of scissors and deduce the analogical determination of its telos" (H XV 14).

13. Husserl does not take up the question, in the *Cartesianische Meditationen*, whether the other or the alien is from the very start a *gendered* other, i.e., whether the neutral '*das Fremde*' is appropriate and should not be instead either '*die*' or '*der*' *Fremde* (see also Waldenfels's article "Experience of the Alien in Husserl's Phenomenology"; originally published as "Erfahrung des Fremden in Husserls Phänomenologie," in *Phänomenologische Forschungen*, Band 22.) Accordingly, he does not inquire into the variations or nuances that unfold in the constitution of sense between bodies that have different genders. If similarity is the basis for positing uniqueness, what takes place when we begin from difference? Furthermore, if we assert, as Husserl does, that the primordial ego under consideration in the constitutional account is an adult, does being dissimilar mean exclusion from the sense "constituting subjectivity"? Likewise, must *Einfühlung* or *Einverstehen* always take place? Is there really an act of intropathy when a child sees her or his parents making love, when this action does not "make sense" to the child bodily? And finally, keeping the level of analysis on the lived-body, is there a relation of intropathy between humans and animals?

These are questions that belong to genetic and generative phenomenologies. In a manuscript from 1931, Husserl notes that there must be essentially different concepts of intropathy, for interrelations between, e.g., humans and animals, adults and children, early childhood and animals, and animals within their species. When noting that the universe of animals is still a psycho-physical analog to that of humans, that animals have lived-bodies with sensuous organs like humans, he even raises the question concerning plants! "But where does the analogy end?" he asks. "Are individual [animals] not also psycho-physical, do they not also have their lived-bodies as organs of their 'ego-pols'? But here the analogy reaches its limit" (H XV 173, Ms. B III 4, 36 f.; see also H XV 605).

14. Held, "Das Problem der Intersubjektivität und die Idee einer phänomenologischen Transzendental-philosophie," see esp. 34–45; hereafter "Das Problem."

15. H IV 158 f. See chapter 7 under the heading "Lifeworld: Earth-as-Ground."

16. Held points to the following texts where Husserl began to differentiate these modes for the theory of intropathy: H XIV 498 ff., H XV 245 ff., 643.

17. See H X §§ 19–23.

18. Notice, for example, the title of the § 53 (H I): "The Potentialities [*Potentialitäten*] of the Primordial Sphere and Their Constitutive Function in the Apperception of the Other."

19. Held, "Das Problem," 35.

20. See H I 150. Husserl uses the presentification of temporality as a metaphor for understanding the other. But it is only a metaphor; whereas the future can never remain future when it becomes present, the other can be simultaneously with my present, as co-existing.

Levinas takes this insight even more radically: For Husserl temporality is merely an "illustrative similitude" for the relation with the other; the other is an other I. But for Levinas, there is no metaphor: The encounter with the Other [*autrui*] is the origin of time. When the future as other, which reveals our finitude, i.e., death, becomes present, there is no time and no encounter with the other. When death as future mystery comes, it negates the Present, the Self as ontological solitude. Only when the exteriority of the future as Other comes face-to-face with the Present, can there be a *simultaneity* of Future and Present, an intersubjective context, a "plurality" that is the origin of temporality. See Levinas, *Le temps et l'autre,* esp. lectures 3 and 4.

21. Held, "Das Problem," 37.

22. Carr, *Interpreting Husserl,* 58.

23. H VIII 62 ff., 134 ff., 180 ff., 188 ff.

24. In the earlier account the lived-body of the other is described as intuitively accessible, whereas in the Fifth Meditation Husserl describes the necessity of appresenting the other's lived-body that is not given originally.

25. H VIII 181, 188; H I 144, 146, and H VIII 63: "es ist Indikation, aber kein Vorgriff, der zum Selbstgriff werden könnte. Diese indizierende Intention fordert und ermöglicht nicht eine einlösende Wahrnehmung, wie das bei allen vordeutenden Momenten innerhalb der raumdinglichen Wahrnehmung der Fall ist."

26. Derrida, *La voix et le phénomène,* 32. See 42: "Pour expliquer le caractère irréductiblement indicatif de la manifestation, même dans le discours, Husserl propose déjà des motifs dont la cinquième des *Méditations cartésiennes* développera minutieusement le système." For a discussion of Derrida's reading in *La voix et le phénomène* of Husserl, see Evans, *Strategies of Deconstruction: Derrida and the Myth of the Voice.*

27. I want to argue that difference between the other and the alien is not just a difference of founding and founded, but a difference in kind. Ricoeur seems to go in this direction, but awards too much sense to a complex and inconsistent text: see "La cinquième méditation cartésienne," 217 ff.

28. Merleau-Ponty, *Le visible,* 113 f.

Section 2

1. From "Kant und die Idee der Transzendental-philosophie," in H VII 247.

2. From Merleau-Ponty, *The Visible and the Invisible*, ed. Claude Lefort, trans. Alphonso Lingis (Evanston: Northwestern University Press, 1968), 6 (*Le visible*, 21).

Chapter 5

1. On the notion of "type" and "typicality" see Alfred Schutz, "Type and Eidos in Husserl's Late Philosophy," in Collected Papers III, 92–115.

2. David Carr, *Phenomenology and the Problem of History*, 69; hereafter *Problem of History*. Cf. H I § 29, the title of which reads "Die material- und formalontolgoischen Regionen als Indices transzendentaler Systeme von Evidenzen," also cited by Carr.

3. As I will note below, the "natural concept of the world" is a predecessor of the expression "lifeworld."

4. See chapter 6, n. 19.

5. Examples of such investigations range from the "Origin of Geometry" to the "Origin of the Spatiality of Nature." See pages 112ff.

6. For a brief survey of the popular philosophical and logical concept of presuppositionlessness used around the time of Husserl's early work, see Klaus Rosen, *Evidenz in Husserls deskriptiver Transzendentalphilosophie*, 138–42.

7. It is interesting to follow the consistent usage of the term "*pregiven*" [*vorgegeben*] and its cognates when (1) the world is at issue and when (2) it is a matter of a regressive questioning back. To cite just one striking example, in a text Boehm dates to be at least from 1924, Husserl uses the cognates of pregivenness in the context of world no less than *15 times* in the short space of four pages. See H VIII 266–70.

8. Cf. H VII 245; H VIII 267–69, H VI esp., Part III A.

9. On the distinction between *Reflexion* and *Besinnung* see also Carr, *Problem of History*, esp. 59 ff.

10. See the process of explication and clarification [*Verdeutlichung und Klärung*] in *Ideen III* §20.

11. See H VIII 259–74, "[Der] Weg durch die Kritik der positiven Wissenschaften zur transzendentalen Phänomenologie, der cartesianische Weg der 'Ideen' [und das Problem der vorgegebenen Lebenswelt]." See also "Weg in die transzendentale Phänomenologie als absolute und universale Ontologie durch die positiven Ontologien und die positive erste Philosophie," 219–28. See also H VII 258 and H VIII 4.

12. I explain this relation in sections 3 and 4 of my "The New 'Crisis'."

13. H VI esp., Beilage XVI from 1937 and §§41–42.

Chapter 6

1. We need not adjudicate Husserl's charges here. See Kern, *Husserl und Kant*, 51–178. On the relation between Husserl and Kant see also Thomas Seebohm, *Die Bedingungen der Möglichkeit der Transzendental-Philosophie.*

2. And Beilage III, "Die Frage nach dem Ursprung der Geometrie als intentionalhistorisches Problem."

3. See Carr, "Husserl's Problematic Concept of the Life-world," 334; hereafter "Problematic Concept."

4. Gurwitsch, "Problems of the Life-world," 47 ff.

5. For the genesis of the notion of lifeworld, see Guy van Kerckhoven, "Zur Genese des Begriffs 'Lebenswelt' bei Edmund Husserl"; hereafter "Zur Genese." See also Kern, "Die Lebenswelt als Grundlagenproblem der objektiven Wissenschaften und als universales Wahrheits-und Seinsproblem"; hereafter "Die Lebenswelt."

6. See the lectures on "transcendental aesthetic" from 1919 that Husserl "inappropriately" entitled "Natur und Geist," Ms. F I 35, cited by van Kerckhoven, "Zur Genese," 191. See also the lecture "Natur und Geist" from 1927 and A IV 5, cited by Kern, "Die Lebenswelt," 69.

7. See Beilage XIII, esp. 374–76. To this one should also add Ms. D 13 I, 173a (about 1918) and Ms. A IV 22, 70 (1920), cited by Kern in "Die Lebenswelt."

8. See Cairns, *Conversations with Fink and Husserl,* 63. Cairns records one of his conversations with Husserl and Hans Reiner from 1931. "Husserl objected that Heidegger did not mention either Avenarius or Husserl when speaking of the natural world-picture, but treated it as a matter of common knowledge rather than something developed by these two philosophers. Husserl acknowledges his own debt to Avenarius." See also H IX 62 f. and 93 ff.; and Kern, "Die Lebenswelt," 68, n. 2, as well as Soffer, *Question* 146.

9. See, for example, Janssen, "Die Problematik der Rede von der Lebenswelt als Fundament der Wissenschaft," hereafter *Lebenswelt und Wissenschaft*; Boehm, "Husserls drei Thesen über die Lebenswelt"; Brand, *Die Lebenswelt: Eine Philosophie des konkreten Apriori;* Claesges, "Zweideutigkeiten in Husserls Lebenswelt-Begriff," hereafter "Zweideutigkeiten"; Mohanty, Essay Eight, " 'Life-world and 'a priori' in Husserl's Later Thought," in *The Possibility of Transcendental Philosophy,* 101–19; and Waldenfels, "Die Abgründigkeit des Sinnes: Kritik an Husserls Idee der Grundlegung" (15–33), and "Die verachtete Doxa: Husserl und die fortdauernde Krisis der abendländischen Vernunft" (34–55) in *In der Netzen der Lebenswelt,* hereafter *Netzen.*

10. Ricoeur, for example, does sketch a systematic view of the lifeworld concepts by isolating an epistemological function of the lifeworld, which is developed in terms of relations of contrast that points to the primacy of the idea of science and to questions of validity, and an ontological function, developed in terms of their relations of dependence, suggesting the anteriority of the lifeworld. See Ricoeur, "L'originaire et le question-en-retour dans la *Krisis* de

Husserl." In a similar manner, Claesges designates a "diagnostic function" in the theory of the lifeworld, and a "therapeutic function." See his "Zweideutigkeiten."

11. At this point in *Krisis 1*, Fink interpolates that one has never scientifically inquired into the way in which the lifeworld constantly functions as a foundation [*Untergrund*], how its manifold prelogical validities are founding for logical and theoretical truths (H VI 127; cf. 50). See David Carr's remark in his translation of *Krisis 1* (*The Crisis of European Sciences and Transcendental Phenomenology* [Evanston: Northwestern University Press, 1970] 124) noting that this passage was in Fink's hand (Carr's translation hereafter *Crisis*).

12. Ms. C 16 78a: "Phänomenologische Archäologie, das Aufgraben der in ihren Baugliedern verborgenen konstitutiven Bauten, der Bauten apperzeptiver Sinnesleistungen, die uns fertig vorliegen als Erfahrungswelt. Das Zurückfragen und dann Bloßlegen der Seinssinn schaffenden Einzelleistungen bis zu den letzten, den 'Archai', um von diesen aufwärts wieder im Geist erstehen [zu] lassen die selbstverständliche Einheit der so vielfach fundierten Seinsgeltungen mit ihren relativen Seienden. Wie bei der gewöhnlichen Archäologie: Rekonstruktion, Verstehen im 'Zick-Zack'!"

Also compare Ms. B III 3, 33a: "In der *phänomenologischen Rekonstruktion* findet unter dem Titel einer Enthüllung der dunklen Hintergründe eine 'ursprüngliche' Zeitigung, ich meine eine wirkliche als Seinskonstitution von solchem statt, das vorher 'schon war', aber nicht als seiend konstituiert war und als das nicht zu einer Zeitigung gekommen war." Notice here a possible genetic interpretation of reconstruction.

13. H VI 135. Here I follow Carr's translation, *Crisis*, 132.

14. Ms. F I 32, 109b, cited by Kern, "Die Lebenswelt," 72 fn. 2: "Ist denn nicht Wissenschaft selbst Funktion des Lebens . . . ? Ist sie nicht ein Stück selbst der einheitlichen Lebenswelt?"

15. H XIV 397: "Ob klare oder unklare, vollgültige oder ungültige Wissenschaften, wie alle guten oder schlechten Werkgebilde der Menschheit gehören sie zum Bestand der Welt als Welt *reiner Erfahrung*" (my emphasis).

16. Carr, "Problematic Concept," 335; see also H VI 125 f.

17. "Problems of the Life-world," 49 f.; hereafter "Problems."

18. On Soffer's reading there is a distinction to be made between the *pluralism* of the lifeworld (which concerns the contents of the lifeworld) and the *relativism* of the lifeworld (which concerns the reference to specific intersubjective constitutive communities). Accordingly, not only does each individual live in several worlds (i.e., pluralistically), but also some worlds are "valid" for some communities but not for others. (Soffer, *Question*, 152). This description is on the way to a deeper sense of the lifeworld than the third provisional sense I am sketching here.

But because Soffer does not treat the lifeworld transcendentally as world-horizon and as earth-ground, because she does not explicate the normative dimensions of the lifeworld (suggestively working through an initial stage i.e., *Einstimmigkeit*, but without connecting it to normality and abnormality), and because the normative lifeworld is never exfoliated in terms of the generative concepts homeworld and alienworld (though she does mention these terms, e.g., 184 ff.) her analysis, while extremely well wrought given the self-imposed boundaries of her work, has to remain a provisional analysis of the lifeworld and the problem of relativism. That is, her analysis remains confined to an ontological and static constitutional analysis and only at times does she engage a genetic one; however, it does not yet enter the deeper dimension of intersubjective geo-historical constitution peculiar to a *generative* phenomenology. In fact, I would argue that the only way she can really put to use the distinctions she has so incisively presented is to bring them into the context of generativity. Here, the distinctions themselves would have to be modified and reinterpreted.

19. For a more nuanced and schematic understanding of a lifeworld ontology, see the second volume of Husserl's *Krisis* writings, H XXIX, text Nr. 11. And see my "The New 'Crisis'," esp. section 4.

20. Gurwitsch, "Problems," 57 f., my emphasis. Gurwitsch makes this transition from the pluralist cultural worlds to the singular structure of the perceptual world exceptionally clear.

21. H VI 144: "die große Aufgabe einer reinen *Wesenslehre von der Lebenswelt*" (my emphasis).

Chapter 7

1. The world as a universe of things is another formulation of the world as totality. This notion is taken up explicitly in Husserl's writings which are included in the supplementary volume of the *Krisis* texts. The world as a totality of things or "facts" [*Tatsachen*] is mundane and is contrasted with a phenomenological-teleological interpretation of the world. See H XXIX, texts Nrs. 25 and 26. See also my "The New 'Crisis'," esp. section 3.

2. I would like to thank Donn Welton for bringing these two motives clearly to my attention.

3. *Metaphysics,* Book Gamma, 1003a. "ἔστιν ἐπιστήμη τις ἣ θεωρεῖ τὸ ὂν ᾗ ὂν καὶ τὰ τούτῳ ὑπάρχοντα καθ' αὑτό."

4. Held, "Der griechische Anfang der Philosophie und seine Erneuerung in Husserls Phänomenologie." On phenomenology as openness to the world, see also Held's article "Husserl und die Griechen" and his "Husserls These von der Europäisierung der Menschheit," esp. 18, 32; hereafter "Husserls These." See also Elmar Holenstein's rejoinder to Held's article in the same collection of essays, "Europa und die Menschheit: Zu Husserls kulturphilosophischen Meditationen."

5. Kern, *Husserl und Kant,* 140 f.

6. See Held, "Finitude of the World: Phenomenology in Transition from Husserl to Heidegger," 190 f.; hereafter "Finitude."

7. Thus, Husserl draws a phenomenological distinction between a "noema" and an "essence," or methodologically between phenomenology and ontology. See, for example, H V, chapter 3.

8. George Schrader has argued that even in Kant's *Kritik der reinen Vernunft*, there is a distinction to be made between the dogmatic-*metaphysical* opposition between the noumenon and phenomenon and a *critical* relation that obtains between the in-itself and the appearance. See Schrader, "The Thing in Itself in Kantian Philosophy."

Dogmatically and metaphysically, he claims, the thing-in-itself is noumenal insofar as Kant treats it as a cause or ground of appearances, assumes that the categories can be applied to it and writes as if a privileged faculty, practical reason, could have access to them. The concept of the thing-in-itself is critical insofar as it functions as a limiting concept; it is given in its appearances, i.e., it is the object which appears and is not a second object.

This distinction can be helpful in understanding Husserl's notion of the in-itself and the phenomenon. It is helpful because Husserl never rejected the notion of the in-itself. In fact, the in-itself is essentially understood as the object's "objective sense" or "identical core." See H III §§ 131 ff. And see H XI, Division 4, "Das Ansich des Bewußtseinsstroms."

9. Husserl, "Notizen zur Raumkonstitution," published posthumously in *Philosophy and Phenomenological Research* 1, no. 1 (1940/41), 32 f.; hereafter "Notizen."

10. On the role of teleology in Husserl see Guillermo Hoyos, "Zum Teleologiebegriff in der Phänomenologie Husserls"; hereafter "Teleologiebegriff."

11. H VII 251: "die Welt as gegenständlichen Sinn und als uns geltende Wirklichkeit."

12. H VII 274 f.: "Der kontinuierliche Fortgang der Erkenntnis ist wie für das Universum ein in mannigfaltigen Sonderprozessen verlaufender Gesamtprozess der Erfüllung. . . . Sie ist Erfüllung, die in einer übergreifenden Einstimmigkeit und in fortschreitender Gesamtkraft der Erfahrungsbewährung alle gelegentlichen Enttäuschungen in eine höhere Harmonie auflöst."

13. The term Husserl uses here for "ground" is *Boden* and not *Grund*. For the distinction between these two terms and the explanation of the meaning of *Boden* as ground, see below, "Lifeworld: Earth-as-Ground."

14. As Husserl reminds us, he has already invoked the notion of the pregiven lifeworld as horizon and ground prior to this passage. But he did so without explicitly distinguishing between a mundane and a transcendental analysis.

15. It goes to Waldenfels's credit to have identified the import of the concepts "horizon" and "ground" in Husserl's concept of the lifeworld. This is itself a peculiar feat: Despite their prominence in Husserl's texts, they are seldom mentioned together in secondary literature, or set apart as belonging uniquely to a lifeworld analysis.

The difficulty I find in Waldenfels's interpretation, however, lies not so much in his pervasive identification of horizon with the "whither to" [*woraufhin*] and ground with the "whence" [*woher*] of sense determination (see his "Weltliche und soziale Einzigkeit bei Husserl," 160, and "Die Abgrundigkeit des Sinnes," in *Netzen*, 17). Disturbing is his equation of horizon with an ultimately regulating process as a synthetic totality, and ground with what is first given in intuitive presence (cf. "Die Verachtete Doxa," *Netzen*, 52).

16. See Husserl, "Grundlegende Untersuchungen zum phänomenologischen Ursprung der Räumlichkeit der Natur," published posthumously in *Philosophical Essays in Memory of Edmund Husserl*; hereafter "Ursprung."

See also H XV 206 ff., and text 27. And see Ms. K III 10, 4b: "In dieser Welt hat unsere Menschheit ihr Territorium—ihr beschränktes Feld der heimischen Lebenstätigkeit, ihr Feld heimatlich praktischer Interessen." See, too, H XXIX 41: "Die innen-historische Welt gleich Welt im Territorium in der geschlossenen, der Allgemeinschaft 'Nation'."

17. H VI 146: "Andererseits ist Welt nicht seiend wie ein Seiendes, wie ein Objekt, sondern seiend in einer *Einzigkeit*, für die der Plural sinnlos ist. Jeder Plural und aus ihm herausgehobene Singular *setzt den Welthorizont voraus*" (my emphasis).

18. See H III 83, 200–203; H VI 161, 163, 165, 267. Cf. H XI 11, 21. See also EU 28, William James, *The Principles of Psychology*, vol. 1, 249–51, 260, 447, and his article "On Some Omissions of Introspective Psychology," 18 f.

19. EU 28 ff., 114, 171 ff.; H VI 165, 267; H XI 11.

20. See the Third Logical Investigation in LU II/1, 225–93.

21. I am indebted to Klaus Held for this distinction between falsifying the horizon character by grasping it, as he says, *in* its non-thematicity, and the phenomenological task of thinking the horizon *as* what is non-thematic as such. (Conversation, July 1989, Wuppertal.) See also his "Finitude." Donn Welton also made a similar point in his lecture "Margins of the World," presented at the Society for Phenomenology and Existential Philosophy, Memphis State University, October 1991.

22. See H VIII 123 ff., 168 ff., 294 and more specifically H XI 5 ff., 19 ff.

23. Held, "Finitude," 192.

24. Husserl seems to go in this direction in his later manuscript from 1934, "Notizen zur Raumkonstitution," 21–37. And see the continuation of the article in No. 2 of this same series, 217–26.

25. "Ursprung," 320; cf. 307.

See also Merleau-Ponty's working notes in *Le visible*, esp. 223, 230, and 305, which appear to be distinctive reflections on these pages of Husserl.

26. See also Ms. B I 10 I (1932/33), 7 (from transcription): For the natural-scientific attitude: "Die Naturobjekte sind im engeren Bereiche wirklicher Erfahrung von vornherein apperzipiert als Objekte in Raum-Zeitlichkeit, und diese als Horizontsinn ist ins Unendliche mit Objekten wirklich oder möglicherweise besetzt. . . . Hier soll nur betont werden, daß der Seinssinn, in dem in jeder Erfahrung . . . Weltliches bewußt ist, notwendig eine implizite Unendlichkeit, eine offene Endlosigkeit aus Induktion in sich schließt."

27. Compare Aristotle, *On the Heavens*, book 2, 297b.

28. Calvino, *Cosmicomics*, 14.

29. H VI 158: "Beginnen wir unseren neuen Weg, indem wir der 'Lebenswelt' als dem allgemeinen 'Boden' menschlichen Weltlebens nun ein ausschließliches,

konsequent theoretisches Interesse zuwenden, und zwar gerade der Weise, wie ihr diese allgemeine 'Boden' Funktion eignet." See also H VI 157: "So machen wir sie jetzt konsequent thematisch, als Boden aller unserer Interessen."

30. See, for example, H XXIX 38, 141, 191, 193–94, 217.

31. These have been cited above as "Ursprung" and "Notizen."

32. H IV 29, 36, 54.

33. Thinking along with, say, the natural-scientific attitude is commonplace in Husserl's meditations. We see it not only, for example, in *Ideen II*, but in his later writings as well. In this respect, Husserl follows with programmatic intent the basic assumption of Descartes; that is, he describes the physical-body according to the naturalistic or physical scientific attitude of which the physical-body is a correlate. See, for instance, H XXIX 19; and B I 10 I, 4 (from transcription): "Beginnen wir uns tiefer als naturwissenschaftlich Eingestellte auf das uns in dieser Einstellung auf unser Thema Natur schon Selbstverständliche."

34. See especially H IV 58 ff.

35. See H XI 3 ff. Summarizing the relevant passages in *Ideen II*, Merleau-Ponty writes: "Non seulement la permanence de mon corps n'est pas un cas particulier de la permanence dans le monde des objets extérieurs, mais encore la seconde ne se comprend que par la première; non seulement la perspective de mon corps n'est pas un cas particulier de celle des objets, mais encore la présentation perspective des objets ne se comprend que par la résistance de mon corps à toute variation perspective." *Phénoménologie*, 108.

36. Merleau-Ponty, *Phénoménologie*, 292, 358, 442, 490 f.

37. The brackets are inserted by Schutz for clarity.

38. This accounts for the fact that "I walk," or "I move" kinaesthetically ["*Ich gehe*," "*'Ich bewege mich' kinästhetisch*"] in a different sense than physical-bodies, and as we will see, than the earth-ground (cf. Ursprung, 314).

39. This seems to be a reference to Aristotle, *De Caelo*. See book 2, chapters 13–14. See also Husserl's comments on how the Earth becomes a mere finite thing among things through idealization (H XXIX 141).

40. Ursprung, 317: "Aber das ist eben die Frage, ob und wie ich zur Körperlichkeit käme, in dem Sinne, daß die Erde 'astronomisch' eben ein Körper unter den anderen, darunter den Himmelskörpern wäre."

41. Ursprung, 312: "Aber es ist doch alles zunächst auf den Boden aller relativen Bodenkörper, auf den Erdboden bezogen."

42. Ursprung, 320: "Ohne weiteres wird die Homogenisierung von uns so verstanden, daß die Erde selbst ein Körper sei, auf dem wir zufällig herumkriechen."

43. Ursprung, 319: "Aber jedes Volk und seine Historizität und jedes Übervolk (Übernation) ist selbst beheimatet letztlich natürlich auf der 'Erde,' und alle Entwicklungen, alle relativen Historien haben insofern eine einzige Urhistorie, deren Episoden sie sind."

44. See Merleau-Ponty, *Phénoménologie*, 198 f.

45. Ursprung, 318: "ist Erde mit Leiblichkeit und Körperlichkeit konstituiert, so ist auch 'Himmel' notwendig als Feld des äußerst [reading 'äußerst' for

'äuserst'] noch räumlich Erfahrbaren für mich und uns alle—vom Erdboden aus." See also 317 and 324.

46. Ursprung, 317. I take up the notion of *stamm* in relation to generative sense-constitution in chapter 12.

47. Cf. Ursprung, 310, 312, 313, 318, 320, 323, 324.

48. Ursprung, 324: "Alle Tiere, alle Lebewesen, alles Seiende überhaupt hat Seinssinn nur von meiner konstitutiven Genesis and diese 'irdische' geht voran."

Section 3

1. See Canguilhem, *Le normal et le pathologique,* esp. part 1; hereafter *Le normal.* One of the cornerstone phenomena for this interpretation was diabetes. Cf. *Le normal,* 34 ff.

2. In Freud's early theory abnormality included (1) "perversion," which is a deviation of energy from the proper (sexual) object and from the proper goal, i.e., the release of tension; (2) "neurosis," which is the negation of perversion; and (3) "psychosis." He is not always clear about the status of "inversion" or homosexuality. In any case, it does not seem to be an inversion of nature. See Freud, *Gesammelte Werke,* vol. 16, 233 ff. and vol. 5, 59 ff. ("Drei Abhandlungen über Sexualtheorie"). I would like to thank Karmen MacKendrick for many engaging discussions on Freud and the problem of normality and abnormality.

3. Durkheim, *The Rules of Sociological Method,* esp. 48 f., 55, 61, 79 in the chapter entitled "The Normal and the Pathological"; hereafter *Sociological Method.*

4. Cf. H XIV 325; H XIV, 132 fn.; H XV 155; and Ms. D 13 I (1915/1916/1917), 186a: "ja es sind wohl mancherlei Stufen, entsprechend mancherlei Normalitäten."

5. "Normalität in ihrer konstitutiven Bedeutung." These are the opening words for Husserl's general description of the contents of manuscripts D 13 I, 121a–214a.

6. See H XIII 360 and H XIV 131. See also Ms. D 13 I (1921/1910), 123a: "Es wird auch hier notwendig sein, vom Limes-Fall des solipsistischen Ich auszugehen und von der Annahme, daß sich in einer Kontinuität des Erfahrens als Korrelat eine einheitliche Welt konstituiert." See also, e.g., manuscripts D 13 I (1917), 214a: " 'Zuerst' hat das solipsistische Ich seine Welt, es konstituiert sie als normale Welt"; and D 13 I, 174a: "Denken wir uns nun ein solipsistisches Ich mit orthoaesthetischer und logischer Normalität."

Chapter 8

1. See Ms. F I 9 (1898/1904–5), "Anfänge über Wahrnehmung."

2. See Freud, "Drei Abhandlungen über Sexualtheorie."

3. Ms. F I 9, 69a/66b: "Unter einer normalen Wahrnehmung verstehen wir eine solche, in welcher der präsentierende Empfindungskomplex der *eigentlich präsentierten Erscheinung (dem direkt präsentierten Merkmalkomplex)* ähnlich ist." Also, "Als *normal* kann man vorerst eine Wahrnehmung bezeichnen, die den Gegenstand bzw. die *Seite des Gegenstandes 'zeigt, wie sie wirklich aussieht'*. Das tut sie aber, wenn der in der Wahrnehmung erlebte Komplex sinnlicher Inhalte (ich meine die präsentierende Empfindungskomplexion) ein korrektes, angemessenes *Abbild ist für* den *direkt präsentierten Komplex von Bestimmtheiten*, den wir die erscheinende Seite des Gegenstandes nennen."

4. Here Husserl assumes that the tactile dimension is the consistent, standard measure of reality.

5. Ms. F I 9, 67b: "Aber die [d.i. Tast- und Gesichtsinhalten] widerstreiten einander nicht. Die Sinne streiten nicht, sondern die Deutungen."

6. See, for example, H XI 34 f. This view is confirmed in a text written by Husserl after 1930 (Ms. A VII 31, 5) concerning the differentiation of modalization and discordance in normality and abnormality: "Unterscheidung von Modalisierung und Unstimmigkeit zwischen normalen und anomalen Menschen im Konnex," H XV 52. He writes, "*Diese Stimmigkeit und Unstimmigkeit ist aber wohl zu unterscheiden von der im eigenen Gang der Konstitution der Natur für das Einzel-Ich und wieder in der normalen Vergemeinschaftung eintretenden Modalisierung und Ausscheidung von Schein.*" See also H XV 157.

7. Furthermore, if evidence is the experience of truth, and if truth is understood through a theory of coherence, then evidence cannot be punctual or explicated through a theory of adequation. It must take place over time via the internal concordance of sense unity.

8. Ms. D 13 I, 213a: "Die Idee der Normalität im vorhin angegebenen Sinne ist eine solche, daß die Welt der für die wahre Natur konstitutiven Phänomene, also auch die Welt der Naturwissenschaft genau dieselbe wäre für Subjekte, für welche es keine wandelbare Sinnlichkeit gäbe."

9. See Ms. D 13 II, 16a: "und er findet die Dinge (auch Leiber als Dinge) in einem Relativismus der Kausalität, wechselnd in seinen sinnlichen Beschaffenheiten je nach Umständen."

10. Ms. D 13 II (Göttingen period, probably between 1907 and 1912), 73b: "In der Physik enthüllt sich das reale, objektive Wesen der Dingwelt: jedes Subjekt kann sich das identische physikalische Wesen herausarbeiten, wenn es in normaler oder mindestens verallgemeinert normaler leiblicher Verfassung ist, also daß es einstimmige Erscheinungen hat, ausreichend die Dingeigenschaften darzustellen, (und einen logischen Verstand)."

See also Ms. D 13 XIII, 3: "Idee von 'Menschen', die zwar anomale Phänomene haben, aber nur hinsichtlich der sinnlichen Qualitäten, die also alles Quantitative bestimmen können, nachmessen können etc., die soweit also normal sind, daß sie hinreichend deutlich sehen oder tasten. . . . Kurzum trotz anomaler Phänomene ist ihnen eine Physik zugänglich."

11. Ms. D 13 II, 16a: "Natürlich ist die Fiktion einer Gemeinschaftsphysik, die nie die Anomalität der Leiblichkeit kennenlernen [würde], nicht

durchzuführen, da sie ja Leiber als Dinge behandelnd bald auf das Anomale stoßen würde, es selbst mit erzeugen würde. Aber das Stück Versuch, die Fiktion auszuführen, zeigt doch schon, daß im Felde der physikalischen Thematik das Anomale und die Leibbeziehung nicht liegt, und daß der Physiker ein geschloßenes Thema als physikalische Natur hat, wenn er das Anomale auschaltet. Natürlich ist das nicht zufällig."

12. Ms. D 13 II, 15b: "Muß man also nicht sagen: der Physiker ist rein objektiv gerichtet; d.h. er nimmt die in einstimmiger normaler Erfahrung gegebene Welt als Wirklichkeit und interessiert sich nicht, *wie mit dem Fungieren der Leiblichkeit die sinnlichen Gegebenheiten zusammenhängen*, nicht dafür, daß eine gewisse Leiblichkeit in gewissen Umständen, in gewisser Verfassung erforderlich ist, damit das Subjekt der Erfahrung die jeweiligen Erfahrungen und *bald normal, bald anomal* hat . . . er betrachtet auch die Leiber nicht als Sinnesfunktion übende Organe, sondern als Gegenstände normaler Erfahrung" (my emphasis).

13. Canguilhem, *Le normal*, 148.

14. Ibid., 57.

15. Cf. Ibid., 81 ff.

16. Freud, "Drei Abhandlungen über Sexual theorie," 40, 60, 65.

17. The only exceptions to Husserl's otherwise consistent employment of the term '*anomal*', with which I am familiar, date, first, from 1898/1905: "Indessen dürften es sich doch zeigen, daß auch rein phänomenologisch über den Unterschied zwischen Normalem und *Abnormalem* allerlei auszumachen ist" (my emphasis). Ms. F I 9, 69a/66b. The other exceptions occur around 1930–31 (H XV 139): "abnormer Menschen einer abnormen Umwelt" and (H XV 159): "dem radikal Abnormen."

18. See H XIII 364. In fact, at one point, Husserl goes so far as to say that the activity of rupturing or interrupting is the genuine sense of anomaly. Ms. D 13 I (1921), 122a: "Demgegenüber ist das eigentliche Anomale das, was Einstimmigkeit der Erfahrung . . . nach gewissen Seiten durchbricht."

19. H IV 66. Where the visual field is concerned, Husserl's examples include getting struck in the eyes, putting on colored glasses, ingesting santonin (which makes one see things yellow), etc. In the tactile sphere, Husserl often focuses on suffering a burn.

See Ms. D 13 I, 174a: "Nun kommen aber Durchbrüche der Einstimmigkeit. Alle Dinge erscheinen plötzlich geändert, auch der Leib. Ich habe Santonin genossen oder einen Schlag in die Augen erhalten, oder ich habe eine farbige Brille aufgesetzt. Die radikale Änderung betrifft die visuelle Sphäre. Ich habe mir die Hand verbrannt: die Änderungen betreffen alle Tasterscheinungen, soweit diese Hand tastend fungiert usw."

20. Freud, *Gesammelte Werke*, vol. 14, 113–205.

21. Ms. D 13 I, 125b: "Hierbei ist das Erscheinungssystem, das der freien Möglichkeiten des Durchlaufens, auf mein waches Ich bezogen, das Ich des 'Ich kann das und das tun' "; and "Also wenn sich die Freiheit des Ich-kann ungehemmt verwirklicht, so führt das eine endlose Zukunft mit sich. Aber die Zukunft ist nicht völlig offen."

22. Husserl describes *Anomalität* as "das Problem der Erfahrungsunterbrechung" (Ms. D 13 I, 123a).

23. Ms. D 13 II, 42a: "der Leib ist normal, wenn dieses Vorgehen ungehemmt ist und die zugehörigen Erfahrungsreihen für alle in Funktion zu setzenden Sinne einstimmig laufen. . . . Es gibt demgegenüber ein anomales Funktionieren, bei Hemmungen, oder das sonstige Fungieren ist normal, aber das Organ selbst ist geändert." There is a similar qualification earlier in this manuscript, p. 39b.

24. Nevertheless, phenomena like pain and grief do occupy the field of psychological anomaly for Husserl. Cf. H XIV 69.

25. Ms. D 13 I, 123b f.: "Aber diese 'Hemmung' des Augenschliessens (die nicht zur konstituierenden Erfahrung gehört) ist eine freie Hemmung. . . . Aber Schlaf ist eine andere Unterbrechung als das Augenschliessen; und so ist die Lösung des zum letzteren gehörigen Problems noch keine des Schlafproblems. In den Schlaf versinke ich unwillkürlich, obschon ich ihm in gewissem Grade widerstehen kann; aber das spielt kaum eine Rolle." See also p. 123a: "Als Schlaf, Ohnmacht und dergleichen kennen wir solche vollständige Unterbrechungen."

26. For example, there is an equation of normality with being awake and "activity" on the one hand, and sleep, unconsciousness, etc., with passivity on the other. As a consequence, not only would sleep "interrupt" activity (and be abnormal), but passivity, too, would have to be seen as abnormal. This implication is clearly contrary to the sense of Husserl's analyses of passive syntheses and their special role in the constitution of normality. In conjunction with Ms. D 13 I, 121a ff., see H XV 154.

27. Ms. D 13 I, 161b: "sondern weil die neuen Fälle isoliert sind und der bestimmt geordneten Beziehung auf die Umstände entbehren."

28. Ms. D 13 II, 16b: "Die Erfahrung selbst mit dem in ihr genetisch entwickelten Erfahrungssinn überwindet alle Relativismen."

29. Ms. D 13 I (1921), 232a f.: "Aber 'normal' heißt das erst durch Kontrast mit Anomalitäten, die von diesem ersten, notwendig zuerst konstituierten System der Einstimmigkeit abweichen. Wenn nun Abweichungen eintreten und dann eventuell wieder verschwinden, so bleibt die erste Konstitution wirksam, . . . so heißt die Wahrnehmung normal und das Wahrgenommene das Normale und Wahre, wenn alles erwartungsmäßig im System der ursprünglichen Einstimmigkeit verläuft."

See also Ms. D 13 II, 14a: "wir sprechen von Verbrennen des Fingers, in Folge dessen die Tasterscheinungen desselben krankhaft abweichen von den normalen." See too D 13 II (1921), 60b: "Sie sind bloße Ausnahmen, Abweichungen von der Normalität, und die anomalen Erscheinungen werden aufgefaßt als solche Abweichungen und bezogen auf Krankheit, auf geänderte Leiblichkeit."

30. Ms. D 13 I, 161a: "Diese Unstimmigkeiten sind wirklich Unstimmigkeiten, wenn das Subjekt seine Apperzeptionen entwickelt hat im Rahmen einer *beständig sich erhaltenden* Normalität, auf die also ein System der Einstimmigkeit bezogen ist, tritt die Unstimmigkeit auf und zwar so, daß im Kontrast zu den normalen und

motivierten Umständen geänderte, andersartige Umstände merklich werden; und wird in wiederholter Erfahrung dieses Zusammenhanges die unstimmige Erscheinung auf die geänderten Umstände bezogen, dann entwickelt sich motiviert eine neue Apperzeption, wonach eben zu den normalen Umständen die normale Erscheinung, zu den anomalen die anomale gehört. Vorausgesetzt, daß in den neuen Umständen wieder *Einheit* der Erscheinung durch *mannigfaltig* frei motivierte Erscheinungen durchzuhalten ist und die Rückkehr in die alten Umstände unter Festhaltung derselben Einheit möglich ist, haben wir dann eben wieder eine *erweiterte Einstimmigkeit* und der alten Apperzeption hat sich nur eine neue apperzeptive Schicht, eine neue Richtung der Abwandlung von Erscheinungen angereiht" (my emphasis).

31. Ms. D 13 I, 186a f.: "nun treten aber gelegentlich und wiederholt, schon in der ersten Sphäre (der der Genesis der normalen Aesthesie) 'anomale Wahrnehmungsbedingungen' auf; wir sehen durch ein farbiges Glas. Das farbige Glas durchbricht das erste System der *normalen Orthoaesthesie,* aber das geänderte Weltbild ist *wieder einstimmig,* solange das blaue Glas vor dem Auge ist. . . . So oft es vor das Auge gesetzt wird, ist die Modifikation wieder da, ein neues, in sich *ortho[aesthetisches],* wenn auch beschränktes System" (my emphasis). See also Ms. D 13 I, 161b.

32. René Leriche, *Physiologie et pathologie du tissu osseux* (Paris: Masson, 1939), 11, cited by Canguilhem, in *Le normal,* 56.

33. Durkheim, *Sociological Method,* 52. The difference between 'anomaly' and a new concordance might be seen in the difference between the Spanish verbs "to be," *estar* and *ser.* For example, one could say "El está rico" and mean "he is (i.e., has just become) rich" or "El es rico" and mean "he is rich" (as a permanent characteristic). Or again, one could say "Estoy grande" and mean "I am tall (for my age) or one might assert "Soy grande" and imply that "I am (always) tall." I would like to thank Leslie Brown for her suggestion of using the verbs *ser* and *estar* to illustrate this difference between discordance *qua* anomaly and concordance.

34. From "La méthode pathologique," in *Encyclopédie française 8, 1938,* cited by Canguilhem, in *Le normal,* 71.

35. Durkheim, *Sociological Method,* 66.

36. Ibid., 49, 55, 61.

Chapter 9

1. H XIII 379; H XIV 123, 134. See the text cited below in n. 9 this chapter.

2. See Ms. D 13 I, 168a: "das Sehen bei hellem Tageslicht z.B. ist bevorzugt für die kindliche Entwicklung; ist es dunkel, schläft das Kind"; and Ms. D II, 13a: "weniger günstig, wie das Sehen im Dunkeln gegenüber dem Sehen im hellen Tageslicht."

3. Ms. D 13 I, 160b: "Das Tageslicht, der helle Tag läßt die Dingmerkmale *am reichsten und differenziertesten* hervortreten, in ihm betätige ich mich daher mit Vorliebe" (my emphasis).

4. Ms. D 13 I, 206b: "im Schatten sieht man nicht so viele Unterschiede; das Hellere, Belichtete gilt als das Bessere und die Norm."

5. Husserl anticipated such a discussion of the normal as optimal in 1905 when he characterized it as that which is "maximum." Cf. Ms. F I 9, esp. 42a–48a. He writes, for example (42a): "Geht das kontinuierliche Wahrnehmen in der betreffenden Richtung hinreichend weit fort, so kommen wir schließlich zu einem *Höhe*-und zugleich *Wendepunkt*, in welchem die Steigerung der erfüllenden Klarheit in Minderung übergeht, m.a.W. wir kommen zu einem *Maximalpunkt* der perzeptiven Klarheit."

Writing of the difference between direct and indirect presentation (45a): "Wir könnten es auch so tun, daß wir uns so jenes vielgegliederte Reihensystem in 'unbewußter' Weise reproduziert dächten und nun weiter fingierten: es durchlaufe—unbewußt—unser durch den präsenten Empfindungsinhalt in seiner Richtung fixiertes Interesse zunächst die erste Gruppe von Leitungsbahnen, die Linien kontinuierlicher Steigerung der das Interesse primär erregenden Momente, bis es in den *Maximalwerten* befriedigt ruht. Hier ist der Verlauf durch Ähnlichkeit bestimmt. Aber nun folgt das Interesse der Kontiguität, es überfließt auf die mitverbundenen Momente, erhält durch sie neue Intentionen, die dann wieder in die Linien der Steigerung und Ähnlichkeit überführen und in den neuen *Maximalmomenten* terminieren" (my emphasis).

6. Ms. D 13 I, 242b: "Das normale Ding fungiert im Leben zugleich in dem anderen Sinne als normal, als es zur Norm für die anomalen Erscheinungen dient." Also Ms. D 13 II, 72b: "Der Typus normaler Erfahrung bestimmt bevorzugte optimale Erscheinungen unter motivierenden Umständen, auf die alle zur Erfahrungseinheit zusammengehenden Erscheinungen zurückbezogen sind." See also H XIII 364.

7. H XI 23 f. See p. 150 and n. 3.

8. Ms. D 13 I, 175a: "Es ist eine 'Modifikation' sie weist auf normale Erscheinungen zurück, als Normen, als Optima." Cf. above, chapter 8, n. 29. As we will see, there is still a possibility of a "deviation" instituting a new normality, and thus at the same time pointing to and pointing beyond a particular norm.

9. Ms. D 13 II, 44b: "Zu berücksichtigen ist aber, daß der Begriff der Anomalität nicht ein ganz willkürlicher oder an das Faktum gebundener ist: anomal ist eine Wahrnehmung, wenn sie *nicht nur* das Wahrgenommene *ungewöhnlich*, sondern '*schlechter*' gibt, mit einem *geringeren Reichtum an sachlichen Differenzen*. Im Faktum der gewöhnlichen und nur ausnahmsweise durchbrochenen Normalität, wie wir sie kennen, liegt also eine *Teleologie*" (my emphasis). On the role of teleology within so-called "facts," see *Krisis 2*, text nos. 24, 26, 27, and my "The New 'Crisis'," 567–70.

10. Ms. D 13 I, 179a f.: "Aber zum Ding gehört es, daß diese normale Farbe doch wieder sich wandelt, eben je nach Auftreten von belichtenden Körpern bei Tageslicht oder bei fehlendem Tageslicht. . . . Es scheidet sich also Farbe als Erscheinungsfarbe (im Vollschema) und Farbe an sich, ein Ansich aber, das eigentlich mit gesehener Farbe keine Ähnlichkeit hätte, wenn nicht die *optimale*

Farbe das *Telos* wäre, *und* eine *wirkliche* Farbe im ursprünglichen Sinn eben *erscheinender* Farbe" (my emphasis).

11. Ms. D 13 I, 179b: "Aber in der Wahrnehmung, in der Auffassung des Körpers als eines perzeptiv farbigen dient eben jede aktuelle 'Farbe' als zu ihren *Umständen* gehörig und zugleich als *Index* für die *normale* (*optimale*) Farbe, die sozusagen der Generalnenner ist" (my emphasis). Also Ms. D 13 I, 180b: "Es zentrieren sich also in der optimalen Farbe geordnete Mannigfaltigkeiten von Zuständen in intentionaler Implikation."

See also Ms. D 13 I, 182a: "Das Optimum oder der Typus von Umständen, der für die gewöhlichen Interessen Optima ergibt (diesen wechselnden Interessen entsprechende mit weiteren Umstandswandlungen, aber innerhalb dieses Typus, etwa Tageslicht) wird nur zum zentrierenden Index der intentionalen Mannigfaltigkeiten."

12. Cf. n. 10 above.

13. Ms. D 13 I, 232b: "*Genetisch* muß eine harmonische Urkonstitution vollzogen sein und muß also *zum Norm werden*, und es muß dann die normale 'wahre' Dingwelt, wenn sie als Nullsystem und Gleichgewichtslage fungiert, in die alle Abweichungen zurückzukehren pflegen, zwar als Bezugssystem fungieren, aber doch zu bloßer Erscheinung werden" (my emphasis).

14. Husserl asks, for example (Ms. D 13 I, 69a): "warum sagen wir, wie immer die Kinästhesen zum Stillstand bringend . . . 'das' sei der eine und selbe Gegenstand; aber einmal erführen wir ihn, sehen wir ihn deutlicher, das andere Mal undeutlicher, und die einen Erscheinungsweisen seien *besser*, die anderen *schlechter*, und nur im Zentralbild, da sei der Gegenstand selbst gegeben, im Zentralbild, da erscheine er, wie er selbst ist (oder vielmehr im kontinuierlichen *Ineinanderüberführen* der Zentralbilder, wodurch alle 'Punkte' eines jeden und damit auch mittels aller unterscheidbaren Punkte die Fernbilder in den Zentralpunkt *übergeführt sind als optimalen*)" (my emphasis).

See also Wilhelm Schapp, *Beiträge zur Phänomenologie der Wahrnehmung*, 63 f. This work was written as his Inaugural-Dissertation for Husserl in 1909.

15. Merleau-Ponty, *Phénoménologie*, 348 f. (my emphasis).

16. See Ms. D 13 I, 206a: "Also Beziehung auf optimale Erscheinungen und optimale Verhältnisse, bzw., auf die als normale *bevorzugt* werden; in bezug auf die normalen sind die Verhältnisse anomalen sekundär: die unter ihnen gegebenen Erscheinungen haben symbolischen Charakter, Anzeigen deutend auf Normales."

17. Merleau-Ponty, *Phénoménologie*, 367 f., my emphases.

18. Ms. D 13 I, 241a: "Zu beachten ist dabei, daß Beziehung auf dasselbe bei einem Funktionieren verschiedener Organe vermittelt ist durch ihr 'übereinstimmendes Gerichtetsein'. Jedes System der Kinästhese ist in Wahrnehmungsfunktionen auf jedes andere in bestimmter Weise bezogen; jedes System hat in jedem sein Entsprechendes, wobei aber zu berücksichtigen ist, daß, was die Sache sehr kompliziert macht, z.B. jeder Finger seine eigene Kinästhese hat, aber als Finger der Hand an ihrer Kinästhese teilnimmt und daß nun zu seinem kinästhetischen System auch all die Bewegungsmöglichkeiten

gehören durch Bewegung der ganzen Hand; dann weiter ebenso durch Armbewegung usw."

19. H XIII 365; H IV 66, 69; and see Ms. D 13 I, 175a: "Die Änderung des ausgezeichneten Sinnesorganes bedingt in Bezug auf ihn [der Leib] eine Gruppe anomaler Dinggegebenheiten; ich erfahre dabei, es ist dasselbe Ding, das mit der kranken Hand modifiziert gegeben ist, mit der gesunden Hand normal gegeben. Die Zusammenstimmung ist nicht ganz aufgehoben."

20. Ms. D 13 I, 215b: "aber wenn [sie] im einzelnen anomal werden, so geschieht das derart, daß sie 'für einander eintreten' können; und daß das allgemein möglich ist, das besagt selbst wieder eine Art Normalität höherer Stufe und darin eine gewisse normale Harmonie zu den fungierenden Organen, wonach immer normale verbleiben und die anomalen zu ihnen harmonieren." Cf. H XIII 364, 368.

21. Canguilhem, *Le normal*, 73–75.

22. Ms. D 13 I, 215b: "Ich kann dasselbe Ding in verschiedener Weise wahrnehmen und scheide die Wahrnehmungen nach den 'Sinnen' als optische, haptische etc., und als haptische verschiedener haptischer 'Organe'. Alle Organe fungieren '*normal', das sagt, sie stimmen zusammen*" (my emphasis).

23. See n. 18 this chapter. Let me cite more completely a passage I noted above (see chapter 8, n. 23). Ms. D 13 II, 42a: "der Leib ist normal, wenn dieses Vorgehen ungehemmt ist und die zugehörigen Erfahrungsreihen für alle in Funktion zu setzenden Sinne einstimmig laufen, so daß, was der eine Sinn als funktionierender (oder ein Partialsinn in einem Gesamtsinn) als gegenständliches Korrelat zeigt, von jedem anderen Sinn (in seiner 'Sprache'), gezeigt werden könnte und gezeigt wird, wenn er herangezogen wird, oder wenn das gezeigt wird, was von der Einheit der Gegenständlichkeit, die sich immerfort einstimmig durchhält, zu erwarten ist."

24. Minkowski, *Lived Time: Phenomenological and Psychopathological Studies*, 285.

25. Husserl writes, for example: "Für den Normalen hat das Ding nicht einen dinglichen Aufbau aus Sehding und Tastding; . . . Das Ding ist durch beide Erscheinungsgruppen nicht getrennt, sondern in einheitlicher Apperzeption, konstituiert" (Ms. D 13 I, 177a). See also H XIII 363, 365.

26. What the latter means simply is that I see at 20 feet what someone else sees at 20 feet; accordingly 20/200 vision means that I see at 20 feet what someone else sees at 200 feet. Why 20 feet became normative is itself a qualitative judgment and need not concern us at this time.

27. See Wittgenstein, *Bemerkungen über die Farben*, vol. 3, 54, 170, 278, and 286.

28. Ms. D 13 II, 63b: "wie die anschauliche sich anschaulich im Fortleben in der Natur und Naturerfahrung sich erweitert, sich neu und besser bestimmt, vielleicht *neue Optima* hervortreten läßt, so schafft die Wissenschaft sicherlich auch Bereicherung der Erfahrungskenntnis und baut darauf" (my emphasis).

29. See Sacks, *The Man Who Mistook His Wife for a Hat and Other Clinical Tales*, 195–213. Let me thank Eva Kittay for bringing this example to my attention.

30. I take the term "optimalizing" from Husserl. See Ms. D 13 I (1921), 65b:

"Erzielung von Bildern als optimalen erwächst durch Einübung. Ferner muß gezeigt werden, wie durch die Erfahrung vom Übergang aller Bilder in den Zentrallagen und der damit gegebenen *Optimalisierung* jedes ruhende Bild zum Index für sein Optimum wird und für einen besten 'direkten' Weg dahin" (my emphasis).

31. Ms D 13 II, 63a: "Die *normale* Leiblichkeit bedeutet dann diejenige, die einen Kreis von *Optima herstellt oder ermöglicht*" (my emphasis).

32. See Canguilhem, *Le normal,* 130, and cf. 132–33: "L'homme ne se sent en bonne santé—qui est la santé—que lorsqu'il se sent plus que normal—c'est-à-dire adapté au milieu et à ses exigences—*mais normatif,* capable de suivre de nouvelles normes de vie" (my emphasis).

33. In particular, falciparum malaria. I would like to thank Claudia Roussos for this example.

34. See Canguilhem, *Le normal,* 91.

35. Thus Husserl writes, Ms. D 13 II, 206b: "wieder das Normale: Sehen mit Brille, wo ich scharfe Konturen sehe etc., und wieder ist das Anomale bildlich oder äußerlich signitiv bezogen auf das Normale." See also H IV 69.

36. Ms. D 13 I, 233a: "Ein normales System muß sich also ursprünglich konstituieren. Die Frage ist nur, ob es notwendig ist, daß ein solches System immer als Bezugssystem verbleiben muß."

37. Ms. D 13 I, 175a: "(Doch ist denkbar, daß die leibliche Änderung auch 'bessere' Erscheinungen ergibt.) Wer ein pathologisches Sinnesorgan *ursprünglich* hatte, wer seine erste Konstitution mit Erscheinungen geleistet hat, die normal sind,—aber bei nachträglicher Gesundung des Organs wird eine *neue optimale* Erscheinungsgruppe derselben Dinge konstituiert, und die bestimmt nun *trotz der Rückbeziehung auf die frühere Norm,* die für die Durchhaltung desselben notwendig ist, im weiteren Leben (was das Ding selbst ist)" (my emphasis).

38. See Scheler, *Gesammelte Werke 2: Der Formalismus in der Ethik und die Materiale Wertethik,* 160; hereafter *Formalismus.* See also Canguilhem, *Le normal,* 91.

39. Ms. D 13 II, 63a: "Dann wäre eine 'feinere' Sinnesorganisation, mit gesteigerten Sehleistungen etc., nicht anomal, *sondern erst recht normal, gesteigert normal,* und, was vorher normal hieß, wäre anomal" (my emphasis).

40. Instructive here is Husserl's analysis of the "law of propagation" published in the supplementary edition of *Krisis* writings. Here he examines the formation of a new teleology out of what becomes the "previous" one in terms of normality and abnormality in relation to species. See H XXIX, text Nr. 27. See also my "The New 'Crisis'," section 3.

Chapter 10

1. This excerpt is found as a marginal note to Ms. D 13 (3. Teil), 151a of Husserl's stenographic manuscripts. It is included in an appendix to Part III of the D 13 series entitled "Auszüge" and edited by Ulrich Claesges. Husserl's

comment to which I refer runs as follows: "[am Rande] Tendenz auf das Optimum als *Auswahlprinzip* der praktischen Möglichkeiten" (my emphasis).

2. I began to articulate this structure in my "Totalitarianism, Homogeneity of Power, Depth: Towards a Socio-Political Ontology," esp. 639 ff. For the role of selection and exclusion in the contexts of speech and action see Waldenfels, *Ordnung im Zwielicht,* esp. part B. I will take up some implications of Waldenfels's highly original work in the final section.

3. H XI 23 f. Cf. "Auszüge" from D 13 (Teil III) to 27a: "[am Rande] Optimale Gegebenheit und praktische Interessen."

4. See above pp. 146–47 and chapter 9, n. 38.

5. Canguilhem, *Le normal,* 79 (my emphasis).

6. Ibid., 84.

7. Ibid., 121.

8. Scheler, *Formalismus,* 164–66.

9. Ibid., 165, (my emphasis).

10. Ibid., 166.

11. Ibid., 159; see also 167.

12. Ibid., 159.

13. We could say, moreover, that even for perception, a blank cube is not given with six equal sides as if they could be homogeneously splayed out before us.

14. See Ms. D 13 I, 51a–74b. This part of the manuscript of over forty stenographic pages is entitled "Typologie des visuellen Feldes und die zugehörige Kinästhese. Grundstück zu einer Lehre von den Kinästhesen. Das Doppelfeld. Theorie des Reliefs." See, for example, his comment (p. 64b): "denn in der Gradualität der Abhebung wird etwas anfangen können, sich abzuheben, *was vorher nicht abgehoben war,* und so dann weiter." See also H XI 163 ff.

15. H XI 164 (my emphasis). Does this mean, in turn, that the constitution of temporality and the process of temporalization is in essence an ongoing self-affection, or again, that self-affection is the origin of temporality?

16. Cf. H XI 172 and H XI 168 (my emphasis).

17. Ms. D 13 I, 65a: "Wir nehmen an, daß Bilder, Abgehobenheiten in der Empfindungssphäre das Ich 'affizieren', auf es Reize üben, und daß die Stärke des Reizes funktionell abhängig ist von der beschriebenen Gradualität. *Das Optimum ist also ein relatives Maximum* des geübten Reizes, dem nun auch ein 'Interesse', eine Zuwendung des Ich, folgen mag. Das Ich ist nun bei dem es affizierenden" (my emphasis).

18. See Ms. D 13 I, 69a, cited above in chapter 9, n. 14.

19. Scheler, *Formalismus,* 160 f.

20. See, for example, W. B. Clapham, Jr., *Natural Ecosystems,* 90 f.; hereafter *Ecosystems.*

21. Husserl tends to define the typical as a vague or morphological essence and thus ontologically (e.g., H XIII 370), and the optimal as an "in-itself" and thus phenomenologically. But given Husserl's tendency to understand normality also as a "typical constancy [*typische Konstanz*] in the comportment of

lived-corporeality" or "a typical condition [*typischer Stand*] in the whole typicality [*Typik*] of lived-corporeality," I believe it makes more sense to understand the systematic connection between optimality and typicality in the following way: The typical is the concordant repetition of the optimal. (Cf. H XIV 121).

22. This typical stylization of comportment plays itself out in the lived-body itself. Anyone who has tried speaking a foreign language knows how the typical is not a *mere* repetition, and how it functions selectively and exclusively by "forecasting" or "preempting" the concordant integration of sounds. Pronouncing the French "*fumer*" is easier for an American than the past participle "*vu*," even though abstractly the "u" is the same sound. The juxtaposition of the vowel and the consonant are so "atypical" for Americans that initially they make no auditory or vocal distinction between "*vous*" and "*vu*" even though it is explicitly emphasized that there is one.

23. See Goldstein, *The Organism*, esp. chapter 10.

24. Schutz, *The Phenomenology of the Social World*, 194; hereafter *Social World*.

25. Ibid., 186 f.

26. Ibid., 181 ff.

27. Ibid., 182.

28. Ibid., 184.

29. Schutz, *Collected Papers III: Studies in Phenomenological Philosophy*, esp. 92–116, 124–30; hereafter *Collected Papers III*. See also Schutz, *Collected Papers I: The Problem of Social Reality*. See also Schutz's letter to Gurwitsch from December 1957 in which he is extremely sensitive to the formation of types and how a type becomes an "habitual acquisition" in *Alfred Schütz, Aron Gurwitsch: Briefwechsel, 1939–1959*.

30. Cf. Schutz, *Collected Papers III*, 96.

31. Husserl, *Erfahrung und Urteil*, 139 (my emphasis). See Schutz, *Collected Papers III*, 97.

32. Sorre, *Les fondements biologiques de la géographie humaine: essai d'une écologie de l'homme*, 415; hereafter *Géographie humaine*. See also Canguilhem, *Le normal*, 110 f.

33. Sorre, *Géographie humaine*, 415 f. Cf. 78 and chapter 3, "La formation de l'oekoumème."

34. Ibid., 412.

35. Here we might want to characterize, along with Schutz, the typical as the origin of the familiar. Cf. *Collected Papers III*, 110.

36. See Canguilhem's discussion on Quetelet and Halbwachs in *Le normal*, 100 ff. and 196 f.

37. See H XXIX text Nr. 27. See also Ms. D 13 I, 161a: "Die Normalität bezieht sich auf die Spezies." See also H XV 155, 159.

38. See Canguilhem, *Le normal*, 90.

39. The eagle's vision is optimally different than human vision and figures into the very form of life; the dog's sense of smell is typically different from an eagle's. In an earlier text (1915–17), Husserl seems on the verge of limiting normality to a species. He writes: "Zuerst erscheint das als eine wichtige

Ergänzung zum Begriff der Normalität. Aber auch als Idee ist das Optimum wohl kaum verwendbar. Oder kann sie begrenzt werden? Auge des Adlers, Geruch des Hundes etc.? Die Zahl der Sinne? Oder soll man hier eine "*transzendentale Idee*" im Kantischen Sinne supponieren?" (H XIII 380).

40. On this point see Scheler, *Formalismus*, 161 ff.

41. Contrary to Derrida, who takes "de-limitation" to mean literally the dissolution of limits, I use this expression here as the *process of limit formation*. (See Derrida, "Les fins de l'homme," in *Marges*, 129–64.) Delimitation is a new level of selection and exclusion or "discriminating" experience. I discuss delimitation in the final section as the process of appropriation/disappropriation.

42. Waldenfels, "Grenzen der Legitimierung und die Frage nach der Gewalt," in *Der Stachel des Fremden*, 115; hereafter *Stachel*.

Section 4

1. From *Paul Celan: Poems*, 152 ff.

RADIX MATRIX
Wie man zum Stein spricht, wie
du,
mir vom Abgrund her, von
einer Heimat her Ver-
schwisterte, Zu-
geschleuderte, du,
du mir vorzeiten,
du mir im Nichts einer Nacht,
du in der Aber-Nacht Be-
gegnete, du
Aber-Du—:

Damals, da ich nicht da war,
damals, da du
den Acker abschrittst, allein:

Wer,
wer wars, jenes
Geschlecht, jenes gemordete, jenes
schwarz in den Himmel stehende:
Rute und Hode—?

(Wurzel.
Wurzel Abrahams. Wurzel Jesse. Niemandes

Wurzel—o
unser.)

Ja,
wie man zum Stein spricht, wie
du
mit meinen Händen dorthin
und ins Nichts greifst, so
ist, was hier ist:
auch dieser
Fruchtboden klafft,
dieses
Hinab
ist die eine der wild-
blühenden Kronen.

2. Concerning the role of generativity for Husserl's "Crisis" project in particular, see my "The New 'Crisis'," esp. section 4.

Chapter 11

1. Natanson, "Philosophische Grundfragen der Psychiatrie I: Philosophie und Psychiatrie"; hereafter "Psychiatrie."
2. Ibid., 924. See also on this point Grathoff, "Über Typik und Normalität im alltäglichen Milieu," 90; hereafter "Typik und Normalität."
3. For example, "Psychiatrie," 909, 910, 916.
4. Grathoff, "Typik und Normalität," 90.
5. Natanson, "Psychiatrie," 914.
6. Ibid., 910, 913 f., 924.
7. Ibid., 914.
8. Ibid., 919 f.
9. Ibid., 916 f.
10. Grathoff, "Typik und Normalität," 91; see also 89.
11. Ibid., 91. Cf. Natanson, "Psychiatrie," 917.
12. Ibid., 92.
13. See Gurwitsch, *Die Mitmenschlichen Begegnungen in der Milieuwelt,* esp. 82–95.
14. On the distinction between "other" and "alien," see chapter 3.
15. I have already suggested that generative problems were addressed in Husserl's writings on intersubjectivity and in the context of his "Crisis" reflections. A selection of the latter are included in *Krisis 2* (H XXIX), and feature prominently in texts nos. 1 and 4.
16. See Foucault, *Histoire de la folie à l'âge classique,* 94.
17. Cf. chapter 4 above, and compare chapter 12, esp. under the heading "Language, Expressive Communication, Narrative."

18. H XV 139: "Ist jeder *normale* Mensch historisch, konstituiert als seiend in einer historisch dauernden Gemeinschaft, so ist seine Umwelt, die Welt, die für ihn konkret konstituiert ist, *umgrenzt* als historische, unerachtet eines offenen Horizontes einer 'leeren' Raumzeitlichkeit und Welt; so, wenn wir die totale historische Gemeinschaft nehmen, die als totale sich in Sondergemeinschaften gliedert."

19. H XV 431: "Das *normale* Leben als *generatives* hat nun *seine* Geschichtlichkeit und zunächst die jeder Generation eigene Lebenszeitlichkeit und Weltzeitlichkeit, die selbst ihre Horizonte der Bekanntheit und Unbekanntheit hat" (my emphasis).

20. See Waldenfels, *Stachel,* 29f.

21. Ibid., 30.

22. H XV 214: "Es konstituiert sich also fremdes Menschentum, eine fremde Menschheit, als fremdes Volk etwa. *Eben damit* konstitutiert sich für mich and für uns '*unsere eigene*' Heimgenossenschaft, Volksgenossenschaft in Beziehung auf unsere Kulturumwelt als Welt unserer menschlichen Geltungen, unserer besonderen" (my emphasis).

23. H XV 176 n. 1: The remark runs as follows: "Meine Heimwelt, mein Volk. Das Universum in erster Form als Heimwelt *kommt nur zur Abhebung,* wenn schon andere Heimwelten, andere Völker mit im Horizont sind. Die Lebensumwelt im Horizont von fremden Lebensumwelten, mein Volk umgeben von fremden Völkern" (my emphasis).

24. H XV 165 f.: "*Die Auszeichnung, die im Wir und Jedermann steckt, ist die Normalität,* die aber *als solche sich erst abhebt* durch das Mitvorkommnis des Anomalen" (my emphasis added to Husserl's). But being no less uncomfortable with this conclusion he must draw—because it departs too radically from a theory of normality in which abnormality is its intentional modification—he quickly amends his formulation: H XV 166: "Oder vielmehr, von dem Normalen als an sich Erstem hebt das Anomale sich ab und tritt auf als intentionale Modifikation des Normalen."

Notice also that Husserl does experiment with a constitutive one-sidedness of home and alien. See for example H XV 235 and 215: "Hier ist also eine Aufgabe, die Fundierung der Seinsgeltungen aufzuklären, die ich und die irgendein Subjekt einer zunächst bloßen Heimwelt in Vollzug haben muß, um Welt und Heimwelt zu unterscheiden, bzw. um eine anderes, fremdes Menschentum mit seiner fremden Heimwelt im Unterschied von der meinen zu verstehen."

25. This is primarily the fault I find with Klaus Held's otherwise sagacious synthesis of material from vol. XV of the *Husserliana* focusing on the theme of homeworld and alienworld. See "Heimwelt, Fremdwelt, die eine Welt."

26. H XV 431: "Zwar gehört der Kontrast von heimisch oder vertraut und fremd zur beständigen Struktur jeder Welt, und zwar in einer beständigen Relativität." See also H XV 226 and 432 n.

27. H XV 212: "Wir sind nur, und für uns ist Welt nur in der Relativität von Normalitäten und Anomalitäten."

28. H XV 604: "Wie erhält sich diese Kontinuität in der Relativität von Vertrautheit und Fremde oder von verschiedene Stufen von Heimat und Fremde, Dorf und fremdes Dorf, Heimatland und fremdes Land mit fremder Heimgenossenschaft, eigenes Volk und fremdes Volk und doch 'europäische' Menschheit?"

Chapter 12

1. Calvino, *Invisible Cities*, 86.
2. Ms. A V 10 (ca. 1920), 77a: "Die niederste Stufe ist der Mensch in seinem Heim im engsten Sinne, wie primitiv oder 'kultiviert' es auch sein mag."
3. Ms. A V 10, 76–79, entitled "*Umwelt, Heimwelt.*" See, for example, 77a: "Diese Heimwelt ist Korrelat seines eigenen Daseins, er ist personales Subjekt für diese Welt und ist Subjekt seines 'Lebens'—das hier nicht eine momentane Lebens gegenwart bezeichnet, sondern das Leben in weitem Horizont (schließlich, mindest auf höherer Stufe des Menschentums: sein gesamtes Leben als Ganzheit), das Leben, das ihm 'vergönnt ist' oder ihm schicksalsmäßig 'auferlegt' ist." See also note 4 below. The fact that this is the first mention of homeworld in Husserl's writings is confirmed by René Toulemont, *L'essence de la société selon Husserl*, 184, n. 6.
4. Ms. A V 10, 77a: " 'Umwelt' ist die 'Welt', in die der Mensch bewußt hineinlebt, als die für ihn als Menschen konstituierte, die Welt, in der er im weitesten Sinne *heimisch* ist, die er sich als sein *Heim* gestaltet oder gestalten möchte, die danach immer neuen Inhalt, ein immer neues Gesicht für ihn hat" (my emphasis).

It was also in the context of revising the *Cartesianische Meditationen* that Husserl began to take up the problematic of "homeworld." See, for example, H XV 67 (from 1930): "Ferner, es konstituiert sich intersubjektiv eine gemeinsame Heimwelt, eine gemeinsame Umwelt."

It is perhaps no coincidence that Eugen Fink—Husserl's close personal assistant who was entrusted with the task of revising the *Cartesianische Meditationen* for German publication—echoed the generative expressions such as *Heim, Heimwelt,* and *Heimgenosse* found in Husserl's manuscripts in the planned German edition of the Fifth Cartesian Meditation (1932). See Eugen Fink, *VI. Cartesianische Meditation. Teil 2: Ergänzungband,* 270 ff.

5. Ms. B III 3 (1931), 41b: "Das erste Normale ist also [das] der einstimmigen Heimwelt und das der ihr zugehörigen Subjekte, die in Beziehung auf sie stimmen."
6. H XV 142: "Der Normale ist normal in und vermöge der normalen Gemeinschaft." See also H XV 155: "Die erste und universale Normalität ist die, daß die transzendental Intersubjektivität überhaupt eine Welt konstituiert als normale *Erfahrungs*welt der normalen Menschheit." See also H XV 138 ff., and 233.
7. Ms. C 8 (1929), 11a: "Treten wir nun von der transzendentalen Egologie in die *transzendentale Soziologie* über bzw. vom abstraktiv solipisistisch gedachten

Ego zur Menschengemeinschaft und ihrer Welt, so erweitert sich für mich als Ego (und dann für jedes Ich) in neuer Weise die seiende Welt, die nun einen intersubjektiven Seinssinn annimmt."

8. H XI 377–81, Beilage VIII: "Das Fortleben und das Ich, das fortlebt, ist unsterblich." And "Freilich ist mit der Unsterblichkeit des Ich, wie sie jetzt sich gibt, als Undurchstreichbarkeit der sich immer neu erfüllenden Gegenwart, noch nicht eine unendliche künftige Zeit gesetzt." Note also "Wieder ist undenkbar, daß das transzendentale Ich aufhört."

9. Ms. C 8 7a: "Ich betrachte das Historische in der primordialen Welt, und dabei führen die Fragen der 'Historie' des Seinsinnes dieser Welt auf die Limesprobleme, 'Geburt' rein von innen gesehen als erwachendes Ich, das für sich noch nicht Menschenich ist, noch nicht Ich in einer realen Umwelt, und 'Tod' als Aufhören des Bewußtseinsich als solchen, als Limes des Alterns oder eines 'Erkrankungs'prozesses, der kein Altern ist. Das ist 'Historie' im Sinne von konstitutiver Genesis."

10. Ms. C 17 (1931), 74b: "Schlaf, Geburt, Tod—sind wohlgemerkt Probleme als Vorkommnisse in der faktischen Welt und in der Fraglichkeit, ob sie *wesenmäßig* zu einer Welt überhaupt gehören müssen, ihre Weisen der *ursprünglichen* Konstitution haben" (my emphasis).

11. Ms. C 17 76b: "Kann sich objektive Zeiträumlichkeit und Welt ohne all das konstituieren, sind Tod etc. zufällige faktische Vorkommnisse der Welt? Merkwürdige Fakta!"

12. Ms. C 17 V, 92a: "Kann die transzendentale Subjektivität, in der Welt sich konstituiert mit Geburt und Tod, in ihrer Absolutheit anfangen und aufhören?" Also, Ms. C 17 93a: "Tod aber und nach dem Tod [—] das ist für niemand Sein und so auch Vor-der-Geburt-Sein also Nichtsein. . . . Aber Schlafpausen habe ich primordial und intersubjektiv konstituiert; das Vor-der-Geburt-Sein habe ich primordial und intersubjektiv nicht konstituiert."

13. The title for Beilage VIII in H XV reads: "Problem: Generativität—Geburt und Tod als Wesensvorkommnisse für die Weltkonstitution" (H XV 171).

14. Ms. C 17 85a: "Transzendental ist die Welt konstitutives Produkt transzendental wacher Subjekte als miteinander in Wach-Konnex stehender Personen und in einer *Einheit der Tradition*,—in der Welt selbst sich konstituierende Tradition ist *über die 'Pausen' Geburt und Tod des Einzelnen hinaus*" (my emphasis).

15. Ms. C 17 86a: "neue Geburt gehört zu jeder Gegenwart als weltliches und dann doch als transzendentales Vorkommnis."

16. Cf. H XI 126–32.

17. These expressions have become familiar to us especially from the *Krisis I* and its appendices. See, e.g., Beilage III, the famous "Origin of Geometry" text.

18. See H XXIX, text 30, 344–45.

19. Ms. C 17 84b: "so Vererbung ursprünglich generativ und Vererbung der gewöhnlichen Tradition, historisch. Alles Assoziation. Deckung ist Sinnübertragung. Da kommen wir auf Merkwürdigkeiten." See also Ms. A VII 9 (1933), 2a: "Die Weckung der fernen Vergangenheiten—generativ."

20. Cf. Ms. C 17 84a–84b.

21. It is *tradiert* or *tradierbar* through *sinntradierende Fortpflanzung.*

22. H XV 138 n. 2: "Die Konstitution einer verharrenden Mitmenschlichkeit, allgemeinen Gesellschaftlichkeit in korrelativer Bezogenheit zu einer praktischen Umwelt, kann *abstrakt* schon *vor der Generation* behandelt werden, und so liegt vermöge der Art der Zeitigung dieser praktischen Umwelt als *personal* bedeutsamer schon *eine abstrakte Historizität* darin beschlossen. Wird die *Generation* ins Spiel gesetzt, so ist dieser Fortschritt in der *Konkretion* auch eine *Konkretisierung* der bleibenden Mitmenschlichkeiten, Mutter bzw. Eltern und Kind etc., und zugleich haben wir eine *konkreter, generativ* geformte Zeitgung und *historische* Umwelt" (my emphasis).

23. See above p. 181, chapter 11, n. 19.

24. Corresponding to a "unity of historicity" there is a generative "remembrance" [*Gedächtnis*], just as corresponding to a unity of a life there is genetic "remembering" [*Erinnerung*]. While the latter can reawaken sense of a personal past, making it present, the former can reawaken the sense a communal past. See "Geschichte und Erinnerung" from January 1937 (text Nr. 30) in H XXIX.

25. See H XI 377–81.

26. Cf. Ms. C 17 84b: "Mutter und Kind; das Generative überhaupt." See also H XV, Beilage XLV from 1935.

27. Ms. C 17 85b: "Dazu kommt die transzendentale Aufklärung der generativen Erbschaften, *nicht der biophysischen,* sondern der psychischen und somit transzendentalen" (my emphasis). See also H VI 320 f.

28. Cf. the final heading of this chapter, "Language, Expressive Communication, Narrative."

29. Because I find no singular satisfactory rendition of the German expression "*Stamm,*" for the purposes of this work I will anglicize it and write it as "stamm."

30. H XV 433: "*aus ihrer vertrauten Umwelt her stammenden Sinn.*" See note 33 below.

31. I am indebted to Irene Klaver for many fruitful conversations at our *Stammtisch* on this sense of *Stamm* as an enduring origin.

32. Scheler, *Wesen und Formen der Sympathie. Gesammelte Werke, Band 1,* 173.

33. Cf. H XV 463: "Rückgewendet sehe ich alsbald, daß, was vordem für mich als Welt in Geltung war, seinerseits immer schon Bestände hat, die aus solcher Tradition stammen." See also H XV 165.

34. H XV 463: "*ich übernehme* sozusagen sein ihm als wirklich Geltendes als meine Geltung, seine Urteile als meine." See also H XXIX 34, 373–75.

35. Ms. C 17 84b: "Wir stehen in der Tradition; durch Andere werden wir anders, ihr Personales in uns aufnehmend, in uns notwendig umbildend. Generativ: es vererbt sich nicht nur die leer-formale, monadisch-ichliche Struktur, sondern die vererbten Charaktereigenschaften; wie das? Mit der Erweckung der neuen Monade ist erweckt oder vor-erweckt die elterliche Habitualität aber die neue Monade hat eine neue Hyle und die elterliche

ihre eigene Habitualität. . . . Das alles in sedimentierter Überdeckung und sich 'mischend', verschmelzend. Eine andere Frage ist—obschon eine verwandte—die von Geburt und Tod."

See also H XXIX 88 where Husserl contends that even *my* "innate" characteristics stem from the *generative* framework.

36. Casey, "Forgetting Remembered," esp. 286, 289, 293 ff.

37. See Scheler, *Formalismus*, 581: "Wir werden so, *wie* das Vorbildexemplar als Person ist, nicht, was es ist." See also Scheler, "Vorbilder und Führer," *Gesammelte Werke*, Band 10, 257–344.

38. See H XXIX 4–5, but also pp. 69, 87 where Husserl speaks of the animal environing-world as "*geistig*" or "spiritual," as well as the animal as "transcendental subject." For the purposes of this work, I wish to hold Husserl's assessment of animals in abeyance. I would however like to use his comments to the extent that they help sharpen the focus on what he considers to be the distinguishing traits of a homeworld. See also chapter 13.

39. See H XV 160 n. 1 and 181, but compare 179.

40. Ms. C 11 (1934), 23b: "Menschliche Sozialität ist nicht Herde, sondern eine verbundene und offene Gemeinschaft von seienden Personen und wieder schon Gemeinschaften—Stämme unter Stämmen, Völker unter Völkern. Als Mensch lebt er in seiner in relativ fester Normalität geformten Umwelt."

41. This point will be taken up below.

42. See Habermas, *Theorie des kommunikativen Handelns*.

43. Of these three only the first article appeared in both German and Japanese, the remaining two appeared only Japanese translation. The final two articles were withheld and left in draft form. See the editors' (Thomas Nenon and Hans Sepp's) introduction to the *Husserliana* edition in which these articles have been included, H XXVII xi f.

44. Welton, "Husserl and the Japanese," 577. Note also that the fifth article, provisionally entitled "Formale Typen der Kultur in der Menschheitsentwicklung," treats many themes that were to become prevalent in his famous Vienna Lecture of 1935. I have in mind here the role of rational teleology, the central place of Europe, primordial institution of philosophical science with ancient Greeks, etc.

45. Reading "*unsere*" for "*ihre.*"

46. Cf. H XXVII 12 ff. and H XXVII 89.

47. Self-regulation, according to Husserl, is the ability to evaluate the sense of one's life in terms of its actualities and possibilities. In a Kantian vein it entails prescribing general life goals and submitting oneself to norms which one has "freely" generated. See H XXVII 26 ff.

48. I would like to thank Tom Nenon for highlighting this important distinction between perceptual and ethical optima implicit in Husserl's descriptions.

49. Welton, "Husserl and the Japanese," 594 f.

50. Cf. H XXVII 33: "Ein solches jeweils *bestmögliches* Leben ist für sein Subjekt selbst charakterisiert als das absolut Gesollte." See also H XXVII 29, 37–39 as well as H XV 144 f.

51. See especially H VI §15.

52. See 62 ff., 77 ff. Here Husserl defines critique as the conscious differentiation between the heteronomous and autonomous motives of certainty and the position of the knowing subject against all motivations of the heart [*Gemüt*] for a judgmental certainty, and against other motivations that have become standardized [*normierten*] without insight through prejudices.

53. Here I have reformulated and adapted one of Welton's explanations of critique for my purposes. See Welton, "Husserl and the Japanese," 587.

54. See Appendix VII, "Radikale Kritik," H 27, p. 107.

55. Benhabib, *Critique, Norm, Utopia: A Study of the Foundations of Critical Theory*, 8.

56. See also H XV 235: "Kritik einer universalen Erfahrung, die über alle synthetisch zu verbindenden Heimwelten Einheit herstellen soll."

57. See Waldenfels, *Ordnung im Zwielicht*, esp. sections A and B.

58. H XV 224–25 (from approximately 1931): "*Die Heimwelt des Menschen . . . ist grundwesentlich von der Sprache her bestimmt*" (Husserl's emphasis).

59. Ms. A VII 23, 12 (from transcription): "der durch Einfühlung sich herstellenden Kommunikation."

60. Ms. D 13 I (1921), 122a: "Aber es ist nicht ausgeschlossen, daß *erst im Herstellen der Kommunikation* Differenzen zwischen eigener und fremder 'Normalität' . . . *aufgrund einer Gemeinsamkeit sich herausstellen*" (my emphasis).

61. Let me note also that when Husserl discusses the interrelation between various dimensions of homeworld, he appeals again to the prospect of linguistic communication to account for how one can move from a family home to a hometown or to a home state, etc. (H XV 220).

62. H XV 472 (from 1932): "Wie nun, wenn wechselseitige aktiv eingehende Einfühlung hergestellt ist? *Damit ist noch keine soziale Einigung, keine kommunikative, hergestellt*" (Husserl's emphasis). See also H XV 136–38.

63. The role that communication plays in instituting a community, Husserl reminds us, is captured by the Latin term *communicatio* (H XV 472 f.).

64. H XV 462. On Husserl's view animals pose no questions and thus give no answers. Ms. C 11, 24a: "das Tier hat keine Fragen und somit keine Antworten."

65. Ms. A VII 23, 9a f.: "Jede Gemeinwelt und somit jede Heimwelt ist schon aus Mitteilung konstitutiert und schafft immer neue Möglichkeiten der Mitteilung. Gemeinwelt als vertraute traditionale Lebensumwelt einer im gemeinen Leben verbundenen Völkerschaft entstammt nicht nur aus der Mitteilungsfunktion der verbundenen Personen, sondern sie ist verharrende Heimwelt nur in der Weise, daß zu ihr selbst als mitkonstituiert eine Mitteilungssitte gehört, ein gewohnter Mitteilungsstil, in den jedermann hineinerzogen ist—im weitesten Sinne eine Sprache."

66. See chapter 4.

67. "*und sonstige anomale Modi, wohin wir jetzt auch monologische Aussagen im stillen Denken rechnen*" (H XV 220 f., my emphasis). I realize that the term for "expression" used here is *Aussage* and not *Ausdruck* (as in the *Logische Untersuchungen*). Nevertheless, given the context of these remarks, which

directly point to Husserl's formulation of an expressive soliloquy in the First Investigation, the treatment of *Aussage* as expression is justified in this discussion.

68. Of course, even dialogue in this sense already takes place generatively. Waldenfels makes this case clearly in his *Zwischenreich*. He writes, for example, that generativity is the means by which we find each other in the world, the way in which the individual emerges in communal life as well as interacts in dialogue. See esp. 345–53.

69. Hereafter *Narrative*.

70. Carr's thesis more precisely is that narrative is our primary way of organizing our experience of time where we are individual and social subjects of action, experience, and history. My point is that narrative is a particular way of reconstituting a homeworld historically or generatively and that the home history is co-constituted in part through narrative.

Moreover, Carr, for his part, considers the socio-historical dimension of narrative experience to go beyond phenomenology itself—at least a phenomenology centered on an "ego" (cf. *Narrative*, 5). Nevertheless, I take his work as a contribution to a generative *phenomenology* and more specifically what might be called from the perspective of this work a "phenomenology of narrative."

71. Carr, *Narrative*, 115.

72. For such an account see Ibid., chapters 1–4.

73. Ricoeur, *Temps et récit: I*, esp. 19–53. Cf. Carr, *Narrative*, 14 f.

74. MacIntyre, *After Virtue*, 201, 198.

75. Carr, *Narrative*, 83–85.

76. Foucault, "Qu'est-ce qu'un auteur?".

77. Similarly, Carr writes that what counts in the complex interrelationship of storytelling is not authorship at all, but narratorship. *Narrative*, 85, 112.

78. See Merleau-Ponty, *Le visible*, esp. the chapter "L'entrelacs—le chiasme."

79. Carr, *Narrative*, 89.

80. See p. 194 above. See also H XV 431 fn. 1: "Ja, diese Geschichtlichkeit besagt Konstitution der Umwelt als einer erstlichen, mythischen Welt—alles darin ist mythisch geformt." See also H XV 436 f.; H XXVII, 59 ff.

Chapter 13

1. From Calvino, *Invisible Cites*, 27.

2. Held, "Heimwelt, Fremdwelt, die eine Welt," 307 ff.; hereafter "Heimwelt."

3. I.e., when he interjects the possibility of something like a "national intropathy." Cf., for example, H XV 436.

4. See Carr, *Interpreting Husserl*, 281 ff. See also Carr, *Narrative*, 130 ff.

5. Cf. Carr, *Narrative*, 120–22. See also *Interpreting Husserl*, chapter 3, 14.

6. See for example H XV Text 11, 148–70, or Text 14, 196–214, or Text 27, 428–37, as well as their accompanying appendices. Let me also note that despite Carr's formulation of the "We," he is sensitive to describing experience as precisely *our* experience and does invoke it in his analyses. Cf., for example, *Interpreting Husserl*, 286 and *Narrative*, 149.

7. The expression "homecomrade" is used throughout Husserl's writings on normality and homeworld. Cf. note 6 above, and H VI 320 f.

8. On the notion of "operative concepts," see Eugen Fink, "Operative Begriffe in Husserls Phänomenologie."

9. H XV 164: "Auch die ganze indirekte Tradition unbekannter Menschengenerationen rechnet mit."

And H XV 218–19: "Die gemeinschaftliche Erfahrung übersteigt mein und eines jeden endliches Leben, sie erstreckt sich durch unser aller Leben und durch die offene Kette der Generationen hindurch. Sie reicht auch hinaus über die mir bekannten Anderen und die mir durch die Historie hindurch individuell bekannt werdenden." See chapter 12, n. 9.

10. They would be aliens with whom I am acquainted [*bekannte Fremdvölker*] (H XV 177). Compare discussion in chapter 11 under the heading "Toward Intersubjective Normality and Abnormality."

11. "Le monde et le sujet," 69; hereafter "Le monde."

12. Within a genetic framework where *intropathy* is invoked, Husserl writes "durch Einfühlung in die Säuglinge, die ich äußerlich sehe und nicht besser verstehe als junge Katzen!" (Ms. B III 3, 36a). But he cannot hold this and related positions in a generative framework. See also H XV 231.

13. See Canguilhem, *Le normal*, 122 ff.

14. Ibid., 124.

15. Ey and Rouart also make this point, cf. *Le normal*, 124–25. See also Husserl, Ms. B III 3, 41b: "Das Anomale jedes Typus tritt in der normalen Welt auf: die neugeborenen Kinder, die Irrsinnigen, der Delirierende, der Schlafende, der Primitive."

16. This later text stems from Ms. K III 11 (1935).

17. Here Husserl sketches this in terms of speaking and especially *naming* things held in common, first and foremost, "mother" and "father" or "mama" and "papa" (H XV 605 f.). He observes that the mother does not say to the child, for example, "*I'm* coming right now" or "*I'm* bringing it," but "mama's coming," "mama's bringing," etc. Thus, it is an important constitutional problem for Husserl to understand "*how* the child arrives at saying 'I'," and interpersonal pronouns for that matter, "you," "he," "we," etc., as well as "here," "now," "near," "far," "right," "left," "present," "past," "future," etc. (H XV 606).

18. H XV 214: "Das Sein der Welt hat nur einen Anschein von Festigkeit, in Wahrheit ist es Festigkeit eines Normalgebildes."

19. MacIntyre, *After Virtue*, 204.

20. See Bernet, "Le monde," 70 f. See also H XXIX 87 and H XV 167: "Doch es fragt sich, ob das wirklich so richtig ist, da man einwenden könnte, daß, wenn die Tiere verstanden sind als sich auf die Welt beziehend, dieselbe, die die unsere ist, sie auch *gelegentlich als Welt mitkonstituierend* fungieren können. Wenn der Hund als ein Wild witternd verstanden wird, so belehrt er uns gleichsam von dem, was wir noch nicht wußten (my emphasis)."

21. Ms. A V 10 (1931), 4a: "Der Kampf gegen die Tradition, gegen die vermeinten Selbstverständlichkeiten der 'Lebenserfahrung', die in Wahrheit

keine Selbstgebung ist. Es ist immer und im vollen Sinne Kampf gegen die 'Situation', gegen die sedimentierten Erwerbe von höchst mittelbaren Seinsgeltungen, die zu 'Selbstverständlichkeiten' geworden sind. Was aus der Situation herausgeholt wird und zur Aussprache kommt, gilt in 'Selbstverständlichkeit', zumal wenn es, wie normaler Weise, gemeinschaftliche Situation ist bzw. Tradition."

22. Kozol, *The Night Is Dark and I Am Far From Home,* 151 (my emphasis).

23. Merleau-Ponty, *Phénoménologie,* 187.

24. In the second volume of Husserl's *Krisis* writings, Husserl describes the elderly as the keepers of the tradition, of the past historicity, as the meditators for the appropriation of the tradition in the new young ones (H XXIX 40).

25. See Carr, *Narrative,* 132 f.

26. See also H XXIX 9: "There are already within a nation differences of homeland and alien." See also H XXIX 198.

27. I interpret the phenomenon of homelessness in terms of this discussion of homeworld and alienworld in an article entitled "Homelessness and The Homeless Movement: A Clue to the Problem of Intersubjectivity."

28. Husserl, "Ursprung," 319.

29. The French language has no easy task in translating the German "*Heimwelt.*" To capture the senses of being "*chez soi,*" or "*provenance,*" as well as "*l'appartenance généalogique,*" Raphaël Célis, in a sensitive rendition of Held's article "Heimwelt," has translated Heimwelt as "le monde natal" (cf. "Le monde natal, le monde étranger, le monde un").

To be sure, the generative aspect of home is done better service here than with the expression "*le monde familier*" (Toulemont). I would only like to insist that the home cannot be equated with the world of my birth. It could also be the world of my death or the world in which I live now, and not the world in which I was born.

30. See Ms. A V 10, 78a: "Jedes Heimland ist 'Territorium' einer Heimmenschheit, der Wohnsitz. Das bedeutet nicht im gewöhnlichen Sinne Seßhaftigkeit, aber in einem weiteren ist auch der Nomade 'seßhaft', nämlich er hat sein Territorium, in dem er wandert und das er als sein Land, sein Herrschaftsgebiet, Nahrungsgebiet etc. ansieht."

31. Cf. Held, "Husserls These," 37. But even here would we not have to say along with Husserl's "Ursprung" reflections that home is at least limited geo-graphically to the earth?

32. From Calvino, *Invisible Cities,* 30–31.

Chapter 14

1. From Calvino, *Invisible Cities,* 28.

2. H XV 210, 214 f., 217, 437.

3. On one occasion Husserl explicitly imports this structure from the Fifth Meditation and imposes it on the structure of homeworld and alienworld. He writes of making the alienworld a homeworld by grasping it "as if it were a homeworld" (H XV 625).

4. See Ms. A VII 9 (1933), 13a: "Natürlich da der Mensch seiende Welt nur hat in Modis der Heimweltlichkeit und Fremde . . . , so ist es ohne weiteres ersichtlich, daß jede konkrete, den konkreten Menschen seines Volkes und seiner Heimwelt betreffende Ethik oder Religion . . . durchaus umweltliche Bezogenheit hat. . . . Universale Ethik und Religion ist offenbar nur reine Form, in ihrer universalen Allgemeinheit abstrakt, offen unbestimmt lassend die Konkretionen von Mensch und Umwelt. Eben damit aber die Norm der Echtheit, die stets mitverstanden sein muß in der Weise, wie jedes Konkrete nur konkret ist in seinem allgemeinen und doch nicht herausabstrahierten Typus. Doch wäre da manches Besondere zu sagen."

5. H XV 430: "Die Sache ist so, daß, wenn eine Umwelt voll ausgebildet ist, sie nicht den Charakter eines geschlossenen endlichen Raumes hat, für den kein Draußen konstituiert ist, wie wenn ein Kind hineingeboren wäre in einen Kerker ohne Türen und Fenster."

6. Holenstein, "Europa und die Menschheit," 49; hereafter "Europa."

7. Ibid., especially the section entitled "Das Kultur-Modell: Kugel oder Bastelei," 48 ff.

8. In a genetic context, Husserl writes (Ms. A VII 9, 14b): "Aber zunächst ist hier kein Streit, wenn ich im fremden Land fremde Kultur und Menschen kennen lernen soll. Denn die fremden Kulturobjekte und die fremden Menschen apperzipiere ich nicht in heimatlicher Typik."

9. Levinas, *Totalité et infini* and *Le temps et l'autre;* hereafter *Le temps.*

10. I plan to work out this theme in an article entitled "The Other and the Alien: Levinas and Husserl on Intersubjectivity."

11. Cf. Ms. A VII 9, 14b: "Im Unverstandenen und in Bestimmtheit Unverständlichen das *Mythische.*" See also H XXIX, text Nr. 4 and text Nr. 20.

12. Ms. A V 10, 96: "generativ fremden Menscheiten"; and H XV 432 n. 1.

13. Ms. A VII 9, 2b: "Verstehen des Chinesen—Verstehen seiner Heimwelt. Ich müßte in sie wie ein Kind in die Welt des Erwachsenen 'hineinwachsen', schließlich seine Geschichte verstehen lernen."

14. Waldenfels, "Experience of the Alien in Husserl's Phenomenology," 26, translation slightly modified; hereafter "Experience of the Alien."

15. H XV 631: "Im mittelbaren Horizont sind die fremdartigen Menschheiten und Kulturen; die gehörigen dazu als fremde und fremdartige, aber Fremdheit besagt Zugänglichkeit in der eigentlichen Unzugänglichkeit, im Modus der Unverständlichkeit." See also H XXIX 42.

16. See p. 182 and n. 22, chapter 11.

17. Cf. Waldenfels, "Experience of the Alien," 29; see also 28, 31.

18. See p. 196 and n. 35, chapter 12.

19. H XV 214: "Ich habe also (wenn ich das *quasi* oder wirklich genetisch-historisch verstehe) *eine Änderung meiner und unserer Welterfahrung und Welt selbst*" (my emphasis).

20. Also, writes Husserl in a generative context, my own perception and remembering are completed through alien perception and remembering. H XXIX 7.

21. See above, "Introduction."

22. See Waldenfels, *Stachel*, 31, who makes a similar distinction between occupation and transgression.

23. See pp. 238 and 246 above.

24. Waldenfels, *Stachel*, 39.

25. Accordingly, in a different article on violence and legitimation, Waldenfels rightly speaks of violence as denying claims [*Ansprüche*]. Cf. "Grenzen der Legitimierung und die Frage nach der Gewalt," in *Stachel*, 115.

26. See Adorno et al., *The Authoritarian Personality;* Lowenthal and Guterman, *Prophets of Deceit;* Adorno, "Freudian Theory and the Pattern of Fascist Propaganda."

27. See my "Totalitarianism, Homogeneity of Power, Depth: Towards a Socio-Political Ontology"; hereafter "Totalitarianism."

28. *Über soziale Differenzierung*: *Soziologische und psychologische Untersuchungen*, 13.

29. *Allgemeine Soziologie als Lehre von den Beziehungen und Beziehungsgebilden der Menschen.*

30. *Individuum und Gemeinschaft. Grundlegung der Kulturphilosophie*, 221.

31. *Man in Reciprocity: Introductory Lectures on Culture, Society and Personality.*

32. *Crime and Custom in Savage Society*, chapter 9. I owe these references to R. J. de Folter, *Normaal en abnormaal: Enkele beschouwingen over het probleem van de normaliteit in het denken van Husserl, Schütz en Foucault*, who treats these authors in historical perspective. See esp. Hoofdstuk III, 53–81.

33. Mead, *The Philosophy of the Present*, 165.

34. Schutz, *Collected Papers: I*, 10 ff., *Social World*, 154 ff.

35. Cf. my "Totalitarianism," 631 ff.

36. See Waldenfels, "Eigenkultur und Fremdkultur: Das Paradox einer Wissenschaft vom Fremden"; hereafter "Paradox."

37. Levinas, *Ethique et infini*, 94–95. See also Levinas, *Le temps*, 75 ff.

38. See Whitehead, *Science and the Modern World*, 49 ff., 58 ff., 91.

39. Cf. Waldenfels, *Stachel*, 33 f.

40. Cf. my "Totalitarianism," esp. 639 ff.

41. See, for example, H XXIX 41.

42. Cf. Waldenfels, "Paradox," 21 f.

43. Cf. Waldenfels, *Stachel*, 113.

Chapter 15

1. See Spiegelberg, *The Phenomenological Movement: A Historical Introduction*, 340–47; hereafter *Phenomenological Movement.*

2. Heidegger dedicated and presented a copy of *Sein und Zeit* to Husserl on his (Husserl's) birthday (April 8, 1926). See, for example, Georg Misch's "Nachwort" in his *Lebensphilosophie und Phänomenologie: Eine Auseinandersetzung der Diltheyschen Richtung mit Heidegger und Husserl*, 328; hereafter *Lebensphilosophie und Phänomenologie.*

3. Schuhmann, ed., *Husserl-Chronik: Denk- und Lebensweg Edmund Husserls*, 303 f. and 349; hereafter *Husserl-Chronik*.

4. It would be an interesting project to consult Husserl's marginal notes in *Sein und Zeit* in order to understand the influence of Heidegger on Husserl. See "Randbemerkungen Husserls zu Heideggers *Sein und Zeit* und *Kant und das Problem der Metaphysik*," ed. Roland Breeur, *Husserl Studies* 11 (1994), 3–63. One would find, however, expressions of incredulity on Husserl's part, that is, statements protesting that he (Husserl) had already done what Heidegger claimed to do, and that Heidegger, instead, is simply appropriating Husserl's work only without deep thinking.

See also D. Souche-Dagues's Herculean task of interpreting Husserl's marginal responses to Heidegger's *Sein und Zeit* in "La lecture husserlienne de Sein und Zeit."

5. See Carr, *Narrative*, 102–10.

6. See Martin Heidegger, *Sein und Zeit*, for example 377. For Heidegger's relation to Dilthey see Spiegelberg, *Phenomenological Movement*, 395 f.

7. Their personal contact seems to have been instigated by Husserl's discovery that Dilthey was lecturing on his own (i.e., Husserl's) second volume of the *Logische Untersuchungen*. At this point, Husserl traveled to Berlin to see Dilthey. By December 1910, Dilthey sent Husserl a copy of his work, *Der Aufbau der geschichtlichen Welt in den Geisteswissenschaften*. But it was only after Husserl completed his *Logos* article (February 1911) and Dilthey objected to Husserl's accusation of "historicism" that Husserl gave a thorough reading of Dilthey's book (September/October 1911). See *Husserl-Chronik*, 87–88, 151, 159, 161. See also Husserl's correspondence with Dilthey, esp. the letter from June 29 and July 5/6, 1911.

8. See *Husserl-Chronik*, 321.

9. See Sepp, ed., *Edmund Husserl und die phänomenologische Bewegung*, 344. Apparently, Misch initiated a correspondence with Husserl by sending Husserl the first part of his work. See *Husserl-Chronik*, 346.

10. *Husserl-Chronik*, 282. David Carr also reminds us that 1927 was the year volume 7 appeared containing the piece Husserl had originally received from Dilthey, namely, *Der Aufbau der geschichtlichen Welt in den Geisteswissenschaften*. See *Narrative*, 103.

11. On Dilthey and Husserl see Makkreel and Scanlon, eds., *Dilthey and Phenomenology*; Orth, ed., *Dilthey und der Wandel des Philosophiebegriffs seit dem 19. Jahrhundert*. See also Makkreel, "Husserl, Dilthey, and the Relation of the Life-World to History," and Borsen, *Zur Phänomenologie des Bewußtseinsstromes: Bergson, Dilthey, Husserl, Simmel und die lebensphilosophischen Antinomien*.

12. Carr makes a similar point concerning the question of history in his *Problem of History*, chapter 2.

13. Derrida, *L'écriture*, 230.

14. See H III 362.

15. See Derrida, *L'écriture*, 243 f.

16. Ibid., 231.

17. See H XXIX (*Krisis 2*), text Nr. 28 (1936). Understood in light of leading clues, there is an important difference in the so-called mundane disciplines, in particular, between psychology and anthropology. Whereas psychology can provide leading clues to the genesis of individual life, anthropology can offer leading clues to the generation socio-geo-historical life. On this view, one could not equate psychology and anthropology as Husserl does at times in the tradition of Kant (see "Phänomenologie und Anthropologie," (from 1931) in H XXVII).

This line of thought, and the phenomenological import of the "anthropological world" and anthropology, become prominent in Husserl's *Krisis* writings (see "The Anthropological World," text Nr. 28, H XXIX from 1936). I discuss the role of anthropology in relation to a lifeworld ontology, psychology, generative phenomenology, and the general "crisis" problematic in "The New 'Crisis'," section 4.

18. Derrida, *L'écriture,* 231.

19. See chapter 2, under the heading "Leading Clue."

20. H XV 138 n. 2; cf. chapter 12, note 22 above.

21. Let me recall the discussion from chapter 2 that according to Husserl's Third Logical Investigation (§17 and H III §15) that which is non-independent was considered abstract, and independent or simple, concrete. Here we see that just the reverse is the case.

22. See pp. 178–79, chapter 11, n. 15.

23. See H VI 176, H XI 345, and H XVII 257.

24. I have developed this thought further, comparing the generative Husserlian phenomenologist to a Hegelian phenomenologist of spirit in an article entitled "The Role of the Phenomenologist: Hegel and Husserl."

25. My emphasis. H XV 393: "Aber der Phänomenologe und die Phänomenologie stehen selbst in dieser Geschichtlichkeit."

26. See H XXIX 73, 79–80.

27. See Waldenfels, *Einführung in die Phänomenologie,* 9. See also Ricoeur, "Sur la phénoménologie," in *A l'école de la phénoménologie,* 156.

Selected Bibliography

Bibliography of Husserl's Works

Husserliana (In Order of Publication):

Cartesianische Meditationen und Pariser Vorträge. Ed. S. Strasser. The Hague: Martinus Nijhoff, 1950. Husserliana Vol. I.

Die Idee der Phänomenologie. Fünf Vorlesungen. Ed. W. Biemel. The Hague: Martinus Nijhoff, 1950. Husserliana Vol. II.

Ideen zu einer reinen Phänomenologie und phänomenologischen Philosophie. Erstes Buch: Allgemeine Einführung in die reine Phänomenologie. Ed. W. Biemel. The Hague: Martinus Nijhoff, 1950. Husserliana Vol. III.

Ideen zu einer reinen Phänomenologie und phänomenologischen Philosophie. Zweites Buch: Phänomenologische Untersuchungen zur Konstitution. Ed. W. Biemel. The Hague: Martinus Nijhoff, 1952. Husserliana Vol. IV.

Ideen zu einer reinen Phänomenologie und phänomenologischen Philosophie. Drittes Buch: Die Phänomenologie und die Fundament der Wissenschaften. Ed. W. Biemel. The Hague: Martinus Nijhoff, 1952. Husserliana Vol. V.

Die Krisis der europäischen Wissenschaften und die transzendentale Phänomenologie. Eine Einleitung in die phänomenologische Philosophie. Ed. W. Biemel. The Hague: Martinus Nijhoff, 1954. Husserliana Vol. VI.

Erste Philosophie (1923/24). Erster Teil: Kritische Ideengeschichte. Ed. R. Boehm. The Hague: Martinus Nijhoff, 1956. Husserliana Vol. VII.

Erste Philosophie (1923/24): Zweiter Teil: Theorie der phänomenologische Reduktion. Ed. R. Boehm. The Hague: Martinus Nijhoff, 1959. Husserliana Vol. VIII.

Phänomenologische Psychologie. Vorlesungen Sommersemester 1925. Ed. W. Biemel. The Hague: Martinus Nijhoff, 1962. Husserliana Vol. IX.

Zur Phänomenologie des inneren Zeitbewußtseins (1893–1917). Ed. R. Boehm. The Hague: Martinus Nijhoff, 1966. Husserliana Vol. X.

Analysen zur passiven Synthesis. Aus Vorlesungs-und Forschungsmanuskripten 1918–1926. Ed. M. Fleischer. The Hague: Martinus Nijhoff, 1966. Husserliana Vol. XI.

Zur Phänomenologie der Intersubjektivität. Texte aus dem Nachlaß. Erster Teil: 1905–1920. Ed. Iso Kern. The Hague: Martinus Nijhoff, 1973. Husserliana Vol. XIII.

Zur Phänomenologie der Intersubjektivität. Texte aus dem Nachlaß. Zweiter Teil: 1921–1928. Ed. Iso Kern. The Hague: Martinus Nijhoff, 1973. Husserliana Vol. XIV.

Zur Phänomenologie der Intersubjektivität. Texte aus dem Nachlaß. Dritter Teil: 1929–1935. Ed. Iso Kern. The Hague: Martinus Nijhoff, 1973. Husserliana Vol. XV.

Ding und Raum. Vorlesungen 1907. Ed. U. Claesges. The Hague: Martinus Nijhoff, 1973. Husserliana Vol. XVI.

Formale und transzendentale Logik. Versuch einer Kritik der logischen Vernunft. Mit ergänzenden Texten. Ed. P. Janssen. The Hague: Martinus Nijhoff, 1974. Husserliana Vol. XVII.

Aufsätze und Rezensionen (1890–1910). Ed. B. Rang. The Hague: Martinus Nijhoff, 1979. Husserliana Vol. XXII.

Phantasie, Bildbewußtsein, Erinnerung. Zur Phänomenologie der anschaulichen Vergegenwärtigungen. Texte aus dem Nachlaß (1898–1925). Ed. E. Marbach. The Hague: Martinus Nijhoff, 1980. Husserliana Vol. XXIII.

Aufsätze und Vorträge (1911–1921). Ed. T. Nenon und H.-R. Sepp. Boston: Kluwer, 1986. Husserliana Vol. XXV.

Aufsätze und Vorträge (1922–1937). Ed. T. Nenon und H.-R. Sepp. Boston: Kluwer, 1989. *Husserliana* Vol. XXVII.

Die Krisis der europäischen Wissenschaften und die transzendentale Phänomenologie: Ergänzungsband. Texte aus dem Nachlaß 1934–1937. Ed. Reinhold N. Smid. Boston: Kluwer, 1993. Husserliana Vol. XXIX.

Works Consulted Appearing outside of Husserliana

Briefe an Roman Ingarden. Ed. Roman Ingarden. The Hague: Martinus Nijhoff, 1968.

"Grundlegende Untersuchungen zum phänomenologischen Ursprung der Räumlichkeit der Natur" (1934) in *Philosophical Essays in Memory of Edmund Husserl.* Ed. M. Garber. Cambridge: Harvard University Press, 1940, pp. 307–325.

Erfahrung und Urteil. Untersuchungen zur Genealogie der Logik. Ed. L. Landgrebe. Hamburg: Meiner, 1948.

Logische Untersuchungen. Band I: Prolegomena zur reinen Logik. Tübingen: Niemeyer, 1968.

Logische Untersuchungen. Band II: Untersuchungen zur Phänomenologie und Theorie der Erkenntnis, I. Teil, Tübingen: Niemeyer, 1968. *II. Teil,* Tübingen: Niemeyer, 1968.

"Notizen zur Raumkonstitution" (1934). Ed. A. Schütz. In *Philosophy and Phenomenological Research* 1, no. 1 (1941), pp. 21–37.

"Die Welt der lebendigen Gegenwart und die Konstitution der außerleiblichen Umwelt," in *Philosophy and Phenomenological Research* 6, no. 3 (1946), pp. 323–43.

Unpublished Manuscripts

A. Mundane Phänomenologie

A V 10 I (ca. 1920) "Umwelt. Heimwelt"

A V 10 I (November 1931) "Situationsurteil, Traditionsurteil, Erfahrungsurteil"

A VII 6 "Struktur der Erfahrungswelt, Episteme und Doxa—Bekanntheit und Fremde"

A VII 9 (November 6, 1933) "Horizont"

A VII 23 "Zur prinzipiellen Scheidung der Relativitäten. Die entsprechenden Relativitäten der Horizontstruktur"

B. Die Reduktion

I. Wege zur Reduktion

B I 10 I (New Year 1932/1933) "Rückfrage Naturerkenntnis, Welterkenntnis"

II. Die Reduktion selbst und ihre Methodologie

B II 3 (1934) "Trieb, Trieb-Instinkleben-Aktleben, Askese, Epoché"

B II 6 (1930) "Phänomenologie der Phänomenologie"

III. Vorläufige transzendentale Intentionalanalytik

B III 3 (1931) "Das Problem des Anfanges der (primordialen) Subjektivität—Anfangende Affektion als instinktive"

C. Zeitkonstitution als formale Konstitution

C 3 III (March 1931) "Reduktion auf die lebendige Gegenwart"

C 8 I (October 1929) "Zur Konstitution der Intersubjektiven Welt"

C 11 II (September 1934)

C 13 I (January 1934) "Bekanntheit und Neuheit . . . Instinkte und Universale Teleologie sich auswirkend als Weltkonstitution"

C 13 III (March 1934) "Konstitution von Seienden in Zeitmodalitäten . . ."

C 14 (January 13, 1933) "Elementares zur Zeitkonstitution. Konstitution jedes Körpers durch Nah-Fernerscheinungen . . ."

C 15 "Urassociation und Urzeitigung, zunächst in der hyletischen Kernsphäre behandelt"

C 17 II (1930–31) "Weltzeitigung und Weltzeitmodalitäten . . ."

C 17 IV (1930) "Zur lebendigen Gegenwart. Passive Zeitigung des Erlebnisstromes"

C 17 V (1931) "Konstitution der Einheit einer realen Zeiträumlichkeit Rolle des Schlafes, dann Geburt u. Tod für die Konstitution der Welt"

D. Urkonstitution

D 13, Part I (October, St. Märgen) "Typologie des visuellen Feldes und die zugehörige Kinästhese . . ."

D 13, Part I (1928) "Orientierungsstruktur, Orientierung und Zugangspraxis"

D 13, Part I (St. Märgen, 1921) "Normalität in ihrer konstitutiven Bedeutung . . ."

D 13, Part I (1915/1916/1917) "Objektivität und Intersubjektivität"
D 13, Part I (1917) "Normalität. Idee"
D 13, Part I (St. Märgen, 1921) "Normalität in ihrer konstitutiven Bedeutung und sekundäre Qualitäten"
D 13, Part II (1918/1910) "Raumkonstitution . . ."
D 13, Part II (St. Märgen 1921) "Natur und Normalität"
D 13, Part II (Göttingen, probably between 1907 and 1912) "Sonne, Mond, Himmel kein blosses Phantom? . . ."
Auszüge to D 13, Part III (edited by Claesges)

F. Vorlesungen und Vorträge

Vorlesungen und Teile aus Vorlesungen
F I 9 (1904–5/1898) "Anfänge über Wahrnehmung"

G. Writings from Husserl's Privatbibliothek

Lévy-Bruhl. *Die Geistige Welt der Primitiven.* München: Bruckmann, 1927.

H. Correspondence

Husserl. La lettre de Husserl à Lévy-Bruhl. Trans. Philippe Soulez. Presented in "Les cahiers de l'education," November 1985.
"Der Briefwechsel Dilthey-Husserl." In *Man and World* 1, no. 3 (1969), pp. 428–46.

Secondary Literature

Abraham, Nicolas. *Psychoanalyse et Phénoménologie.* Conference of January 5, 1959.
———. *Psychoanalyse et Phénoménologie.* Conference of February 11 and 16, 1959.
Adorno, Theodor W., et al. *The Authoritarian Personality.* New York: Harper and Brothers, 1950.
———. "Freudian Theory and the Pattern of Fascist Propaganda." In *The Essential Frankfurt School Reader.* Ed. Andrew Arato and Eike Gebhardt. New York: Continuum, 1982, pp. 118–37.
———. *Zur Metakritik der Erkenntnistheorie.* Frankfurt: Suhrkamp, 1971.
Aguirre, Antonio F. *Genetische Phänomenologie und Reduktion: Zur Letztbegründung der Wissenschaft aus der radikalen Skepsis im Denken E. Husserls.* The Hague: Martinus Nijhoff, 1970.
———. *Die Phänomenologie Husserls im Licht ihrer gegenwärtigen Interpretation und Kritik.* Darmstadt: Wissenschaftliche Buchgesellschaft, 1982.
Aristotle. *On the Heavens.* Trans. W. K. C. Guthrie. Cambridge: Harvard University Press, 1986.
———. *The Nicomachean Ethics.* Trans. H. Rackham. Cambridge: Harvard University Press, 1975.
Becker, Howard Paul. *Man in Reciprocity: Introductory Lectures on Culture, Society and Personality.* New York: Praeger, 1956.

Benhabib, Seyla. *Critique, Norm, and Utopia: A Study in the Foundations of Critical Theory.* New York: Columbia University Press, 1986.

Bernet, Rudolf. "Différence ontologique et conscience transcendantale." In *Husserl.* Ed. Eliane Escoubas and Marc Richer. Grenoble: Millon,1989, pp. 89–116.

———. "Le monde et le sujet." *Philosophie* no. 21 (1989), pp. 57–76.

Bernet, Rudolf, Iso Kern, and Eduard Marbach. *Edmund Husserl: Darstellung seines Denkens.* Hamburg: Meiner, 1989.

Bernstein, Richard J. *Beyond Objectivism and Relativism: Science, Hermeneutics, and Praxis.* Philadelphia: University of Pennsylvania Press, 1983.

———. *The Restructuring of Social and Political Theory.* New York: Harcourt Brace Jovanovich, 1976.

Biemel, Walter, ed. *Phänomenologie Heute: Festschrift für Ludwig Landgrebe.* The Hague: Martinus Nijhoff, 1972.

Boehm, Rudolf. "Husserls drei Thesen über die Lebenswelt." In *Lebenswelt und Wissenshaft in der Philosophie Edmund Husserls.* Ed. Elisabeth Ströker. Frankfurt: Klostermann, 1979, pp. 23–31.

———. *Vom Gesichtspunkt der Phänomenologie.* The Hague: Martinus Nijhoff, 1968.

Borsen, Peter. *Zur Phänomenologie des Bewußtseinsstromes: Bergson, Dilthey, Husserl, Simmel und die lebensphilosophischen Antinomien.* Bonn: Bouvier,1966.

Brand, Gerd. *Die Lebenswelt: Eine Philosophie des konkreten Apriori.* Berlin: de Gruyter, 1971.

———. "Die Normalität des und der Anderen und die Anomalität einer Erfahrungsgemeinschaft bei Edmund Husserl. In *Alfred Schütz und die Idee des Alltags in den Sozialwissenschaften.* Ed. Walter M. Sprodel und Richard Grathoff. Stuttgart: Enke, 1979, pp. 108–24.

———. *Welt, Ich und Zeit: Nach unveröffentlichten Manuskripten Edmund Husserls.* The Hague: Martinus Nijhoff, 1955.

Breeur, Roland, ed. "Randbemerkungen Husserls zu Heideggers *Sein und Zeit* und *Kant und das Problem der Metaphysik.*" *Husserl Studies* 11 (1994), 3–63.

Brentano, Franz. *Psychologie vom empirischen Standpunkt.* Second Edition. Leipzig: Meiner, 1924.

Broekman, Jan M. *Phänomenologie und Egologie: Faktisches und transzendentales Ego bei Edmund Husserl.* The Hague: Marinus Nijhoff, 1963.

Cairns, Dorion. *Conversations with Fink and Husserl.* The Hague: Martinus Nijhoff, 1976.

Calvino, Italo. *Cosmicomics.* Trans. William Weaver. New York: Harvest/HBJ, 1968.

———. *Invisible Cities.* Trans. William Weaver. New York: Harvest/HBJ, 1974.

Canguilhem, Georges. *Le normal et le pathologique.* Paris: PUF, 1966.

Carr, David. "Husserl's Problematic Concept of the Life-world." *American Philosophical Quarterly* 7 (1970), pp. 331–39.

———, trans. *The Crisis of European Sciences and Transcendental Phenomenology.* Evanston: Northwestern University Press, 1970.

———. *Interpreting Husserl: Critical and Comparative Studies.* Boston: Martinus Nijhoff, 1987.

Carr, David, and Edward S. Casey, eds. *Explorations in Phenomenology: Papers of the Society for Phenomenology and Existential Philosophy.* The Hague: Martinus Nijhoff, 1973.

———. *Phenomenology and the Problem of History: A Study of Husserl's Transcendental Philosophy.* Evanston: Northwestern University Press, 1974.

———. *Time, Narrative, and History.* Bloomington: Indiana University Press, 1991.

Casey, Edward S. "Forgetting Remembered." *Man and World* 25 (1992), pp. 281–311.

———. "Imagination and the Phenomenological Method." In *Husserl: Expositions and Appraisals.* Ed. F. Elliston and P. McCormick. Notre Dame: Notre Dame University Press, 1977, pp. 70–82.

———. *Imagining: A Phenomenological Study.* Bloomington: Indiana University Press, 1976.

Celan, Paul. *Paul Celan: Poems. A Bilingual Edition.* Ed and trans. Michael Hamburger. New York: Persea Books, 1980.

Claesges, Ulrich. *Edmund Husserls Theorie der Raumkonstitution.* The Hague: Martinus Nijhoff, 1964.

———. "Zweideutigkeiten in Husserls Lebenswelt-Begriff." In *Perspektiven transzendental-phänomenologischer Forschung.* Ed. Ulrich Claesges and Klaus Held. The Hague: Martinus Nijhoff, 1972, pp. 85–101.

Claesges, Ulrich, and Klaus Held, eds. *Perspektiven transzendental-phänomenologischer Forschung.* The Hauge: Martinus Nijhoff, 1972.

Clapham, W. B., Jr. *Natural Ecosystems.* 2d ed. New York: Macmillan, 1983. Conrad-Martius, Hedwig, "Die transzendentale und die ontologische Phänomenologie." *In Edmund Husserl: 1859–1959.* The Hague: Martinus Nijhoff, 1959, pp. 175–84.

Courtine, J. François. "Intersubjectivité et analogie." Presented at "Phänomenologie im Widerstreit," Bochum, Germany, October 7, 1988.

———. "Différence ontologique et analogie de l'être: Le tournant suarézien." *Bulletin de la Société Française de Philosophie* 83, no. 3 (1989), pp. 41–67.

Crowell, Steven Galt. "Husserl, Heidegger, and Transcendental Philosophy: Another Look at the Encyclopaedia Britannica Article." *Philosophy and Phenomenological Research* 1, no. 3 (March 1990), pp. 501–18.

Dastur, Françoise. "Réduction et intersubjectivité." In *Husserl.* Ed. Elaine Escoubas and Marc Richir. Grenoble: Millon, 1989, pp. 43–64.

De Almeida, Guido Antônio. *Sinn und Inhalt in der Genetischen Phänomenologie E. Husserls.* The Hague: Martinus Nijhoff, 1972.

Derrida, Jacques. *De la grammatologie.* Paris: Minuit, 1967.

———. *L'écriture et la différence.* Paris: Seuil, 1967.

———. *Marges.* Paris: Minuit, 1972.

———. *La problème de la genèse dans la philosophie de Husserl.* Paris: PUF, 1990.

———. *La voix et le phénomène.* Paris: PUF, 1967.

Diemer, Alwin. *Edmund Husserl: Versuch einer systematischen Darstellung seiner Phänomenologie.* Meisenheim am Glan: Hain, 1956.

Dilthey, Wilhelm. *Gesammelte Schriften. Band 5. Die Geistige Welt.* Ed. Georg Misch. Göttingen: Vandenhoeck & Ruprecht, 1957.

Dupré, Louis. "The Concept of Truth in Husserl's *Logical Investigations.*" *Philosophy and Phenomenological Research* 24 (September 1963–64), pp. 345–54.

Durkheim, Émile. *Les règles de la méthode sociologique.* Paris: PUF, 1960.

———. *The Rules of Sociological Method.* Trans. Sarah A. Solovay and John H. Mueller. Chicago: University of Chicago Press, 1938.

Eley, Lothar. *Die Krise des Apriori in der transzendentalen Phänomenologie Edmund Husserls.* The Hague: Martinus Nijhoff, 1962.

Escoubas, Elaine, and Marc Richer, eds. *Husserl.* Grenoble: Millon, 1989.

Evans, Joseph Claude. *Strategies of Deconstruction: Derrida and the Myth of the Voice.* Minneapolis: University of Minnesota Press, 1991.

Fink, Eugen. *VI. Cartesianische Meditation: Die Idee einer transzendentalen Methodenlehre. Husserliana Dokumente: Ergänzungband II/1.* Ed. Hans Ebneling, Jann Holl, and Guy van Kerckhoven. Boston: Kluwer, 1988.

———. *VI. Cartesianische Meditation. Husserliana Dokumente: Ergänzungband II/2.* Ed. Guy van Kerckhoven. Boston: Kluwer, 1988.

———. "Operative Begriffe in Husserls Phänomenologie." In *Nähe und Distanz: Phänomenologische Vorträge und Aufsätze.* Ed. Frank-Antib Schwarz. Freiburg: Alber, 1976, pp. 180–204.

———. "Die phänomenologische Philosophie Edmund Husserls in der gegenwärtigen Kritik." In *Kant-Studien.* Band 38, 1933, pp. 319–83.

Folter, R. J. de. *Normaal en abnormaal: Enkele beschouwingen over het probleem van de normaliteit in het denken van Husserl, Schütz en Foucault.* Groningen: Historische Uitgeverji Groningen, 1987.

Foucault, Michel. *L'archéologie du savoir.* Paris: Gallimard, 1971.

———. *Histoire de la folie à l'âge classique.* Paris: Gallimard, 1972.

———. "Qu'est-ce qu'un auteur?" *Bulletin de la Société française de philosophie* 64 (1969), pp. 73–104.

Frank, Didier. *Chair et corps: Sur la phénoménologie de Husserl.* Paris: Minuit, 1981.

Freud, Sigmund. "Drei Abhandlungen über Sexualtheorie." In *Gesammelte Werke* Vol. 5. Frankfurt: Fischer, 1972, pp. 33–145.

———. *Gesammelte Werke.* Vol. 14. Frankfurt: Fischer, 1972.

———. *Gesammelte Werke.* Vol. 16. Frankfurt: Fischer, 1972.

Giddens, Anthony. *Central Problems in Social Theory: Action, Structure and Contradiction in Social Analysis.* Berkeley: University of California Press, 1979.

Goldstein, Kurt. *The Organism: A Holistic Approach to Biology Derived from Pathological Data in Man.* New York: American Book Company, 1939.

Granel, Gérard. *Le sens du temps et de la perception chez E. Husserl.* Paris: Gallimard, 1968.

Grathoff, Richard. *Milieu und Lebenswelt. Einführung in die phänomenologische Soziologie und die sozialphänomenologische Forschung.* Frankfurt: Suhrkamp, 1989.

———. "Selbst-Thematisierungen des Gesellschaftssystems." In Luhmann, *Soziologische Aufklärung Band II*, pp. 72–102.

———. "Über Typik und Normalität im alltäglichen Milieu." In *Alfred Schütz und die Idee des Alltags in den Sozialwissenschaften.* Ed. Walter M. Sprodel und Richard Grathoff. Stuttgart: Enke, 1979, pp. 89–107.

Gurwitsch, Aron. *The Field of Consciousness.* Pittsburg: Duquesne University Press, 1964.

———. *Die mitmenschlichen Begegnungen in der Milieuwelt.* Berlin: de Gruyter, 1977.

———. "On the Intentionality of Consciousness." In *Philosophical Essays in Memory of Edmund Husserl.* Ed. Martin Farber. Cambridge: Harvard University Press, 1940, pp. 65–83.

———. "Problems of the Life-world." In *Phenomenology and Social Reality: Essays in Memory of Alfred Schutz.* Ed. Maurice Natanson. The Hague: Martinus Nijhoff, 1970, pp. 35-61.

———. *Studies in Phenomenology and Psychology.* Evanston: Northwestern University Press, 1966.

Habermas, Jürgen. *Theorie des kommunikativen Handelns. Band 1. Hanglungsrationalität und gesellschaftliche Rationalisierung.* Frankfurt: Suhrkamp, 1987.

———. *Theorie des kommunikativen Handelns. Band 2. Zur Kritik der funktionalistischen Vernunft.* Frankfurt: Suhrkamp, 1987.

Hartmann, Nicolai. *Wege der Ontologie.* Stuttgart: W. Wohlhammer, 1949.

Harvey, Charles W. *Husserl's Phenomenology and the Foundations of Natural Science.* Athens, Ohio: Ohio University Press, 1989.

Hegel, G. W. F. *Phänomenologie des Geistes.* Hamburg: Meiner, 1952.

Heidegger, Martin. *Sein und Zeit.* Tübingen: Niemeyer, 1979.

Held, Klaus. "Einleitung." In Edmund Husserl, *Die phänomenologische Methode: Ausgewählte Texte I.* Stuttgart: Reclam, 1985, pp. 5–51.

———. "Einleitung." In Edmund Husserl, *Phänomenologie der Lebenswelt: Ausgewählte Texte II.* Stuttgart: Reclam, 1986, pp. 5–53.

———. "Finitude of the World: Phenomenology in Transition from Husserl to Heidegger." Trans. Anthony J. Steinbock. In *Ethics and Danger: Essays on Heidegger and Continental Thought.* Ed. Arleen Dallery et al. New York: SUNY Press, 1992, pp. 187–98.

———. "Der griechische Anfang der Philosophie und seine Erneuerung in Husserls Phänomenologie." Unpublished manuscript.

———. "Heimwelt, Fremdwelt, die eine Welt." In *Perspektiven und Probleme der Husserlschen Phänomenologie. Band 24/25.* Freiburg: Alber, 1991, pp. 305–37.

———. "Husserl und die Griechen." In *Phänomenologische Forschungen, Band 22.* Freiburg: Alber, 1988, pp. 137–76.

———. "Husserls These von der Europäisierung der Menschheit." In *Phänomenologie im Widerstreit: Zum 50. Todestag Edmund Husserls.* Ed. C. Jamme und O. Pöggeler. Frankfurt: Suhrkamp, 1989, pp. 13–39.

———. *Lebendige Gegenwart: Die Frage nach der Seinsweise des transzendentalen ich bei Edmund Husserl, entwickelt am Leitfaden der Zeitproblematik.* The Hague: Martinus Nijhoff, 1966.

———. "Le monde natal, le monde étranger, le monde un." Trans. Raphaël Célis. In *Husserl-Ausgabe und Husserl-Forschung.* Boston: Kluwer, 1990, pp. 1–21.

———. "Das Problem der Intersubjektivität und die Idee einer phänomenologischen Transzendental-Philosophie." In *Festschrift für Ludwig Landgrebe.* Ed. Ulrich Claesges und Klaus Held. The Hague: Martinus Nijhoff, 1972, pp. 3–60.

Henry, Michel. "Réflexions sur la cinquième méditation cartésienne de Husserl." In *Phénoménologie matérielle.* Paris: PUF, 1990, pp. 138–59.

Hobbes, Thomas. *Leviathan.* Ed. E. B. MacPherson. New York: Penguin, 1980.

Holenstein, Elmar. "Europa und die Menschheit. Zu Husserls kulturphilosophischen Meditationen." In *Phänomenologie im Widerstreit: Zum 50. Todestag Edmund Husserls.* Ed. C. Jamme und O. Pöggeler. Frankfurt: Suhrkamp, 1989, pp. 40–64.

———. *Phänomenologie der Assoziation: Zu Struktur und Funktion eines Grundprinzips der passiven Genesis bei E. Husserl.* The Hague: Martinus Nijhoff,1972.

Hoyos, Guillermo. "Zum Teleologiebegriff in der Phänomenologie Husserls." In *Perspektiven transzendental-phänomenologischer Forschung.* Ed. Ulrich Claesges and Klaus Held. The Hague: Martinus Nijhoff, 1972, pp. 61–84.

Huneman, Philippe. *Intuitionnisme et formalisme en mathematiques.* Unpublished manuscript.

James, William. "On Some Omissions of Introspective Psychology." Mind 9 (January 1884), pp. 1–26.

———. *The Principles of Psychology.* Vol. 1. Cambridge: Harvard University Press, 1981.

Jamme, Christoph, and Otto Pöggeler, eds. *Phänomenologie im Widerstreit.* Frankfurt: Shurkamp, 1989.

Janssen, Paul. *Geschichte und Lebenswelt: Ein Beitrag zur Diskussion von Husserls Spätwerk.* The Hague: Martinus Nijhoff, 1970

———. "Die Problematik der Rede von der Lebenswelt als Fundament der Wissenschaft." In *Lebenswelt und Wissenshaft in der Philosophie Edmund Husserls.* Ed. Elisabeth Ströker. Frankfurt: Klostermann, 1979, pp. 56–67.

Kant, Immanuel. *Kritik der reinen Vernunft.* Ed. Raymund Schmidt. Hamburg: Meiner, 1956.

Kern, Iso. "Die Lebenswelt als Grundlagenproblem der objektiven Wissenschaften und als universales Wahrheits-und Seinsproblem." In *Lebenswelt und Wissenschaft in der Philosophie Edmund Husserls.* Ed. Elisabeth Ströker. Frankfurt: Suhrkamp, 1979, pp. 68–78.

———. *Husserl und Kant: Eine Untersuchung über Husserls Verhältnis zu Kant und zum Neukantianismus.* The Hague: Martinus Nijhoff, 1964.

———. "The Three Ways to the Transcendental Phenomenological Reduction in the Philosophy of Edmund Husserl." In *Husserl: Exposition and Appraisals.*

Ed. F. Elliston and P. McCormick. Notre Dame: University of Notre Dame Press, 1977, pp. 126–49.

Kockelmans, Joseph J. *Edmund Husserl's Phenomenological Psychology: A Historico-Critical Study.* Pittsburgh: Duquesne University Press, 1967.

Kohák, Erazim. *Idea and Experience: Edmund Husserl's Project of Phenomenology in Ideas I.* Chicago: University of Chicago Press, 1978.

Kozol, Jonathan. *The Night Is Dark and I Am Far from Home.* New York: Bantam Books, 1975.

Kuhn, Helmut. "The Phenomenological Concept of 'Horizon'." In *Philosophical Essays in Memory of Edmund Husserl.* Ed. Marvin Farber. New York: Greenword Press, 1968, pp. 106–23.

Landgrebe, Ludwig. *Der Weg der Phänomenologie: Das Problem einer ursprünglichen Erfahrung.* Gütersloh: Mohn, 1967.

———. "World as Phenomenological Problem" [*Welt als phänomenologisches Problem*]. *Philosophy and Phenomenological Research* 1, no. 1 (1940), pp. 38–126.

Larrabee, Mary Jeanne. "Husserl's Static and Genetic Phenomenology." *Man and World* 9, no. 2 (June 1976), pp. 163–74.

Lefort, Claude. "Esquisse d'une genèse de l'ideologie dans les sociétés modernes. In *Les formes de l'histoire.* Paris: Gallimard, 1978, pp. 278–329.

———. "La naissance de l'idéologie et l'humanisme." In *Les formes de l'histoire.* Paris: Gallimard, 1978, pp. 234–77.

Legros, Robert. "Husserl et la critique de l'evidence (Sur la phénoménologie des *Reserches logiques*)." *EPOCHE,* 1, no. 1 (1990), pp. 229–40.

Levinas, Emmanuel. *Le temps et l'autre.* Paris: PUF, 1979.

———. *Théorie de l'intuition dans la phénoménologie de Husserl.* 6th ed. Paris: J. Vrin, 1989.

———. *Totalité et infini.* The Hague: Martinus Nijhoff, 1984.

Litt, Theodor. *Individuum und Gemeinschaft: Grundlegung der Kulturphilosophie.* 3d ed. Leipzig: Teubner, 1926.

Locke, John. *An Essay concerning Human Understanding.* Ed. Alexander Campbell Fraser. Vol. 1. New York: Dover, 1959.

Lowenthal, Leo, and Norbert Guterman. *Prophets of Deceit.* Palo Alto: Pacific Books, 1970.

Löwit, Alexandre. "L"époche de Husserl et le doute de Descartes." *Revue de métaphysique et de morale,* no. 4 (1957), pp. 399–415.

Luhmann, Niklas. *Soziologische Aufklärung: Aufsätze zur Theorie sozialer Systeme. Band 1.* Cologne: Westdeutscher Verlag, 1970.

———. *Soziologische Aufklärung: Aufsätze zur Theorie der Gesellschaft. Band 2.* Cologne: Westdeutscher Verlag, 1975.

MacIntyre, Alasdair. *After Virtue.* Notre Dame: University of Notre Dame Press, 1988.

———. *Whose Justice? Which Rationality?* Notre Dame: University of Notre Dame Press, 1988.

Makreel, Rudolf A., and John Scanlon, eds., *Dilthey and Phenomenology*. Washington, D.C.: University Press of America, 1987.
Makkreel, Rudolf A. "Husserl, Dilthey, and the Relation of the Life-World to History." In *Husserl and Contemporary Thought*. Ed. John Sallis. Atlantic Highlands, N.J.: Humanities Press, 1983, pp. 39–58.
Malinowski, Bronislaw. *Crime and Custom in Savage Society*. London: Routledge & Kegan Paul, 1978.
Marbach, Eduard. *Das Problem des Ich in der Phänomenologie Husserls*. The Hague: Martinus Nijhoff, 1974.
Marx, Werner. "The Life-World and the Particular Sub-worlds." In *Phenomenology and Social Reality: Essays in Memory of Alfred Schutz*. Ed. Maurice Natanson. The Hague: Martinus Nijhoff, 1970, pp. 62–72.
Mead, George Herbert. *The Philosophy of the Present*. Chicago: Open Court, 1959.
Melle, Ulrich. "Objektivierende und nicht-Objektivierende Akte." In *Husserl-Ausgabe und Husserl-Forschuung*. Ed. Samuel Ijsseling. Boston: Kluwer, 1990, pp. 35–49.
———. *Das Wahrnehmungsproblem und seine Verwandlung* in *phänomenologischer Einstellung*. The Hague: Martinus Nijhoff, 1983.
Merleau-Ponty, Maurice. *Phénoménologie de la perception*. Paris: Gallimard, 1946.
———. *La Structure du comportement*. Paris: PUF, 1942.
———. *Le visible et l'invisible*. Ed. Claude Lefort. Paris: Gallimard, 1964. Trans. Alphonso Lingis as *The Visible and the Invisible*. Evanston: Northwestern University Press, 1968.
Minkowski, Eugène. *Lived Time: Phenomenological and Psychopathological Studies*. Trans. Nancy Metzel. Evanston: Northwestern University Press, 1970.
Misch, Georg. *Lebensphilosophie und Phänomenologie: Eine Auseinandersetzung der Diltheyschen Richtung mit Heidegger und Husserl*. Darmstadt: Wissenschaftliche Buchgesellschaft, 1975.
Mohanty, J. N. *Phenomenology and Ontology*. The Hague: Martinus Nijhoff, 1970.
———. *The Possibility of Transcendental Philosophy*. Boston: Kluwer, 1985.
Natanson, Maurice. "Philosophische Grundfragen der Psychiatrie I: Philosophie und Psychiatrie." In *Psychiatrie der Gegenwart: Forschung und Praxis*. Ed. H. W. Gruhle et al. Berlin: Springer, 1963, pp. 903–25.
Olafson, Frederick A. *The Dialectic of Action*. Chicago: University of Chicago Press, 1979.
Orth, Ernst Wolfgang, ed. *Dilthey und der Wandel des Philosophiebegriffs seit dem 19. Jahrhundert*. Freiburg: Alber, 1984.
Paci, Enzo. *The Function of the Sciences and the Meaning of Man*. Evanston: Northwestern University Press, 1972.
Patočka, Jan. *Le monde naturel comme problème philosophique*. Trans. Jaromir Danek and Henri Declève. La Haye: Martinus Nijhoff, 1976.
———. *Qu'est-ce que la phénoménologie?* Trans. Erika Abrams. Grenoble: Millon, 1988.
Patzig, Günter. "Kritische Bemerkungen zu Husserls Thesen über das Verhältnis von Wahrheit und Evidenz." *Neue Hefte für Philosophie* 1 (1979), pp. 12–32.

Ricoeur, Paul. "La cinquième méditation cartésienne." In *A l'école de la phénoménologie.* Paris: J. Vrin, 1987, pp. 197–225.

———. "L'originarie et le question-en-retour dans la *Krisis* de Husserl." In *A l'école de la phénoménologie.* Paris: J. Vrin, 1987, pp. 285–95.

———. "Sur la phénoménologie." *A l'école de la phénoménologie* (Paris: J. Vrin, 1987), 141–59.

———. *Temps et récit: I.* Paris: Seuil, 1983.

———. *Temps et récit: II.* Paris: Seuil, 1984.

———. *Temps et récit: III.* Paris: Seuil, 1985.

Römpp, Georg. *Husserls Phänomenologie der Intersubjektivität: Und ihre Bedeutung für eine Theorie intersubjektiver Objektivität und die Konzeption einer phänomenologischen Philosophie.* Boston: Kluwer, 1992.

Rorty, Richard. *Philosophy and the Mirror of Nature.* Princeton: Princeton University Press, 1979.

Rosen, Klaus. *Evidenz in Husserls deskriptiver Transzendentalphilosophie.* Meisenheim am Glan: Hain, 1977.

Sacks, Oliver. *The Man Who Mistook His Wife for a Hat and Other Clinical Tales.* New York: Harper & Row, 1985.

Schapp, Wilhelm. *Beiträge zur Phänomenologie der Wahrnehmung.* Wiesbaden: B. Heymann, 1976.

Scheler, Max. *Gesammelte Werke, II. Der Formalismus in der Ethik und die. Materiale Wertethik: Neuer Versuch der Grundlegung eines ethischen Personalismus.* Ed. Maria Scheler. Bern: Franke, 1954.

———. *Schriften aus dem Nachlaß: Zur Ethik und Erkenntnislehre.* Ed. Maria Scheler. Bern: Francke, 1957.

———. "Die Stellung des Menschen im Kosmos." In *Späte Schriften, Gesammelte Werke. Band 9.* Ed. Manfred S. Frings. Bern: Francke, 1976, pp. 9–71.

———. *Vom Ewigen im Menschen: Gesammelte Werke. Band 5.* Ed. Maria Scheler. Bern: Francke, 1954.

———. *Wesen und Formen der Sympathie. Gesammelte Werke. Band 1.* Ed. Manfred S. Frings. Bern: Franke, 1973.

Schrader, George. "The Thing in Itself in Kantian Philosophy." In *Kant: A Collection of Critical Essays.* Ed. Robert Paul Wolff. Notre Dame: University of Notre Dame Press, 1968, pp. 172–88.

Schuhmann, Karl. *Die Fundamentalbetrachtung der Phänomenologie: Zum Weltproblem in der Philosophie Edmund Husserls.* The Hague: Martinus Nijhoff, 1971.

———. ed. *Husserl-Chronik: Denk- und Lebensweg Edmund Husserls.* The Hague: Martinus Nijhoff, 1977.

Schutz, Alfred. *Collected Papers I. The Problem of Social Reality.* Ed. Maurice Natanson. The Hague: Martinus Nijhoff, 1962.

———. *Collected Papers II. Studies in Social Theory.* Ed. Arvid Brodersen. The Hague: Martinus Nijhoff, 1976.

———. *Collected Papers III. Studies in Phenomenological Philosophy.* Ed. I. Schutz. The Hague: Martinus Nijhoff, 1975.

———. *The Phenomenology of the Social World.* Trans. George Walsh and Frederick Lehnert. Evanston: Northwestern University Press, 1967.

Schütz, Alfred, and Aron Gurwitsch. *Briefwechsel 1939–1959.* Munich: Fink, 1985.

Seebohm, Thomas. *Die Bedingungen der Möglichkeit der Transzendental-Philosophie: Edmund Husserls transzendental-Phänomenologischer Ansatz, dargestellt im Anschluß an seine Kant-Kritik.* Bonn: H. Bouvier, 1962.

Sepp, Hans Rainer, ed. *Edmund Husserl und die phänomenologische Bewegung.* Freiburg: Alber, 1988.

Simmel, Georg. *Über soziale Differenzierung: Soziologische und psychologische Untersuchungen.* Leipzig: Duncker & Humbolt, 1980.

Smith, David Woodruff. *The Circle of Acquaintance: Perception, Consciousness, and Empathy.* Boston: Kluwer, 1989.

Soffer, Gail. *Husserl and the Question of Relativism.* Boston: Kluwer, 1991.

Sokolowski, Robert. *The Formation of Husserl's Concept of Constitution.* The Hague: Martinus Nijhoff, 1964.

———. *Husserlian Meditations: How Words Present Things.* Evanston: Northwestern University Press, 1974.

———. *Presence and Absence: A Philosophical Investigation of Language and Being.* Bloomington: Indiana University Press, 1978.

Sorre, Max. *Les fondements biologiques de la géographie humaine: essai d'une écologie de l'homme.* Paris: Colin, 1943.

Souche-Dagues, D. "La lecture husserlienne de Sein und Zeit." *Philosophie,* No. 21, pp. 7–36.

Spiegelberg, Herbert. *Doing Phenomenology.* The Hague: Martinus Nijhoff, 1975.

———. *The Phenomenological Movement: A Historical Introduction.* The Hague: Martinus Nijhoff, 1984.

Sprondel, Walter M., and Richard Grathoff, eds. *Alfred Schütz und die Idee des Alltags in den Sozialwissenschaften.* Stuttgart: Enke, 1979.

Stein, Edith. *Zum Problem der Einfühlung.* Munich: Kaffke, 1980.

Steinbock, Anthony. "Homelessness and the Homeless Movement: A Clue to the Problem of Intersubjectivity." *Human Studies* 17 (1994), 203–23.

———. "The New 'Crisis' Crontribution: A Supplementary Edition of Edmund Husserl's Crisis Texts." *Review of Metaphysics* 47 (March 1994), pp. 557–84.

———. "Totalitarianism, Homogeneity of Power, Depth: Towards a Socio-Political Ontology." *Tijdschrift voor Filosofie* 51, no. 4 (December 1989), pp. 621–48.

Thao, Tran Duc. "Marxisme et phénoménologie." *Revue Internationale,* 2 (1946), pp. 168–74.

Theunissen, Michael. *Der Andere: Studien zur Sozialontologie der Gegenwart.* Berlin: de Gruyter, 1977.

Toulemont, René. *L'essence de la société selon Husserl.* Paris: PUF, 1962.

Tugendhat, Ernst. *Der Wahrheitsbegriff bei Husserl und Heidegger.* Berlin: de Gruyter, 1967.

Valéry, Paul. *Cahiers II, Pléiade.* Paris: Gallimard, 1974.

Van Kerckhoven, Guy. "Zur Genese des Begriffs 'Lebenswelt' bei Edmund Husserl." *Archiv für Begriffsgeschichte*, pp. 182–203.

Von Wiese, Leopold. *Allgemeine Soziologie als Lehre von den Beziehungen und Beziehungsgebilden der Menschen.* Leipzig: Duncker & Humbolt, 1924.

Waldenfels, Bernhard. "Eigenkultur und Fremdkultur: Das Paradox einer Wissenschaft vom Fremden." Unpublished manuscript.

———. *Einführung in die Phänomenologie.* Munich: Fink, 1992.

———. "Experience of the Alien in Husserl's Phenomenology." Trans. Anthony J. Steinbock. *Research in Phenomenology* 20 (1990), pp. 19–33.

———. *In der Netzen der Lebenswelt.* Frankfurt: Suhrkamp, 1985.

———. "Lebenswelt zwischen Alltäglichem und Unalltäglichem." In *Phänomenologie im Widerstreit: Zum 50. Todestag Edmund Husserls.* Ed. C. Jamme und O. Pöggeler. Frankfurt: Suhrkamp, 1989, pp. 106–18.

———. *Ordnung im Zwielicht.* Frankfurt: Suhrkamp, 1987.

———. *Der Stachel des Fremden.* Frankfurt: Suhrkamp, 1990.

———. "Weltliche und soziale Einzigkeit bei Husserl." *Zeitschrift für philosophische Forschung* 25 (1971), pp. 157–71.

———. *Das Zwischenreich des Dialogs: Sozialphilosophische Untersuchungen in Anschluß an Edmund Husserl.* The Hague: Martinus Nijhoff, 1971.

Welton, Donn. "Husserl and the Japanese." *Review of Metaphysics* 44 (March 1991), pp. 575–606.

———. "Margins of the World." Presented at the Society of Phenomenology and Existential Philosophy, October 1991.

———. *The Origins of Meaning: A Critical Study of the Thresholds of Husserlian Phenomenology.* The Hague: Martinus Nijhoff, 1983.

———. "Structure and Genesis in Husserl's Phenomenology." In *Husserl: Exposition and Appraisals.* Ed. F. Elliston and P. McCormick. Notre Dame: University of Notre Dame Press, 1977, pp. 54–69.

———. "Verbindende Namen–Verbundene Gegenstände: Frege und Husserl über Bedeutung." In *Phänomenologie im Widerstreit: Zum 50. Todestag Edmund Husserls.* Ed. Christoph Jamme and Otto Pöggeler. Frankfurt: Suhrkamp, 1989, 141–91.

Whitehead, Alfred North. *Science and the Modern World.* New York: Free Press, 1967.

Wittgenstein, Ludwig. *Bermerkungen über die Farben (Remarks on Colour).* Ed. G. E. M. Anscombe. Berkeley: University of California Press, 1977.

Wolff, Robert Paul. *Kant's Theory of Mental Activity.* Gloucester, Mass.: Peter Smith, 1973.

Yamaguchi, Ichiro. *Passive Synthesis und Intersubjektivität bei Edmund Husserl.* The Hague: Martinus Nijhoff, 1982.

Index